EDUCATIONAL PLANNING IN INDIA

CONCEPTS IN COMMUNICATION
INFORMATICS & LIBRARIANSHIP (CICIL)

For a list of titles in this series,
see pp. 487-490 at the end of the book.

ABOUT THE AUTHORS

J.C. AGGARWAL (*b.* 1928), retired Deputy Director of Education/Executive Director of Delhi Bureau of Textbooks, Delhi Administration, has a varied experience in the field of education. He has singly/jointly authored about 130 books on Education, Social Sciences and Current Problems. In collaboration with Shri S.P. Agrawal, he has written *Documentation Encyclopaedia of UNESCO and Education* (in two parts); *Women's Education in India; National Policy on Education: Agenda for India 2001; Indian Writings on Education 1979 to 1986* and *Vocational Education in India.*

His other recent publications on Education include: *Yearbook of Indian Education, 1991: World Overview; Ramamurti Report 1990 on National Policy on Education in India; and Survey of Educational Documents in the World Since 1983*, etc.

S.P. AGRAWAL (*b.* 1929) was Member Secretary, Indian Association of Social Science Institutions and Director, National Social Science Documentation Centre, ICSSR. He was also the Vice-Chairman of the Asia and Pacific Information Network in Social Sciences (APINESS). In 1988 he was awarded the degree of Doctor of Philosophy in Education (Honoris Causa) by International University Foundation. Presently, he is Member, Round Table on Research in Reading, IFLA, and Member, International Committee for Social Science Information and Documentation. He is also Member, Board of Studies, National Archives of India, and Member, Hindi Advisory Committee, Ministry of Coal, Government of India. He has written extensively on various aspects of education as well as of library and information science.

Concepts in Communication
Informatics & Librarianship-39

General Editor: **S.P. Agrawal**

EDUCATIONAL PLANNING IN INDIA

With a Slant to Educational Financing and Administration

VOLUME I

Reports of Committees and Commissions, Five Year Plans, Statistical Tables

J.C. AGGARWAL
Former Deputy Director of Education
Delhi

S.P. AGRAWAL
Former Member Secretary
Indian Association of Social Science Institutions, New Delhi

CONCEPT PUBLISHING COMPANY PVT. LTD.
NEW DELHI-110059

ISBN: 978-81-7022-438-9

Edition 2023

Published and Printed by

Concept
Since 1974

Concept Publishing Company Pvt. Ltd.
A/15-16, Commercial Block, Mohan Garden,
New Delhi-110059 (India)
T : 91-11-41101460
E : publishing@conceptpub.com, *W*: www.conceptpub.com

PREFACE

The book, intended to serve as a reference guide, is organised into three sections. Section I incorporates in it the observations and recommendations on educational planning and financing of 15 documents beginning with Post-War Plan of Educational Development, 1944. It also includes an introductory chapter on overview of Educational Planning and Financing in India. Section II provides complete texts of almost all the Five Year Plans relating to Education. Section III provides relevant tables on educational statistics covering financial allocations in Plans, population and density, literacy, expansion of educational institutions and enrolments at all levels, teachers and teacher training institutions, education of scheduled castes and tribes, expenditure per pupil, etc., and education in India in 1989-1990.

Primary reference sources for the matter contained in the book include publications of the Ministry of Human Resource Development, Department of Education, Government of India; University Grants Commission; Controller of Publications, Government of India and Registrar General and Census Commissioner, India. The authors extend their gratefulness to them.

It is hoped that the book will be of great use to advanced students of education, educational administrators, planners and research scholars.

J.C. AGGARWAL
S.P. AGRAWAL

GENERAL EDITOR'S INTRODUCTION

In India–may be, as elsewhere too–in every sphere of developmental activity, there always remained a big gap between what we say or propose and what we actually do. No where this gap between idea and action is more visible than in the sphere of education. We have had a number of Committees and Commissions set-up from time to time by Government of India that have, on the face of it, thoroughly examined almost all facets and levels of our educational system and which have recommended remedial measures to overcome the ills of the system and to improve the situation both in term of quantitative and qualitative development. However, political-will and planner-initiative have not been forthcoming in this regard. While reforms suggested by these august bodies have been appreciated and lip sympathy paid by publicly promising support to them, actually when if comes to allocation of financial resources for working out these meaningful reforms, both – political leaders and educational planners – become indifferent and tend to provide inadequate funds for implementation of the educational programmes and plans. As a matter of fact in their scheme of things education is assigned lowest priority. It was at one time reasonably thought that the National Policy on Education (1986), which was formulated by the Union Education Ministry after a nation-wide debate on educational problems and issues and in consultation with distinguished educationists and seasoned educational administrators would improve educational situation and pave the way towards enlightened and egalitarian society. But due to serious resource constraints it could not be implemented effectively and thus failed to produce the desired results.

One of the glaring defects in the thinking of our policy-makers and planners is that the crucial role of the education in the human resources development has not been recognised by them, although an investment in education is, in the long run, an investment for development of competent manpower, which can improve our economy and bring about general prosperity in the country. 'Education has tended to be given comparatively low priority in the matter of sectoral allocation of resources. Allocation for education cannot wholly be treated either investment outlay or as consumption outlay. Gestation period for investment in education to yield results is also too long. Difficulties are encountered in accurately estimating or quantifying the returns on investment in education. Reason is that, the functioning relationship between inputs and outputs in education is indeterminate. The net result is that, in India also as in other developing economies, education is treated as a social service sector and often gets for itself only the residual resources after allocations to the so-called productive sectors. As regards educational planning too much accent is given in centralisation of planning which unduly ignores the claims of other bodies. Since we have a federal democracy which is predominantly rural in character what is needed is that the process of educational planning should be the right blend of the centralisation in the appropriate sectors, with a judicious decentralisation in other sectors and especially in administration. J.P. Naik Committee also maintained that there is need to adopt a broad-based and decentralised system of educational planning and, to that end, to prepare well-coordinated plans of the Institutional, District, State and National levels.

The present CICIL volume makes it possible to have a comprehensive view of the educational planning and financing by presenting at one place observations and recommendations pertaining to education, of the Committees and Commissions on education in the post-Independence period, important documents brought out by the Union Education Ministry, recommendations of an important National Seminar on Institutional Planning (1968) and by reproducing complete texts relating to education of all the Five Year Plans (including Draft Approach to Eighth Five-Year Plan). It will enable the planners, policy-makers and the serious students of education to see for themselves defects in educational planning and to find out how the financial constraints have played upside down with the plans and programmes which if worked out effectively would have helped to achieve the goals and objectives. The other feature of this reference guide is that it not only furnishes relevant information on the subject but has also provided a brief overview of and relevant tables on educational planning on different aspects of education in India.

S.P. AGRAWAL

CONTENTS

SECTION III
Selected Educational Statistics and Classified Index to Tables

SECTION I

OVERVIEW AND OFFICIAL DOCUMENTS: REPORTS OF COMMITTEES, COMMISSIONS, ETC.

1

OVERVIEW OF EDUCATIONAL PLANNING IN INDIA

The Planning Process

The Planning Commission is a high-powered Central agency constituted in March 1950 to prepare a blue-print for development of the country. It has been entrusted with the task of assessing the resources of the country, drawing up Plans for the development and utilisation of resources within the framework of specified national priorities, and determining conditions, modalities and adjustments needed for the success of the planning process. The Commission also appraises the progress of the Plans from time to time.

The Prime Minister is the Chairman of the Commission. In order to achieve co-ordination among the States in implementing the Plans and to achieve targets set in the Plans, an advisory body called National Development Council (NDC) was set up in 1952, with the Prime Minister as Chairman and Chief Ministers of all the States and Administrators of the Union Territories as members.

Broadly speaking the national Plans are formulated and finalised in three stages. In the *First* stage, the rough projections and estimates, prepared by the Planning Commission in consultation with the Central Ministries and State Governments against the background of the long-term perspective, are approved and modified, if necessary, by the NDC in the form of preliminary instructions.

In the *Second* stage, State Governments/Union Territories prepare their own Plans and send them to the Planning Commission, which dovetails these schemes, programmes and projects into an integrated Plan called the "Draft Plan". The Draft Plan is then released for public discussion.

The *Third* stage consists of prolonged discussions between the members of the Planning Commission and the representatives of different Central Ministries, State Governments and Union Territories, for arriving at an agreement on the nature and the size of the Plan.

These tentative agreements are sent to the NDC after examination by the Union Cabinet. In the light of the recommendations of the NDC, the Planning Commission gives the final shape to the Plan, which subsequently becomes the official national plan.

The Five-Year Plan specifies the allocation, chalks out the policies and the programmes, and sets targets of achievements. There is a provision for periodic appraisal of the Plan performance and every year 'Annual' Plan is drawn up with due modification but within the framework of the Five-Year Plan.

Under the Constitution, education is a concurrent subject and educational planning, therefore, is done at two levels—Central and State. At the Central level, the Planning Commission and the Ministry of Human Resource Development prepare a national plan of educational development which consists of two parts—first a, central plan dealing with the direct responsibilities with the Government of India regarding education including schemes of financial assistance to State Governments for educational development in certain specific areas known as the Centrally-sponsored Schemes; and second, an integrated summary of the State Plans of educational development. At the State level the Planning and Education Departments prepare detailed plans of educational development in the State concerned.

In the course of four decades, an elaborate organizational machinery has grown at the Central and State levels for the formation of Five-Year Plans. To assist in the formulation of the plans at the Central level, the Education Division of the Planning Commission works in close liaison with the Education Division of the Ministry of Human Resource Development.

In the planning of higher education, Education Department of the Ministry is assisted by the University Grants Commission. Similarly for school education, it is assisted by the National Council of Educational Research and Training.

A glance at Table 1.3, shows that over the years, the percentage of GNP spent on education has been increasing. At the inception of planning (1950-51) India was spending 1.2 per cent of GNP on education, and this increased approximately to 4 per cent (1986-87). While the increase is significant, the actual requirements of the system exceed the present provisions. The total expenditure as a proportion of GNP is far below the general target of 6 per cent.

TABLE 1.1: Financial Allocation to Education in Five Year Plans: First Plan to Seventh Plan

(Rs. in Crores)

Plan	Total Plan Outlay	Expenditure	Outlay on Education	Expenditure on Education	Percentage of Plan Outlay on Education to Total Plan
First Five Year Plan (1951-56)	2,356	1,960	169	153	7.2
Second Five Year Plan (1956-61)	4,800	4,672	277	273	5.8
Third Five Year Plan (1961-66)	6,209	8,557	560	589	7.5
Annual Plans (1966 to 1969)	6,756	6,625	331	321	4.8
Fourth Five Year Plan (1969-74)	24,882	16,160	822	786	5.2
Fifth Five Year Plan (1974-79)	53,411	42,300	1,285	912	3.3
Sixth Five Year Plan (1980-85)	1,72,210	1,49,750	2,524	2,943	2.6
Seventh Five Year Plan (1985-90)	1,80,000	—	5,733	—	—

Source: *Handbook of Educational and Allied Statistics, 1987*, Ministry of Human Resource Development, Government of India, New Delhi 1987.

Universalisation of Elementary Education (UEE)

Article 45 of the Constitution stipulates, as a Directive Principle of State Policy, that the State shall endeavour to provide for, within a period of ten years from the commencement of the Constitution, free and compulsory education for all children until they complete the age of 14 years. Para 5.12 of the National Policy on Education (NPE) 1986 says:

> "The New Education Policy will give the highest priority to solving the problem of children dropping out of school and will adopt an array of meticulously formulated strategies based on micro-planning, and applied at the grassroots level all over the country, to ensure children's retention at school. This effort will be fully co-ordinated with the network of non-formal education. It shall

TABLE 1.2: Sectorwise Percentage of Plan Outlay and Expenditure : First Plan to Seventh Plan

(Rs. in crores)

Sector	I Plan		II Plan		III Plan		IV Plan		V Plan		VI Plan		VII Plan
	Outlay	Exp.	Outlay	Exp.	Outlay	Exp.	Outlay	Exp.	Outlay	Exp.	Outlay	Exp.	Outlay
Elementary	55	56	34	35	37	34	31	30	32	35	36	30	34
Secondary	13	13	18	19	15	18	14	18	19	17	16	25	
University	9	9	17	18	15	15	22	25	23	22	19	18	
Other Educational Programmes	9	9	12	9	5	11	16	12	11	11	13	12	52
Cultural Programmes includes General Education	1	1	2	1	2	2	3	3	4	4	2		
Total: General Education	86	87	82	82	74	79	85	87	88	88	88	89	88
Total: Technical Education	14	13	18	18	26	21	15	13	12	12	12	11	12
Total: Education	100	100	100	100	100	100	100	100	100	100	100	100	100

Source: *Handbook of Educational and Allied Statistics, 1987*, Ministry of Human Resource Development, Government of India, New Delhi, 1987.

be ensured that all children, who attain the age of about 11 years by 1990, will have had five years of schooling, or its equivalent through the non-formal stream. Likewise, by 1995 all children will be provided free and compulsory education up to 14 years of age".

Over the years, the Centre and the States have made considerable investments in promoting Elementary Education. Tables 1.6, 1.7 and 1.8 bring out the status of expansion of elementary education since 1950-51.

TABLE 1.3: Share of Education in GNP (Percentage), 1950-51 to 1986-87

Years	Share of Education
1950-51	1.2
1960-61	2.5
1970-71	3.1
1980-81	3.1
1984-85	3.7
1985-86	4.0
1986-87	3.9

Source: *Education for All by 2000*, NIEPA, New Delhi, 1990, p. 105.

TABLE 1.4: Literacy Rate, 1951-1991

Year 1	Persons 2	Males 3	Females 4
1951	18.33	27.16	8.86
1961	28.31	40.40	15.34
1971	34.45	45.95	21.97
1981	43.56 (41.42)	56.37 (53.45)	29.75 (28.46)
1991	52.11	63.86	39.42

Notes: 1. Literacy rates for 1951, 1961 and 1971 relate to population aged five years and above. The rates for the years 1981 and 1991 relate to the population aged seven years and above. The literacy rates for the population aged five years and above in 1981 have been shown in brackets.

2. The 1981 rates exclude Assam where the 1981 Census could not be conducted. The 1991 Census rates exclude Jammu & Kashmir where the 1991 Census is yet to be conducted.

Source: *Census of India 1991*, Registrar General, India, New Delhi.

TABLE 1.5: Number of Literates and Illiterates among Population Aged Seven Years and Above, 1981-1991

(in '000s)

Literates/Illiterates	Persons	Males	Females
Literates			
1981	233,947	156,953	76,994
1991	352,082	224,288	127,794
Increase in 1991 over 1981	118,135	67,335	50,800
Illiterates			
1981	301,933	120,902	181,031
1991	324,030	126,694	197,336
Increase in 1991 over 1981	22,097	5,792	16,305

Notes: 1. The figures exclude Assam and Jammu & Kashmir. For Assam, the 1981 figures are not available as the 1981 Census could not be held there, while for Jammu & Kashmir, the 1991 figures are not yet available as the 1991 Census is yet to be conducted there.

2. Figures of literate population for 1991 are as per the provisional results of the 1991 Census. The figures of illiterate population aged seven years and above are estimated figures based on certain assumptions on population age structure and are likely to undergo change.

Source: *Census of India 1991*, Registrar General, India, New Delhi.

TABLE 1.6: Expansion of Elementary Education, 1950-51 and 1989-90

	1950-51	1989-90
Number of primary schools	2.10 lakhs	5.50 lakhs
Number of middle schools	0.14 lakhs	1.44 lakhs
Enrolment in classes I to V	19.15 million	97.3 million
boys	13.77 million	57.7 million
girls	5.38 million	39.6 million
Enrolment in classes VI to VIII	3.13 million	32.2 million
boys	2.59 million	20.4 million
girls	0.54 million	11.8 million
Enrolment in classes I to VIII	22.28 million	129.5 million
boys	16.36 million	78.1 million
girls	5.92 million	51.4 million

TABLE 1.7: Gross Enrolment Ratios: Percentage of Enrolment in the Respective Age-group Population, 1989-90

Classes/Age-group	Boys	Girls	Total
I-V (6-11 yrs)	115.5	83.6	99.9
VI-VIII (11-14 yrs)	73.0	44.6	59.1

TABLE 1.8: Gross Enrolment Ratios: Scheduled Castes and Scheduled Tribes, 1989-90

	Scheduled Cast			Scheduled Tribes		
Classes/Age group	Boys	Girls	Total	Boys	Girls	Total
I-V (6-11 yrs)	120.93	78.81	100.44	127.53	77.55	103.22
VI-VIII (11-14 yrs)	59.70	31.08	45.75	49.63	24.02	37.15

TABLE 1.9: High School/Senior/Secondary/Pre-University/Intermediate Education: Institutions and Enrolment 1950-51 and 1989-90

Institutions and Enrolment	1950-51	1989-90
(1) High/Post Basic/Senior Secondary schools/10+2 Pattern	7,416	70,663*
(2) Enrolment in classes IX to XII	1,219,917	17,211,264 (High schools: 13,789,333 10+2 Pattern: 3,421,931)
(3) Pre-university/Intermediate/ Junior colleges	128	5,486
(4) Enrolment in Pre-university/ Intermediate class/Junior college	221,337	2,758,946
High schools	57,973	
Higher Secondary schools (New Pattern)	12,660	

TABLE 1.10: Higher Education: Institutions and Enrolment: 1950-51 and 1989-90

	1950-51	1989-90
(1) Universities, Institutions Deemed to be universities and Institutions of National Importance	27	184
(2) Colleges for General Education and degree alone	542	4,755
(3) Enrolment at the university stage (Arts, Science and Commerce college	3.6 lakhs	40.75 lakhs

Source: 1. *A Handbook of Educational and Allied Statistics, 1987*, Ministry of Human Resource Development, Government of India, New Delhi, 1987.
2. *Selected Educational Statistics (1989-90)*, Ministry of Human Resource Development, Government of India, New Delhi, 1991
3. *Annual Report, 1990-91*, Part I, Ministry of Human Resource Development, Government of India, New Delhi, 1991.

TABLE 1.11: Teachers, 1950-51 and 1989-90

Sl. No.	Category	Number of teachers	
		1950-51	1989-90
1.	Primary	537,918	1,601,554
2.	Middle	85,496	1,047,588
3.	High and Higher Secondary	126,504	1,264,249
4.	Higher Education	18,648	250,000

TABLE 1.12: Percentage of Trained Teachers, 1950-51 and 1989-90

Sl. No.	Category	1950-51	1989-90
1.	Primary school	58.8	89.84
2.	Middle school	53.3	91.74
3.	Secondary and Senior Secondary Schools	55.5	92.60

2

POST-WAR PLAN OF EDUCATIONAL DEVELOPMENT, 1944*

Introduction

In 1944, while in England Butler's White Paper on Education was passing into an Act, the Central Advisory Board of Education (CABE) in India published a comprehensive report on the Post-War Educational Development of the country. This was a first systematic and national level attempt at tackling the problems of education as a whole. In fact, work on the problems of education had started in 1938 when a National Planning Committee had taken up the assessment of educational reconstruction at national level. The World War interrupted the effort. The CABE had also started that work in 1938 but the piecing together of the report of various committees could be done only in 1943-44.

The report reveals that whereas the pre-war Britain was spending Rs. 33.20 per head on education, India's comparable expenditure was only Rs. 0.89 per head. The merits of this report are obvious. It is concise, comprehensive and workable. It champions basic education for children from 6 to 14 and pleads for effective teaching at the primary level. It finds that a national system of education would take 30 to 40 years to be evolved.

Unfortunately it was drafted when the techniques of perspective planning were not known and the research available on planning was meagre, nor were the national goals precisely known. The projections of population, the rate of economic growth, the likely price levels are not there. Then, the plan could be acceptable neither to the aspiring State Governments who could ill afford to have a four-year period of

---

* *Post-War Educational Development in India: Sargent Report*, Manager of Publications, Delhi, 1944.

preparation and 30 to 35 years of implementation nor to the Centre because of the colossal expenditure involved because per capita cost was to be Rs. 11 in 30 years, exclusive of the cost of building. One reason why the Plan suffered unmerited neglect was the suspicion of its being British inspired and modelled. It is, however, clear that the forecast of the report was by no means far from the figures known today. The Education Commission's estimates of cost are Rs. 12 per head as against Sargent report's Rs. 11. The number of years would be about the same from 1951 to 1981. It is in explicable that the report was shelved.

REPORT BY THE CENTRAL ADVISORY BOARD OF EDUCATION ON THE POST-WAR EDUCATIONAL DEVELOPMENT IN INDIA, 1944[1]

Chairman
Jogendra Singh

Members

W.H.F. Armstrong	Sayidur Rahman
P.N. Banerjea	Renuka Ray
C.V. Chandrasekharan	M. Ruthnaswamy
Maurice Gwyer	Mohd. Samin Jan
M. Afzal Husin	H.N. Sen
Pir Illahi Bakhsh	Shah Alam
Mirza M. Ismail	Leonard G.D. Silva
W.A. Jenkins	Ujjal Singh
Abdus Samad Khan	R.M. Statham
Tamizuddin Khan	Malini B.Sukthankar
V.T. Krishnamachari	John Sargent

The report in its introduction began with following words from the White Paper containing proposals for the post-war expansion of the British education which was laid before Parliament:

> "Upon the education of the people of this country the fate of this country depends."

1. (i) Popularly known as the Sargent Report after the name of John Sargent, the then Educational Adviser to the Government of India
   (ii) Original Table Number has been changed to conform to this chapter number.

Type of Education Desired for India

In the introductory remarks the report sets out the aim of education in following words:

> While the aim throughout has been to devise a system which is essentially Indian, the Board at the same time believe that there are certain fundamental principles which must determine the training of the future citizen, wherever in the world he or she may happen to dwell, and they cannot conceive that any form of social or political community will ever prosper unless the importance of fostering in the rising generation such attributes as physical fitness, intelligence and integrity of character receives the fullest recognition. In particular they are anxious not to expose themselves to the criticism that they have ignored the moral or spiritual side of education; they wish to state with all the emphasis in their power that at all stages of education the training of the intellect and the training of character must proceed side by side.

Basic Education/Primary Education

The report observed:

> Basic (Primary and Middle) education as envisaged by the Central Advisory Board, embodies many of the educational ideas contained in the original Wardha Scheme, though it differs from it in certain important particulars. The main principle of learning through activity has been endorsed by educationists all over the world. At the lower stages the activity will take many forms, leading gradually up to a basic craft or crafts suited to local conditions. So far as possible the whole of the curriculum will be harmonised with this general conception. The three R's by themselves can no longer be regarded as an adequate equipment for efficient citizenship. The Board, however, are unable to endorse the view that education at any stage and particularly in the lowest stages can or should be expected to pay for itself through the sale of articles produced by the pupils. The most, which can be expected in this respect, is that sales should cover the cost of the additional materials and equipment required for practical work.
>
> Basic education, while preserving its essential unity, will consist of

> two stages—the junior (or Primary) stage covering a period of five years and the senior (or Middle) stage covering three years. Those, who find the term "Basic" unattractive and prefer the existing nomenclature of "Primary" and "Middle" for these two stages, are of course at liberty to retain these, provided they accept the essential unity of the two stages and the necessity of so planning the Primary course that it leads up naturally to the Middle. The main reason for this division is that at about the age of eleven to twelve, with the onset of adolescence, certain mental and physical changes occur in boys and girls which necessitate a corresponding adjustment both in the content of the curriculum and in the methods of instruction. "Hence", as the second Basic Committee says, "arises the need for treating the instruction given before and after this psychological break as forming two well defined stages, each with its own scope, aim and technique though inspired by the same fundamental aim.

The Sargent Report endorsed the recommendations of the two committees of the Central Advisory on Basic Education.

Two committees of the Central Advisory on Basic Education made the following recommendations:

(a) *First Committee*

(1) The scheme of 'basic' education should first be introduced in rural areas.
(2) The age range for compulsion should be six to fourteen years, but children can be admitted to the 'basic' school at the age of five.
(3) Diversion of students from the 'basic' school to other kinds of schools should be allowed after the 5th class or about the age of eleven plus.
(4) The medium of instruction should be the mother tongue of the pupils.
(5) A common language for India is desirable. This should be Hindustani with both the Urdu and Hindi scripts. Option should be given to children to choose the script and provision should be made for teaching them in that script. Every teacher should know both scripts, *viz.*, Urdu and Hindi. Some members of the Committee suggest that the adoption of Roman script might prove a solution to the language difficulty and greatly minimise the work of both scholar and teacher.

(6) The Wardha Scheme of basic education is in full agreement with the recommendations made in the Wood-Abbott Report so far as the principle of learning by doing is concerned. This activity should be of many kinds in the lower classes and later should lead to a basic craft, the produce from which should be saleable and the proceeds applied to the upkeep of the school.

(7) Certain elements of cultural subjects, which cannot be correlated with the basic craft, must be taught independently.

(8) The training of teachers should be reorganized and their status raised.

(9) No teacher should receive less than Rs. 20 per mensum.

(10) Efforts should be made to recruit more women teachers and to persuade girls of good education to take up teaching.

(11) Basic schools should be started only when suitable trained teachers are available.

(12) The curriculum will need revision in the light of experience.

(13) English should not be introduced as an optional subject in basic schools.

(14) The State should provide facilities as at present for every community to give religious teaching, when so desired but not at the cost of the State.

(15) No external examinations need be held. At the end of the basic school course a leaving certificate based on the internal examination should be given.

(16) Pupils wishing to join other schools at the end of the 5th class (age eleven plus) should also be granted a leaving certificate.

(17) Promotion from class to class will be determined by the school, though the results of the internal examinations should be subject to the supervisor's inspections.

(b) *Second Committee*

(1) While the provision of 'pre-basic' education in Nursery and infants schools and classes is highly desirable, it is not practicable at this stage, in view of the lack, both of money and of trained women teachers, to advocate its introduction on a compulsory basis. Provincial Governments should aim in the first place (a) at providing model infants and Nursery Schools in suitable centres, (b) at increasing the supply of properly trained infants' teachers, who should be women, (c) at encouraging the enrolment in 'basic' schools of children below

the minimum age for compulsory attendance, and (d) at stimulating the provision by voluntary agencies of efficient pre-basic schools.

(2) 'Basic' education should comprise a course of eight years from the age of six to fourteen years and that this course while preserving its essential unity should consist of two stages—the first stage, the 'Junior' stage, covering a period of five years and the second stage, the 'Senior', three years.

(3) The transfer of children from the 'basic' school to other forms of post-primary education should be allowed after the 5th grade, i.e., at the conclusion of the 'Junior basic' stage.

(4) The various types of post-primary school (other than the 'senior basic' school) to which suitable children may be transferred at the end of the 'junior basic' stage should provide a variety of courses extending over a period of at least five years after the age of eleven. These courses, while preserving an essential cultural character, should be designed to prepare pupils for entry to industrial and commercial occupations as well as to Universities.

(5) Special arrangements should be made in these schools for assimilating pupils who decide to continue their education after competing the full course in the 'basic' school, i.e., after reaching the 8th class.

(6) Suitable courses should be framed for girls attending 'senior basic' schools which should include such subjects as cookery, laundry work, needle work, homecrafts, the care of children and first aid, the remainder of the institutions to be correlated with this course of domestic science in accordance with the general principles of the 'basic education' scheme.

(7) A standing committee of the Central Advisory Board of Education should be appointed to watch new educational experiments carried on in the provinces as well as the progress of educational developments generally, with special reference to 'basic' eduation, and to make recommendations to the Board for ncessary action. There should be a representative of the Hindustani Talimi Sangh on this committee.

(8) Subject to such conditions as are set out in the report, the Central Government should contribute not less than half the amount of the approved net recurring expenditure on 'basic' education in each province, the balance to be found by the Provincial Government and the local bodies entrusted by it with the administration of compulsory education. For capital expenditure on buildings, equipment,

etc., a loan system should be adopted.
(9) A Central agency should be established in each province for the disposal of marketable articles produced in schools.

High School and Its Function

The Report says:

> the function of the High School is to cater for those children who are well above the average in ability. It will, therefore, only admit pupils selected on the basis of abilities, aptitudes, and general promise.
> High school education should on no account be considered simply as preliminary to University education, but as a stage complete in itself. . . . While it will remain a very important function of the High Schools to pass on their most able pupils to Universities or other institutions of equivalent standard, the large majority of High School leavers should receive an education that will fit them for direct entry into occupations and professions . . . though a certain percentage of them may be expected to require further training for a period of one to three years, either full-time or part-time in order to qualify themselves for posts that require special skill.

Types of High Schools

The reorganised High Schools, according to the Report, should be of two main types—the Academic and the Technical.

> The Academic High School will impart instruction in the Arts and pure Sciences; while the Technical High School will provide training in the applied sciences and industrial and commercial subjects. In both types the course in the Junior departments covering the present Middle stage will be very much the same and there will be a common core of the 'humanities' throughout. Art and Music should form an integral part of the curriculum, in both and all girls should take a course in domestic science. . . . Transfer from one type to the other should be made as easy as possible at any rate up to the end of the Junior courses. . . . In smaller centres which can only be served economically by single High Schools, the individual schools should be required to offer as wide a choice of

courses as possible. In rural areas . . . an agricultural bias should be given to the curriculum.

University Education

The Report summarises its recommendations on University education in the following words:

> Indian Universities, as they exist today, despite many admirable features do not fully satisfy the requirements of a national system of education. In order to raise standards all round, the conditions of admission must be revised with the object of ensuring that all students are capable of taking full advantage of a University course. The proposed reorganization of the High School System will facilitate this. Adequate financial assistance must be provided for poor students. The present Intermediate Course should be abolished. Ultimately the whole this course should be covered in the High School, but as an immediate step the first year of the course should be transferred to High School and the second to Universities. The minimum length of a University Course should be three years (in certain subjects longer). The tutorial system should be widely extended and closer personal contacts established between teachers and students. The importance of establishing a high standard in post-graduate studies and particularly in pure and applied research should be emphasised. Steps should be taken to improve the conditions of service, including remuneration of University and College Teachers where those now in operation are not attracting men and women of the requisite calibre.

Technical and Vocational Education

The Report divided the workers needed by Indian Arts and Industries into four categories:

(a) *Chief Executives and Research Workers of the Future*

> These will normally have their preliminary training in a Technical High School and will then pass to the Technological Department of a University or to a full-time course of the National Diploma

type in a Technical Institution. The admission to these courses should be the outcome of a very strict process of selection. They will not be many.

(b) *Minor Executives, Foremen, Charge Hands, etc.*

It is the main aim of the Technical High School to satisfy this need; but the Technical High School pupil will be required to continue his technical education either by taking a National Diploma or Certificate Course or by attending part-time classes of a fairly advanced description.

(c) *Skilled Craftsmen*

These may be recruited from Technical High School pupils; but as a rule after passing through the Senior Basic School where they will have mastered the rudiments of craft work, they will go to Junior Technical Trade or Industrial Schools for a further two or three years, full-time course.

(d) *Semi-skilled and Unskilled Labour*

They will be recruited mostly directly from Senior Basic (Middle) Schools where they will have done some craft work. It is important to afford these persons facilities both for continuing their general education and for improving their skills, so that the best of them may ultimately ascend to the skilled class.

Role of Adult Education

The role of Adult Education, according to the Report is

> to make every possible member of a State an effective and efficient citizen and thus to give reality to the ideal of democracy. . . . In India, so far the general attitude has been to regard adult education as connoting adult literacy. The reason is obvious, for the problem in this country is vastly different from what it is in Western countries. A child must learn to walk before he can run; an adult must be literate before he can hope to derive any benefit from facilities for education in the wider sense. . . . The main em-

phasis in this country must, for some time to come, be on literacy, although from the very beginning some provision must be made for adult education proper, so that those made literate may have an inducement as well as an opportunity to pursue their studies.

The Report made many observations regarding the organisation of a programme of Adult Education.

SUMMARY OF MAJOR RECOMMENDATIONS

(1) **Basic Education**

(a) A system of universal, compulsory and free education for all boys and girls between the ages of six and fourteen should be introduced as speedily as possible though in view of the practical difficulty of recruiting the requisite supply of trained teachers it may not be possible to complete it in less than forty years.
(b) The character of the instruction to be provided should follow the general lines laid down in the reports of the Central Advisory Board's two Committees on Basic Education.
(c) The Senior Basic (Middle) School, being the finishing school for the great majority of future citizens, is of fundamental importance and should be generously staffed and equipped.
(d) All education depends on the teacher. The present status and remuneration of teachers and especially those in Primary Schools, are deplorable. The standards in regard to the training, recruitment and conditions of service of teachers prescribed in the report of the Committee approved by the Central Advisory Board in 1943 represent the minimum compatible with the success of a national system, these should be adopted and enforced everywhere.
(e) A vast increase in the number of trained women teachers will be required.

(2) **Nursery Education**

(a) An adequate provision of pre-primary instruction in the form of Nursery Schools or classes is an essential adjunct to any national system of education. The provision in this respect at present is negligible.
(b) In urban areas, where sufficient children are available within a

reasonable radius, separate Nursery Schools or departments may be provided; elsewhere Nursery classes should be attached to Junior Basic (Primary) Schools.
(c) Nursery Schools and classes should invariably be staffed with women teachers who have received special training for this work.
(d) Pre-primary education should in all cases be free. While it may not be feasible to make attendance compulsory, no efforts should be spared to persuade parents to send their children to school voluntarily, particularly in areas where housing conditions are unsatisfactory and/or mothers are accustomed to go out to work.
(e) The main object of education at this stage is to give young children social experience rather than formal instruction.
(f) On the basis of normal age-range of three to six years provision has been made for 1,000,000 places in Nursery Schools and classes.

(3) **High School Education**

(a) The High School course should cover six years and the normal age of admission should be about eleven.
(b) Entry to High Schools should be on a selective basis; only those pupils should be admitted who show promise of taking full advantage of the education provided. Additional places may be provided for those not selected provided that no cost falls on public funds.
(c) In accordance with the general principle set out in (b) above, places in High School should be provided for at least one child in every five of the appropriate age-group.
(d) In order to secure the right children, the methods of selection to be employed will require the most careful considerations. Special arrangements will have to be made for the transfer from Senior Basic (Middle) Schools to High School of suitable children and particularly of those who show signs of late development.
(e) High Schools should be of two main types—(i) Academic (ii) Technical. The objective of both should be to provide a good all-round education combined with some preparation in the later stages for the careers which pupils will enter on leaving school.
(f) The curriculum in all cases should be as varied as circumstances permit and should not be unduly restricted by the requirements of Universities or examining bodies.
(g) In order that no poor child of ability may be excluded, liberal assistance in the form of free places, scholarships and stipends should

be available throughout the course.

(h) In order to secure teachers of the right type, the salaries paid in all recognised schools, whether maintained by the State or by private bodies, should not be less than those prescribed by the Central Advisory Board of Education.

(4) **University Education**

(a) Indian Universities, as they exist today, despite many admirable features do not fully satisfy the requirements of a national system of education.

(b) In order to raise standards all round, the conditions for admission must be revised with the object of ensuring that all students are capable of taking full advantage of a University Course. The proposed reorganisation of the High School system will facilitate this. Adequate financial assistance must be provided for poor students.

(c) The present intermediate course should be abolished. Ultimately the whole of this course should be covered in the High School but as an immediate step the first year of the course should be transferred to High Schools and the second to Universities.

(d) The minimum length of a University degree course should be three years.

(e) The tutorial system should be widely extended and closer personal contacts established between teachers and students.

(f) The importance of establishing a high standard in post-graduate studies and particularly in pure and applied research should be emphasised.

(g) Steps should be taken to improve the conditions of service, including remuneration, of University and College teachers where those now in operation are not attracting men and women of the requisite calibre.

(h) An Indian University Grants Committee should be constituted for the purposes and with the terms of reference set out in this chapter.

(i) To provide for the increased number of able and well-prepared students, which a national system of High School may be expected to produce, approximately 240,000 places, or double the existing number, should be available in Universities.

(5) Technical, Commercial and Art Education

(a) In view of the prospective needs of post-war industry and commerce for skilled technicians, and in order to cater for the aptitudes of those who will derive greater benefit from a practical course, the establishment of an efficient system of technical education at all stages, on the lines set out in the report of the Technical Education Committee, is a matter of great urgency.

(b) Due regard should be had to the recommendations of the Abbot-Wood Report in respect of the scope and content of Technical instruction.

(6) Adult Education

The main conclusions and recommendations of the Adult Education Committee of the Central Advisory Board of Education, together with the decisions of the Board thereon, are reproduced below:

(1) To secure an early and effective solution of India's educational problems, the provision of facilities for adult education on the widest scale and the introduction of a free and compulsory system of primary education are of equal urgency and must be treated as complementary to one another.

(2) While the literacy campaign is only one aspect of the adult education movement, the prevalence of illiteracy in India at the present time makes it the aspect to which immediate attention must be devoted.

(3) Literacy is a means to further education and must not be regarded as an end in itself. The primary aim of the campaign must be not merely to make adults literate but to keep them literate. To achieve its object, the attack must be launched on the widest possible front with the help of every agency, human or material, which can in any way contribute to its success. Continuous and effective propaganda of all kinds is essential.

(4) Efforts should be directed in the beginning to persuade illiterates voluntarily to undergo instruction. If a voluntary system fails to achieve its object, ways and means of bringing pressure to bear on illiterates should be explored.

(5) In a movement of this character the utmost freedom must be allowed to experiment, and regard must be had at all times to local

conditions. No useful purpose would be served by attempting to prescribe methods or draw up a code applicable to India as a whole. Valuable assistance might, however, be afforded to Provincial Governments and other authorities responsible for adult education if a committee of experts were appointed to report on questions of teaching technique and survey the results of experiments.

(Board's Decision on No 5: "The Board were of opinion that it would be premature at this stage to appoint a Committee as suggested. It is too early as yet to survey the progress of the movement as a whole or to assess the results of the experiments which are being carried out in many areas. The Educational Commissioner was asked to collect information from Provincial Education Authorities as and when available and to prepare a statement for the Board.")

(6) Whatever subjects are introduced into the curriculum and whatever the teaching methods adopted, the form in which instruction is given must be intelligible and interesting to the student, and the instruction itself should be closely related to his occupation, his personal interests and the social and economic conditions under which he lives.

(7) It is unnecessary and inexpedient in view of the circumstances prevailing in India to draw any rigid distinction between adult education in the strict sense and technical, commercial or art instruction or to regard the latter as falling outside the sphere of the former. The easiest way of approach to many adult students may be through subjects of a vocational character.

(8) With a view to defining what is meant by an adult it is recommended

(a) That a boy under the age of twelve should not be admitted to an adult centre under any circumstances;

(b) That a boy, so long as he is attending a full-time day school, should not be encouraged to attend evening classes as well; and

(c) That subject to (b) above and wherever the numbers justify it, separate classes should be organized for boys between twelve and sixteen.

It is unnecessary to fix any age limits in the case of girls who wish to join adult classes for women.

(9) Every effort should be made to enlist the help of voluntary agencies. Classes run by reputable associations should receive every encouragement and bodies whose primary objects are not educational need not be excluded if adequate safeguards are provided

against any risk of the movement being used for religious or political propaganda.

(10) Universities should be urged to expand and popularize the work of their extra-mural departments and provide opportunities for adult students of exceptional ability to take a University course.

(11) An extension in the number and scope of institutions providing technical, commercial and art instruction is urgently needed, and subjects of a cultural or recreational kind should be included in their curricula.

(12) Adult education is a branch of social reconstruction. Social science in a practical form should be taught in all Universities.

(13) The possibility of making a period of social service obligatory on all students in Universities and pupils in the upper forms of High Schools should be carefully examined. Pending the setting up of a special committee for this purpose a strong appeal should be made to all educated persons, and in particular to Government servants, to render voluntary service in connection with the literacy campaign.

(*Board's decision on Nos. 10, 12 and 13:* "The Board decided, without endorsing them, to ask Provincial Governments to bring them to the notice of Universities in their areas for such action as they might think fit.")

(14) Mechanical aids to learning such as the radio, the cinema, the gramophone and the magic lantern can be used with great effect in adult education. To enable them to be employed much more widely than at present, steps should be taken to increase the supply and reduce the cost. Information on this and other points should be collected and distributed by the Bureau of the Central Advisory Board of Education.

(15) An adequate supply of trained and competent teachers is the fundamental need in adult as in every other branch of education. Teachers in day school may be expected to form the nucleus of this supply but in view of the fact that teaching methods which are successful with children are not always suitable for adults, they will require a special course of training. It is recommended that the course of training in the normal schools should include instruction in the technique of teaching adults.

(16) It will be necessary to supplement the professional teachers by a large body of helpers drawn from other occupations. The training of these is an essential preliminary to their employment, particularly if they are to be in charge of classes.

(17) Every Province should appoint Inspectors and Organizers, expert in and able to devote their whole time to adult education. The appointment, by at least one Province, of a number of full-time teachers of adult work only is a commendable experiment.

(18) The movement so far as depended very largely on unpaid service but it is reasonable to anticipate that it will soon require a very considerable portion of paid workers, especially when the demand arises for instruction beyond the stage of mere literacy. The financial implications of this, including the rates of pay and conditions of services to be offered, are matters for local consideration.

(19) A library is an essential adjunct to every adult education centre. Liberal grants should be given to increase the number and size of libraries, particularly in rural areas, and to assist the production of suitable literature. The Central Government should help in the distribution of books and other literature by granting special postal concessions. Provincial Governments should take immediately steps to deal with the present unsatisfactory state of affairs so far as the supply of text-books is concerned.

(*Board's Decision*: "While in full agreement as to the need for extending libraries and providing suitable literature, the Board felt that no useful purpose would be served by asking the Central Government for special concessions as suggested by the Committee")

(20) The importance of a wide expansion of facilities for adult education is even more important in the case of women than that of men. The methods of approach in the case of women must be at once more varied and less formal.

(21) Illiteracy is not confined to the village; a large proportion of the workers in urban areas is also illiterate. In this connection it is essential to secure the co-operation of employers of labour and associations of workers. The question of levying a tax on those employers of labour, who do not make adequate provisions for the education of their employees, is worthy of consideration.

(*Board's Decision on No. 21:* "The Board felt that practical difficulties would arise with regard to the levying of a tax on those employers who do not make provision for the education of their employees.")

(22) It should be obligatory on all Government departments, Central and local, to ensure that their staffs are literate.

(*Board's Decision on No. 22:* "While agreeing as to the desirability of all Government departments giving every encouragement to their staffs to become literate, the Board did not agree that this should be made obligatory under existing circumstances.")

(23) The progress of the Adult Education Movement can only be ensured if its control in each Province is vested in a single authority. That authority should be the Education Department. It should be the duty of the Education Department (a) to establish satisfactory contacts with other authorities in the province concerned with social reconstruction, of which adult education is a part and (b) to delegate authority to such subordinate bodies and to appoint such officers as local circumstances may require for the effective organization and supervision of the movement.

(24) The cost of the literacy campaign alone apart from other essential developments in adult education will impose a very severe strain on the resources of most Provincial Governments. In view of the extreme importance of bringing the campaign to a successful conclusion at the earliest possible date, the Central Government should afford financial assistance to those Provincial Governments which are prepared to carry out approved schemes within the next five years.

(*Board's Decision:* "In view of the prior claims of primary education to any financial assistance which might be forthcoming from the Central Government towards educational development in the Provinces, the Board were unable to accept the recommendation of the Committee that the Central Government should make a specific grant to Provincial Government for carrying out approved schemes of adult education.")

(25) In each Province there should be established a Bureau to collect and distribute information with regard to the adult education movement. There should also be a Central Bureau to collect, collate and publish at regular intervals information as to the progress of the movement in all parts of the country. The Bureau of the Central Advisory Board of Education should be equipped to undertake this latter function.

(*Board's Decision:* "The Board were in sympathy with the general policy outlined but thought it advisable to wait for action by Provincial Governments before expanding their own Bureau for this purpose.")

(26) The returns as to literacy in the Census Report should be so amended as to make them more useful for educational purposes.

(a) Comprehensive arrangements on the general lines set out in the Adult Education Committee's report should form an integral part of any national system of education. These are particularly important in India today in view of the very high percentage of illiterates.

(b) Literacy is a means not an end in itself. Although the main emphasis in the beginning may be placed on the liquidation of illiteracy, adult education in the full sense must be provided for those already literate. The amount of this should progressively increase as illiteracy disappears.

(c) It is estimated that even with the introduction of a universal system of Basic education there will be over 9 crores of illiterates (age 10—40) to be dealt with. Plans should be made to solve this problem by a campaign spread over twenty years. Before this campaign opens, five years should be devoted to the necessary preparations, including the recruitment and training of the staff of teachers required.

(d) In this as in all branches of education the quality of the teacher is of supreme importance. The difficulty of obtaining a sufficient number of teachers of the right type, particularly women, must on no account be under-estimated.

(e) The responsibility for adult education must rest with the State but every effort should be made to enlist the aid of suitable voluntary organisations wherever available.

(7) Training of Teachers

(a) The existing training institutions are barely sufficient to meet wastage among existing teachers and to train those hitherto untrained.

(b) New Training Colleges (including University Education Departments) must be provided to supply the additional teachers whom a national system will require. These will amount to over 2,000,000 non-graduates for schools of all types and 180,000 graduates for high schools.

(c) Arrangements should be made to pick out suitable boys and girls towards the end of the high school course. This is particularly important in girls' high schools in view of the vast increase in the number of women teachers required.

(d) The courses provided should be essentially practical and should be specially related to the needs of the schools in which the trainees will subsequently serve.

(e) No fees should be charged in training colleges; liberal assistance should be available for the maintenance of poor students.

(f) Refresher courses are of the utmost importance and should be provided for all types of teachers but particularly for those in remote rural areas. Facilities should be provided for research and selected teachers should be encouraged to study educational methods in foreign countries.

(8) **Health of the School Child**

The main conclusions of the Joint Committee of the Central Advisory Board of Education and Health are set out below:

Introduction and Historical

(1) The Committee wish to draw special attention to the frequency with which a system of medical inspection has been started in a Province only to be abandoned after a shortwhile as a measure of economy. This indicates that there has not been a clear appreciation of the fundamental necessity for and the essential characteristics of a school medical scheme. The Committee emphasise that satisfactory arrangements for school medical inspection and treatment form an essential part of any efficient system of public education.

Aims and Objects of a School Medical Service

(2) The Committee consider that the aims and object of a school medical service, as defined by Sir George Newman, are applicable to India and that it is absolutely essential that steps be taken to ensure that children attending school are healthy and kept healthy. This is necessary not only from the medical but also from the educational point of view.

(3) In developing a school medical service in India a big difficulty is the inadequate number of qualified doctors and nurses. However, in some of the large cities it should be possible to organise school health work on as wide a basis as in the West.

Medical Inspection

(4) Probably fifty per cent of the children attending school would be found to require medical attention or medical observation.

(5) Too much weight cannot be given to health consideration in

determining age at which children should be admitted to school. The age of school entry should be not more than six and preferably five.
(6) Many routine examinations of school children in some parts of India are unnecessary. The routine examinations should be (a) on entry into a primary school at approximately the sixth year, (b) at the eleventh year and, (c) at the fourteenth year. For children in high schools when leaving at the age of seventeen a final examination is desirable. Children going from a private school without a medical inspection scheme to a secondary school should be given a routine examination as soon as possible after admission.
(7) A whole-time doctor may reasonably be expected to carry out 5,000 routine inspections in a year.
(8) A medical record will have to be maintained for each child, which will go with the child when he goes from one school to another.
(9) Height and weight records should be taken not less than twice a year. This work should be done by the teacher.
(10) Medical inspection should only be carried out by a qualified doctor with special training for the work.
(11) Medical inspection should take place in the school during school hours and if possible the parents should be present. In schools with a physical instructor, he should as far as possible be available during the inspection. The doctor should go through the inspection results with the teachers.

Treatment and Follow-up

(12) A scheme for medical inspection without provision for treatment and follow-up is of little or no use. Schemes for treatment must include provision for supplementary nourishment. Special arrangements will be necessary for treating dental defects, tonsils and adenoids and for correcting the more serious defects of vision and hearing.
(13) In urban areas accommodation for school clinics should be provided at convenient centres. In many towns, buildings suitable for the purpose already exist, such as maternity and child welfare centres. Where it is not possible to provide special school clinics, the next best plan is a special session for school children at the local hospital or dispensary.
(14) Much of the minor elementary treatment can be done by the teacher provided he has received the requisite instruction.

(15) Any campaign for the reduction and prevention of disease amongst school children must be carried into the home, if sound progress is to be achieved.
(16) Every effort should be made to secure the interest and co-operation of health visitors in following up the defective school children in their homes.
(17) The lack of contact in every type of school between teachers and parents is a regrettable feature of school life in India, which the Committee feel should be remedied as soon as possible.
(18) As the teacher is the solution of so many of the problems of school health, the Committee urge the vital importance of making the conditions of employment more attractive to the right type of man and woman.

Nutrition

(19) The children of primary schools are not generally included in the schemes for mid-day meals. The effects of malnutrition on primary school children are not less serious than on children of higher ages. All the children should be given a mid-day meal, whether it is brought from their homes or provided at the school. Parents able to pay should contribute to the scheme.
(20) Simple text-books embodying the fundamental principles of nutrition should be made available in the different Indian languages.

Personal and Environmental Hygiene

(21) The practice of personal hygiene by school children depends largely on the example set by the teacher. Not only must the teacher's personal cleanliness be of a high standard but his physique and general health must also be good. All candidates for admission to training colleges and schools should be medically examined. The teacher should be medically examined at intervals as much to protect his own health as to eliminate any danger to the school population.
(22) A daily parade before the school starts gives an opportunity of judging cleanliness standards. It should be a health and cleanliness parade.
(23) Where it is necessary to use ordinary buildings as schools, the responsible educational authority should obtain the advice of the local health officer as to their suitability.

(24) The appointment of a body of experts to report on suitable standards for lighting, ventilation and heating of schools is recommended.

(25) In each school some type of container should be provided in which wholesome water kept under lock and key is made available.

(26) Regarding the provision of latrines, the bored-hole latrine offers a satisfactory solution in most rural and suburban areas.

(27) The effect of posture on the child's health and growth with special reference to the use of desks and seats is a matter of great importance and requires special investigation by experts.

(28) Co-operative effort among the children for the cleaning up of the school and its surrounding areas should be encouraged and suggestions are made for carrying this out.

Teaching of Hygiene in Schools and in Training Colleges

(29) Instruction to school children in hygiene should begin at the earliest age possible and at the beginning should be made wholly on practical lines and devoted mainly to personal hygiene.

(30) The Junior Red Cross Health Game is an appropriate and valuable means of laying the foundations of a healthy life during the primary school years.

(31) Hygiene should be a compulsory subject in all courses for the training of teachers.

(32) Practical demonstrations should form an important part of the course of training in hygiene for teachers. They should be taught by practice to recognise defects in children and to do elementary treatment.

(33) Text-books on hygiene dealing with Indian conditions are indispensable.

Physical Education

(34) The Education Department headquarters staff should include a well qualified and experienced officer to organise the scheme for physical instruction in colleges and schools. He should have an Inspector for each District.

(35) The physical instructor should have training in the elementary principles of physiology, of the hygienic mode of life and of nutrition.

(36) Health education should find a prominent place in the

programme of study of the physical instructors, the aim being to develop in them the incentive and the ability to train children to practise healthful living and enable them to co-operate intelligently in medical inspection.

(37) Every secondary school should have a fully trained physical instructor, and his appointment should be a condition for a grant-in-aid.

(38) District Inspectors should organise training camps for physical instruction, lasting about a month for primary school teachers.

(39) A special effort should be made to accelerate the rate of progress of physical education in girls' schools.

(40) Some period, everyday during school hours, should be devoted to organise physical activity but undue emphasis on drill is undesirable.

Organised games should form an important part of the curriculum for physical education.

Corporate Activities

(41) The Education Department should be strongly represented on the Junior Red Cross Committees in order that the potential benefit of this important movement may become more widespread throughout the schools.

(42) The curriculum of the school should be arranged to provide at least one period a week for some corporate activity in addition to physical training and organised games.

(43) A sustained campaign to interest the parents in the school activities and to increase the opportunities of contact between the parents and the school authorities must be undertaken.

(44) Much can be done through education to improve existing health conditions, and the simultaneous education of the child and his parent is an important part of the corporate activities of the school.

Administration

(45) School medical services should be created in the provinces.

(46) The administrative control of these, including the necessary budget provision, should be under the Education Department.

(47) In each major province there should be Chief School Medical Officer to administer the school medical service, which should con-

tain sufficient number of doctors for the administrative and executive duties, medical inspection and treatment of school children.

(48) In order to promote co-ordination in regard to school medical work between the Education Department and the Medical and Public Health Departments, a co-ordination committee consisting of the Director of Public Instruction, Surgeon-General or Inspector-General of Civil Hospitals and the Director of Public Health should be set up in major provinces.

(49) In making the recommendation for the appointment of a Chief School Medical Officer the Committee do not regard it as necessarily involving the appointment of a third administrative medical officer at Provincial headquarters. They are of opinion that, in order to secure as much co-ordination as possible and to facilitate the economic use of doctors already in the employment of the Provincial Governments, it may be found convenient for the Surgeon-General or the Inspector-General of Civil Hospitals as the case may be, or the Director of Public Health to act as Chief School Medical Officer under the Minister for Education. Whether one of these officers acts as Chief School Medical Officer or a separate appointment is made is obviously a matter for each Provincial Government to decide.

(50) Government control over the efficiency of local school medical inspection schemes should be exercised through the judicious distribution of grants-in-aid to the responsible local bodies. Government grant-in-aid should be at least 50 per cent of the cost.

(51) The expenditure on the supervising staff maintained at Provincial and District headquarters should be a charge on the Provincial funds.

(52) Continuity in school medical work is vital and the period of deputation of a doctor for this work should be at least four to five years.

(53) In the larger towns the employment of whole-time school medical officers is essential for efficient service and such officers should not be permitted to engage in private practice. A scheme should include primary and secondary schools and it should be a condition of recognition that each school takes part in the scheme.

(54) Medical inspection and treatment should be provided free for the children of all primary schools and of the primary departments of secondary schools.

(55) In secondary schools, particularly in urban areas, the fees charged should include a contribution towards the cost of medical in-

spection and treatment.

(56) Before a school medical inspection scheme can be drawn up for rural areas a preliminary survey should be made of the medical facilities available and of the ways of supplementing them.

9. Education of the Handicapped

(a) Provision for the mentally or physically handicapped should form an essential part of a national system of education and should be administered by the Education Department.

(b) Hitherto in India, Governments have hardly interested themselves at all in this branch of education, what has been done has been due almost entirely to voluntary effort.

(c) Wherever possible, handicapped children should not be segregated from normal children. Only when the nature and extent of their defect make it necessary, should they be sent to special schools or institutions. Partially handicapped children should receive special treatment at ordinary schools.

(d) The blind and deaf need special educational arrangements including specially trained teachers. It may be desirable to establish Central institutions for training the teachers required.

(e) Particular care should be taken to train the handicapped, wherever possible, for remunerative employment and to find such employment for them. Aftercare work is essential.

(f) In the absence of any reliable data, it is impossible to estimate what would be the cost of making adequate provision for the handicapped in India; 10 per cent of the total expenditure on basic and high schools has been set aside for special services, which include such provision, and it is hoped that this will suffice.

10. Recreative and Social Activities

(a) The provision of recreative and social activities on an adequate scale is an essential feature of any modern educational system.

(b) Apart from the needs of boys and girls in schools and colleges special attention should be paid to those in the 14-20 age group who are no longer attending school. To serve these a Youth Movement on an All-India basis should be set up.

(c) A Youth Movement should aim at co-ordinating and supplementing rather than superseding the work of organisations already dealing with aspects of this problem.

(d) The main need of a Youth Movement will be for leaders, both men and women, who will have to be specially trained. The possibility of finding suitable recruits among demobilised officers and N.C.O.'s should be explored.

(e) The provision of social and recreative facilities for adults should form an important part of any Social Service scheme.

11. Employment Bureaux

(a) Employment Bureaux form an essential part of educational administration, they are especially necessary in India in view of the restricted openings at the moment for progressive employment.

(b) Employment Bureaux, if they are to fulfil successfully the functions set out in this chapter, must be staffed by trained experts with practical experience of teaching and of industrial conditions.

(c) While contact should be maintained with Employment Exchanges, Labour Tribunals, etc., established by other Departments, Employment Bureaux, which deal with the output of educational institutions, should be under the control of the Education Department.

12. Administration

(a) The provinces should remain the main units for educational administration except in regard to University and higher technical education, the activities of which should be co-ordinated on an All-India basis.

(b) In the event of the Indian States taking part in educational development on an All-India scale, it may be necessary, in order to form economic educational units, to group the smaller ones or attach them to larger States or contiguous provinces.

(c) A national system of education will require much closer co-operation, financial and otherwise, between the Central and Provincial Governments.

(d) Provincial Governments should be left to make such changes in their administrative arrangements as the carrying out of education developments on the scale contemplated may require. Experience, however, suggests that they would be well-advised to resume all educational powers from local bodies, except where these are functioning efficiently.

(e) In order to enlist local interest in education, School Managing Bodies, School Boards and District Education Committees may be constituted, if and when sufficient people of the right type are available to serve on them. An Education Advisory Board for the whole Province may be desirable.

(f) A strong Education Department will be required at the Centre and in its connection the scope and functions of the Central Advisory Board should be enlarged.

(g) Steps should be taken in accordance with the recommendations of the Board's Committee on the Recruitment of Education Officers (1943) to check the present deterioration in the status and calibre of the educational administrative service and to enable it to secure the services of the type of officer who will be capable of carrying a scheme of the kind contemplated into successful operation.

(h) Arrangements should be made for the exchange of officer between the Centre and the Provinces and between one Province and another. The desirability of establishing a senior educational administrative service on an All-India basis should receive consideration.

(i) The Director of Public Instruction should be directly responsible for the general administration of education, other than University and higher technical education, throughout the Province. He should also be Secretary for Education, should it be thought necessary to keep in existence a separate post of this kind.

(j) Provision has been made under each separate branch of education for the cost of administration which may be estimated at 5 per cent of the gross annual expenditure.

TABLE 2.1: Financial Estimates in 1944

(Rupees in lakhs)

	Estimated gross annual expenditure	Estimated income from sources other than public funds	Estimated net expenditure to be met from public funds
1. Basic (Primary and Middle) Education	200,00	...	200,00
2. Pre-Primary Education	3,20	...	3,20
3. High School Education	79,00	29,00	50,00
4. University Education	9,60	2,90	6,70
5. Technical, Commercial and Art Education	10,00	2,00	8,00
6. Adult Education	3,00	...	3,00
7. Training of Teachers	6,20	1,70	4,50
8. School Medical Service	...	...	...
9. Education of the Handicapped	...	...	...
10. Recreative and Social Activities	1,00	...	1,00
11. Employment Bureaux	60	...	60
12. Administration	...	...	...
Total	312,60	35,60	277,00

3

COMMITTEE ON THE WAYS AND MEANS OF FINANCING EDUCATIONAL DEVELOPMENT, 1950*

Introduction

In the 14th meeting of the Central Advisory Board of Education (CABE) and the All-India Educational Conference held in January, the issue of future development and planning was discussed. It was generally agreed that the period of forty years laid down in the report of 'Post-War Educational Development in India, 1944, must be curtailed and if necessary for the purpose, stage up to which compulsion should be enforced, may also be reduced. It was, therefore, decided by the Government of India to appoint a Committee to examine the existing financial resources and the programme for educational development for all Provinces and States and to make suggestions to ensure that educational development may not be held up for want of funds. The Committee made fourteen recommendations on Central Grants, Levy of an Education Cess and Educational Loans.

Agenda

1. To consider in the light of present conditions the finances (recurring and non-recurring) required for the different stages of a comprehensive system of education for India.
2. To consider the ways and means of raising the necessary finances by means of any or all of the following methods:

(i) *Central Grants:* Allocation of the sources of revenue between

* Manager of Publications, Delhi, 1950.

the Central and the Provincial Governments under the new Constitution; scope and extent of grants from Central Revenues:

(a) To Provincial Governments;
(b) For Central all-India schemes of development;
(c) To Universities and other all-India institutions.

(ii) *Levy of an Education Cess:* Its feasibility and details of its levy, administration and distribution.
(iii) *Educational Loans:* Purposes for which educational loans may be raised and the terms on which they should be raised and applied.

3. To consider any other feasible suggestions for raising the finances for educational development programme.

Composition of the Committee

The Government of India accordingly appointed a Committee consisting of the following members:

(a) Hon'ble Shri B.G. Kher, M.A., LL.B., Premier, Bombay Province.
(b) Dr. B.P. Adarkar, M.A. (Cantab), Ministry of External Affairs & Commonwealth Relations.
(c) Dr. Tara Chand, M.A., D. Phil. (Oxon.), Educational Adviser to the Government of India.
(d) Acharya Narendra Deo, D.Litt., Vice-Chancellor, Lucknow University.
(e) Prof. Humayun Kabir, M.A. (Oxon.), Joint Educational Adviser to the Government of India.
(f) Shri Rustom P. Masani, M.A.
(g) Shri V. Narahari Rao, Formerly Secretary to the Government of India, Ministry of Finance.
(h) The Hon'ble Shri N.R. Sarkar, Finance Minister, Government of West Bengal.
(i) Prof. K.T. Shah, Member, Constituent Assembly.

Dr. Bina Chatterjee, Assistant Educational Adviser, Ministry of Education, acted as Secretary to the Committee.

SUMMARY OF RECOMMENDATIONS

(i) The State must undertake the responsibility of providing at least Junior Basic Education for everybody without, however, detriment to existing facilities for Secondary and Higher Education. Special attention should be given to the provision of such higher studies as will be necessary for increasing the industrial and agricultural potential of the country.

(ii) The Provinces should aim at introducing universal compulsory education for the children of 6–11 age-group within a period of ten years but if financial conditions compel, the programme may be extended over a larger period but in no circumstances should it be given up.

(iii) The basic minimum salary of trained Basic school teachers should be Rs. 40 per mensem and should on no account be reduced.

(iv) In view of the present emergency, the Committee, with great reluctance, agrees that only for five years, the teacher-pupil ratio may be 1: 40 instead of 1: 30, though from the educational point of view, this change would be most undesirable. The ratio of 1: 30 should be restored earlier, if possible, but in any case the position must be reviewed at the end of five years.

(v) In urban areas, where conditions justify, the same school buildings should be used for two shifts provided different teachers are employed in each shift.

(vi) Some increase in the fees in the post-compulsory stage of education, i.e., Senior Basic, Pre-Secondary and above, may be permitted, provided a substantial number of free places are available to meritorious students in straitened circumstances.

(vii) The Government may enact suitable legislation for ensuring that an adequate percentage of the income of all charitable trusts is allocated for expenditure on education provided that the Government may exempt certain specified types of trust, e.g., a medical trust, etc., from the operation of such law.

(viii) Students after passing their Matriculation or equivalent examination, should, subject to such conditions as may be laid down, be required to serve as teachers for Adult Education for a period of at least six months and Government may enact necessary legislation for the purpose.

(ix) Voluntary efforts should be encouraged for meeting the capital and recurring cost of education and voluntary organisations should be induced to run educational institutions with such assistance from Government as may be feasible.

(x) Wherever conditions permit, loans should be raised for meeting the capital cost of such part thereof as may be necessary.

(xi) A fixed percentage of Central and Provincial Revenues — about 10 per cent of the Central and 20 per cent of the Provincial — should be earmarked for education by the respective Government.

(xii) About 70 per cent of the expenditure on education should be borne by the Local Bodies and Provinces and the remaining 30 per cent by the Centre.

(xiii) All contributions for education approved by the Provincial or Central Government should be exempted from income-tax.

(xiv) The expenditure incurred on education by industrial or business concerns should also, if approved by the Provincial or Central Government, be treated as establishment expenses for purpose of income-tax.

4

SECONDARY EDUCATION COMMISSION, 1952-53
on Financing of Indian Education*

Introduction

The Secondary Education Commission was appointed by the Government of India on September 23, 1952, with Dr. A. Lakshmanswami Mudaliar, Vice-Chancellor, Madras University, as its Chairman, with the following terms of reference:

(a) to enquire into and report on the present position of Secondary Education in India in all its aspects; and
(b) to suggest measures for its reorganization and improvement with particular reference to:

   (i) the aims, organization and content of Secondary Education;
   (ii) its relationship to Primary, Basic and Higher Education;
   (iii) the inter-relation of Secondary Schools of different types; and
   (iv) other allied problems,

   so that a sound and reasonably uniform system of Secondary Education suited to our needs and resources may be provided for the whole country.

The Commission submitted its report in 1953. Its recommendations — almost all of them — including the opening of Multipurpose Schools and transforming High Schools into Higher Secondary

---

* *Report of the Secondary Education Commission*, Manager of Publications, Delhi, 1953, Chapter XIV.

Schools — two priority areas — could not be implemented on account of several constraints.

It also included a Chapter on Finance which is reproduced here.

Finance

Financial Aid to Secondary Education

The question has often been asked whether finances will be available to implement the recommendations that the Commission may make. It has been pointed out that the recommendations of the previous Commissions have not been given effect to, largely because the necessary financial resources could not be made available either by the States or by the Centre. While some of the recommendations that we have made may possibly be implemented without undue strain on the financial resources of the States or the Centre, the most important of our recommendations do require substantial financial help if they are to be worked out successfully.

Responsibilities of Centre and State

We have been told that under the Constitution, Secondary education is a responsibility of the States. We have already expressed the view that the Centre is not absolved of all responsibility in regard to Secondary education, particularly those aspects which have a bearing on the general economic development of the country and the training for citizenship. Moreover the fundamental rights guarantee to every citizen free and compulsory education up to the age of 14; this implies that responsibility in this behalf is shared both by the States as well as the Centre. It seems obvious, therefore, that in all matters connected with the improvement of Secondary education there should be fullest cooperation between the States and the Centre both in regard to the lines on which education should develop as well as the manner in which the recommendations should be implemented.

In this respect we wish to draw attention to the analogy of the United States where, although education is the responsibility of individual States which can carry out their own experiments in education independently, there is an over-all pattern of education for all American youths, which has the approval and support of the Federal Government. The Federal Government has found it necessary to guarantee through legislation substantial financial aid for educational development. The recommendations to which we attach great importance relate to the implementation of vocational education as a part of Secondary education and its expansion to all parts of the country as early as possible and the improvement of the status and conditions of service of the teachers. No progress in Secondary education is possible unless the teaching profession attracts the right type of people and proper conditions of service, including salary, are guaranteed at the different levels of education.

Sources of Revenue

At present, the sources of revenue for educational purposes at the State level are: (1) State Government grants; (2) Grants made by Municipal and other local bodies directly or through an educational cess; (3) Private benefactions and grants made by private managements; and (4) School fees.

An educational cess can be imposed by local bodies under permissive power given to them by State Governments. It is levied on land revenue, as part of the profession tax or on property tax in urban areas. The rate of cess varies and although the local bodies can levy the maximum educational cess permissible under the Act in many cases this has not been done.

State Grants

The grants given for education vary from State to State. Educational institutions under private managements are given grant-in-aid to assist them in the expansion and improvement of their educational facilities. These grants given may be for any of the following purposes:

(1) Payment of stipends to teachers under training;
(2) Payment of medical officers for medical inspection;
(3) Maintenance in boarding homes of orphans;
(4) Construction and extension of school buildings and hostels;
(5) Furniture, apparatus, chemicals and books for library;
(6) For acquisition of lands for school buildings, hostels or playgrounds;
(7) For crafts or industrial education; and

(8) Maintenance grant.

But grants for all these purposes are not given by all States, and the grant-in-aid code would seem to need revision in the light of the new proposals for educational reform.

Vocational Education in the U.S.A.

The way in which Vocational education has been implemented in the United States of America and the reasons which led to its rapid development in that country deserve notice.

In the United States, schools are controlled entirely and supported to a very large degree by the different States. However, the Federal Government has had considerable influence in educational matters and, in recent years, it has increased its grant-in-aid to the States for part of their educational progress. In 1862, an Act called the Morall Act was passed which made a notable change in the educational policy pursued by the Federal Government. It was laid down that the principal objective of such aid should be, without excluding either scientific and classical students, to teach branches of learning as are related to agriculture and the mechanical arts in such a manner as the legislatures of the State may prescribe, in order to afford the industrial classes a liberal and practical education in their various pursuits. This policy has been steadily kept in view. A further impetus to Vocational education was given by the passing of the National Vocational Education Act of 1915 commonly called the Smith-Hughes Act. . . . This Act is intended to provide for the promotion of Vocational education, for co-operation with the States in the promotion of education, agriculture, trades and industries and in the preparation of teachers of vocational subjects and to appropriate money and regulate its expenditure. The detailed provisions of the Act deal with grants to assist the States in paying the salaries of teachers, supervisors and directors of agricultural subjects and teachers of trade, industrial and home economics subjects.

To enable the objectives to be attained, a Federal Board of Vocational Education was created consisting of the Secretaries of Agriculture, Commerce and Labour, the U.S. Commissioner of Education and three citizens of the United States to be appointed by the President with the advice and consent of the Senate. The Board was given the power to co-operate with the State Boards in carrying out the provisions of this Act, and it was the duty of the Federal Board to make or cause to have made, State investigations and reports dealing with the establishment of vocational schools and classes and the giving of instruction in Agriculture, Trades and Industries, Commerce and Home Economics. The funds made available to the Federal Board of Vocational Education could also be utilised for printing and binding of books of reference and periodicals. A series of supplementary acts for the same purposes followed, the most significant being the George Barden Act of 1946, which authorised an additional sum of 28,500,000 dollars to be distributed to the States for Vocational education. In order to receive the federal funds mentioned in the Smith-Hughes Act, the various States and territories were required to match from States, territorial or local funds or both, 100 per cent of the federal money, i.e., grants were made on a dollar to dollar basis paid by the Federal and State Government respectively. It was, however, found that the States and territories actually exceeded their share of the contribution.

As a result of the Smith-Hughes Act and later the George Barden Act, Vocational education received a stimulus which has resulted in a very large increase of trained personnel and much greater industrial prosperity in the United States. We understand that similar Acts have been passed in some other countries also, notably in Canada.

We have referred to this Act in some detail, because, if our country is to make any progress in Vocational education and help agriculture, industry, trade and commerce, it can only be done by passing an Act of Legislature of similar nature, guaranteeing Central funds for the different States for the organization and promotion of Vocational education. At the Centre, different Departments under several Ministries are now expending considerable sums of money for special educational purposes. So far as Secondary education is concerned, the Centre has not given any substantial aid except to those institutions for whose maintenance it has a direct responsibility. We, therefore, recommend that a suitable Act on somewhat similar basis should be passed which will enable the different Ministries concerned to pool their resources in the field of Secondary education and to establish a central organization to supervise the development of Vocational education in the different States. It should be able to assist in their proper organization, equipment and maintenance and in providing properly trained teaching personnel who may be paid adequate salaries. As in the Acts quoted above, the matching of such Central grants with grants from State funds should be laid down as a condition.

The Federal Board for Vocational Education

We recommend that a Board should be constituted at the Centre to be called the Federal Board of Vocational Education. The funds for this board should be contributed by the different Ministries, more particularly the Ministries of Education, Railways and Communication, Food and Agriculture, Industries, Trade and Commerce. The Board should consist of representatives of the different Ministries mentioned above, together with representatives of the Ministries of Finance and Defence. To represent the general public, the President of the Republic may nominate three distinguished persons to it. The Chairman of the Board should be the Minister of Education at the Centre and the Secretary of the Ministry of Education shall be its Secretary. The Board should have power to cooperate with the State Boards in carrying out the provisions of the Act and it should have generally the same functions as the United States Federal Board. The funds at the disposal of the Federal Board shall be distributed to the State concerned taking into consideration the percentage contribution of each State which should be fixed at a definite percentage of the whole grant or with reference to the particular purpose for which the grant is given and the size of the school-going population of each State. The provisions may be incorporated in the Act to guide the Board in its work.

Possible Sources of Finance

(i) *Technical Education Cess:* We have mentioned . . . that the spread of Technical education would directly benefit industry, trade, commerce, transport, etc., and therefore, it is reasonable to expect that industry to contribute towards the training of well qualified technical personnel. The evidence tendered made us feel that industry would welcome this cess if it is taken into full confidence and given a voice in shaping the policy of Technical and Industrial education. At present, a special cess is levied on certain industries to promote development and research in them. While this is of great value, it cannot be denied that the employment of well-trained qualified technicians in all grades of industry will result in much greater improvement, and this would depend largely on the reorientation of the Secondary education as envisaged by us. Among the industries that will largely benefit from employment of such trained personnel, there are the textile industry, steel, ship-building, motor cars, railways and transport, mining, machine tools and other engineering industries, etc. We therefore recommend that a cess called the Industrial Education Cess be levied, the determination of its exact rate and methods of the collection being left to an expert Committee to assess with reference to each industry concerned. This cess should be utilised solely for the furtherance of Technical and Vocational education at the Secondary stage taking into consideration the needs of each industry. Representatives of industry, trade and commerce should be associated with the programme of Technical education. In regard to nationalised industries or concerns such as Railways and Communications, Posts and Telegraphs a certain percentage of the net revenue from these undertakings might be made available for the promotion of Technical education. They should really take the lead in encouraging Technical education in all fields in order to improve the quality of the work turned out in their workshops or elsewhere.

(ii) *Public Philanthropy:* Public philanthropy has played a notable part in the development of every kind of education in our country but in recent years its scope is becoming more and more limited, so that the extent of the aid expected from this source has greatly diminished. We do not want to go into the detailed causes of this change. Many educational institutions owed their inception and continued existence to a class that is fast disappearing. It seems to us that certain special incentives are required to attract philanthropic aid for educational purposes. Taking note of this, the Central Government has already passed certain rules under which contributions made to certain institutions like universities and research institutes are up to a limit of Rs. 25,000 for Secondary education, and up to a limit of Rs. 50,000 for Technical education may be exempted from operation of the Income-tax Act.

(iii) *Religious and Charitable Endowments:* We believe that, in certain States, provision has been made by an Act of the Legislature for some of the income of religious and charitable institutions being used for educational purposes. We consider that it would be a fair utilisation of these funds, if after meeting the necessary charges pertaining to the administration of these trusts, diversion of some of the surplus funds is made to education including secondary education. We trust that similar provisions will be made in other States where such legislation is not already in force.

(iv) *Estate Duties:* We would also recommend that amounts bequeathed to public institutions for general educational purposes in the will of a deceased person should not be subject to any duty by the Centre and that the whole of this amount should be appropriated to the educational purposes for which they are meant.

Other Measures to Relieve the Cost of Secondary Education

(i) *Exemption from Local Taxes on Educational Buildings:* We have been told that certain local bodies levy property tax on educational institutions and on their grounds which seriously affects their finances and restricts the scope of their improvement. If education is a national responsibility, it is not desirable that their buildings and grounds should be taxed and we recommend that whether they are situated in urban or rural areas, in Municipalities or in Corporations, they should be exempted from the levy of this tax. In many countries this is an accepted principle and instead of levying such charges. Municipalities and Corporations have established educational institutions of all grades out of their funds. The importance of educational institutions having adequate playgrounds and open spaces have been stressed by us elsewhere. We recommend, therefore, that State Governments and the Centre should, wherever possible, allot lands to schools for playgrounds, buildings, agricultural farms and other similar purposes, without charging for them. Such allotment is made in the U.S.A. under the land grants scheme.

(ii) *Exemption of Books and Scientific Apparatus from Customs Duty:* Till such time as the necessary scientific apparatus and appliances cannot be manufactured in the country, we recommend that educational institutions which have to obtain scientific apparatus and workshop appliances from abroad should be exempted from customs duty. We realise that this involves some difficulties but, with strict control and the provision of necessary information by the schools to the satisfaction of the Department of Education, it should not be impossible to implement this proposal. We likewise recommend that books for school libraries may be similarly exempted from duty.

Central Aid to Secondary Education

We are of the opinion that in view of the larger interest involved, financial aid from the Centre is necessary and may reasonably be expected. This scheme of vocational education and the introduction of vocational subjects in the school as recommended cannot possibly be implemented in a satisfactory manner unless Central aid is forthcoming. We have referred to some of the methods of augmenting the financial resources needed for Secondary education of diversified types. We feel that so far as the Centre is concerned, certain direct responsibilities may be taken in the field of Secondary education. The Centre may give financial aid for such purposes as the following:

(1) The starting of Secondary schools providing diversified courses, more particularly in the rural areas.
(2) The production of better books for children and teachers.
(3) The establishment of institutions for training teachers in technical subjects.
(4) The establishment of centres for encouraging research in important problems of Secondary education such as:

   (a) Curricula of studies;
   (b) Vocational guidance;
   (c) Physical and health education;
   (d) Methods of teaching;
   (e) Book production research; and
   (f) Technique of examination.

(5) Organisation of refresher courses, seminars and conferences of headmasters and teachers.
(6) Production of suitable educational films and audio-visual aids; and
(7) Encouragement of approved experimental schools.

We feel that the active cooperation of the Centre with the States is essential to promote education in the country, to improve its quality and to carry on the necessary research in the different fields of education which may ultimately be incorporated in the educational system.

SUMMARY OF RECOMMENDATIONS

1. In matters connected with reorganisation and improvement of Secondary education there should be close co-operation between the Centre and the States.

2. In order to promote Vocational education a Board of Vocational education should be constituted at the Centre consisting of the representatives of concerned Ministries and other interests.

3. A cess called the Industrial Education Cess be levied, the amount collected to be utilised for the furtherance of Technical and Vocational education at the Secondary stage.

4. A certain percentage of the net revenue from nationalised industries or concerns such as Railways, Communications, Posts and Telegraphs, etc., should be made available for the promotion of Technical education in certain fields.

5. Contributions for the development of Secondary education should be exempted from the operation of the Income-tax Act.

6. Surplus funds from the religious and charitable endowments should be diverted to educational purposes.

7. The amount bequeathed to public institutions for general educational purposes in the will of a deceased person should not be subject to any duty by the Centre and the whole of it should be appropriated to the educational purpose.

8. All educational institutions and the grounds attached thereto should be exempted from the levy of property taxes.

9. The State Governments and the Centre should, wherever possible, assign lands to schools for playgrounds, buildings or agricultural farms and other necessary purposes without any charge.

10. The educational institutions which have to obtain necessary scientific apparatus, workshop appliances and books for school library should be exempted from customs duty.

11. The Centre should assume a certain amount of direct responsibility for the contemplated reorganisation of secondary education and give financial aid for the purpose.

5

EDUCATION COMMISSION, 1964-66*
on Educational Planning and Educational Financing

Introduction

The Education Commission, 1964-66, was appointed by the Government of India in July 1964 to advise on the national pattern of education and on the general principles and policies of development of education at all stages and in all aspects. The Commission was headed by Prof. D.S. Kothari, Chairman of University Grants Commission, and the report of the Commission is therefore also called the Kothari Commission Report. Shri J.P. Naik was the Member Secretary. The Commission included experts from foreign countries also. The Commission submitted its report in 1966 under the title *Education and National Development*. The unique feature of the Education Commission, 1964-66, was not to limit its enquiry to specific sectors or aspects of education, but to have a comprehensive review of the entire educational system. The Government of India realised that: 'It is desirable to survey the entire field of educational development as the various parts of the educational system strongly interact with and influence one another. It is not possible to have progressive and strong universities without efficient secondary schools and the quality of these schools is determined by the functioning of elementary schools. What is needed, therefore, is a synoptic survey and an imaginative look at education considered as a whole and not fragmented into parts and stages'.

Another unique feature of the Commission was its conviction that education is the most powerful instrument of national development.

---

* *Education and National Development*, Ministry of Education, Government of India, New Delhi, 1966.

Educational and national reconstruction are intimately inter-linked. The crucial role of education in national development appears in all its vividness on every page of the report, appropriately entitled *Education and National Development*. Standing at the critical cross-roads of history, India has to make a choice. The choice lies between education and disaster. The report concludes:

> 'We must either build a sound, balanced, effective and imaginative educational system to meet our development needs and respond to challenging aspirations or be content to be swept aside by the strong currents of history.'

Never before education was given such a niche of national honour, and never before was it conceived as a pivot of nation's progress and prosperity, as revealed in the pages of the Commission's report.

The task before the Commission was of a colossal magnitude and great complexity. A large-scale action was imperative. Mere tinkering with the existing situation would have made things worse than before. In the Foreword to the report, the Commission wrote:

> 'Indian education needs a drastic reconstruction, almost a revolution. We need to bring about major improvements in the effectiveness of primary education; to introduce work-experience as an integral element of general education; to vocationalise secondary education; to improve the quality of teachers at all levels and to provide teachers in sufficient strength; to liquidate illiteracy, to strengthen centres of advanced study and strive to attain, in some of our universities at least, higher international standards; to lay special emphasis on the combination of teaching and research; and to pay particular attention to education and research in agriculture and allied sciences.'

The Commission identified the three important facets of the programme that would bring about the desired 'educational revolution':

- Internal transformation so as to relate it to the life, needs and aspirations of the nation;
- qualitative improvement so that the standards achieved are

adequate, keep continually rising and, at least in a few sectors, become internationally comparable; and

- expansion of educational facilities broadly on the basis of manpower needs and with an accent on equalization of educational opportunities.

For the internal transformation of the system of education the following programmes urged high priority:

(1) Work experience as an integral part of general education; vocationalization of education at the secondary level; improvement of professional education and research, promoting national consciousness;
(2) Introducing a common school system, making social and national service compulsory; developing all modern Indian languages;
(3) Making science education an integral part of all school education and developing scientific research; and
(4) Inculcation of high Values — social, moral and special — at all stages of education.

Full texts of Chapters XVIII and XIX dealing with Educational Planning and Administration, and Educational Finance are given below:

EDUCATIONAL PLANNING AND ADMINISTRATION*

I. *Educational Planning.* (2) The basic problem; (3) Some suggestions for reform; (5) Different levels of priorities; (7) Re-definition of the roles of the different agencies providing education.

II. *The Role of Private Enterprise.* (9) The present position; (11) Recommendations.

III. *The Role of Local Authorities.* (12) The present position; (17) Recommendation; (18) The district and municipal school boards.

IV. *The Role of the Central Government.* (25) The present position; (26) Recommendations; (29) Should education be in the con-

* (i) Para Numbers refer to paras of Chapter XVIII of the document.
(ii) Original Table numbers have been changed to conform to this Chapter number.

current list?

V. *Educational Administration at the National Level.* (32) Ministry of Education; (36) NCERT.

VI. *Educational Administration at the State Level.* (38) Co-ordination; (40) The Education Secretariat; (42) Directorate of Education.

VII. *Personnel.* (44) Indian Educational Service; (50) The State Educational Services; (51) Training of educational administrators; (53) National Staff College for Educational Administrators; (54) Increasing the strength of the department.

VIII. *Procedures.* (55) The present position; (56) Introducing elasticity and dynamism; (57) Education Acts.

18.01 In the present chapter, we shall deal with educational planning and some major aspects of educational administration which have not been dealt with before and in particular with administrative responsibilities and arrangements at the local, State, and national levels and their inter-relationships.

Educational Planning

18.02 **The Basic Problem**. The crux of the problem of educational planning in India is to evolve a national policy in education in spite of the fact that education is largely a State subject in the Constitution and that a multiplicity of authorities at different levels make decisions on all aspects of the situation. This is not an easy task and as there is little similar experience to guide us, we will have to evolve our own techniques in most cases. It is also necessary to review and improve our planning techniques.

18.03 **Some Suggestions for Reform**. A review of the first three Five Year Plans in the different States and at the national level highlights the need to improve the planning techniques in some directions. These have been indicated below:

(1) *Over-emphasis on Enrolment and Expenditure*. There has been an over-emphasis on achievement of targets in enrolments and expenditure. It is true that expansion was badly needed and expansion will have to continue. But an over-emphasis on this aspect leads to the neglect of the still more important aspect of quality. Similarly, an over-emphasis on expenditure targets tends to distort priorities and often leads to wastage. There is thus a need to take a more com-

prehensive view of the problem and to evolve a broader pattern of goals, especially those relating to qualitative improvement.

(2) *The Need for Concentration of Effort and Adoption of a Selective Approach*. Throughout the first three plans, the general policy has been to do something in every sector or for every programme with the result that the meagre resources available were spread thinly over a very large area. This policy involves considerable wastage. It has, therefore, now become important to concentrate on a few crucial programmes such as improvement of the quality of teachers, development of agricultural education provision of good and effective primary education for all children, liquidation of illiteracy, vocationalization of secondary education, establishment of major universities, expansion and improvement of postgraduate education, increase in the number of scholarships and the development of about ten per cent of institutions at each stage to optimum levels of quality.

(3) *Emphasis on Programmes which Need Talent and Hard Work*. The emphasis on reaching expenditure targets to which a reference has been made tends to place a premium on programmes where it is easy to incur expenditure, e.g., construction of buildings or expansion of enrolments. This is unfortunate because there are a number of programmes which call for determined effort, organization, talent and hard work rather than large financial investment. The following are some examples of such programmes:

- production of literature in the modern Indian languages needed for their adoption as media of education at the university stage;
- educational research;
- examination reform;
- preparation of school textbooks and teaching and learning materials;
- in-service education of teachers and officers of the Education Departments;
- improving techniques of supervision;
- improving contact with the local communities and parents;
- providing enrichment programmes and guidance to gifted students and some special assistance to retarded or backward ones.

A number of instances of this type can be cited. What is important to note is that, in the existing situation where the financial resources are limited, it is programmes of this type that need far greater emphasis than those which need heavy financial investment.

(4) *Lack of Adequate Evaluation and Research.* Yet another weakness in our planning is the inadequacy of evaluation and research. Since planning is a comparatively new process and we have to evolve our own techniques it is necessary to evaluate our programme continuously and develop a strong research programme which will enable us to cut down costs and increase the effectiveness of the investment in education. But, by and large, this has not been done. Some attempts at such evaluation have been made recently in the Planning Commission, viz., the COPP Teams have studied three problems,* two of which were not of a major magnitude. What we would recommend is the deep involvement of universities, professional organizations, training colleges, etc., in a periodical evaluation of all major programmes included in the plans and in the development of a large-scale research programme....

(5) *Weakness of Existing Machinery for Educational Planning.* The existing machinery for educational planning leaves much to be desired. It is not adequately staffed nor is the personnel engaged in it suitably trained. There is hardly any educational planning done at the district level. The planning cells in the offices of the Directors of Education are inadequate and staffed mostly by persons who have had no training in the field. Their work also is mostly administrative and financial and confined to the compilation and reporting of educational and financial statistics.

18.04 There is need to improve the organization and methods of educational planning and for training competent personnel to staff the planning unit in the Central Ministry of Education, the State Departments of Education and District School Boards. It should be possible for the Ministry of Education, in collaboration with the Asian Institute of Educational Planning, to undertake studies of educational planning in the different States and to conduct intensive courses for training the personnel involved in the process of educational planning in India. The subject is of such great significance that the UGC should also consider the possibility of setting up an Advanced Centre for Studies in Educational Planning, Administration

---

* These are: teacher training, literacy among industrial workers and rural institutes.

and Finance.

18.05 **Different Levels of Priorities**. Education is essentially a responsibility of the State Governments. But it is also a national concern and in certain major sectors, decisions have to be taken at the national level. This implies the need to regard education as a Centre-State partnership. On the other hand, it is necessary to remember that education which concerns every parent and every family has to be taken as close to the people as possible and that its administration can be best conducted by or in close association with local communities. This implies that educational planning has to be decentralized to the district level and still further down to the level of each institution. The process of educational planning in a federal democracy like ours has thus to be the right blend of centralization, in the appropriate sectors, with a large amount of decentralization in other sectors and especially in administration. Care should, however, be taken that the parts fall coherently into the totality of a broad national plan, and all discordant features and contradictions are eliminated. For this purpose, it will be necessary to devise an effective machinery of coordination. This is the direction in which administration has to strive and planning has to grow.

18.06 One useful suggestion which can be made in this context is to adopt a system of priorities at different levels — national, state and local. Programmes of national significance such as provision of good and effective primary education to every child, vocationalization of secondary education, post-graduate education and research, or education for agriculture and industry may be regarded as *national priorities* in the sense that the decisions regarding them would have to be taken by the Centre in consultation with the States and, once they are taken, it should be obligatory on every State to implement them effectively and vigorously. In several other matters, and these would form the bulk of the decisions to be made, a system of *State-level priorities* should be adopted, i.e., each State may be left to make its own best decision in view of local conditions. These would include problems such as making secondary education free of tuition fees and in such matters, no attempt at a national uniformity need be made. In certain other matters, as for instance, in the provision of amenities in schools, and determining the type and scale of non-teacher costs, a system of *local priorities* may be adopted. The State Governments may create appropriate authorities at the district and school levels and leave them free to take decisions, within the powers delegated, and best suited to the local conditions. There should be no need to expect any uniformity in these matters between one district and another and even between one school and another. A system such as this which centralizes a few essential sectors at the national level would be much better than the present trend to take more and more decisions — crucial or otherwise — at the national and State levels. This sometimes results in the curbing of local initiative and disregard of local conditions.

18.07 **Redefinition of the Roles of the Different Agencies Providing Education.** It is also necessary to redefine the roles of the four different agencies which have been providing educational facilities in the country, viz., the Central Government, the State Governments, the local authorities and the voluntary organizations. Their present roles have arisen, not out of conscious planning, but from historical circumstances many of which have now ceased to have any relevance. For instance, the divorce of the Central Government from education which was so conspicuous a feature of our educational system from 1921 to 1947 arose out of a political necessity, viz., the decision of the British Government to transfer education to Indian control (as a part of the system of Dyarchy introduced in the Provinces in 1921 and of Provincial Autonomy introduced in 1937) while retaining all authority at the Centre in the hands of the Governor-General. This tradition has been considerably modified by the Constitution and even more, by the developments in the first three plans, but it still dominates the scene. The local authorities were first placed in charge of primary education in British India as a part of a programme of transferring power to Indian people, and later on, they were permitted to develop other educational programmes in their discretion. In princely States, however, this political need did not exist and hence local authorities were not generally associated with education. The private educational institutions played an important role in all British Indian Provinces, especially in post-primary education, because direct governmental enterprise was limited and they had to meet almost all the growing demand for education. In the princely States, however, private enterprise was not much encouraged and sometimes it was even discouraged. It is obvious that these traditional roles are out of tune with the massive needs of educational development in the country and that they will have to be modified.

18.08 In the complex process of educational planning and implementation, the State Governments occupy a central and key position. They have to accept, for instance, full responsibility for all school education, but it is advantageous for them to discharge it in collaboration with local authorities. The day-to-day administration of schools, which should be as close to the local communities as possible, may preferably be delegated, with adequate resources, to duly constituted local authorities at the district level. In higher education, on the other hand, they will have to share the responsibilities with the universities, the UGC and the Government of India. In other words:

- school education is predominantly a local-State partnership; and
- higher education is a Centre-State partnership.

In our opinion, it is this basic principle that should guide the evolution of that delicate balance between centralisation and decentralization which our planning needs.

The Role of Private Enterprise

18.09 **The Present Position**. We shall first discuss the role of private enterprise in education. This varies from area to area and also from one stage or sector of education to another . . . statistics of 1960-61, the latest available, throw light on this problem (Table 5.1).

18.10 It will be seen . . . that the percentage of educational institutions managed by voluntary organizations is:

- low in Jammu & Kashmir (1.7), Rajasthan (3.5), Madhya Pradesh (4.6), Punjab (7.4), Andhra Pradesh (8.0) and Assam (19.1);
- high in Kerala (61.6), Orissa (65.3), and Bihar (74.0);
- low at the primary stage: lower primary (22.2) and higher primary (27.1);
- medium in vocational schools (57.4) and colleges for professional education (49.8); and
- high in pre-primary schools (70.9), secondary schools (69.2), special schools (79.0), institutions for higher (general) education (78.8), and colleges for special education (74.9).

TABLE 5.1: Percentage of Non-governmental Educational Institutions to Total Number of Educational Institutions, 1960-61

State	Percentage	Stage or Sector	Percentage
1. Andhra Pradesh	8.0	1. Pre-Primary	70.9
2. Assam	19.1	2. Lower Primary	22.2
3. Bihar	74.0	3. Higher Primary	27.1
4. Gujarat	36.0	4. Secondary	69.2
5. Jammu & Kashmir	1.7	5. Vocational Schools	57.4
6. Kerala	61.6	6. Special Schools	79.0
7. Madhya Pradesh	4.6	7. Institutions for Higher (General) Education	78.8
8. Madras	33.0	8. Colleges of Professional Education	49.8
9. Maharashtra	48.0	9. Colleges for Special Education	74.9
10. Mysore	34.3		
11. Orissa	65.3	Total for all Sectors	33.2
12. Punjab	7.4		
13. Rajasthan	3.5		
14. Uttar Pradesh	14.5		
15. West Bengal	36.3		
Total for India	33.2		

Source: Ministry of Education, Form A.
Note: The local authority institutions are not included.

With such large variations in traditions and in the present position, it is obvious that no single policy can be suitable for all parts of the country. In fact, even in the same State, the policy will have to vary from stage to stage, sector to sector and even from organization to organization. All that we can indicate, therefore, are a few general principles.

18.11 **Recommendations.** In our opinion, the future role of private enterprise in education should be broadly governed by the following principles:

(1) It is true that some forms of private enterprise have made a negative rather than a positive contribution to education. At the same time, we should recognize that private enterprise has played an important role in the development of education in modern India, that a large proportion of our good institutions are in the private sector and that it can continue to make a useful contribution to the development of education in the years ahead. The State should, therefore, make all possible use of the assistance that can come from the private sector for

the development of education.

(2) The growing educational needs of a modernizing society can only be met by the State and it would be a mistake to show any over-dependence on private enterprise which is basically uncertain. As the State has now rightly assumed full responsibility to provide all the needed educational facilities, private enterprise can only have a limited and minor role.

(3) Under the Constitution, private schools have a right to exist and if they do not seek aid or recognition from the State, there need be little or no interference with them. In fact, we have only suggested compulsory registration for unrecognized schools.

(4) The position with regard to private educational institutions which seek financial support from the State is, however, different. Even now, they depend upon Government for the larger part of their expenditure; and when fees, which is their main source of income, are abolished, their dependence on public revenues would be very large. These should, therefore, be gradually assimilated with the system of public education. . . .

(5) In dealing with private enterprise, problems relating to their teachers, grant-in-aid and control are very important. . . .

The Role of Local Authorities

18.12 **The Present Position.** As pointed earlier, there are two historical traditions with regard to the role of local authorities — one of associating local authorities with education which grew up in the British Indian Provinces and the other of not associating them with it which grew up in the Indian princely States. The arguments for and against such association have been repeatedly stated and need only be mentioned here in brief. It is generally agreed that local authorities do succeed in evoking local interest and local enthusiasm and effectively bring local knowledge to bear on the solution of problems. Their financial contribution to the support of education is not large. But it is not negligible either; and it is substantial in the case of richer municipalities like Bombay City. Their main weaknesses, however, are the harassment caused to others through frequent transfers and postings, and through involvement in local regions and politics. This is the one reason why almost all teachers' associations have represented to us that the local authorities should not be placed in-charge of educational institutions. This evil increases as the delegation of authority goes to lower levels, e.g., it is definitely greater when the authority is delegated to the block level than to the district level.

18.13 In the post-Independence period, two attempts have been made to redefine the role of local authorities in education and to evolve a uniform national policy. Unfortunately, these have not succeeded, partly because the two Committees which examined the problem made somewhat conflicting recommendations. The Committee set up under the chairmanship of Shri B.G. Kher rejected the British Indian view that the creation of local authorities and their association with primary education was necessary as a training ground for democratic self-government. It was emphatically of the opinion that education should not be made a guinea-pig on the altar of democracy or decentralization and recommended that the interests of mass education should be the only criteria to decide whether authority over primary education should be delegated to the local bodies, and if so, to what extent. Although aware of the frequent mal-administration of education by local bodies and particularly of the harassment which was often caused to teachers, it felt that these weaknesses could be overcome through appropriate measures and recommended that local bodies should be associated with the administration of primary education, with adequate safeguards to protect the interests of teachers, because 'such associations would further the cause of mass education and bring the goal of universal education near'.*

18.14 Before the recommendations of the Kher Committee could be implemented or even adopted, a different set of recommendations on the subject was made by another Committee, the *COPP Team on Community Development*, which was set up under the chairmanship of the late Shri Balwantrai Mehta to review the community development programme and its future organization. It was of the view that local interest and local initiative in the field of development would not be adequately involved unless 'a single, representative and vigorous democratic institution' was created at the appropriate level 'to take charge of all the aspects of development work in the rural areas' and invested with adequate powers and appropriate finances.

---

* *Report of the Committee on the Relationship between State Governments and Local Bodies in the Administration of Primary Education*, 1951.

Such a body, said the Committee, 'must not be cramped by too much control by Government or Government agencies. It must have the power to make mistakes and to learn by making mistakes, but it must also receive guidance which will help it to avoid making mistakes'. In accordance with this basic approach, the Committee recommended that strong local bodies should be created in rural areas and vested with adequate authority to administer all developmental programmes, including primary education.

18.15 The problem of integrating these two different traditions and the divergent recommendations of these two Committees became urgent when the State reorganization brought together areas from the erstwhile British Indian Provinces and the princely States. But so far it has not been possible to solve it and to evolve a uniform national policy (or, in some cases, even a uniform State policy). The present position shows a mixture of both the traditions, not infrequently, even in the same State. In urban areas, the municipalities have been associated with education in Andhra Pradesh (Andhra area), Bihar, Gujarat (Bombay area), Madhya Pradesh (Maha Koshal area), Madras (Madras area), Maharashtra (Bombay and Vidarbha areas), Mysore* (Bombay and Madras areas) and Orissa (old Orissa province area). In the rural areas, the panchayati raj institutions have been introduced and placed in charge of education in all States except Jammu & Kashmir, Kerala, Madhya Pradesh, Mysore, Nagaland and Punjab. The method of association is also not uniform. The municipalities are generally in charge of primary education; but they can also undertake other educational activities at their discretion. The panchayati raj institutions have been entrusted with lower primary education in some States (e.g., West Bengal); with the whole of primary education in some others (e.g., Madras); and with both primary and secondary education in two States (Andhra Pradesh and Maharashtra). Authority over education has been delegated to the block level in some States (e.g., Rajasthan and Madras); and to the district level in some others (Maharashtra). The systems of administration and grant-in-aid also show similar variations.

18.16 In our opinion, the policy in these matters will have to be decided on a pragmatic basis with reference to ultimate goals and lo-

*. The Mysore Government has recently decided to relieve the municipalities of this responsibility.

cal conditions. The close involvement of schools with their communities is a principle of great educational significance and this is the direction in which we should move. At the same time, the difficulties caused to teachers under local authority management cannot be ignored and at least in the transitional stage, adequate safeguards would have to be provided to teachers. Local authorities should realize their responsibilities and ensure that they help rather than hinder the cause of education. Here we are more inclined to agree with the Kher Committee that the decision to associate local authorities with the administration of education should be taken not on political but on educational grounds and that the only justification for such a decision should be a conviction that it would promote the cause of education and bring the goal of providing universal education nearer. Similarly, local authorities should not be encouraged to think that they can claim to administer education as a matter of right and that this right will continue with them in spite of bad administration or harassment of teachers. The normal practice should be that a local authority is given the right to administer education as a privilege subject to two conditions — promoting the cause of education and good administration — and that this privilege would be withdrawn if either of these conditions is violated. There is no need to insist, as is often done at present, that a uniform policy must be adopted in all parts of the country simultaneously. It would be in the larger interests of education to adjust the experiment to local conditions and to permit each area to progress at a pace and in a manner best suited for its growth.

18.17 **Recommendations**. In view of these broad principles, we recommend that the future role of local bodies in education may be defined as follows:

(1) As an ultimate objective, it is essential that schools and their local communities should be intimately associated in the educational process. This will harness local knowledge, interest and enthusiasm for the development of education. Besides, local bodies can make a significant contribution to the total expenditure on education.

(2) It would, however, not be proper to look upon this democratic decentralization as an end in itself and to press for its universal and immediate adoption without reference to local conditions.

(3) The immediate goal in this respect — and this should be adopted immediately as a national policy in all the States — is to associate the local communities, namely village panchayats in rural areas and the municipalities in urban areas, with their local schools and to make them responsible for the provision of all non-teacher costs with the help, where necessary, of a suitable grant-in-aid from the States...

(4) The ultimate goal to be reached is the establishment, at the district level, of a competent local education authority which may be designated as the District School Board (to be constituted under an Education Act which we are recommending) and which would be in charge of all education in the district below the university level. This should also be accepted as a national policy. The jurisdiction of this authority should cover the entire area of the district with one exception, namely, the big municipalities in the district with a population of 100,000 or more which should preferably have a similar authority for their own areas. The detailed proposals on this subject are discussed below.

(5) The transition from the immediate to the ultimate objective cannot be made in one jump but will have to proceed through a number of carefully planned stages. It cannot also be made simultaneously in all States and perhaps not even simultaneously in all the districts of a State. The difficult decisions regarding the type of local authority to be created, the level at which powers are to be delegated, the extent and nature of delegation, the powers to be retained by the State Government, the system of grant-in-aid, etc., are so complex that each State will have to decide them for itself, not even necessarily for the State as a whole, but perhaps separately for each district. While, therefore, the Centre may advise the States to move towards the ultimate objective as soon as practicable, it would be wrong to pressurize all States to adopt common policies in the matter. There is no inherent virtue in such a uniformity; and it may lead to better administration to recognize that, while the immediate and ultimate objectives may be assumed as national goals, there need be no uniformity with regard to the details of the transition from the immediate to the ultimate objective. These should be left for decision at the State level in view of local conditions.

(6) In all such association of the local authorities with education adequate safeguards should be provided to ensure that the teachers are not harassed and that they do not get involved in local factions and politics. Experience has shown that, for this purpose, it is necessary to vest the control over the teachers, not in the local authority, but in its Administrative Officer (who should be an officer of the Education Department seconded to serve under the local authority), to associate him closely with the District Education Officer in the discharge of this responsibility and to frame a fairly detailed system of rules and regulations to smoothen and guide the day-to-day administration.

(7) It is necessary to remember that it is not enough to decentralise the administration of education and to vest it in the local authority. The programme will not succeed unless intensive steps are taken, to educate local leadership on the right lines, to provide the local authority with trained and competent officers who would have certain independence in the performance of their duties and to make the necessary resources available to the local authority to fulfil the responsibilities placed upon it. This will be a major task for the State Education Departments.

18.18 **The District and Municipal School Boards** . . . We shall now discuss some details about their composition, powers and responsibilities and finances. The jurisdiction of the district school board should cover the entire area of the district with one exception, namely, the big municipalities in the district with a population of about 100,000 or more which should preferably have similar boards for their own areas. A district school board should consist of:

(1) Representatives of the Zila Parishad elected by itself;

(2) Representatives of the municipalities in the district (which do not have a separate school board of their own) elected in the prescribed manner.

(3) Educationists nominated by the State Government or elected by the Zila Parishad from out of the panel approved by the State Governments; and

(4) *Ex-officio* members, such as officers of education, agriculture, industries or other departments which administer vocational schools.

Persons in categories (3) and (4) should be about half of the total membership. A senior officer of the State Government (Class I) should be the whole-time secretary of this board, which should be provided with the necessary administrative and supervisory staff.*

18.19 The functions of this board would cover all school education in the district — general as well as vocational: it will directly administer all government and local authority schools within the district, and it will also remain in charge of giving grants-in-aid to all private institutions in the district in accordance with the rules framed by the State Government for the purpose.

18.20 Within the framework of the instructions given by the State Government it should be a responsibility of the district school board to prepare plans for the development of school education within the district and it should also be the principal agency within the district to develop school education, the finances and guidance required for the purpose being provided by the State Government and the State Education Departments.

18.21 In big towns with a population 100,000 or more, it would be desirable to establish municipal school boards on the above lines, since these would be viable administrative units. It would also give an opportunity to the local people, who are better educated, more well-to-do and vocal, to take positive interest in developing an educational programme for their children. The composition, powers and responsibilities of these boards should be similar to those of the district school boards.

18.22 Each school board will maintain an education fund. The Zila Parishads (or municipalities) will approve the budget of the school boards. They will also raise the resources expected of them and credit them to the school board. In all day-to-day administration, the school board would be autonomous. The same relation would hold good between a municipal school board and its municipality.

18.2[illegible] The recruitment of teachers will be done by a special committee c[illegible]isting of the chairman of the board, its secretary and the district education officer. The transfers should be effected by the same committee, subject to rules framed by the State Government,

* Where Zila Parishads do not exist, the composition of the District School Boards will have to be decided differently to suit local conditions. It may consist of person nominated by the State Government and others representing local interests.

the general policy being to reduce transfers to the minimum and to allow teachers to develop loyalties to individual institutions. The salaries, allowances and service conditions of teachers will be regulated by the State Governments and will be common to all the districts. These measures will provide safeguards to teachers and the fact that all school teachers are serving together under the boards (and not primary teachers alone as at present) will be a further strength and an additional safeguard.

18.24 It may be advantageous, in some cases, not to burden the school boards with full administrative responsibilities all at once. In such cases, the entire administration of the schools may be left with the offices of the Department (especially the personnel administration) and the school board may be given powers with regard to planning and development. Additional powers may be conferred on it as it gains experience and competence.

The Role of the Central Government

18.25 *The Present Position.* Under the Constitution, the Central Government has been specifically vested with several educational responsibilities, and certain other responsibilities also devolve upon it as the Government of the Union. The more important of these are enumerated in the following entries of the Seventh Schedule.

List I — Union List

63. The institutions known at the commencement of this Constitution as the Banaras Hindu University, the Aligarh Muslim University and the Delhi University and any other institution declared by Parliament by law to be an institution of national importance.

64. Institutions for scientific or technical education financed by the Government of India wholly or in part and declared by Parliament by law to be institutions of national importance.

65. Union agencies and institutions for:

(1) professional, vocational or technical training, including the training of police officers; or
(2) the promotion of special studies or research; or
(3) scientific or technical assistance in the investigation or detection of crime.

66. Co-ordination and determination of standards, in institutions for higher education or research and scientific and technical institutions.

List III — Concurrent List

25. Vocational and technical training of labour.

In addition, the Government of India is also responsible for several other educational programmes which include national planning; educational and cultural relations with other countries; participation in the work of the UN and its specialized agencies, especially UNESCO; clearing-house function of collecting and disseminating ideas and information; education in the union territories; propagation, development and enrichment of Hindi; preservation and promotion of national culture, including patronage to national art; special responsibilities for the cultural interests of minorities; responsibilities for the weaker sections of the people such as the Scheduled Castes and Scheduled Tribes; responsibility for promoting national integration through suitable programmes; and grant of scholarship, particularly at the university stage.

18.26 *Recommendations*. We are of the view that education must increasingly become a national concern and we have indicated, in the relevant context, the role that the Government of India should play in the development of education. For instance, apart from its role in the improvement of educational administration which we are discussing in this chapter, we have indicated several other central responsibilities in education for:

- the improvement of teacher status and teacher education;
- manpower planning in crucial sectors like agriculture, engineering, medicine, etc.;
- the development of a programme of scholarships;
- the equalization of educational opportunities with special reference to the reduction of inter-State differences and the advancement of the weaker sections of the community;
- the provision of free and compulsory education as directed by the Constitution;
- the vocationalization of secondary education;
- the improvement of standards at the education;
- the development of higher education and research with special reference to the postgraduate stage;

- the development of professional education in agriculture and industry;
- the promotion of scientific research; and
- the promotion of educational research.

18.27 We are convinced that the radical reconstruction of education which we have recommended in this Report will not be possible unless: (1) the Government of India provides the needed initiative, leadership and financial support and (2) educational administration, both at the Central and State levels, is adequately strengthened.

(1) With regard to the first, we recommend that the Centre should play an important role in the development of educational research. It should make the good work done in one area of the country known to the other areas, through the coordinating and clearing-house functions which cross-fertilize educational thinking, through periodical reviews and through conducting, or offering assistance to conduct, pilot or experimental projects. There is also the need to establish, in special cases, Central institutions which can set the pace for others. It is but proper that, as in the past, the Central institutions thus established should largely be in the scientific and technical sector. But it is also necessary for the Centre to establish institutions specializing in social sciences, including pedagogical sciences and the humanities. These should be established in close association with the universities and be an integral part of the university system. Besides, the Centre can also develop education in the Union Territories, particularly in Delhi, to serve as a pace-setter for the other areas.

(2) As regards the general strengthening of the administration, the constitution of the Indian Educational Service, with the amendments proposed by us, is a step of considerable importance. It is also a Central responsibility to arrange for the in-service training of educational administrators through such programmes as the conduct of an administrative staff college for senior officers of State Educational Services . . . The Centre should scout for talent in different fields and make the services of the best people in the country available to the State Governments for advice and assistance in all matters. It also has a significant role in the preparation of teachers to which we have already made a reference.

18.28 Equally important is the role of the Central Government in providing financial assistance for the development of education. This assistance will take three forms:

(1) Grants-in-aid (including transfer of revenues) made to the State Governments on account of their committed expenditure, through the quinquennial Finance Commissions;
(2) Grants-in-aid for development expenditure given for the plan as a whole, through the Planning Commission; and
(3) Expansion of the Central and the Centrally-sponsored sectors.

With regard to the first, our colleague, Prof. M.V. Mathur, is of the view that it would be a great improvement if the Finance Commission could be a Standing Commission, mostly with part-time membership and a small, compact secretariat. Certain minimum percentages of the proceeds of income-tax and Central excise revenues could be guaranteed to the States and distributed on population basis. For the rest of the flow of funds from the Centre to the States, the Finance Commission should hold annual reviews (this could be done immediately after the annual plan discussions with the States) and make necessary adjustments in transfer of revenues and grants-in-aid on the basis of needs and performance.

With regard to the second, we are not generally in favour of earmarking funds for specific sub-schemes in the educational sector within the State plans. The total allocation for education should not be altered without the approval of the Planning Commission. But within it, the State Governments should be free to use the funds at their discretion.

We attach considerable importance to the third, namely, the expansion of the Central and the Centrally-sponsored sectors. It is through this mechanism and the Centre will be able to stimulate and guide educational developments in the national interests in the crucial sectors referred to above.

18.29 *Should Education be in the Concurrent List?* An important issue raised in regard to the role of the Central Government is the desirability or otherwise of including education in the concurrent list in the Seventh Schedule of the Constitution so that the Centre may be able to control educational developments through legislation. The Committee of the members of Parliament on Higher Education (presided over by Shri P.N. Sapru) which examined the whole issue recommended that higher education at least should be included in the concurrent list. In the same vein, we have received various proposals to include some other sectors of education, e.g., technical education, in the concurrent list. Our colleagues, Shri P.N. Kirpal and Dr. V.S. Jha, are of the view that the whole of education should be included in the concurrent list. In their opinion, the experience of the years since independence has shown that, for the lack of adequate authority at the Centre, national policies could not be implemented satisfactorily and that the excellent recommendations of many commissions and committees, in various fields of education, remained on paper. Even the resolutions unanimously adopted by the conferences of Education Ministers and the Central Advisory Board of Education remained unimplemented. They think that although there is some scope for more effective implementation within the present constitutional set-up by evolving suitable conventions and especially by developing new attitudes to the national character of education, these changes will not be easy to be brought about and they will not be sufficient. They, therefore, think that the Union Government should be invested with legal authority in the field of education, which should appear in the concurrent list of subjects. The constitutional amendment will, of course, take some time to take effect but the process towards this should be started as early as possible.

18.30 We have examined this problem very carefully. We are not in favour of fragmenting education and putting one part in the concurrent and the other in the State list — education should, under any circumstances, be treated as a whole. We also do not agree with our colleagues and are of the view that in a vast country like ours, the position given to education in the Constitution is probably the best because it provides for a Central leadership of a stimulating but non-coercive character. The inclusion of education in the concurrent list may lead to undesirable centralization and greater rigidity in a situation where the greatest need is for elasticity and freedom to experiment. We are convinced that there is plenty of scope, within the present constitutional arrangement to evolve a workable Centre-State partnership in education and that this has not yet been exploited to the full. The case for amending the Constitution can be made only after this scope is fully utilized and found to be inadequate. All things considered, we recommend that an intensive effort be made to exploit fully the existing provisions of the Constitution for the development of education and evolution of a national educational policy. The problem may then be reviewed again after, say, ten years.

Educational Administration at the National Level

18.31 The agencies at the national level concerned with the development of education are the Ministry of Education, the University Grants Commission and the National Council of Educational Research and Training (or the NCERT)... We shall now turn to our proposals for the Ministry of Education and the NCERT.

18.32 *Ministry of Education.* The present convention is that the post of the Secretary to the Government of India is not to be filled from the ICS or IAS pool and that it should be given to an eminent educationist who should be designated as 'Educational Adviser to the Government of India and Secretary to the Ministry of Education'. This is a healthy tradition and should continue. It is also necessary to make it clear that this is a 'selection post' and that it should not go, as a matter of routine, by promotion to the present advisory service or even to the proposed IES. This should be a tenure post, given only for six years in the first instance with an extension, in exceptional cases, for three or four years, but not renewable further. The selection should be made from amongst all persons available, official, non-official, IES, university men, etc. So much depends upon the selection of the right man for this post that no vested interest of any service should be allowed to stand in the way and, through a proper machinery for selection, the best man available in the country should be recruited on a tenure basis. We would like to mention that the present status of the Ministry of Education in the academic world is largely due to the fact that its Secretaries were selected in the post-independence period from outside the services and from among eminent educationists.

18.33 It is extremely important that eminent educationists, outstanding teachers in universities and schools and leading officials from the State Education Departments should be associated with the Ministry of Education so that it can provide the needed leadership and command the confidence of the public and the teaching community. We, therefore, recommend that all the posts at the level of additional or joint secretaries and joint educational advisers should be divided into two categories:

(1) About half the posts should be filled from among the official

ranks by promotion, i.e., from the present education advisory service (or the IES when it is constituted) and officers seconded from the State Education Departments.

(2) The remaining half should be filled from the ranks of eminent educationists and outstanding teachers in universities and schools. The term of each tenure should be five years to be renewable at the most for a second term.

The top level machinery for advising the Union Minister of Education and executing his order will consist of the Educational Adviser and Secretary to the Government of India and all the additional and joint secretaries and joint educational advisers.

18.34 Our proposals to strengthen evaluation and research by the establishment of a Research Council in the Ministry of Education has already been discussed . . . earlier in this chapter. Two other functions of the Ministry of Education also need considerable strengthening and expansion.

(1) The first is the clearing-house function. The Ministry of Education has to function as a national clearing house in education. This is necessary, not only in its own right, but also as an important aid to planning. What is needed is the collection of information on important educational topics from the State Governments, according to a well-planned schedule and its publication, with proper analysis, for the information of all concerned. These data should also be re-collected periodically so that each publication serves as a bench-mark. We recommend that a well-staffed division should be created to perform this function on an adequate scale. It was not possible for us to go into the details of the various types of studies required. Some of these have been indicated in our Report in the appropriate context. We suggest that the Ministry of Education may set up a committee to examine the issue and to prepare a programme for action.

(2) The second is the maintenance of a good statistical service which is another major responsibility of the Ministry of Education, from the point of view of educational planning, policy-making and evaluation. This service should have three main functions: (a) to collect, publish and interpret educational data; (b) to conduct statistical studies, investigations and surveys; and (c) to make projections and forecasts for the future. The existing statistical service leaves a good deal to be desired. At present, only the first function is being performed. There is so much delay in the collection, collation and publi-

cation of the data that it is almost out-of-date for the purpose of planning by the time it is published. Moreover, no worthwhile interpretation of the past data is done and the other two functions have been completely ignored. In order that these functions may be discharged properly, it is essential that the statistical section of the Ministry should be reorganized and strengthened. From this point of view, we make the following recommendations:

(a) A master plan should be prepared for the publication of educational data and for the surveys and investigations which should be conducted from time to time.
(b) The combination of the publication of routine statistics with studies of special problems is not desirable. The publication of routine annual statistics should therefore be the responsibility of a special unit as at present. But it will be desirable to create a new unit for the conduct of special surveys and investigations.
(c) To make this service more efficient, it will be desirable to introduce mechanization to the extent feasible.
(d) The statistical unit should continue its present function of providing training to the statistical staff of the State Governments and universities. However, there is need to tone up the quality and content of this training. The Ministry should also provide opportunities to its own statistical staff to receive training and periodic reorientation at training courses conducted by other expert bodies like the Indian Statistical Institute and the Central Statistical Organization.
(e) The statistical units of the State Departments of Education will have to be reorganized and strengthened likewise to enable them to perform practically the same functions as outlined above for the statistical unit of the Education Ministry.

18.35 Of the various advisory bodies of the Ministry of Education, the most important is the Central Advisory Board of Education which has been functioning since 1935. The Minister for Education, Government of India, is the Chairman of this Board and all the State Ministers of Education are members. The Government of India also nominates a few experts and representatives of different interests on the Board. It has also the representatives of the Planning Commission, the University Grants Commission and the Inter-University

Board of India. We recommend that this organization with all its standing committees be functionally strengthened.

18.36 *NCERT*. The establishment of the National Council of Educational Research and Training (NCERT) has been a step in the right direction. We give below some indications of the lines on which its future development should take place.

(1) *Functions*. The principal function of the NCERT is extension work with the State Education Departments centring round the improvement of school education. It is uniquely suited for this function because the Union Minister for Education is its President and all State Education Ministers are its members. The objective of policy should, therefore, be to develop the NCERT as the principal technical agency functioning at the national level for the improvement of school education and operating through and in collaboration with the National Boards of School Education, State Departments of Education and their technical agencies like the State Institutes of Education.

(2) *Constitution*. The Governing Body of the NCERT should have an all-India character, with a majority of non-officials in particular, it is desirable to have at least one outstanding teacher from secondary schools and a person specializing in primary education, preferably a primary teacher.

(3) *Director and Joint Director*. We recommend that the Council should have its own full-time Director and Joint Director. At present, the Secretary to the Ministry of Education is the Director of the Council and an officer of the Ministry (generally part-time) is the Joint Director. This is not an ideal arrangement, and the size and importance of the Council are such that it would be wrong to leave its leadership in the hands of part-time officers whose loyalties and commitments lie elsewhere. The Council should have a whole-time Director of its own who should be an eminent educationist in the field. His status should be that of a vice-chancellor. His term of office should be five years, renewable for not more than one term. The Joint Director (who may be an officer lent by the Ministry) would be needed mainly for the purposes of assisting the Director and relieving him of routine administrative matters.

(4) *Regional Colleges and CIE*. The NCERT is now running four regional colleges for training of secondary school teachers. . . . The Council is also in charge of the Central Institute of Education, Delhi. We suggest that this institution should be transferred to the Delhi

University; and we hope that the Delhi University will establish a School of Education on the lines of our recommendations and give a lead to the improvement of the programme of teacher education in the country.

(5) *Personnel.* The success of the NCERT will depend upon the extent to which it is accepted by the State Education Departments and their technical wings and upon the extent to which it is able to assist them to solve their technical problems in the field. It would, therefore, be desirable that there is a considerable interchange and flow of officers from the NCERT to the State Departments and *vice versa*. This could be secured by inviting selected offices from the State Education Departments to work in the NCERT on tenure appointments. Arrangements should also be made with the State Governments under which officers of the NCERT could work in State Education Departments for specified periods.

(6) As the NCERT has to play the key-role in promoting qualitative improvements in school education, it is imperative that its campus should be developed speedily and the building programme given the highest priority. The present dispersal of departments and units in distant parts of the city is not conducive to efficient functioning.

Educational Administration at the State Level

18.37 The State Education Departments are the principal agency to prepare and implement educational plans. Unfortunately no adequate attention has been paid so far to their development on proper lines. Their structure, designed during the British period for very limited purposes, continues to be substantially unchanged even to this date. Their procedures and programmes are still largely traditional and the outlook of their officers is, more often than not, rigid and conservative. It is true that there has been some expansion in the Education Departments. But most of this expansion has been on traditional lines and has not implied any qualitative change in their functioning. Moreover, even this numerical expansion has not kept pace with the demands of the situation and has fallen far short of the expansion in the number of educational institutions, their enrolments, or total educational expenditure. In some States, programmes of retrenchment in the strength of the Education Departments have been carried out even when expansion of educational facilities was in full swing. The State Education Departments, as constituted at present, will not be in a position to assume responsibility for the complex and difficult programme of educational reconstruction outlined in this Report. It is, therefore, necessary to accord priority to programmes for the improvement of educational administration at the State level. Our major recommendations in this regard are given below.

18.38 *Co-ordination*. Co-ordination is very often an administrative bottleneck at the State level because educational programmes are spread over a number of departments at present. In most States, general education is in one department and under one Director of Education or Public Instruction. In some States, however, even general education is divided into two parts — college education and school education, and placed under different Directors. Sometimes there are additional directorates for Sanskrit or art education. In three States the education of tribals is separated and placed under a different department. In all States, technical education is under a separate directorate and may or may not form a part of the Education Department. Agricultural education is generally under the Department of Agriculture and medical education under the Medical and Health Services Departments. The industrial training institute are mostly under the Department of Industries. Programmes of adult education are sometimes grouped with general education and, on other occasions, placed under the Community Development Administration. It is obviously necessary that these different programmes of educational development should be co-ordinated properly and viewed as parts of a comprehensive whole.

18.39 To place all these different aspects of education under the 'umbrella' of a single department does not seem to be administratively feasible, and, for some time to come, we shall have to accept the factual position that education will be administered by more than one department. It is, therefore, desirable to create, at the State level, some machinery to coordinate the programmes of all these different sectors of education and to take a unified view for purposes of planning and development. The following two measures may be considered from this point of view:

(1) A statutory *Council of Education* should be created at the State level. As separate arrangements have already been suggested for the development of higher education which is a Centre-State-University partnership, the scope of this Council should be restricted to school education or all education below the university level. It

should have the State Minister for Education as the chairman and its membership should include representatives of universities in the State, all directors in charge of different sectors of education and some eminent educationists. It should meet about three or four times a year and have a small secretariat of its own. Its principal functions should be to advise the State Government on all matters relating to school education, either *suo motto* or on points referred to it, to review educational developments in the State and to conduct evaluation of programmes from time to time through suitable agencies. This should be the most important advisory body at the State level and if necessary, it may form standing or sub-committees for different sectors and programmes. Its annual report, along with its recommendations, should be presented to the State legislature.

(2) It may be desirable to have, in addition, a standing committee at the officers level. It would include all State level officers in charge of different sectors of education and meet periodically under the chairmanship of the Education Secretary.

18.40 *The Education Secretariat.* At present the Education Secretary is generally an IAS officer, except in West Bengal, where he belongs to the Education Service. We are of the opinion that the Education Secretary also, like the Educational Adviser to the Government of India, should be an educationist rather than an administrative officer. It will, therefore, be desirable to make this appointment a tenure post.

18.41 The relationship between the Education Secretary and the Director of Education has been a subject of long controversy since the issue was first highlighted by the Hartog Committee in 1928. The most common complaint is that the Education Secretariat completely dominates over the Directorate of Education and interferes even in purely technical matters. It has also been argued that the dual scrutiny of proposals that now takes place in the Directorate as well as in the Education Secretariat leads to considerable delays. The remedy most frequently suggested is that the Director of Education should be *ex-officio* Secretary or Additional Secretary to the Government. The problem is difficult and there is no easy answer to all the complex relationship. Broadly speaking, the role of the Education Secretariat should be to examine educational problems from the administrative and financial points of view and in the wider context of government policies for development. It should give due weightage to the views of the Directorate in technical matters and assist the Director to function as the effective head of his department. The key to a successful relationship lies, however, in the 'personal equation' between the Director of Education and the Education Secretary; and where this has been of the right type, the results have been satisfactory.

18.42 *Directorate of Education.* At present the Directorates have grown big and there is not enough delegation of powers to the district level. The time of the Director of Education therefore, is so taken up with personnel administration and trivial details that he has no time for his principal responsibility of providing leadership in educational development. We have, therefore, made two important proposals which will alter the entire functioning of the department:

(1) the constitution of district school boards at the district level and the transfer to them of the administration of all education below the university level (including the management of all government schools); and
(2) the strengthening of the office of the district inspector of schools so that he takes over almost all the responsibilities of the Directorate in his area.

When these changes are carried out, the directorate will be a compact and efficient organization concerned mainly with general coordination and supervision over the district education officers and district school boards. It will then be possible for them to vitalize education through a purposeful and dynamic leadership.

Personnel

18.43 Administration is essentially a matter of faith and vision, bold and courageous leadership, and proper handling of human relations. The importance of securing the right type of personnel for it cannot, therefore, be over-emphasized. The major weaknesses of the existing organization of the State Education Departments are largely related to personnel. These include: shortage of personnel at the higher level; lack of specialized staff; unsatisfactory remuneration and conditions of service; unsatisfactory methods of recruitment; inadequate provision of in-service education; and inadequate staffing.

18.44 *The Indian Educational Service.* The creation of the Indian Educational Service or IES is a step in the right direction and if organized on proper lines, such a service would help the progress of education. We are, however, not happy at some of the features of the proposal which is now under the consideration of Government. We shall, therefore, examine this issue in some detail.

18.45 At the very outset, it should be noted that the character of the IES will have to be very different from the IAS or other Central Services. First, in education, administration is a service agency to teaching and research and not their master. Secondly, one cannot be a good educational administrator unless one is also a good teacher. Thirdly, there should always be a possibility for an educational administrator to come back to teaching or research and for a teacher to go over to the administrative side on a tenure assignment. In our opinion, the present proposal for the organization of the IES cuts across these sound principles of educational administration. As proposed at present, two-thirds of the recruitment to the IES will have to be made directly by open competition. The persons selected will not generally have any experience of teaching or research and would have had no opportunity to show their competence in these fields. The remaining one-third of the posts will be filled by promotion from State services and some of these may be teachers in government schools and colleges. But the bulk of the teachers, i.e., all university teachers and teachers in private schools and colleges will be barred entry within its ranks. This can only have a depressing effect upon the body of the teaching profession and ultimately on education itself. We, therefore, strongly feel that the method of recruitment to the IES should be as follows:

(1) Only one-third of the posts should be filled by direct recruitment at the level of the junior scale. Even these selected persons should not be placed in administration direct. Their first assignments, for a minimum period of 2 or 3 years, should be in teaching; and it is only after this initiation that they should be assigned to administration.

(2) The remaining two-thirds of the posts should be filled, partly by direct recruitment and partly by promotion at the level of the senior and higher scales. One-half of these posts (i.e., one-third of the total) would be filled by promotion from the State services. The remaining half should again be filled by direct recruitment — some at the level of the senior scale and other at the level of the higher scales. The age limits for these recruitments should be suitably fixed, say, 35 and 45 years, and

the applicants should have put in a minimum of service as teachers or should have distinguished themselves as research workers.

(3) Some posts in the IES should be available for being filled by tenure appointments of teachers for specified periods. In the same way, some posts in teaching and research should also be available for tenure appointments of persons from the IES.

18.46 The second point which we examined in detail was that of creating a teaching wing in the IES. The present proposal visualizes the encadrement of the posts of the principals of Government colleges (which are regarded more as administrative than as teaching posts). There is also a suggestion that some posts of the principals of higher secondary schools should be encadred. There is no objection to a few posts of principals of Government colleges or of higher secondary schools being encadred. In fact, it would be good to do so. But this does not require the creation of a teaching wing — the posts of these principals can be made inter-changeable, as they are even at present, with some levels of inspecting officers. But there are insuperable difficulties in the creation of a teaching wing as such which, if it is to be created at all, should include a large proportion of the teaching posts in higher education. This will not be possible because all the teaching posts in the universities and the vast bulk of the posts in the government colleges (to say nothing of the posts in private affiliated colleges) will have to be kept out of the IES. The attempt to create a teaching wing by the encadrement of a few posts of the principals of government colleges is, therefore likely to do more harm than good by adversely affecting the morale of the teaching community as a whole. We, therefore, are commend that the idea of creating a teaching wing in the IES should be abandoned and the service should encadre only the following posts:

- All posts of Directors, Additional Directors, Joint Directors, Deputy Directors, etc., District Educational Officers (and equivalent posts) in the State Education Departments (inclusive of the principals of government colleges and a few posts of headmasters of higher secondary schools);
- All gazetted advisory posts in the Ministry of Education;
- suitable post in the NCERT;
- all gazetted posts dealing with educational programmes in

other Ministries of the Government of India;
- suitable gazetted posts in the Education Departments of the Union Territories; and
- suitable posts of principals of higher secondary schools under the scheme of Central Schools.

18.47 Instead of creating a teaching wing in the IES, we recommend that an adequate number of posts comparable to the higher scale of pay in the IES should be created in the universities and colleges. This is justified on educational grounds because the remuneration and status given to teachers and research workers should be at least equal, if not better, than those given to educational administrators. It will also prevent a drain of talent from teaching and research to administration.

18.48 Some thought will have to be given to languages required from the members of the IES. It is true that officers of the IES will need a much better command over the regional language than those in the IAS. But the advantages of the service would be lost to a considerable extent if every member of the IES is recruited and assigned only to the State to which he belongs. It should be a convention that only about 50 per cent of the IES officers are assigned to their own States; and there should also be the possibility of inter-State transfers (in addition to deputation to the Centre). Hence each member of the IES should be required to study and pass, within a given time after recruitment, tests in two other languages (Hindi and one modern Indian language which is not his mother-tongue) at certain prescribed levels.

18.49 The changes we have recommended in the organization of the IES and the corresponding improvement in the remuneration of teachers and research workers are extremely significant. If these are carried out, the IES will strengthen the administration without adversely affecting teaching or research.

18.50 *The State Educational Services.* At present, the State Educational Services are divided into three broad groups — Class I, Class II and others. In the reorganization of these services, the following points will have to be kept in view:

(1) There should be an adequate number of posts at higher levels, namely in Class I and Class II. The secretaries of the district school boards should be in Class I. The District Educational

Inspectors (who will be in the IES) should have adequate assistance from officers of Class I and Class II status.

(2) The methods of recruitment would have to be improved. A disturbing trend now seen is to push fresh recruitment to all posts on the administrative side of the State Education Departments lower and lower down the line. In one State, all fresh recruitment to all the departmental posts is done at the assistant masters' level. In such cases, a young talented graduate from the universities is not attracted to the service and all higher posts come to be gradually occupied by those who have risen from the ranks. What is needed is recruitment at three levels: assistant teachers' level; Class II level (50 per cent for freshers and 50 per cent for promotion); and Class I level (75 per cent for freshers and 25 per cent for promotion). There should be, as in the IES, suitable relaxation in age limit while recruiting at higher levels.

(3) In the pre-independence period, the main functions of the department were two: the control of educational institutions — public and private — and distribution of grant-in-aid. The entire cadre of the department consisted, therefore, of 'generalists' i.e., persons who had some initiation into education (as indicated by the B.T. or a similar degree) or had some experience of teaching. There were a few special posts (e.g., Inspector of Audio-Visual Education), no doubt; but there was no special training for the purpose and anyone could be appointed to the post and expected to learn his job by doing. Even inspections were 'general' in the sense that an officer who inspected the school was expected to guide the teaching of all subjects and look after all aspects of the school life. By and large this tradition has continued to this day. But it has outlived its utility. With the enlargement of the functions of the Education Departments and the heavy responsibilities it has now come to assume for the improvement of education, the need for specialized officers has increased. For instance, curricular reform has assumed great significance; and yet there is not one specialist in curriculum in all the State Education Departments. Similar observations could also be made about other fields of education such as evaluation, textbooks, etc. One of the major reforms now needed is to reorganize the State Education Departments where necessary, on the basis of

specialized functionaries (the need for whom is universally recognized) and, what is even more urgent and important, to make adequate arrangements for their specialized training with the help of the universities. These specialist officers (who will include subject inspectors) will be appointed at two levels — at the directorate and on the district staff.

(4) There are several anomalies in the salaries of departmental staff in the States and Union Territories. Two of these deserve notice:

(1) Should the scales of pay in the administrative wing of the Education Department be the same as in its teaching wing or should they be different? At present, three practices are in vogue. In some States, they are identical; in some, the scales of pay on the teaching side are kept higher while in others, it is the other way round. The ideal position would be to keep the scales of pay identical but to add allowances, either to the teaching or to the administrative side, to make up for the inconveniences, losses or disadvantages, such allowances being payable only so long as the person occupies the post. Such a system would make for easier transferability between the two wings and promote traffic both ways.

(2) The scales of pay of the departmental staff (Class I and II) are made comparable, not with the UGC scales of pay, but with those of similar posts in other departments. This creates difficulties for the transfer of persons from the teaching to the administrative wing. We would recommend that the scales of pay of the departmental staff should be correlated with the UGC scales of pay for university teachers.

18.51 *Training of Educational Administrators*. The existing facilities and arrangements for the training of educational administrators are inadequate. Pre-service education for administrators is neither necessary nor pôssible. It is true that educational administration is one of the subjects taught on an optional basis in the courses of the M.Ed. degree in some training colleges and university departments of education. The number of places available in these courses is very limited. Their standard leaves a good deal to be desired because they are taught by persons who themselves have little experience of administration, because the literature available on Indian conditions and practices is very limited and because there are hardly any facilities for giving practical training to the students. Such pre-service education can only be of limited use and one has largely to rely on in-service education for the training of educational administrators.

18.52 Unfortunately there is little or no provision for such training opportunities at present in any State Education Department. This is all the more surprising because the efficacy of training is the basic assumption in education. Training for an educational administrator is needed, not only because the tasks he is required to perform are difficult and complex, but mainly because it is necessary to orient him to the programmes of educational expansion and improvement which has to be implemented in the next two decades and to the role which educational administration should play therein. From this point of view, we make the following recommendations:

(1) At the non-gazetted level, the number of officers is very large and arrangements for their in-service training would necessarily have to be made at the State level. We recommend that the State Institutes of Education, in collaboration with the universities, where necessary, should organize the in-service education programmes of all the non-gazetted educational staff on the administrative and inspectional side. The objective should be to provide an in-service training of abut two months to every officer in every five years of his service. In addition, they should also organize conferences, seminars, and workshops for the gazetted staff.

(2) At the level of the gazetted officers, the numbers in any given State are not large enough for developing a training institution at the State level. We, therefore, recommend that the Ministry of Education should run a National Staff College for senior educational administrators of the State Departments of Education.

(3) The task of an educational administrator is generally so heavy that he gets no time to read and to keep himself abreast of educational thought. The programmes of in-service education recommended above will correct this weakness to a great extent. In addition, it will be desirable to revive the old practice

of giving three months' leave on full pay for every five years of service, for undertaking special studies in educational problems. Preferably still, the idea of a sabbatical year of leave should be extended to senior posts in administration. He should also have the option to add to this his unutilized privilege leave (which now more or less lapses), if he desires. The only condition attached to this leave should be that the officer should submit a report on his studies at the end of the leave period.

(4) Some incentives should be provided for the officers who improve their qualification materially through programmes of in-service education.

18.53 *National Staff College for Educational Administrators*. We attach importance to the establishment of the National Staff College for Educational Administrators and would like to indicate broadly the manner in which it should function.

(1) The object of the college should be to provide in-service education, for about eight weeks, in every five years of service, to all the senior officers in the education service — IES and State Educational Services (Class I and Class II).

(2) It should have a permanent and whole-time staff of its own. In addition, it should use, as resource personnel, senior officers of the Education Departments and the Ministry of Education. As educational administration cannot function in isolation, competent persons from other departments also should be utilized for purposes of training. This will incidentally serve an important objective of such training, namely, to bring the young recruits to the cadre in living contact with senior officers.

(3) It should have a research wing where studies would be conducted in problems of educational administration. It should maintain a good library of books on the subject, both Indian and foreign. Besides, it should also function as a clearing-house of administrative procedures and practices in the States and Union Territories.

(4) As very little material on Indian conditions is available for purposes of training, the college should be established immediately and its first assignment should be to prepare a number of case studies and other data which can be utilized for conducting the training programmes. This may well take about one or two years. It is only

when a thorough preparation of this type is made that the training programmes should be started.

(5) It should conduct two types of courses; a longish induction course should be provided for new recruits and shorter courses of 3-6 weeks for officers already in service.

(6) In every course conducted at the college, some officers from every State and a few from the Union Territories should be included. It should be an object of policy to cross-fertilize administrative experience.

(7) It should conduct periodical conferences, seminars and workshops on matters relating to educational administration.

(8) It should conduct a journal on educational administration and maintain a publication wing.

18.54 *Increasing the Strength of the Department.* The most common complaints that were placed before us by the State Education Departments were: they are understaffed; the growth in the Departmental staff does not *precede* but *follows* the growth in the number of educational institutions and is never able to keep pace with it; norms fixing the number of officers required on the basis of educational institutions, teachers and students, distances involved, problems of transportation and such other relevant factors are not generally fixed and, even if fixed in theory, are not observed in practice; the expenditure for increasing the Departmental staff always has a low priority and is not sanctioned automatically when programmes of expansion are approved; and the axe of retrenchment within educational falls, more often than not, on the departmental staff. Most of these complaints are genuine. We recommend a reversal of these policies, subject to one reservation. It is better to have a fewer officers at a higher level than a large number of officers at a lower level and on inadequate scales of pay. Our recommendations regarding the new techniques for administration and supervision provide for this; and this point should be kept in view in the proposed reorganization of the State Educational Departments.

Procedures

18.55 *The Present Position.* The existing procedures in educational administration suffers from an excessive emphasis on uniformity and rigidity. In every State, we heard complaints by the headmasters of government schools that almost every detail of the life of a school was regulated by the orders of the Department. The managements of private institutions also complained of rigid Departmental attitudes and attempts at controlling even the smallest details. The need to change these old traditions cannot be over-emphasized. The idea of creating uniformity and regulating the educational process through comprehensive Departmental codes has been overdone and has killed all freedom and initiative and reduced experimentation to the minimum. We must now initiate a new process under which the administration will be distinguished by elasticity and dynamism. As Dr. J.W. Gardner observes: "The rule book grows bigger as the ideas grow fewer. Thus almost every well-established organization is a coral reef of procedures that were laid down to achieve some long-forgotten objective. An organization must therefore objective. An organization must therefore have some means of combating the process by which men become prisoners of their own procedures."

18.56 **Introducing Elasticity and Dynamism.** How can this elasticity and dynamism be introduced in educational administration? We have made a number of suggestions in this regard in the earlier chapters. Here we would like to emphasize some general suggestions:

(1) The first is a change in the attitude of the administrator. He should cultivate an openness of mind and a spirit of inquiry rather than a rule-of-thumb approach which tries to stick to established practices, even when they cease to be meaningful. It is here that research in educational administration and the in-service training of educational administrators can play a significant role.

(2) The second is to establish a practice of holding periodical reviews, say, every three to five years, of important administrative practices, with a view to chopping off dead-wood and putting in fresh grafts, where necessary.

(3) The third is to build up inter-State contacts and to encourage comparative studies in different State practices in all administrative matters. The study of educational administration developed in the USA out of one peculiar feature: the variety of administrative practices in the different States which arose from the fact that education was a State subject. This variety led to a comparative study of different practices in each aspect of administration. This comparison was originally restricted to mere tabulations which showed the dif-

ferences. But it soon led to a discussion about the origin of these differences, the fundamental principles on which each such practice should be based, and a comparison of the relative advantages and disadvantages of different practices. Out of this arose a science of educational administration and when the States were confronted with those comparative studies year after year, they were stimulated to think and to make innovations. This happy and fruitful cross-fertilization of administrative practices has not occurred in India.* There are hardly any comparative studies it has conducted or promoted in educational administration with the result that the intellectual contact between the different State Education Departments is very little. We find officers in every State Education Department who know about the USA, the UK, or the USSR, but they do not know what is happening in other States of India. If periodical comparative studies in educational administration could be prepared and the State Education Departments closely involved with them, the sad picture would soon disappear and administrative efficiency will begin to rise.*

(4) An area in which there is scope for improvement in our administrative practices is that of project preparation. Modern administrative practice in both the armed forces and industry require a systematic analysis and preparation before an operation of a new activity is launched. In education, too often the practice is to describe a scheme in a page or two with some sketch of the budget required and to begin operation with no more preparation than this. Where large sums of money are to be spent, series of preparatory steps are all justified beginning from feasibility studies and going through to detailed, step-by-step., plan of operations for the project. This detailed programming of the planned projects will ensure more economic use of resources and more detailed evaluation of the progress being made in project implementation. The resolution of this technique and the training of officers in them is the responsibility of the State Institutes of Education and the National Staff College for Educational Administrations.

(5) The traditional system of administration is based on the prin-

---

* One illustration may suffice. A comparative study of the systems of grant-in-aid, an important issue, was first made in Indian Education Commission in 1882; it was repeated by Ritchie in 1922, and has not been done since.

ciple of having a few officers who are assisted by a large army of superintendents, assistants and clerks, because it was originally devised at a time when the administration had to be run by a few Englishmen with the assistance of a large number of Indians in subordinate positions. Under a system of this type, most of the work tends to be done by unimaginative persons at a lower level who were described by Burke as the 'tyrants of the desk'. This is one contributory cause to the rigidity of the system. We, therefore, recommend that the modern 'officer-oriented system' where most of the work will be done by officers at their own level with the help of a small secretariat staff should be adopted.

18.57 *Education Acts*. At present the educational legislation in the country presents a motley picture: in most States, it is scattered in a number of laws and the bulk of it is still in the form of executive orders, the only State to have an Education Act being Kerala. We, therefore, recommend that education should be given a statutory basis everywhere and in all sectors and that an Education Act should be passed in all the States and Union Territories. This should be a comprehensive and consolidating measure which will replace all the miscellaneous laws which now exist and which will also provide a statutory basis for certain important aspects of administration (for example grant-in-aid code) which now exist merely in the form of executive orders.

18.58 We also recommend that the Government of India should issue a Statement on the National Policy in Education which should provide guidance to the State Governments and the local authorities in preparing and implementing education plans in their areas. The possibility of passing a National Education Act may also be examined.

EDUCATIONAL FINANCE*

I. *Total Educational Expenditure (1950-65)*. (2–6).
II. *Pattern of Educational Expenditure (1950-65)*. (7–13).
III. *Sources of Educational Expenditure (1950-65)*. (14–17).
IV. *Sources of Educational Expenditure (1965-85)*. (18) Contribu-

* (i) Para Numbers refer to paras of Chapter XIX of the Document.
(ii) Original Table numbers have been changed to conform to this Chapter number.

tions of local authorities; (19) Contributions of voluntary organizations; (20) Centre-State relationship in the financing of education.

V. *Total Educational Expenditure(1965-85)*. (22) Estimate of resources likely to be available for education during the next 20 years.

VI. *Expenditure per Student*. (28) Pattern of cost per student in the first three plans; (30) Pattern of cost per student during the next 20 years; (31) School education; (34) Higher education.

VII. *Adult Education*. (37).

VIII. *Some General Observations*. (39—44).

19.01 In this chapter, we shall examine a few major issues relating to the financing of education. These will mainly include a survey of the growth of educational expenditure in India in the post-independence period and of the sources of educational finance. We shall also refer to the order of financial resources likely to be available for education during the next two decades, their appropriate allocation to various sectors and priorities involved. The questions of fundamental importance that arise are:

- What should be the total level of financial support for education at all levels to ensure achievement of national goals and rapid advancement of national economy, cohesion and security?
- What judgment and guidelines can be formulated, and with what degree of reliability and confidence, about the distribution of funds between different levels or stages of education (including research) and different sectors within a level?
- Although quality and quantity are inseparable, what proportions of the total resources should be broadly devoted to improvement of quality and consolidation and the expansion of education?

These questions, by their very nature, do not permit of precise answers because they are not questions in arithmetic or production engineering but in human dynamics involving complex sociological considerations. Difficulties really arise when one tries to give precise values to quantities which are essentially vague. However, if dealt with the proper perspective, the exercise affords insight and helps the process of decision-making.

Total Educational Expenditure, 1950-65

19.02 The discussion may conveniently begin with an examination of the manner in which the total educational expenditure has increased in the post-independence period. In 1946-47, the total educational expenditure in 'British' India was Rs. 577 million which worked out at only Rs. 11 per head of population. At the end of the third plan, the total expenditure on education is estimated at Rs. 6,000 million or approximately Rs. 12 per capita (at current prices). The details will be found in Table 5.2.

It will be seen that, during the first three plans:

- the total educational expenditure increased from Rs. 1,144 million in 1950-51 to Rs. 6,000 million in 1965-66, which denotes a total increase of 424 per cent in a period of 15 years or a cumulative annual increase of 11.7 per cent. This has varied but little from plan to plan — it stood at 10.6 per cent in the first plan, rose to 12.7 per cent in the second, and dropped to 11.8 per cent in the third;
- the total educational expenditure per capita rose from Rs. 32. at the beginning of the first plan to Rs. 4.8 at the end of the first, Rs. 7.8 at the end of the second and Rs. 12.1 at the end of the third — an overall increase of 278 per cent;
- the total educational expenditure represented 1.2 per cent of the national income in 1951. This proportion rose to 1.9 per cent at the end of the first plan, 2.4 per cent at the end of the second plan and 2.9 per cent at the end of the third. This represents an increase of 142 per cent in 15 years.
- the rate of growth of the educational expenditure in the first three plans (11.7%) is 2.2 times the rate of growth of national income at current prices (5.4%). It is 1.6 times the rate of growth of enrolment and 1.7 times the rate of growth in the number of teachers.*

* During this period, the total enrolment in educational institutions has increased from 24,287 thousand in 1950-51 to 70,292 thousand in 1965-66 which shows an average annual rate of growth of 7.3 per cent per year. The number of teachers has also increased from 798,192 in 1950-51 to 2,168,786 in 1965-66 which shows a rate of growth of 6.9 per cent per year.

TABLE 5.2: Total Educational Expenditure, 1950-51 to 1965-66

	1950-51	1955-56	1960-61	1965-66 (estimated)
1. Total educational expenditure from all sources (Rs. in millions)	1,444	1,897	3,444	6,000
2. Index of growth	100	166	301	524
3. Educational expenditure *per capita* (Rs.)	3.2	4.8	7.8	12.1
4. Index of growth	100	150	244	378
5. Total national income (at current prices) (Rs. in millions)	95,300	99,800	141,400	210,000
6. Index of growth	100	105	148	220
7. National income *per capita* (at current prices) (Rs.)	266.5	255.0	325.7	424.4
8. Index of growth	100	96	122	159
9. Total educational expenditure as percentage of national income	1.2	1.9	2.4	2.9
10. Index of growth	100	158	200	242
	First Plan	Second Plan	Third Plan	All Three Plans
11. Average annual rate of growth of total educational expenditure	10.6%	12.7%	11.8%	11.7%

Source: The educational data for 1950-51, 1955-56 and 1960-61 have been taken from Form A of the Ministry of Education. Those for 1965-66 have been estimated in the Commission's Secretariat. The data relating to National income are taken from CSO (the figure for 1965-66 is a rough estimate).

N.B.: The total educational expenditure given here does not include:

(1) expenditure incurred by the guardians of the students on their education, except fees paid;

(2) the 'opportunity costs' which are defined as the foregone income which would have been earned by the students if they had engaged themselves in some direct or indirect productive activity instead of attending the school;

(3) the expenditure figures of unrecognised institutions;

(4) the expenditure on pensions due to retired employees of Government in the Education Department (inclusive of teaching and non-teaching staff); and

(5) the expenditure on administration and other expenditure of private societies conducting educational institutions.

19.03 Three points need emphasis in this context. The first is that the total educational expenditure given in the Table 5.2 is at current prices. Unfortunately, no effort has been made so far to convert the educational expenditure in the country to constant prices. We began this exercise, but it could not be completed due to absence of necessary data. We, however, recommend that such an exercise should be taken up and completed as early as possible. The UGC may consider giving financial assistance to a well-established department of economics of a university for this purpose. We may, however, point out that, during this period, the wholesale price index has risen by about 53 per cent and the cost of living index for the working classes by about 65 per cent. Although these indices cannot be used to reduce the total educational expenditure to constant prices, they indicate that a good deal of the increase in total educational expenditure is due merely to a rise in the price level.

19.04 The second point is that the proportion of national income devoted to education in India is small in comparison with that in educationally advanced countries of the world. The absolute amount per capita spent by us on education is about one-hundredth of that spent by a highly industrialized country like the USA. This reflects the close interaction and interlocking between the level of education and the level of industrialization. Japan and the USA and the USSR are spending considerably more than 6 per cent of their GNP on education, about twice as much as India. In making international comparisons, however, one should not miss the important point that in countries with low levels of national incomes, the disposable surplus is much smaller and it is, therefore, far more difficult for them to make a given effort for education than for those countries which have a comparatively higher income per capita and in consequence, a larger disposable surplus. For instance, an educational expenditure of 3 per cent of the national income in India, where the national income per head is only about Rs. 400, has to be regarded as a much higher degree of 'effort' than an expenditure on the same or even higher percentage of the national income in the UK or the USA.

19.05 The third point is that the increase of educational expenditure has been much faster than that of the growth of economy. The overall resources available to education are a function of two variables — ability or the national income per head of population and effort or the proportion of national income allocated to education. During the first three plans, ability has shown a relatively lower rate of growth. Between 1950 and 1965, the total national income rose from Rs. 91,400 million in 1950-51 to Rs. 163,600 million in 1965-66 (at 1960-61 prices) which implies that the national economy grew only at about 4 per cent per year and that the income per head of population increased only from Rs. 256.5 to Rs. 330.7 which implies a growth-rate of only 1.7 per cent per year. It is unfortunate, that, in 1965-66, there has been a bad failure of the monsoon so that the net national product in the primary sector has been very adversely affected and the total national income threatens to be about 3 per cent less than that in 1964-65. But even if this year is set aside, the growth in total national income between 1950-51 and 1964-65 would be only 4.5 per cent per year and that in the per capita income (from Rs. 256.5 to Rs. 348.7) only 2.2 per cent per year. Since the precise figures of educational expenditure at constant prices are not available, it is not possible to compare the rate of growth of ability, at constant prices, with the rate of growth of effort. But there is enough indirect evidence available to show that, even at constant prices, the rate of growth in educational expenditure far exceeds that in the national income.

19.06 A more precise comparison is, however, possible at current prices. As shown in Table 5.2 the national economy has grown at 5.4 per cent per year during the first three plans while educational expenditure has grown at the rate of 11.7 per cent per year. The effort or the national income devoted to education has thus increased at more than twice the rate of ability or national income.

Pattern of Educational Expenditure, 1950-65

19.07 We may now pass on to examine how the available financial resources are allocated to different sectors and programmes of education at present. From this point of view, the data regarding educational expenditure by objects for two years — 1950-51 and 1965-66 — are given in Table 5.3.

19.08 It will be seen that the indirect expenditure given in the Table 5.3 is not divided according to different stages or sectors of education. We, therefore, divided this expenditure, on the assumptions given below, into two sectors — schools and university. Our calculations are given in Table 5.4.

19.09 On the basis of the above break-up, the expenditure at the three levels of education will be as shown in Table 5.5.

TABLE 5.3: Educational Expenditure by Objects in India, 1950-51 to 1965-66

Object	Total expenditure (Rs. in 000's)		Percentage of total expenditure		Average annual rate of growth
	1950-51	1965-66	1950-51	1965-66	
A. *Direct Expenditure*					
1. Pre-Primary Schools	1,198	11,000	0.1	0.2	15.9
2. Lower Primary Schools	364,843	1,220,500	31.9	20.3	8.4
3. Higher Primary Schools	76,990	717,500	6.7	12.0	16.0
Total (First Level)	443,031	1,949,000	38.7	32.5	10.4
4. Secondary Schools	230,450	1,181,000	20.1	19.7	11.5
5. Vocational Schools	36,944	250,000	3.2	4.2	13.6
6. Special Schools	23,335	39,920	2.0	0.7	3.6
7. Boards of Secondary/ Intermediate Education	5,338	45,000	0.5	0.8	15.3
Total (Second Level)	296,067	1,515,920	25.9	25.3	11.5
8. Universities	49,052	270,000	4.3	4.5	12.0
9. Research Institutes	6,256	65,000	0.5	1.1	16.0
10. Colleges for Arts and Science	71,714	327,500	6.3	5.5	10.7
11. Colleges for Professional Education	42,194	350,000	3.7	5.8	15.1
12. Colleges for Special Education	2,224	17,500	0.2	0.3	14.7
Total (Third Level)	171,440	1,030,000	15.0	17.2	12.7
Total (Direct)	910,539	4,494,920	79.6	74.9	11.2
B. *Indirect Expenditure*					
13. Direction and Inspection	27,364	114,009	2.4	1.9	10.0
14. Buildings	99,270	666,055	8.7	11.1	13.5
15. Scholarships, Stipends, etc.	34,456	420,035	3.0	7.0	18.1
16. Hostels	18,264	95,463	1.6	1.6	11.7
17. Miscellaneous	53,928	209,518	4.7	3.5	9.5
Total (Indirect)	233,282	1,505,080	20.4	25.1	13.2
GRAND TOTAL	1,143,822	6,000,000	100.0	100.0	11.7

Source: Ministry of Education, Form A.

N.B.: The educational expenditure given in Table 5.3 is divided into two categories — direct and indirect — in accordance with the classification adopted by the Ministry of Education. Some clarifications are, however, necessary to relate this classification to the usual classification of 'recurring' and 'capital' expenditure. All expenditure which is classified as 'direct' is recurring in character. All items of expenditure classified as 'indirect' are also recurring except in the case of 'buildings'. (This head includes all capital expenditure on buildings but does not include expenditure on their maintenance). Expenditure shown under hostels includes only the maintenance charges but does not include the capital expenditure on the construction of hostel buildings and the food charges of the inmates.

TABLE 5.4: Indirect Expenditure at School and University Stages, 1950-51 and 1965-66

	1950-51		1965-66	
	Amount (Rs. in 000's)	Percentage of total expenditure	Amount (Rs. in 000's)	Percentage of total expenditure
School Education				
1. Direction and Inspection	27,364	2.4	114,009	1.9
2. Buildings	39,708	3.5	133,211	2.2
3. Scholarships	24,705	2.2	210,017	3.5
4. Hostels	5,479	0.5	19,093	0.3
5. Miscellaneous	26,964	2.4	104,759	1.7
Total	124,220	10.9	581,089	9.7
Higher Education				
1. Direction and Inspection	—	—	—	—
2. Buildings	59,562	5.2	532,844	8.9
3. Scholarships	9,751	0.9	210,018	3.5
4. Hostels	12,785	1.1	76,370	1.3
5. Miscellaneous	26,964	2.4	104,759	1.7
Total	109,062	9.5	923,991	15.4

N.B.: (1) The expenditure on buildings has been divided, on the basis of general trends noticed, as 40:60 in 1950-51 and 20:80 in 1965-66.

(2) The break-down of the expenditure on scholarships for 1950-51 (actuals) is available. That for 1965-66 is an estimate made in the Secretariat of the Commission on the basis of present trends.

(3) The expenditure on hostels is largely at the university stage. It was divided, on the basis of general trends noticed, as 30:70 in 1950-51 and 20:80 in 1965-66.

(4) The miscellaneous expenditure was divided, on an *ad hoc* basis, in the proportion of 50: 50.

(5) Totals do not tally due to rounding.

19.10 In the initial stages of development, the total expenditure on education is generally low and the bulk of it is spent on school education. As societies become industrialized, the total expenditure on education begins to grow and an increasingly larger part of it comes to be devoted to higher education and research. This broad trend is maintained in spite of the increase that takes place in the expenditure on school education on account of universalization of primary education, expansion (or even universalization) of secondary education, and the qualitative improvement of school education. The growth of educational expenditure in Japan as seen in Table 5.6 will show this clearly.

TABLE 5.5: Educational Expenditure by Level, 1950-51 and 1965-61

(*Percentage*)

	1950-51	1965-66
1. *First level*, i.e., pre-primary, lower primary and higher primary schools	38.7	32.5
2. *Second level*, i.e., secondary, special and vocational schools and Board of Secondary Education	25.9	25.3
3. Indirect expenditure on school education	10.9	9.7
Total	75.5	67.4
4. *Third Level*, i.e., Universities, research institutions, and colleges of general, special and professional education	15.0	17.2
5. Indirect expenditure on higher education	9.5	15.4
Total (University)	24.5	32.6
GRAND TOTAL	100.0	100.0

N.B.: Totals do not tally due to rounding.

19.11 It will be seen that, in 1885, the expenditure on elementary education in Japan was as high as 84.3 per cent of the total. It has now come down to 42.4 per cent. (In Japan, the duration of the elementary course of education is six years as against seven years we are recommending.) The expenditure on secondary education, which was only 2.8 per cent in 1885, has now risen to 42.5 per cent. (The course of secondary education in Japan extends over six years, for the first three years of which education is compulsory.) In higher education, the expenditure has been steadily growing and risen from 8.3 per cent in 1885 to 13.1 per cent in 1960.

19.12 Some idea of the manner in which expenditure is distributed over the different levels of education in other countries can be had from Table 5.7.

19.13 The Indian picture in this context can be seen in the statistics given in Table 5.8.

TABLE 5.6: Educational Expenditure in Japan, 1885 to 1960

Year	Distribution of expenditure by level of education (%)					Percentage of GNP spent on education	GNP in million yen
	Elementary education I-VI	Secondary education VII-XII	Higher education XIII and above	Teacher training	Total		
1885	84.3	2.8	8.3	4.6	100.0	1.8	612
1890	76.9	3.1	10.9	9.1	100.0	1.0	924
1900	67.6	16.5	7.0	8.9	100.0	2.1	1,997
1910	67.4	16.7	10.0	5.9	100.0	3.0	2,888
1920	67.6	17.6	10.9	3.9	100.0	2.5	11,845
1935	61.9	18.7	16.9	2.5	100.0	3.3	15,203
1940	55.7	21.8	20.1	2.4	100.0	2.1	32,183
1950	41.8	46.2	12.0	—	100.0	4.8	3,381,500
1960	42.4	44.5	13.1	—	100.00	5.2	11,821,700

Source: *Japan's Growth and Education*, Ministry of Education, Japan, Tokyo, 1963, Tables 10 and 14.

TABLE 5.7: Percentage Distribution of Recurring Expenditure on Education by Level and Type of Education, 1961

Country	Central adminis-tration	Pre-primary and 1st level	Second level			Third level	Other types of education	Total
			Total	General	Vocational and teacher training			
Brazil	10.1	33.4	19.5	—	—	20.0	17.0	100.0
France	1.9	48.3	29.2	18.0	11.2(a)	8.3	12.3	100.0
Germany (F.R.)	1.5	48.1(b)	35.8	23.1	12.7(a)	13.2	1.4	100.0
Ghana	13.2	26.7	33.1	18.7	14.4	17.2	9.8	100.0
Nigeria	9.4	53.8	29.0	12.6	16.4	5.1	2.7	100.0
Pakistan	5.5	42.9	23.8	19.1	4.7	19.6	8.2	100.0
Turkey	—	61.3	32.4	13.4	19.0	1.4	4.9	100.0
U.K. (England & Wales)	4.1	27.1	38.8	31.5	7.3(a)	14.1	15.9	100.00
U.S.A.	—	72.4(c)	—(d)	—	—	27.6	—	100.0
U.S.S.R.	0.5	71.2(c)	—(d)	—	—	13.3	15.0	100.0
Yugoslavia (e)	4.5	58.3	19.3	—	—	16.1	1.8	100.0

Source: Compiled by the Commission's Study Team from documents available in the UNESCO Secretariat, Paris.

(a) Excludes expenditure on teacher training.
(b) Includes expenditure on special education.
(c) Includes expenditure on second level of education.
(d) Included under pre-school and first level of education.
(e) 1960.

TABLE 5.8: Growth of Educational Expenditure according to Objects, 1881-82 to 1960-61

(Rs. in 000's)

	1881-82	1891-92	1901-02	1911-12	11921-22	1936-37	1946-47	1960-61
1. Primary Schools	7,087 (44.0)	9,614 (31.5)	11,876 (29.6)	20,726 (26.4)	50,908 (27.7)	81,260 (29.9)	181,853 (32.1)	734,461 (21.3)
2. Secondary Schools	3,912 (24.3)	9,896 (32.4)	12,684 (31.6)	20,789 (26.5)	48,727 (26.5)	81,300 (29.9)	170,230 (29.5)	1,118,336 (32.5)
3. Vocational and Special Schools (including training)	453 (2.8)	1,711 (5.6)	2,280 (5.7)	5,374 (6.8)	13,701 (7.5)	18,595 (6.8)	34,657 (6.0)	146,688 (4.3)
4. Boards of Intermediate and Secondary Education	—	—	—	—	—	324 (0.1)	974 (0.2)	24,133 (0.7)
Total (Schools)	11,452 (71.1)	21,221 (69.5)	26,840 (66.9)	46,889 (59.7)	113,336 (61.7)	181,479 (66.7)	390,714 (67.8)	2,023,018 (58.8)
5. Universities	163 (1.0)	473 (1.6)	772 (1.9)	1,588 (2.0)	7,341 (4.0)	13,208 (4.9)	22,977 (4.0)	141,388 (4.1)
6. Arts and Science Colleges	1,332 (8.3)	2,044 (6.7)	2,601 (6.5)	4,799 (6.1)	11,042 (6.0)	16,662 (6.1)	43,915 (7.6)	236,139 (6.9)

Contd.

TABLE 5.8 *Contd.*

	1881-82	1891-92	1901-02	1911-12	11921-22	1936-37	1946-47	1960-61
7. Professional and Special Colleges	—	829	1,197	2,253	5,978	8,138	18,659	167,166
	—	(3.0)	(2.9)	(3.2)	(3.0)	(3.0)	(3.2)	(4.9)
Total (Universities)	1,495	3,346	4,570	8,640	24,361	38,008	85,551	544,693
	(9.3)	(11.0)	(11.4)	(11.0)	(13.2)	(14.0)	(14.8)	(15.9)
8. Direction & Inspection	1,628	2,250	2,545	4,775	9,335	11,407	18,238	70,123
	(10.1)	(7.4)	(6.3)	(6.1)	(5.1)	(4.2)	(3.2)	(2.0)
9. Buildings	838	2,182	2,573	9,730	19,761	18,197	28,453	428,150
	(5.2)	(7.1)	(6.4)	(12.3)	(10.8)	(6.7)	(4.9)	(12.4)
10. Scholarship	399	727	912	1,340	3,170	—(a)	—(d)	200,222
	(2.5)	(2.4)	(2.3)	(1.7)	(1.7)			(5.8)
11. Miscellaneous	298	794	2,681	7,219	13,784	22,766	53,657	171,711
	(1.8)	(2.6)	(6.7)	(9.2)	(7.5)	(8.4)	(9.3)	(5.1)
Total (Indirect)	3,163	5,953	8,711	23,064	46,056	52,370	100,348	870,214
	(19.6)	(19.5)	(21.7)	(29.3)	(25.1)	(19.3)	(17.4)	(25.3)
GRAND TOTAL	16,110	30,520	40,121	78,593	183,753	271,857	576,613	3,443,801
	(100.0)	(100.0)	(100.0)	(100.0)	(100.0)	(100.0)	(100.0)	(100.0)

(a) Included under Miscellaneous.
(b) Includes expenditure on pre-primary schools also.
Note: The figures in parentheses indicate the percentage to total expenditure.

It will be seen that before independence the position remained more or less stationary in India for a period of about sixty years — the direct expenditure on school education decreasing only from 71.1 per cent in 1881-82 to 67.8 per cent in 1946-47 and that on higher education rising only from 9.3 per cent to 14.8 per cent during the same period. The position, however, changed radically with the attainment of independence. Steps began to be taken for industrialization and hence greater expenditure was incurred on higher education, science and scientific research, technical and technological education, etc. By 1965-66, therefore, expenditure on higher education increased considerably. As will be seen from the data given in paragraph 19.09 earlier, the present position is that about one-third of the total expenditure is devoted to the first level of education; another one-third is devoted to the second level and to the indirect expenditure on school education; and the remaining one-third is devoted to higher education.

Sources of Educational Expenditure, 1950-65

19.14 We shall now proceed to examine the sources of educational expenditure during the first three plans. Due to various historical reasons, a multi-source finance system has grown in the country and education is now financed by the Central Government, State Governments and local authorities, and through fees and 'other' sources which include endowments, donations and other voluntary contributions from the public. This has helped to raise more resources in the aggregate than would otherwise have been possible and has also shown a certain resilience in times of difficulties by setting off, to some extent, the shortfalls in one source by increase in others. Table 5.9 shows how the contribution of each source has increased during the first three plan.

It will be seen that the largest increase has taken place in the expenditure from government funds (555 per cent or an average annual growth of 13.3 per cent) — this is only to be expected — and they now contribute 71.2 per cent of the total expenditure as against 57.1 per cent in 1950-51. Consequently, the contribution of all other sources has proportionately declined, although it has increased in absolute terms. The next important source is fees whose contribution has increased by 294 per cent (or 9.6 per cent per year); it now accounts for 15.3 per cent of the total educational expenditure. Then come other sources whose contribution has increased by 225 per cent (or 8.1 per cent per year) and which now bear only 7.2 per cent of the total expenditure. The local authorities whose resources are inelastic, particularly in rural areas, account for 6.3 per cent of the total expenditure only and they also show the lowest increase in contribution — 202 per cent (or 7.3 per cent per year).

TABLE 5.9: Educational Expenditure by Sources, 1950-51 to 1965-66

Source	1950-51	1955-56	1960-61	1965-66 (estimated)
1. *Government Funds*				
(i) Total expenditure (Rs. in 000's)	652,678	1,172,049	2,340,914	4,271,856
(ii) Index of growth	100	179	359	655
(iii) Percentage of total expenditure on education	57.1	61.8	68.0	71.2
2. *Local Authorities' Funds*				
(i) Total expenditure (Rs. in 000's)	124,987	163,548	224,914	378,031
(ii) Index of growth	100	131	180	302
(iii) Percentage of total expenditure on education	10.9	8.6	6.5	6.3
3. *Fees*				
(i) Total Expenditure (Rs. in 000's)	233,272	379,033	590,258	918,077
(ii) Index of growth	100	162	253	394
(iii) Percentage of total expenditure on education	11.6	20.0	17.1	15.3
4. *Other Sources*				
(i) Total expenditure (Rs. 000's)	132,885	181,980	287,715	432,036
(ii) Index of growth	100	137	217	325
(iii) Percentage of total expenditure on education	11.6	9.6	8.4	7.2
	First Plan	Second Plan	Third Plan	All Three Plans
5. *Average Annual Rate of Growth*				
(i) Government funds	12.4	14.8	12.8	13.3
(ii) Local authorities' funds	5.5	6.6	10.9	7.3
(iii) Fees	10.3	9.2	9.2	9.6
(iv) Other sources	6.5	9.6	8.5	8.1

Source: Ministry of Education, Form A.

Sources of Educational Expenditure, 1965-85

19.15 What would be the probable development relating to sources of educational expenditure in the next 20 years? It will be seen from the above that the responsibility for the financing of education at all stages is falling increasingly on government funds (Central and State). This trend will increase in the future. The total revenue from fees will be considerably reduced when, . . . education up to the end of the lower secondary stage is made tuition-free and a much larger provision of free-studentships is made in higher secondary and university education to meet the needs of the young persons from the under-privileged sections of society who are now coming into the universities and colleges. Similarly, the income from other sources would not rise in proportion to the increase in total educational expenditure. The local authorities also may not be able to provide more than a very small percentage of the total expenditure, even after they have made the best effort to raise their contribution. Taking an overall view of the situation, therefore, it appears that the funds of the Central and State Governments would have to bear about 90 per cent (or even more) of the total educational expenditure.

19.16 While it is true that most of the responsibility for the support of education should thus be squarely placed on governmental funds, a total centralization of all financial responsibility for education would also not be desirable, because it deprives the agencies at the school and local levels of all initiative in the matter. Even though the resources thus raised may not be large, the provision of administrative arrangements under which such initiative can exist and is even encouraged is of very great educational significance and will stimulate parental and local interest in education and help to raise standards. We, therefore, recommend that attempts should continue to be made to raise as much contribution as possible from local communities, voluntary organizations and local authorities to support educational development.

19.17 *Contribution of Local Communities* . . . the local communities should be closely associated with all government and local authority schools and that a school fund should be established in every school to meet the whole or part of the non-teacher costs. . . as part of the organization of a nation-wide programme of school improvement, the assistance of the local communities should be fully harnessed for improving the physical facilities in schools on the lines of the school improvement conference organized in Madras State. In the case of private schools, . . . the management should be able to raise a fair proportion of all the non-recurring costs and in addition, a prescribed percentage of recurring costs. Apart from their principal advantages of stimulating local interest in education, these contributions from the local communities and the public will also help to some extent in financing education.

19.18 *Contributions of Local Authorities*. The local authorities — municipalities and zila parishads — will be able to make a fair contribution in support of educational development. In our opinion, it would be possible to maximise these contributions if a suitable system of grant-in-aid is adopted. The broad features of such a system are indicated in Supplemental Note I given at the end of this chapter.

19.19 *Contributions of Voluntary Organizations*. The voluntary organizations conducting educational institutions are also making a contribution to total educational expenditure. This can be stimulated and utilised for the purpose of development through appropriate policies of grant-in-aid. . . .

19.20 *Centre-State Relationship in the Financing of Education*. Between them, the Centre and the State Governments now contribute about 71 per cent of the total educational expenditure; and as stated above, this will rise to 90 per cent by 1985-86. The problem of Centre-State relationship in the financing of education is thus of great importance. We have discussed it, in the appropriate contexts, in the earlier chapters of this Report. A brief reference to it has also been made in Supplemental Note I given at the end of this chapter.

Total Educational Expenditure, 1965-1985

19.21 We now come to the more difficult part of our task, namely, to estimate the magnitude of the resources likely to be available for educational development during the next 20 years, and the best manner of their allocation to different sectors or stages of education.

19.22 *Estimate of Resources Likely to be Available for Education during the Next Twenty Years*. In comparison with the last 15 years, the programme of educational development to be undertaken during the next two decades will be greater in magnitude and hence the total educational expenditure will have to increase much more. This would be possible only if there is increase both in ability and effort. The rate of growth of the economy has to be speeded up during the next two decades and this should be combined with a programme of population control. Also, the effort to increase allocations to education should be intensified. As stated earlier, it is difficult to be precise about these matters. We should, however, broadly work towards increasing the educational expenditure *per capita*, in a period of 20 years, to between 4 and 5 times the present level of Rs. 12 (at constant prices). This could be reached by a variety of combinations of different assumptions about the three variables involved, namely, economic growth (varying from 5 per cent to 7 per cent per annum), population growth (varying from 1.5 per cent to 2.5 per cent per annum), and the proportion of national income devoted to educational expenditure (varying from 4 per cent to 6 per cent). What we have in view, however, are developments on the following lines (Table 5.10).

TABLE 5.10: Total Educational Expenditure, 1965-66 to 1985-86

	1965-66	1970-71	1975-76	1980-81	1985-86
1. National income at 1965-66 prices — Increase assumed at 6 per cent per annum (Rs. in millions)	210,000	281,000	376,000	503,000	673,000
2. Index of growth	100	134	179	240	320
3. Population estimates (Medium projection in millions)	495	560	630	695	748
4. Index of growth	100	113	127	140	151
5. National Income per head of population (Rs.)	424	502	597	724	900
6. Index of growth	100	118	141	171	212
7. Total educational expenditure (Rs. in millions) (increase assumed at 10 per cent per annum)	6,000	9,663	15,562	25,063	40,364
8. Index of growth	100	161	259	418	673
9. Percentage of total educational expenditure to national income	2.9	3.4	4.1	5.0	6.0
10. Index of growth	100	117	141	172	207
11. Educational expenditure per capita (Rs.)	12.1	17.3	24.7	36.1	4.0
12. Index of growth	100	143	204	298	44

19.23 It will be seen that we have assumed a middle position with regard to the growth of national income (at 6 per cent per year as between the two other estimates of 5 and 7 per cent per year). Our assumption regarding the growth of population is also a medium estimate (2.1 per cent per year between 1966 and 1985 as against the two other estimates of 1.5 and 2.5 per cent per year). With regard to the proportion of national income devoted to education, we have assumed the highest rate of 6 per cent (out of the three possible assumptions of 4, 5 and 6 per cent) because we should accord the highest priority to education and allocate the largest proportion of GNP to it. We thus get a medium estimate of Rs. 54 per head of population by 1985-86 . . .

It should, however, be noted that these assumptions cover a wide range of *per capita* costs:

(1) If national income grew at 5 per cent per year, population at 2.5 per cent per year, and 4 per cent of national income were allocated to education, the expenditure on education in 1985-86 would be only Rs. 27.5 *per capita*.
(2) If national income grew at 7 per cent per year, population at 1.5 per cent per year and 6 per cent of the national income were allocated to education, the expenditure on education in 1985-86 would be as high as Rs. 75.1 *per capita*.

The figure of 6 per cent of GNP invested in education by 1986 may seem to be an ambitious target. We do not quite hold this view. It is only in recent years that nations, realising the deep and symbiotic link between education and national prosperity, have been increasing rapidly their investments in education and this trend is likely to continue. At the beginning of this century even 'advanced' countries such as the USA spent no more than a small fraction of their GNP on education. By 1986, it is likely that a figure of 10 per cent of GNP invested in education will become commonplace in most countries. If total and comprehensive disarmament is achieved by then, as we all hope it will be, the figure for the developing countries may even exceed 10 per cent; and it is only through some such action that the dismal and dangerous gap between the poor and rich countries can be reduced to tolerable dimensions.

19.24 It has been suggested that in early stages of educational development the rate of growth of educational expenditure ought to be approximately twice the rate of growth of national income. In our exercise, however, we have postulated a relatively more modest annual rate of growth of 10 per cent for educational expenditure relative to the assumed rate of growth of 6 per cent in national income. It should thus be possible to implement the schemes of educational expenditure at postulated levels even in the face of shortfalls in the rate of growth of national income. It may be added that the basis of such projections is the expected pattern of individual and collective consumption behaviour as incomes increase, combined with the educational effort needed for sustaining higher levels of economic activity.

19.25 What will be the pattern of allocation of resources to different sectors of education in future? In our view, this pattern will change from decade to decade.

(1) In the first decade, an emphasis on a larger allocation to the school stage is needed. In the first place, it is necessary to upgrade the salaries of school teachers. The allocation needed for this purpose will be very large, partly because of the large numbers involved and partly because of the size of the increment which has to be given without delay. Secondly, we are proposing to transfer the PUC and the Intermediate classes from the university to the school stage. Thirdly, there is an urgent need to provide at least five years of effective education to all children in the country. Fourthly, it is equally necessary to vocationalise secondary education.

(2) In the second decade, seven years of effective primary education will have to be provided. Secondly, emphasis will have to be placed on adding one year to the school stage and vocationalising secondary education. But the additional allocation required for the purpose is not relatively so large as in the first decade and the emphasis will shift a little in favour of higher education.

(3) In the third decade, the programmes at the secondary stage will be nearing completion and the emphasis will shift very largely to the development of higher education and research. As time passes, this trend is likely to continue. . . .

19.26 A tentative estimate of the expenditure required for school and higher education in 1975-76 and 1985-86 has been attempted and will be found in the Supplemental Notes II and III given at the end of this chapter. It will be seen therefrom that about 72 per cent of the total expenditure in 1975-76 will be allocated to school education and that higher education will get about 27 per cent instead of about 33 per cent as at present. We would like to point out, however, that this reduction in the proportion of educational expenditure devoted to higher education is more apparent than real. A large part of the expenditure on higher secondary (PUC) stage which has been shown here under 'school' is at present classified as being under 'university'. If due allowance is made for this — this expenditure is of the order of 4 or 5 per cent of the total — will be seen that the school gets only about two-thirds of the total expenditure as in the past. In the second decade, the expenditure of school education is reduced to 65.9 per cent or about two-thirds of the total. Consequently, higher education will receive a larger allocation.

19.27 It has been argued before us that, in view of the urgency to develop higher education, it may be desirable to go slow with primary education for some time and to invest more of the available resources in secondary and higher education. Some have also argued the other view that we should develop primary education as rapidly as possible and at any cost. The Sargent Plan, for instance, allocated two-thirds of the total resources to primary education. These are extreme views. We realise the need for the development of higher education and for the allocation of more resources to it. But it would not be proper to cut down for this purpose the expenditure on primary education. As we have repeatedly stressed in the Report, the provision of universal primary education is vital on grounds of social justice and to help the process of transformation of the national economy. Again, development of higher education and research is central to the entire developmental programme; and without an adequate provision for higher education there will be no adequate supply of competent teachers for primary and secondary education. What we want is a balanced growth of education. There seems to be no alternative but to adopt the broad pattern of allocation of resources suggested above.

Expenditure Per Student

19.28 *Pattern of Cost Per Student in the First Three Plans*. We shall now turn to a consideration of the expenditure per pupil at each level of education. This depends upon three factors: the average annual salary of a teacher (a); the pupil-teacher ratio (t); and the expenditure on all non-teacher costs which can be expressed as a percentage of the average salary of a teacher (*r*). Symbolically, it can be stated as follows:

$$\text{Cost per pupil} = \frac{a\,(l + r)}{t}$$

where a = average annual salary of a teacher
r = ratio of non-teacher costs to teacher's salary
t = pupil-teacher ratio

All these factors have undergone changes in each sector during the last fifteen years with the result that the overall cost per student (direct expenditure only) has increased from Rs. 37 per student in 1950-51 to Rs. 64 per student in 1965-66 (at current prices) or by 73 per cent. But if allowance is made for the rise in the cost of living (which is about 65 per cent), the rise in real terms becomes almost negligible. The detailed statistics in this regard are given in Tables 5.11 and 5.12.

19.29 . . . With regard to the other factors, some important conclusions arise from these data:

(1) The cost per pupil/student does not show appreciable increase, except in professional colleges and vocational schools. Even here, if allowance is to be made for the rise in prices, there is actually a fall in expenditure in real terms.
(2) At the pre-primary stage, the cost per pupil has remained almost stationary. It implies that in real terms, the investment per student has gone down very greatly.
(3) At the lower primary stage the cost per student has gone up by 50 per cent. But, at constant prices, this also implies a fall in real terms. The non-teacher costs per pupil have actually fallen, even at constant prices. That is why our primary schools are so dull and drab. In fact in many primary schools, we give hardly anything except the teacher! The picture at the higher primary stage is similar.
(4) Expenditure per student in colleges of arts and science shows some increase in current prices, but a fall in real terms.

19.30 *The Pattern of Cost Per Student During the Next Twenty Years.* A tentative estimate of expenditure in the different sectors of school education during the next twenty years is discussed in Supplemental Note II at the end of the chapter. A similar but still more

TABLE 5.11: Average Annual Cost per Pupil, 1950-51

Type of institution	Average annual salary per teacher (Rs.)	Number of pupils per teacher	Percentage of non-teacher costs to teacher costs	Average annual cost per pupil (Rs.)		
				Due to teacher costs	Due to non-teacher costs	Total
Pre-Primary Schools	914	25	51.3	37	19	55
Lower Primary Schools	545	34	24.6	16	4	20
Higher Primary Schools	682	24	32.0	28	9	37
Secondary Schools	1,258	25	44.8	50	23	73
Schools for Vocational Education	1,705	16	86.8	106	92	197
Schools for Special Education	715	13	98.5	55	54	109
Universities (Teaching Departments)	3,759	10	N.A.	N.A.	N.A.	N.A.
Colleges of Arts & Science	2,696	20	73.7	133	98	231
Colleges of Professional Education	13,948	11	118.1	357	422	779
Colleges of Special Education	1,656	8	48.6	203	99	301
Total (Direct Expenditure)				25	12	37

N.B.: Totals do not tally on account of rounding of figures.
Source: Ministry of Education, Form A.

TABLE 5.12: Average Annual Cost Per Pupil, 1965-66

Type of institution	Average annual salary per teacher (Rs.)	Number of pupils per teacher	Percentage of non-teacher costs to teacher costs	Average annual cost per pupil (Rs.)		
				Due to teacher costs	Due to non-teacher costs	Total
Pre-Primary Schools	1,000	31	56.3	35	20	55
Lower Primary Schools	1,046	38	11.1	27	3	30
Higher Primary Schools	1,087	31	12.4	40	5	45
Secondary Schools	1,959	25	37.0	78	29	107
Schools for Vocational Education	2,887	15	100.0	208	208	417
Schools for Special Education	991	12	66.7	81	54	135
Universities (Teaching Departments)	6,500	12	N.A.	N.A.	N.A.	N.A.
Colleges of Arts & Science	4,000	20	63.8	200	128	328
Colleges of Professional Education	6,410	11	100.0	583	583	1,167
Colleges of Special Education	2,918	12	42.9	245	105	350
Total (Direct Expenditure)				46	18	64

N.B.: Totals do not tally on account of rounding of figures.
Source: Ministry of Education, Form A.

tentative estimate for higher education has been given in Supplemental Note III at the end of the chapter. We shall now briefly discuss their implications and limitations.

19.31 *School Education*. It is comparatively easy to estimate the expenditure on school education because (1) the teacher costs form a proportionately larger part of the total expenditure, (2) the non-teacher costs can be more accurately estimated, (3) there is no variety of courses to be provided at the primary stage, and (4) even at the secondary stage, the variety of courses to be provided in vocational education is comparatively limited and does not show wide variations of costs. These estimates, therefore, are more reliable and better guides to the formulation of educational policies.

19.32 Table 5.13 gives the total estimated expenditure on school education and Table 5.33 gives its implications in terms of teachers' salaries, pupil-teacher ratios, levels of non-teacher expenditure, and maintenance of quality institutions.

19.33 We would specially invite attention to the following implications of these estimates:

(1) *Total Expenditure on School Education*: The total expenditure on school education is expected to increase from Rs. 4,046 million (or 67.4 per cent of the total expenditure) in 1965-66 to Rs. 11,262 million (or 72.4 per cent of the total expenditure) in 1975-76, and Rs. 26,588 million (or 65.9 per cent of the total expenditure) in 1985-86.

(2) *Capital Expenditure on School Education*: The bulk of this expenditure will be recurring. The capital expenditure on school education will increase from Rs. 133 million (or 2.2 per cent of the total expenditure) in 1965-66 to Rs. 389 million (or 2.5 per cent of the total expenditure) in 1975-76, and to Rs. 1,009 million (or 2.5 per cent of the total expenditure) in 1985-86.

(3) *Pre-Primary Education*: The average annual salary of teachers is expected to rise from Rs. 1,000 in 1965-66 to Rs. 1,800 in 1975-76 and Rs. 2,500 in 1985-86. The pupil-teacher ratio is proposed to be raised from 31 in 1965-66 to 40. The average annual cost per student which was Rs. 55 in 1965-66, would be raised to Rs. 74 in 1975-76, and Rs. 103 in 1985-86. It will be noticed that the cost per student is higher at the pre-primary stage than at the primary stage because of the need to provide meals and other health services.

TABLE 5.13: Expenditure on School Education, 1975-76 and 1985-86

Object	Total expenditure (Rs. in 000's)		Percentage of total expenditure	
	1975-76	1985-86	1975-76	1985-86
1. *Recurring (Direct)*				
Pre-Primary	236,965	488,531	1.5	1.2
Lower-Primary	3,749,220	6,129,616	24.1	15.2
Higher Primary	2,451,567	5,140,287	15.8	12.7
Total	6,437,743	11,758,434	41.4	29.1
Lower Secondary:				
General	2,072,510	4,490,088	13.3	11.1
Vocational	359,800	2,582,550	2.3	6.4
Total	2,432,310	7,072,638	15.6	17.5
Higher Secondary:				
General	488,436	1,281,299	3.1	3.2
Vocational	823,900	2,362,250	5.3	5.8
Total	1,312,336	3,643,549	8.4	9.0
Total Recurring (Direct)	10,182,389	22,474,621	65.4	55.7
2. *Recurring (Indirect)*				
Direction and Inspection	389,050	1,614,560	2.5	4.0
Scholarships	301,680	1,490,240	1.9	3.7
Total Recurring (Indirect)	690,730	3,104,800	4.4	7.7
3. *Recurring (Direct and Indirect)*	10,873,119	25,579,421	69.9	63.4
4. *Capital*				
Buildings and Equipment	389,050	1,008,890	2.5	2.5
GRAND TOTAL (3+4)	11,262,169	26,588,311	72.4	65.9

N.B.: Totals do not tally due to rounding of figures.
For details, see Supplemental Note II at the end of the chapter.

(4) *Lower Primary Education*: The average annual cost per student was only Rs. 20 in 1950-51 and it rose to Rs. 30 in 1965-66 (at current prices). If allowance is to be made for increase in prices, there would be an actual fall. What is now proposed is to raise this cost substantially, at constant prices to Rs. 52 in 1975-76 and to Rs. 80 in 1985-86.

It should be remembered that, at this level of expenditure, all that is possible is to provide free books to all children and the necessary contingencies to primary schools. The provision has been made in these estimates for school meals, school uniforms or health services. The average annual salaries of teachers will rise from Rs. 1,046 in 1965-66 to Rs. 1,800 in 1975-76 and Rs. 2,500 in 1985-86. This, we regard, is the minimum essential. The pupil-teacher ratio is proposed to be raised from 38 in 1965-66 to 50 in 1975-76 by the adoption of the three-hour session system. This is inescapable if a living wage is to be given to the primary teachers. If smaller classes are considered desirable, either additional funds will have to be found or the rate of expansion will have to be deliberately slowed down.

It may be incidentally pointed out that the average class-size in compulsory primary education bears a definite proportion to the effective birth-rate (i.e., children per thousand of population entering the age-group 5-6 when admission to primary school begins). In other words, class-size (on the assumption that the salary of a primary school teacher is 3 to 4 times the per capita GNP) in compulsory education generally lies between 1.5 and 2.0 times the effective birth-rate. When the birth-rate in India falls down to somewhere between 15-20, it will be easily possible to reduce the class-size to somewhere between 30 and 35. But smaller class-sizes at the present level of birth-rate will be costly and beyond the economic capacity of the country.

It should also be emphasised that we have provided 10 per cent of the primary schools at optimum levels of quality, i.e., at about twice the cost per pupil than in the average school. It will be possible to maintain these schools at a level of efficiency of the next higher stage i.e. higher primary education and to provide them with trained graduates as headmasters and larger grants for non-teacher expenditure.

(5) *Higher Primary Education*. The general picture at this stage is

similar to that at the lower primary stage.

We expect the headmasters of these schools to be trained graduates (it has been assumed that there would be one trained graduate to three other teachers) and hence the average annual salary of a teacher is a little higher than that at the lower primary stage.

The pupil-teacher ratio is proposed to be raised from 31 to 35 and maintained at that level.

The cost per pupil will rise from Rs. 45 to Rs. 87 by 1975-76 and still further to Rs. 199 by 1985-86 (at 1965-66 prices).

As at the primary stage, provision has only been made for free supply of books and contingencies and there is no provision for school meals, uniforms or health services.

It has been assumed that 20 per cent of the total enrolment would be in part-time courses.

(6) *Lower Secondary Education*: The average annual salary of teachers which stood at Rs. 1,959 in 1965-66 is proposed to be increased to Rs. 3,150 by 1975-76 and Rs. 4,150 by 1985-86. The pupil-teacher ratio remains unchanged at 25. The cost per pupil which rose from Rs. 73 in 1950-51 to Rs. 107 in 1965-66 (at current prices) is expected to rise, at constant prices, to Rs. 203 in 1975-76 and to Rs. 268 in 1985-86.

(7) *Higher Secondary Education*: At this stage, the average annual salary of teachers will be Rs. 4,500 in 1975-76 and Rs. 5,500 in 1985-86. The pupil-teacher ratio has been assumed at 20. The cost per student is expected to rise to Rs. 363 in 1975-76 and to Rs. 444 in 1985-86.

(8) *Vocational Education*: Provision has been made for vocational courses both at the lower secondary and higher secondary stages as recommended in the relevant chapters of the Report. The cost per pupil has been assumed on an *ad hoc* basis. To be accurate, it will be necessary to cost each vocational course separately. But the necessary data for this were not available to us.

(9) *Quality Institutions*: As at the lower primary stage, provision has been made to maintain about 10 per cent of the institutions at each stage at optimum levels of efficiency. In other words, it is assumed that in 10 per cent of the institutions at

each stage, the cost per pupil will be about doubte that in the ordinary schools at that stage.

The levels of expenditure per pupil given above certainly mark a great improvement over the existing situation. But they are by no means, what can be wished for. It is, however, evident that these are probably the highest levels of expenditure which we might be able to afford.

19.34 *Higher Education*: We must confess that in the case of higher education it is even more difficult to prepare reliable estimates and forecasts of costs. All the same we have made a tentative exercise in costing the programme of higher education for 1975-76 and 1985-86 at the constant prices of 1965-66. The details, as stated earlier, will be found in Supplemental Note III at the end of this chapter. Its main conclusions are shown in Tables 5.38 and 5.14.

19.35 The following comments about Table 5.14 are in order. We have assumed that –

(1) at the undergraduate stage, the cost per student will be Rs. 733 for about 40 per cent of the enrolment (in arts and commerce courses) and Rs. 1,500 for 60 per cent of the enrolment (in quality institutions in courses in arts and commerce and in science and vocational courses) in 1975-76. For 1985-86 the corresponding figures would be Rs. 917 and Rs. 2,000 respectively. Even these costs will be possible in fulltime education only if at least 30 per cent of the total enrolment is in courses of part-time and correspondence education.

(2) at the postgraduate stage, the cost per student will be Rs. 3,000 for about 40 per cent of the enrolment (in arts and commerce courses) and Rs. 5,000 for the remaining 60 per cent of the enrolment (in quality institutions in arts and commerce and in science and vocational courses) in 1975-76. The corresponding figures for 1985-86 would be Rs. 3,600 and Rs. 6,000 respectively. As at the undergraduate stage, these expenditures would be possible in full-time postgraduate education if at least 30 per cent of the enrolment is provided for in part-time and correspondence courses.

(3) The funds available for capital expenditure are far from adequate, especially in the next few years. Ordinarily, about 20 to 25 per cent of the total expenditure on higher education

TABLE 5.14: Average Annual Cost Per Pupil in Higher Education, 1950-51 to 1985-86

Type of institution	Average annual salary per teacher (Rs.)	Number of pupils per teacher	Percentage of non-teacher costs to teacher costs	Average annual cost per pupil (Rs.)		
				Due to teacher costs	Due to non-teacher costs	Total
Undergraduate						
(a) Arts and Commerce						
1950-51*	2,696	20	73.7	133	98	231
1965-66*	4,000	20	63.8	200	128	328
1975-76	6,000	15	66.7	440	293	733
1985-86	7,500	15	66.7	550	367	917
(b) Science and Vocational						
1950-51**	3,948	11	118.1	357	422	779
1965-66**	6,410	11	100.0	584	583	1,167
1975-76	—	—	—	—	—	1,500
1985-86	—	—	—	—	—	2,000
Postgraduate						
(a) Arts and Commerce						
1975-76	10,000	8	118	1,375	1,625	3,000
1985-86	12,000	8	118	1,650	1,950	3,600
(b) Science and Vocational						
1975-76	—	—	—	—	—	5,000
1985-86	—	—	—	—	—	6,000

* All types of Colleges for Arts & Science (Intermediate to Postgraduate).

** All types of Vocational/Professional Colleges.

N.B.: For details, see Supplemental Note III at the end of the Chapter. Some actual costs per student in a few universities and colleges are given in Supplemental Note IV at the end of the chapter.

should be available for buildings and major equipment. Instead of this, only 15.8 per cent of the total expenditure on higher education will be available for capital programmes in 1975-76. Fortunately, the position improves by about 1985-86 when the proportion of capital expenditure rises to about 25 per cent.

19.36 From the data we have been able to collect regarding cost per student in institutions of higher education which are known to maintain good standards, it appears that this order of expenditure per student will be far from adequate. At the undergraduate stage, we broadly require an expenditure of the order of Rs. 1,000 per student; and if 10 per cent of the institutions are to be maintained at optimum levels of quality, i.e., at abou\u0131 ten times the cost per pupil, the average cost per student at the undergraduate stage will have to be about Rs. 2,000. The capital cost at this stage will be about Rs. 5,000 per student. At the postgraduate stage, a capital expenditure of the order of about Rs. 25,000 to Rs. 30,000 per student is needed and the recurring cost will have to be as high as Rs. 6,000 to Rs. 7,000 per student. As at the undergraduate stage, this expenditure also would be doubled if 10 per cent of the institutions are to be maintained at optimum levels of quality i.e., at about ten times the cost per student. It is thus obvious that if an earnest attempt is to be made to maintain adequate levels of quality in higher education and to raise at least a few institutions to international standards, we will have to find large additional resources. If that is not possible, we shall have to come to grips with difficult problems of the following type:

(1) Would it be possible to reduce the total enrolment in higher education? This will involve the consideration of a number of problems such as relating the output of educational institutions to forecasts of manpower needs; improving organisation and administration in the public and private sectors to ensure that every educated person is fully and properly utilised; reducing unemployment among the educated; increasing the participation rates among the educated persons; revising the present policies which are based on 'over education', e.g., educating an engineer and using him for jobs which can really be done by technicians; etc.

(2) Would it be possible to reduce the number of places to be

provided in full-time education so that a larger expenditure per place could be incurred? This will involve a serious attempt to expand part-time and correspondence education and to provide these facilities to about 50 per cent of the total enrolment as is done at present, for instance, in the USSR.

(3) Would it be possible to economise the expenditure in terms of physical and financial investment without affecting standards? This will involve problems of intensive utilisation of existing facilities; cooperative use of costly equipment by a number of institutions: manufacture of equipment in the country itself; etc.

These and other problems of this type are as important as they are difficult. At the moment we run away from them by diluting standards and maintaining the expenditure per student at low levels — a device which provides an easy escape valve. In any attempt to raise standards and the expenditure per pupil, these problems will have to be squarely faced and resolutely tackled.

19.37 *Adult Education*. . . . For these programmes we propose an increasing provision which will rise to about Rs. 78 million a year (or 0.5 per cent of the total expenditure) in 1975-76 and Rs. 404 million a year (or 1.0 per cent of the total expenditure in 1985-86.

19.38 *Total Expenditure* Table 5.15 gives the total estimated expenditure recurring as well as capital — on all stages and sectors of education for 1975-76 and 1985-86.

Some General Observations

19.39 Whatever the assumptions one might make regarding the growth of national income or the proportion of GNP to be allocated to education, it is evident that, in the foreseeable future, it will not be possible to provide monetary resources for education which can compare with what is being done in the industrialised countries. We have assumed that the total educational expenditure would rise, at constant prices, from about Rs. 12 per capita in 1965-66 to about Rs. 54 per capita in 1985-86. But even this can bear no comparison to the level of educational expenditure already reached in same industrialised countries. For instance, this expenditure is about Rs. 244 (11,700 yen) in Japan, Rs. 295 (193.63 francs) in France; Rs. 378 (45.35 roubles) in the USSR; Rs. 515 (24.55 pound) in the UK and

Rs. 1,175 (156.73 dollars) in the USA.* The gulf between these levels of educational expenditure and ours is and will continue to be so wide that we cannot hope to solve our problems by the mere adoption of the techniques of the industrialised countries.

TABLE 5.15: Educational Expenditure by Objects, 1975-76 and 1985-86

Object	Total expenditure (Rs. in 000's)		Percentage of total expenditure	
	1975-76	1985-86	1975-76	1985-86
Recurring				
Pre-Primary	236,956	488,531	1.5	1.2
Lower Primary	3,749,220	6,129,616	24.1	15.2
Higher Primary	2,451,567	5,140,287	15.8	12.7
Lower Secondary	2,432,310	7,072,638	15.6	17.5
Higher Secondary	1,312,336	3,643,549	8.4	9.0
Direction and Inspection	389,050	1,614,560	2.5	4.0
Scholarships	301,680	1,490,240	1.9	3.7
Total (School)	10,873,119	25,579,421	69.9	63.4
Undergraduate	1,892,766	4,238,963	12.2	10.5
Postgraduate	1,124,200	4,043,400	7.2	10.0
Scholarships	628,200	2,416,200	4.0	6.0
Total (Higher Education)	3,645,166	10,698,563	23.4	26.5
Adult Education	77,810	403,640	0.5	1.0
Total (Recurring)	14,596,095	36,681,624	93.8	90.9
Capital				
School Education	389,050	1,008,890	2.5	2.5
Higher Education	576,855	2,673,486	3.7	6.6
Total (Capital)	965,905	3,682,376	6.2	9.1
GRAND TOTAL	15,562,000	40,364,000	100.0	100.0

Note: Totals do not tally due to rounding of figures.

* All figures are for 1962. The conversion into rupees has been done at the post-devaluation rates of exchange.

19.40 In a situation of this type, we can hope to obtain optimum results only if we adopt action on two lines. The first is that we should strive to allocate the largest proportion of GNP possible to educational development. Since additional resources are generated largely through the process of economic growth, the fact that education tends to augment the flow of national product, though with some time-lag, is of crucial importance. It follows, therefore, that in the long run education to some extent is self-financing because the increased incomes generated by a relatively better educated labour force would provide resources for greater allocations to education.

19.41 The second is the need to realise the simple but elementary point that it is impossible to create an educational system which would meet the individual and national needs if conventional techniques, existing practices of under-utilisation and wastage were to continue. It would, therefore, be necessary to make every rupee go the longest way possible by adopting measures for economy, for reduction of wastage, and for intensive utilisation. These should receive the greatest emphasis and the most earnest consideration. The manner in which this can be done has been indicated in the appropriate context in earlier chapters. Even at the risk of some repetition, however, we would enunciate a few of the points which are significant from the financial point of view:

(1) The utmost economy possible should be practised in the construction of building.
(2) The cost of equipment could be reduced considerably by better designing, large-scale production, improvisation and careful handling to increase its life.
(3) Techniques in which certain facilities could be shared in common by a group of schools (i.e. a circulating library for rural primary schools) should be encouraged and adopted on a large-scale.
(4) Where equipment and facilities become costly and sophisticated, they should be intensively and cooperatively utilised for the largest part of the day and throughout the year.
(5) Whenever possible, educational buildings should be put to use for as long as possible in the day and wherever needed, at night as well.
(6) Larger classes and higher pupil-teacher ratios are inevitable for some years to come, and it would only be a disservice to

education to adopt the practices of affluent societies in this regard. In a developing economy, we must accept these as facts of life and meet their challenge through the development of appropriate techniques and hard work.

(7) There is no justification for the continuance of the large wastages which now prevail at every stage. Their reduction should be a definite national target and to that end, programmes for the active involvement of each individual institution in the process should be encouraged. This is the only way to meet the situation.

(8) The working day should be longer and the number of working days should be increased. The vacations should be utilised as fully as possible and designated as vacation 'terms'.

(9) Programmes of part-time and own-time education should be organised on as large a scale as possible to meet the increasing demand for education from workers as well as from those who cannot be provided with a place in full-time institutions.

(10) The education of the gifted children should be attended to on a top priority basis.

(11) With a view to raising quality all round and in all institutions in the shortest time possible, it is essential to concentrate resources, in the immediate future, on the development of some centres of excellence and quality institutions at all stages of education, particularly in secondary and higher education. This programme should be given a very high priority.

(12) Places in full-time institutions of secondary and higher education should be provided with due regard to manpower needs and maintenance of standards; and admissions to them should be made on the basis of an egalitarian selection.

(13) Sectors of education which have a multiplying effect like postgraduate studies or teacher education or those which have a direct relationship with an increase in productivity such as agricultural and technical education, or those which tend to decrease wastage or intensify utilisation.

(14) Wasteful expenditure which often arises from rigidities of administrative and financial procedures should be avoided by introducing flexibility and adequate decentralisation of authority.

(15) Greater emphasis should be placed on programmes which need more of human talent, dedication and hardwork (such as

preparation of textbooks, teaching and learning aids, research, etc.) than on those which involve large investment of physical and financial resources.

(16) A vigorous attempt should be made to establish institutions of optimum size at all levels of education because these would be more efficient and less costly.

19.42 Since an underdeveloped economy cannot aspire to match the levels of per capita educational expenditure of the developed ones, the problems of educational reconstruction in India can be tackled only on the basis of an approach which meets our special situation. A mere imitation of some of the techniques and programmes of education in developed societies will not meet our requirements. The complexity of our problems, and the necessity of connecting education with life, particularly productivity, have to be identified and solutions worked out which take care of the specific needs of the country. It is our firm view that while a careful study of major educational developments in other countries is essential to enable us to draw upon their experiences, there is no substitute for original, hard and serious thinking involved in a sustained and serious effort to make our meagre resources go the longest way possible.

19.43 This implies emphasis on research in all sectors of education. . . . Here, we would only highlight the need to conduct research in the problems of economics and financing of education which are only just receiving the attention of economists and educationists in our country. Among other things, there is urgent need to examine continually the relationship between cost and quality and to develop programmes which would obtain the highest possible quality for a given level of input (or minimise inputs for a given level of quality). We recommend that the UGC should provide financial support for the development of such studies in a few selected universities and that a similar programme for the school stage should be developed in the NCERT and the State Institutes of Education.

19.44 The estimates of total educational expenditure given above are admittedly tentative. As we have emphasised extensive research is needed on the study of unit costs and educational productivity. In the light of these studies, these estimates will have to be continually revised. Moreover, it is likely that they will be attacked on both sides. On the one hand, some persons would argue that they are on the low side and that they will have to be upgraded substantially if education of the appropriate quality and in adequate quantity is to be provided. On the other hand, they will also be attacked on the ground that they are over-ambitious and unrealistic. What is important, however, is that a national system of education on the lines indicated in the Report is organised without delay and an earnest effort is made to provide all the needed resources for the purpose. In doing so, of course, many hard choices will have to be faced and risks taken. But in an age of science, there can be no greater risk than a policy of drift and niggardliness in education.

SUPPLEMENTAL NOTE I

Grant-in-Aid from State Governments to Local Authorities — Urban and Rural: Central-State Relationship in Financial Support to Education

1\. . . . the administration of school education in a district should be transferred to District School Boards and that in areas of bigger municipalities to Municipal School Boards. We have further suggested that even smaller municipalities should be associated with the administration of education within their areas and be made to bear a certain portion of the expenditure thereon. In this note, we shall make a few suggestions regarding the manner in which grant-in-aid to these authorities, for educational purposes, shall be used to stimulate local contributions and thereby get larger revenues for education. Incidentally, we shall also discuss briefly the Centre-State relationship in the financing of education.

2\. *Grants-in-Aid to District School Boards*. The zila parishads have an authority to levy a cess on land revenue for purposes of education. In this context, we recommend that the State should prescribe the minimum cess to be levied by a zila parishad and also authorise it to raise the same voluntarily up to a prescribed maximum. In order to stimulate the use of this authority, a grant-in-aid proportionate to the additional revenues thus raised should be guaranteed. A device of this type has been adopted in Maharashtra State and it is found that most of the zila parishads have raised the cess substantially. It is possible that a similar result may be obtained elsewhere also.

3\. The existing system of grant-in-aid to local authorities needs revision. An analysis of the existing practices on the subject shows considerable variation. In some States, the grants are given on a deficit basis, and it is the general experience that, under this system, the politically important and vocal districts, rather than the needy or backward areas, get the most benefit and there is no incentive to economise. When 'proportional' grants are given as a percentage of the total expenditure, the richer districts tend to get larger grants; and innumerable problems arise regarding the 'approved' or 'admissible' expenditure. The 'block' grants tend to be inelastic and particularly unsuitable in a situation when expenditure in education is rising fast. On an overall view of the existing practices, therefore, we suggest that a reform of the grant-in-aid procedures in respect of zila parishads be carried out on the broad outlines indicated below:

(1) The grant-in-aid for the salaries and allowances of teachers and other administrative and supervisory staff sanctioned by Government should be on a 100 per cent basis; some definite rules should be prescribed regarding the basis on which the number of teachers required should be calculated (e.g., on the basis of enrolment). The administrative and supervisory staff could be related to the number of teachers.

(2) For the non-teacher costs, a block grant per child in attendance should be given. The amount of this grant should be fixed separately for each category of schools and should be revised every three to five years.

(3) The resources raised locally by the zila parishad, as well as the State grant thereon, should be left with the zila parishad for such developmental programmes as it deems necessary.

(4) Grants-in-aid for non-recurring expenditure should be given separately, preferably at about two-thirds of the expenditure.

The major objective of the system of grant-in-aid to zila parishads should be to equalise educational opportunities. This should be kept in view while sanctioning the posts of teachers or deciding the recurring grant-in-aid per pupil or the proportion of the non-recurring grant to be given. Moreover, the amounts of grant-in-aid should be allowed to be funded and not made to lapse at the end of the financial year, as this encourages economy and a careful use of resources.

4. *Grant-in-Aid to Municipalities*. From the quantitative point of view, the municipal funds are even more important than the contributions of the zila parishads because they are growing rapidly on account of industrialisation, urbanisation, and the increasing con-

centration of wealth in urban areas. In the erstwhile British Indian Provinces, the municipalities were made to pay for the support of primary education as early as in 1882. A tradition has thus grown up and we now find municipalities like Bombay spending a few million a year on primary education. On the other hand, in the erstwhile Princely States, the municipalities were not entrusted with primary education nor paid for it. Thus, even the big municipalities like Hyderabad, Bangalore or Gwalior make no contribution in support of primary education. There is no reason why the richer urban areas should be exempted from responsibility for education. We recommend that all municipalities should be compelled to pay for a portion of the cost of education in their areas by the levy of a cess on land and buildings. Even a minimum cess of two per cent of the annual letting value of real property in urban areas can secure a fair and increasing contribution to the support of education.

5. In devising a system of grants to municipalities for school education, it is essential to remember that the municipalities show an immense variation in their wealth and capacity to support education. For instance, a small municipality in a semi-rural township of 5 to 15 thousand population has a very limited capacity to raise funds in support of education compared with a big corporation like that of Bombay. It is, therefore, necessary to devise a system of grant-in-aid which will vary from one group of municipalities to another; and in our opinion, the best procedure would be to adopt a method under which the municipalities could be classified on the basis of their wealth and the poorer municipalities given a higher rate of grant-in-aid than the richer ones. This principle was enunciated, as early as in 1937, by the Kale Committee of the then Bombay State, and a good deal of experience in its implementation has been gained in the States of Gujarat and Maharashtra. This could be of considerable use to other areas adopting the programmes.*

6. The cases of the larger corporations like Bombay, Madras, Calcutta or Delhi, which form the wealthiest group among the municipalities, would have to be considered separately. At present, the position shows great variation. For the Bombay Corporation, the State Government gives a block grant which now stands of Rs. 6.8 million in a total educational expenditure of Rs. 54 million. In Cal-

* A similar recommendation was made by the Committee of Ministers constituted by the Central Council of Self-Government, 1963.

cutta, the corporation spends about Rs. 3.8 million and gets no grant-in-aid. In Madras, an identical grant-in-aid formula applies to all municipalities, from the smallest to the biggest. At present, the Government grant to the Madras Corporation is equal to Rs. 4.1 million in a total expenditure of Rs. 13.4 million. Several big corporations like Hyderabad have no financial responsibility at all in education. It would be desirable to make all corporations responsible at least for primary education and give them grant-in-aid on a proportional basis, i.e., at a certain percentage to be fixed for a corporation depending upon its resources. The same principle would apply to other large municipalities which have a School Board, the only difference being that the grant-in-aid would be generally at a higher percentage than that in regard to corporations.

7. The smaller municipalities will be able to contribute even less. By and large, they should be made responsible for all non-teacher costs (the teacher costs being borne fully by the State Governments) and should be required to meet them by the levy of a local cess on lands and buildings in their areas and a suitable grant-in-aid towards it given by the State Government, on an equalisation basis.

8. *Equalisation*. We have recommended grants-in-aid from the State Government to the zila parishads and the municipalities on the basis of equalisation. It is necessary to explain this new concept of grant-in-aid which has been in successful operation in the USA for a number of years. The central concept of equalisation is that, for a given local effort, the local authority must be able to reach a given level of expenditure per child. For instance, in the case of two municipalities — A and B — let us assume that

— the level of equalisation in primary education has been fixed at a recurring expenditure of Rs. 50 per child per year;

— it has also been decided that each municipality should contribute to the expenditure on primary education, at the rate of two per cent of the annual letting value of the real property within its area; and

— this rate produces an income of Rs. 10 per child in municipality A and B and Rs. 20 per child in municipality B. Under these circumstances, the grant-in-aid of the State Government to municipality A would be Rs. 40 per child and to municipality B, Rs. 30 per child.

9. *The Role of the Central Government in the Financing of Education*. It has been stated above that the contribution of 'Government funds' to total educational expenditure may have to be increased from the present level of 71 per cent to about 90 per cent.* This is the contribution for the Central and State Governments taken together. For a clarification of the position, however, it is necessary to discuss the contribution of the Central Government separately. The State Governments have the residual responsibility to finance education i.e. they must find all the funds required for education after allowance is made for contributions by the Central Government, the local authorities and other sources.

10. The Government of India gave special grants to the Provinces for educational purposes from 1870 (when authority over education was first decentralised to them) to about 1921. These were particularly large between 1902 and 1914 which was a period of comparative boom in the Central revenues. They were, however, discontinued in 1921 when education was transferred to Indian control in the Provinces. One of the outstanding events of the post-independence period is the resumption of assistance by Central Government for education and these have continuously increased during the first three plans. In addition, the Central Government has been incurring considerable direct expenditure on education. These two forms of Central financial support to education will have to be considered separately.

11. *Direct Central Expenditure on Education*. Table 5.16 shows the growth of direct central expenditure on education from 1950-51 to 1960-61, the latest period for which statistics of expenditure are available.

It will be seen that the total educational expenditure from the funds of the Central Government has increased from Rs. 35 million in 1950-51 to Rs. 296 million in 1960-61 which implies an average annual increase of 23.7 per cent which is considerably greater than that in the total educational expenditure which increased at an average annual rate of 11.7 per cent only. It will be seen further that the bulk of the Central expenditure on education is incurred on higher education and on buildings and scholarships which are also mostly meant for higher education only. This is in keeping with the constitutional

* We except that the balance of 10 per cent would be made by fees (3%), contribution of local authorities (4%) voluntary contributions and donations from the people (3%).

responsibility of the Government of India to coordinate and maintain standards in higher education.

TABLE 5.16: Educational Expenditure through Central Government Funds by Objects, 1950-51 to 1960-61

Type of Institution/Object	Expenditure on Education through Central Government Funds			
	Amount (Rs. in 000's)		Percentage of expenditure on the object to total expenditure Central Govt. Funds	
	1950-51	1960-61	1950-51	1960-61
Direct Expenditure				
Pre-Primary Schools	—	187	—	0.1
Lower Primary Schools	468	17,943	1.3	6.1
Higher Primary Schools	308	11,914	0.9	4.0
Secondary Schools	2,229	6,412	6.3	2.2
Schools for Teacher Training	—	1,778	—	0.6
Schools for Vocational Education (excluding Teacher Training)	1,720	9,241	4.9	3.1
Schools for Special Education	104	1,087	0.3	0.4
Universities and Institutions for Higher Education	11,591	58,962	32.9	19.9
Colleges for Teacher Training	136	1,100	0.4	0.4
Colleges for Professional Education (excluding Teacher Training)	7,928	30,255	22.5	10.2
Colleges for Special Education	127	1,378	0.4	0.5
Total (Direct Expenditure)	24,611	140,259	69.8	47.4
Indirect Expenditure				
Direction and Inspection	—	673	—	0.2
Buildings	8,278	111,447	23.5	37.7
Scholarships and other financial concessions	1,769	32,478	5.0	11.0
Hostel charges	158	1,106	0.4	0.4
Miscellaneous	431	9,815	1.2	3.3
Total (Indirect Expenditure)	10,636	155,519	30.2	52.6
GRAND TOTAL	35,247	295,778	100.0	100.0

N.B.: Totals do not tally due to rounding.
Source: Form A of the Ministry of Education, Government of India.

12. In the third plan, Central expenditure on education increased still further at about 18 per cent per year as shown in Table 5.17. Its detailed distribution over different sectors is not available.

TABLE 5.17: Budgeted Central Expenditure on Education in the Third Plan, 1961-62 to 1965-66

(*Rs. in 000's*)

Year	Budgeted Expenditure of the Government of India (excluding grants to States)
1961-62	333,428
1962-63	459,636
1963-64	428,794
1964-65	617,938
1965-66	756,194

13. In the days ahead, the Centre will have to assume a still larger financial responsibility for education through the expansion of the Central sectors. Our proposals on this subject have been detailed in the appropriate context in the earlier chapters of this Report. By way of reference, we give below some of the programmes which we have recommended for inclusion in the Central sector:

(1) Expansion of the programme of national scholarships;
(2) Expansion of the programmes of scholarships for the backward classes;
(3) Larger allocations to the UGC for

- development of Centres of Advanced Study and major universities;
- developing Schools of Education in a few selected universities;
- developing postgraduate education and research;
- provision of maintenance grants to State universities;
- establishment of the Central Testing Organisation; and
- development of literature in modern Indian languages.

(4) Development of agricultural, engineering and medical education.
(5) Promotion of educational research.

14. *Central Grants to States for Education*: The Central grants to States under the awards of the Finance Commission are not discussed here because they are not earmarked for education. It is only the developmental grants given under the five-year plans that are so earmarked and the data about these are given in Table 5.18.

TABLE 5.18: Expenditure on Education (Revenue Account) from Central and State Government Funds, 1951-52 to 1965-66

(*Rs. in millions*)

Year	Revenue expenditure on education			Combined revenue expenditure of the Centre, States & Union Territories	Grant-in-aid from Centre to States (col. 4 minus col. 5)
	Centre	States & Union Territories	Total (Centre & States) including grants		
1	2	3	4	5	6
1951-52	40.8	602.8	643.6	641.3	2.3
1952-53	33.2	688.0	721.2	714.4	6.8
1953-54	43.0	757.5	800.5	785.8	14.7
1954-55*	24.3	859.6	883.9	899.7	-15.8
1955-56	142.3	1,037.9	1,180.2	1,104.3	75.9
1956-57	194.4	1,142.4	1,336.8	1,134.2	202.6
1957-58	209.8	1,304.4	1,514.2	1,477.6	36.6
1958-59	278.9	1,472.4	1,751.3	1,634.7	116.6
1959-60	366.9	1,709.0	2,075.9	1,897.0	178.9
1960-61	437.9	1,954.1	2,392.0	2,152.2	239.8
1961-62	513.3	2,344.8	2,858.1	2,604.0	254.1
1962-63	500.2	2,505.9	2,006.1	2,788.3	217.8
1963-64	570.8	2,833.3	3,404.1	3,138.1	266.0
1964-65 (Revised Estimates)	741.0	3,293.6	4,034.6	3,693.3	341.3
1965-66 (Budget Estimates)	880.4	3,759.8	4,640.2	4,268.2	372.0

Source: *Indian Economic Statistics*, Part II, *Public Finance*, Ministry of Finance, New Delhi.

Note: 1. The figures relate to expenditure on education through the Ministry of Education only and exclude the expenditure on education incurred by other Ministries and Departments.

2. *The figures for 1954-55 seem to be wrong. As the details are not available, these could not reconciled.

15. *The Centrally Sponsored Sector.* These grants can be subdivided into two sub-categories: (1) grants-in-aid for schemes in-

cluded in the State plans; and (2) grants-in-aid under the Centrally-sponsored sector. We do not propose to discuss the first category which forms a part of the Central assistance to the State plans as a whole and whose quantum and character vary from plan to plan. We are particularly concerned with the second category, namely, grants-in-aid under the Centrally-sponsored sector. It will be recalled that we have recommended large expansion in the Centrally-sponsored sector and that the following are some of the schemes to which we have recommended aid under this sector:

(1) Training of teachers;
(2) Introduction of vocational education at the secondary stage;
(3) Development of the State Institutes of Education;
(4) Production of literature for children and teachers; and
(5) Development of quality institutions at the school stage.

Other programmes of a similar type which can be assisted have been indicated in the appropriate context in the different parts of the Report.

16. Some problems relating to the administration of the Centrally-sponsored sector need attention. In this context, we make the following recommendations:

(1) In selecting programmes to be included in Centrally-sponsored sector the State Governments should be consulted.
(2) One criterion for including programmes in the Central sector is that they should be of crucial importance and national in character. Programmes which need the adoption of a common policy in all parts of the country should preferably be included in the Centrally-sponsored sector.
(3) The local needs of the States vary considerably. It would, therefore, be desirable to include, in the Centrally-sponsored sector, some programmes which may vary from State to State. One method of doing so would be to divide the total funds available in the Centrally-sponsored sector into two parts, about half of them being allocated to national programmes which are referred to above. The other half should be made available to the State Governments, on some equitable basis, and they should be free with the approval of the Government of India, to use them for any scheme which is significant and

urgent in their local situation.

(4) The assistance to Centrally-sponsored schemes generally continues for the plan period. Very often it is nor possible to start new Centrally-sponsored schemes in the beginning of the Plan; and if they are started late, the State Governments are unwilling tq accept them because they would not get full financial assistance. It would, therefore, be desirable to make Central assistance for Centrally-sponsored schemes available to the States, on a five-year basis rather than on the basis of a plan period. For some important schemes in the Centrally-sponsored sector, assistance may even be continued for a longer period, say 10 years.

SUPPLEMENTAL NOTE II

Tentative Estimates of Expenditure on the Development of School Education, 1966-85

1. The object of this note is to give a tentative estimate of expenditure on school education — recurring and capital. The estimate is attempted for two years only — 1975-76 and 1985-86.

Pre-Primary Education

2. The proposals for the development of pre-primary education have been detailed. . . .

3. The estimated enrolments at this level would be the following:

(a) In 1965-66, the enrolment in pre-primary education proper was 250,000. We expect this to rise to 0.5 million in 1975-76 and to 2.4 million in 1985-86.

(b) The enrolment in the second category (i.e. Class I of those States where the school course is of 11 years up to the matriculation and in Infant A and B of Assam and Nagaland) was 11.5 million in 1965-66. But this contains, not only children in the age 5-6, but also some children below five and a large proportion of those who are above six. The attempt to be made in future is to introduce the system of pre-registration, i.e., this class will admit children only of 5. At the same time, all older children will be promoted to regular Class

I of the primary school. As this process goes on, more and more children in the age-group 5-6 will come in (the target to be reached by 1985-86 being 50 per cent of the age-group 5-6) and older children will go up to Class I. As the two processes will be simultaneous, we have assumed that the enrolments at this level will be constant at 10 million each in 1975-76 and 1985-86. The break-down of this enrolment will be as given in Table 5.19.

TABLE 5.19: Break-down of Enrolment in Primary Education, 1975-76 and 1985-86

(000's)

	1965-66	1975-76	1985-86
Pre-Primary Proper: Age-group 3-5	250	513	2,352
Pre-Primary (Other types): Age group 5-6	11,523 (contains a large part of overage children)	9,487 (contains overage children)	7,648 (About 50 per cent of the age-group 5-6)
Total	11,773	10,000	10,000

4. The cost of pre-primary education proper is estimated as in Table 5.20.

TABLE 5.20: Cost of Pre-Primary Education, 1975-76 and 1985-86

(Amount in Rs.)

	1975-76	1985-86
1. Average annual salary of a teacher	1,800	2,500
2. Add 10 per cent for retirement benefits	180	250
Total (Teacher Costs)	1,980	2,750
3. Non-teacher costs at one-half of the above	990	1,375
Total Cost	2,970	4,125
4. Pupil-teacher ratio	40	40
5. Cost per pupil	74.3	103.1

5. For other types of pre-primary education, cost has been assumed at Rs. 20 per pupil for 1975-76 and Rs. 30 per pupil for 1985-86.

6. The total recurring cost of the programme would thus be as given in Table 5.21.

TABLE 5.21: Total Recurring Cost of Pre-Primary Education Programme, 1975-76 and 1985-86

(*Rs. in 000's*)

	1975-76	1985-86
1. State level Centres @Rs. 100,000 per centre	1,600	1,600
2. District level Centres @ Rs. 50,000 per centre (150 in 1975-76 and 300 in 1985-86)	7,500	15,000
3. Pre-primary education of the standard type	38,116	242,491
4. Pre-primary education — other types	189,740	229,440
Total	236,956	488,531

Lower Primary Education

7. At this level, we have recommended a pay scale of Rs. 150-250 with a selection grade rising to Rs. 300. The average of this scale by 1975-76 will be Rs. 1,800 (as against Rs. 1,046 in 1965-66) and Rs. 2,500 for 1985-86.

8. The non-teacher expenditure per student (which is only Rs. 3 at present) will have to be increased to Rs. 12 by 1985-86 as given in Table 5.22.

TABLE 5.22: Estimated Non-Teacher Expenditure Per Student, 1985-86

	Rs.
1. Free supply of books and writing materials	5
2. Equipment (at Rs. 30 per student with an average estimated life of 10 years)	3
3. Contingent expenditure	4
Total	12

We have assumed that it would be possible to raise the cost to about Rs. 8 per child by 1975-76 and to about Rs. 12 per child by

1985-86.

9. We have suggested a pupil-teacher ratio of 40 with an upper limit of 50 for each class. During the next ten years, however, larger classes would be inevitable. We, therefore, suggest the adoption of the three-hour session system in Classes I and II. As more resources become available, it may be gradually discontinued. This will enable us to have a pupil-teacher ratio of 50 by 1975-76 which will be reduced to 45 by 1985-86.

10. We have also recommended that 11 per cent of the schools should be upgraded to the optimum standard, (i.e., to about double the cost per pupil).

11. The objective at this stage is to provide universal full-time education to all children.

12. On these assumptions the cost per student at the lower primary stage would be as given in Table 5.23.

TABLE 5.23: Estimated Cost Per Student at the Lower Primary Education Level, 1975-76 and 1985-86

(*Amount in Rs.*)

	1975-76	1985-86
1. Average annual salary of a teacher	1,800	2,500
2. Add 10 per cent for retirement benefits	180	250
Total (Teacher Costs)	1,980	2,750
3. Non-teacher costs (Rs. 8 per pupil in 1975-76 and Rs. 12 per pupil in 1985-86)	400	540
Total Cost	2,380	3,290
4. Pupil-Teacher Ratio	50	45
5. Cost per pupil	47.6	73.1
6. As 10 per cent of the schools are to be raised to a higher standard of quality (say, double the cost per pupil) the cost would be	52.4	80.4

13. The cost of the programme will then be as shown in Table 5.24.

TABLE 5.24: Estimated Cost of Pre-Primary Education Programme, 1975-76 and 1985-86

	1975-76	1985-86
1. Total enrolment (in 000's)	71,550	76,239
2. Cost per pupil (Rs.)	52.4	80.4
3. Total cost (Rs. in 000's)	3,749,220	6,129,616

Higher Primary Education

14. At this stage, we expect facilities for about 90 per cent of the age-group by 1985-86. Of these, part-time education will be provided for 20 per cent of the children, both in 1975-76 and in 1985-86. In the first decade, the part-time classes will be of two types. (1) for those who have already completed the lower primary stage and want to continue their studies further; and (2) literacy classes for those who have not been to school or have not been able to complete the lower primary stage. In the second decade, only the first category of part-time facilities will remain. But the numbers enrolled therein would increase . . .

15. We also make the following assumptions:

(1) The average annual salary of a teacher would be Rs. 2,100 in 1975-76 (One trained graduate teacher with an average annual salary of Rs. 3,000 for three primary school teachers with an average annual salary of Rs. 1,800), and Rs. 2,875 in 1985-86 (One graduate trained teacher with an average annual salary of Rs. 4,000 for three primary school teachers with an average annual salary of Rs. 2,500).

(2) The non-teacher costs would be 20 per cent of the teacher costs.

(3) The average pupil-teacher ratio would be 35 in both the years.

16. The cost per pupil will be as given in Table 5.25.

17. As 10 per cent of the schools have to be upgraded to optimum standards (i.e., to about double the cost per pupil), the cost per student would be Rs. 87.1 in 1975-76 and 119.4 in 1985-86.

18. For part-time education, we have assumed that the cost per pupil per year will be Rs. 30 in 1975-76 and Rs. 50 in 1985-86.

TABLE 5.25: Estimated Cost per Pupil, 1975-76 and 1985-86

(*Amount in Rs.*)

	1975-76	1985-86
1. Average annual salary of a teacher	2,100	2,875
2. Add 10 per cent for retirement benefits	210	288
Total (Teacher Costs)	2,310	3,163
3. Non-teacher costs at 20 per cent of the above	462	633
Total Cost	2,772	3,796
4. Pupil-teacher ratio	35	35
5. Cost per pupil	79.2	108.5

19. The total costs will be as given in Table 5.26.

TABLE 5.26: Estimated Total Cost of Higher Primary Education, 1975-76 and 1985-86

	1975-76	1985-86
1. Enrolment (in 000's)		
Full-time	25,915	38,971
Part-time	6,479	9,743
Total	32,394	48,714
2. Cost (Rs. in 000's)		
Full-time	2,257,197	4,653,137
Part-time	194,370	487,150
Total	2,451,567	5,140,287

20. The total estimated recurring expenditure on the first level of education in 1975-76 and 1985-86 would,. therefore, be as given in Table 5.27.

21. It will be seen that the cost proposed above are extremely austere. The pupil-teacher ratios we have proposed will be objected to by many. There is no provision made here for mid-day meals, for maintaining school health services, for free supply of school

uniforms, and yet, the total cost required for this programme goes much beyond our proposed target in 1975-76, although it remains within manageable limits thereof by 1985-86. This is one of the reasons why we have proposed that programme of addition of one year to the school stage should be mainly postponed to the second decade.

TABLE 5.27: Total Estimated Recurring Expenditure on First Level of Education, in 1975-76 and 1985-86

(*Rs. in 000's*)

	1975-76	1985-86
1. Pre-primary	236,956	488,531
2. Lower primary	3,749,220	6,129,616
3. Higher primary	2,451,567	5,140,287
Total	6,437,743	11,758,343
4. Percentage of total anticipated expenditure of Rs. 15,562 million in 1975-76 and of Rs. 40,364 million in 1985-86	41.4	29.1

Lower Secondary Education

22. For the purpose of estimating costs we make the following assumptions:

(1) Ninety per cent of the teachers would be trained graduates whose average annual salary will be Rs. 3,000 in 1975-76 and Rs. 4,000 in 1985-86. The remaining 10 per cent of the teachers would have post-graduate qualifications — their average annual salary would be Rs. 4,500 in 1975-76 and Rs. 5,500 in 1985-86.

(2) The pupil-teacher ratio will be 25.

(3) Non-teacher costs will be at the rate of one-third of the teacher costs.

23. On these assumptions the cost per pupil will be as given in Table 5.28.

TABLE 5.28: Estimated Cost Per Pupil at Lower Secondary Education Level, 1975-76 and 1985-86

(*Amount in Rs.*)

	1975-76	1985-86
1. Average annual salary of a teacher	3,150	4,150
2. Add 10 per cent for retirement benefits	315	415
Total (Teacher Costs)	3,465	4,565
3. Non-teacher costs at one-third of the above	1,155	1,522
Total Cost	4,620	6,087
4. Pupil-teacher ratio	25	25
5. Cost per pupil	184.8	243.5

24. As 10 per cent of the schools at this level are to be maintained at optimum standard (i.e., at about double the cost per student), the average cost per student at this stage will be Rs. 203.3 in 1975-76 and Rs. 267.9 in 1985-86.

25. We have suggested . . . that 20 per cent of the enrolments will be in part-time education. In general education, the cost per student in such education has been assumed at Rs. 60 for 1975-76 and Rs. 80 for 1985-86.

26. We have further assumed that the enrolments in vocational education will be 6.4 per cent by 1975-76 and 20 per cent by 1985-86 and the cost will be Rs. 500 in 1975-76 and Rs. 600 in 1985-86.

27. About 20 per cent of the enrolments in vocational education would also be on a part-time basis. The cost per student in such education has been assumed at Rs. 200 by 1975-76 and Rs. 250 by 1985-86.

28. On these assumptions, the total cost of education at this stage will be as given in Table 5.29.

Higher Secondary Education

29. We have recommended . . . that the duration of this stage should be one year till about 1975-76 and that in the following decade, it should be raised to two years. We have also recommended . . . that 50 per cent of the enrolment at this stage should be in vocational

courses and that 25 per cent of the total enrolment should be on a part-time basis.

TABLE 5.29: Estimated Total Cost of Education at Lower Secondary Stage (General Education and Vocational Education), 1975-76 and 1985-86

	1975-76	1985-86
1. Enrolment (in 000's)		
General education		
Full-time	9,494	15,596
Part-time	2,373	3,899
Total	11,867	19,495
Vocational education		
Full-time	654	3,898
Part-time	164	975
Total	818	4,873
2. Cost (Rs. in 000's)		
General education		
Full-time	1,930,130	4,178,168
Part-time	142,380	311,920
Total	2,072,510	4,490,088
Vocational education		
Full-time	327,000	2,338,800
Part-time	32,800	243,750
Total	359,800	2,582,550
GRAND TOTAL (Lower Secondary)	2,432,310	7,072,638

30. On the basis of the salary scales recommended by us, the average annual salary of a teacher at this stage would be Rs. 4,500 in 1975-76 and Rs. 5,500 in 1985-86.

31. The non-teacher costs will be one-third of the teacher costs.

32. The pupil-teacher ratio will be 20:1.

33. On these assumptions, the cost per student in higher secondary education (general) would be as given in Table 5.30.

TABLE 5.30: Estimated Cost Per Student in Higher Secondary Education (General), 1975-76 and 1985-86

(*Amount in Rs.*)

	1975-76	1985-86
1. Average annual salary of a teacher	4,500	5,500
2. Add 10 per cent for retirement benefits	450	550
Total (Teacher Costs)	4,950	6,050
3. Add Non-teacher costs at @1/3 of the teacher costs	1,650	2,017
Total Cost	6,600	8,067
4. Pupil-teacher ratio	20	20
5. Cost per pupil	330.0	403.4

34. As 10 per cent of these institutions are to be upgraded to optimum standards (i.e., about double the cost per pupil), the cost per student would be Rs. 363.0 in 1975-76 and Rs. 443.7 in 1985-86.

35. We have also assumed that the cost in the vocational courses will be Rs. 700 in 1975-76 and Rs. 800 in 1985-86.

36. The costs in part-time education (general) would be Rs. 120 in 1975-76 and Rs. 160 in 1985-86. In vocational courses, these costs have been assumed at Rs. 300 in 1975-76 and Rs. 350 in 1985-86.

37. On these assumptions, the cost of education at this stage will be as given in Table 5.31.

Indirect Expenditure on School Education

38. *Direction and Inspection*. The expenditure on direction and inspection is now 1.9 per cent of the total. In order to give effect to the various recommendations we have made to strengthen administration and supervision, including in-service education of teachers, we propose to increase this expenditure to 2.5 per cent of the total in 1975-76 and to 4 per cent in 1985-86.

39. We have made the following assumptions regarding scholarships at the school stage:

(1) At the higher primary stage, 2.5 per cent of the students would get scholarships in 1975-76 and 5 per cent in 1985-86. The

average amount of the scholarships would be Rs. 60 per annum. The bulk of scholarships will be needed for meeting indirect costs, but a few larger scholarships will be provided to cover hostel charges also.

TABLE 5.31: Estimated Cost of Education at Higher Secondary Stage (General Education and Vocational Education), 1975-76 and 1985-86

	1975-76	1985-86
1. Enrolment (in 000's)		
General education		
Full-time	1,212	2,578
Part-time	404	859
Total	1,616	3,437
Vocational education		
Full-time	1,030	2,577
Part-time	343	859
Total	1,373	3,436
2. Cost (Rs. in 000's)		
General education		
Full-time	439,956	1,143,859
Part-time	48,480	137,440
Total	488,436	1,281,299
Vocational education		
Full-time	721,000	2,061,600
Part-time	102,900	300,650
Total	823,900	2,362,250
GRAND TOTAL (Higher Secondary)	1,312,336	3,643,549

(2) In general secondary education both lower and higher, 5 per cent of the students will receive scholarships by 1975-76 and 10 per cent by 1985-86. The average amount of the scholarship will be Rs. 150 per year. As said earlier, some of these scholarships would cover indirect costs and others would cover hostel charges also.

(3) In vocational secondary education 30 per cent of the students will get scholarships by 1975-76 and 50 per cent by 1985-86. The amount of the scholarships should be Rs. 300 per year at the lower secondary stage and Rs. 400 per year at the higher secondary stage.

40. On these assumptions, the cost of the scholarships programme would be as given in Table 5.32.

TABLE 5.32: Estimated Cost of the Scholarships Programme at School Stage, 1975-76 and 1985-86

Type of education	Total enrolment in full time (000's)	% of students getting scholarship	Total number of scholarships (000's)	Average annual value of scholarships (Rs.)	Total cost on scholarships (Rs in 000's)
1975-76					
Higher primary	25,915	2.5	648	60	38,880
Lower secondary:					
General	9,494	5.0	475	150	71,250
Vocational	654	30.0	196	300	58,800
Higher secondary:					
General	1,212	5.0	61	150	9,150
Vocational	1,030	30.0	309	400	123,600
Total	38,305		1,689		301,680
1985-86					
Higher primary	38,971	5.0	1,949	60	116,940
Lower secondary:					
General	15,596	10.0	1,560	150	234,000
Vocational	3,899	50.0	1,950	300	585,000
Higher secondary:					
General	2,578	10.0	258	150	38,700
Vocational	2,577	50.0	1,289	400	515,600
Total	63,621		7,006		1,490,240

41. *Buildings*. We have made an *ad hoc* provision of 2.5 per cent for buildings. It is less than the present allocation, although the amount, in absolute terms, will be much bigger. This highlights the need to economise on buildings.

TABLE 5.33: Average Annual Cost of School Education Per Pupil, 1950-51 to 1985-86

Year	Average annual salary per teacher (Rs.)	Number of pupils per teacher	Percentage of non-teacher costs to teacher costs	Average annual cost (Rs.)		
				Due to teacher costs	Due to non-teacher costs	Total
1	2	3	4	5	6	7
Pre-Primary Education						
1950-51	914	25	51.3	37	19	55
1965-66	1,000	31	54.3	35	20	55
1975-76	1,800	40	50.0	50	25	74
1985-86	2,500	40	50.0	69	34	103
Lower Primary Education						
1950-51	545	34	24.6	16	4	20
1965-66	1,046	38	11.1	27	3	30
1975-76	1,800	50	20.2	43	9	52
1985-86	2,500	45	19.6	67	13	80
Higher Primary Education						
1950-51	682	24	32.8	28	9	37
1965-66	1,087	31	12.4	40	5	45
1975-76	2,100	35	20.0	73	14	87
1985-86	2,875	35	20.0	99	20	119

Contd.

TABLE 5.33 *Contd.*

1	2	3	4	5	6	7
Lower Secondary Education (General)						
1950-51*	1,258	25	44.8	50	23	73
1965-66*	1,858	25	37.0	78	29	107
1975-76	3,150	25	33.3	152	51	203
1985-86	4,150	25	33.3	201	67	268
Lower Secondary Education (Vocational)						
1950-51**	1,705	16	86.8	106	92	197
1965-66**	2,887	15	100.0	208	208	417
1975-76	—	—	—	—	—	500
1985-86	—	—	—	—	—	600
Higher Secondary Education (General)						
1975-76	4,500	20	33.3	272	91	363
1985-86	5,500	20	33.3	333	111	444
Higher Secondary Education (Vocational)						
1975-76	—	—	—	—	—	700
1985-86	—	—	—	—	—	800

* High/Higher secondary schools.

** All types of vocational and technical schools.

Note: 1. The costs for the years 1950-51 and 1965-65 are at current prices and those for 1975-76 and 1985-86 are at constant prices of 1965-66.

2. Totals do not tally on account of rounding of figures.

42. *Total Expenditure.* We can now sum up the total expenditure on school education—recurring and capital — as anticipated for the years 1975-76 and 1985-86. This has been done in Table 5.13.

43. The implications of these estimates in terms of teachers' salaries, pupil-teacher ratios, levels of non-teacher expenditure, etc., have been given (along with comparisons for earlier years) in Table 5.33.

SUPPLEMENTAL NOTE III

Tentative Estimates of Expenditure on the Development of Higher Education, 1965-85

1. We have recommended . . . that the admission in higher education should be on selective basis and the expansion would be related to manpower needs. We have recommended that more emphasis should be laid on professional education and that quality of education should be improved. We have also recommended that 30 per cent of the enrolment both at the undergraduate and postgraduate stages should be in part-time courses.

2. *Undergraduate Education.* On the basis of salary scales recommended by us, the average annual salary of a teacher at this stage would be Rs. 6,000 in 1975-76 and Rs. 7,500 in 1985-86. The corresponding salary of a teacher in arts and science colleges in 1965-66 was Rs. 4,000.

3. The non-teacher costs will be two-thirds of the teacher costs.

4. The pupil-teacher ratio will be 15 : 1.

5. On these assumptions, the cost per student at undergraduate level (excluding science and professional courses) will be as given in Table 5.34.

6. For costing purposes we make the following assumptions:

(1) The enrolment in arts and commerce courses will be 40 per cent of the total. Of this, 70 per cent would be on a full-time basis and cost at the above rates. The remaining 30 per cent will be on a part-time basis and cost Rs. 300 in 1975-76 and Rs. 400 in 1985-86.

(2) Sixty per cent of the total enrolment would be in professional and science courses and in quality institutions in the arts and commerce courses. This will cost roughly at double the cost

per pupil in the ordinary courses for arts and commerce i.e., at Rs. 1,500 per student in 1975-76 and Rs. 2,000 per student in 1985-86. It must be noted that these are 'average' costs and that in quality and pace-setting institutions, the cost might be much higher, i.e., about as much as 10 times than in the ordinary institutions.

(3) Of the total enrolment in professional and science courses given in (2) above, 30 per cent would be in part-time courses. This will cost Rs. 750 in 1975-76 and Rs. 1,000 in 1985-86.

TABLE 5.34: Estimated Cost Per Student at Undergraduate Level (excluding Science and Professional Courses), 1975-76 and 1985-86

(*Amount in Rs.*)

	1975-76	1985-86
1. Average annual salary of a teacher	6,000	7,500
2. Add 10 per cent for retirement benefits	600	750
Total (Teacher costs)	6,600	8,250
3. Add non-teacher costs @2/3 of the teacher cost	4,400	5,500
Total Cost	11,000	13,750
4. Pupil-teacher ratio	15	15
5. Cost per pupil	733.3	916.7

7. On the above assumptions, the recurring cost of the programme at the undergraduate stage in 1975-76 and 1985-86 will be as given in Table 5.35. The details of the enrolments assumed here have been discussed earlier . . .

8. *Postgraduate Education*. At the post-graduate stage, costing becomes even more difficult because the range of variation is very large — from course to course and from institution to institution. For purposes of these estimates, we have made the following assumptions:

(1) 40 per cent of the total enrolment at the postgraduate stage would be in courses of arts and commerce. Of these, 30 per cent would be in correspondence and part-time education.

(2) The remaining 60 per cent of the enrolment would be in science and professional courses. Of this also 30 per cent

would be in part-time and correspondence education.

(3) The 'average' cost per student in courses in arts and commerce has been assumed at Rs. 3,000 for 1975-76 and Rs. 3,600 in 1985-86. In part-time courses, the cost assumed is Rs. 900 in 1975-76 and Rs. 1,200 in 1985-86.

(4) In courses of science and professional education the 'average' cost per student has been assumed at Rs. 5,000 in 1975-76 and Rs. 6,000 in 1985-86. In part-time courses the cost is assumed at Rs. 2,500 in 1975-76 and Rs. 3,000 in 1985-86.

TABLE 5.35: Estimated Cost on Undergraduate Education, 1975-76 and 1985-86

	1975-76	1985-86
1. Enrolment (in 000's)		
Arts and Commerce		
Full-time	526	896
Part-time	226	384
Total	752	1,280
Science and Vocational Education		
Full-time	790	1,344
Part-time	339	576
Total	1,129	1,920
2. Cost (Rs. in 000's)		
Arts and Commerce		
Full-time	385,716	821,363
Part-time	67,800	153,600
Total	453,516	974,963
Science and Vocational Education		
Full-time	1,185,000	2,688,00
Part-time	254,250	576,000
Total	1,439,250	3,264,00
GRAND TOTAL	1,892,766	4,238,963

9. On these assumptions, the estimated expenditure on post-

graduate education in 1975-76 and 1985-86 would be as given in Table 5.36. The estimates regarding enrolment have been discussed earlier . . .

TABLE 5.36: Estimated Expenditure on Post-Graduate Education, 1975-76 and 1985-86

	1975-76	1985-86
1. Enrolment (in 000's)		
Arts and Commerce		
Full-time	90	269
Part-time	38	115
Total	128	384
Science and Vocational Education		
Full-time	135	403
Part-time	58	173
Total	193	576
2. Cost (Rs. in 000's)		
Arts and Commerce		
Full-time	270,000	968,400
Part-time	34,200	138,000
Total	304,200	1,106,400
Science and Vocational Education		
Full-time	675,000	2,418,000
Part-time	145,000	519,000
Total	820,000	2,937,000
GRAND TOTAL	1,124,200	4,043,400

Scholarships

10. For costing scholarships, we have made the following assumptions:

(1) In courses in arts and commerce at the undergraduate stage, the average value of a scholarship will be Rs. 75 per month and it would be awarded to 15 per cent of the full-time enrolment in 1975-76 and to 25 per cent of that in 1985-86.

(2) In courses in science and professional education at the undergraduate stage, the value of the scholarship will be Rs. 125 per month and it will be awarded to 30 per cent of the enrolment in full-time courses in 1975-76 and to 50 per cent of that in 1985-86.

(3) At the post-graduate stage, the average value of the scholarship will be Rs. 300 per month and it would be awarded to 25 per cent of the students in full-time education in 1975-76 and to 50 per cent of those in 1985-86.

11. On these assumptions, the total expenditure on the programme would be as shown in Table 5.37.

TABLE 5.37: Estimated Cost on Scholarships/Stipends to Students in Higher Education, 1975-76 and 1985-86

Type of education	Total enrolment in full time courses (000's)	% of students getting scholarships	Total number of scholarships (000's)	Average annual value of scholarships (Rs.)	Total cost on scholarships (Rs in 000's)
1975-76					
Undergraduate					
Arts and Commerce	526	15	79	900	71,100
Science and Vocational	790	30	237	1,500	355,500
Postgraduate	224	25	56	3,600	201,600
Total	1,540		372		628,200
1985-86					
Undergraduate					
Arts and Commerce	896	25	224	900	201,600
Science and Vocational	1,344	50	672	1,500	1,005,600
Postgraduate	672	50	336	3,600	1,209,600
Total	2,912		1,232		2,416,200

12. In the light of the above discussions, the total estimated cost on higher education in 1975-76 and 1985-86 will be as given in Table 5.38. Its implications in terms of average annual salaries of teachers, pupil-teacher ratios, level of non-teacher costs and cost per student are given in Table 5.14.

TABLE 5.38: Expenditure on Higher Education, 1975-76 and 1985-86

Type of education	Total expenditure (Rs. in 000's)		Percentage of total expenditure	
	1975-76	1985-86	1975-76	1985-86
1. *Recurring (Direct)*				
Undergraduate				
Arts and Commerce	453,516	974,963	2.9	2.4
Science and Vocational	1,439,250	3,264,000	9.3	8.1
Total	1,892,766	4,238,963	12.2	10.5
Postgraduate				
Arts and Commerce	304,200	1,106,400	1.9	2.7
Science and Vocational	820,000	2,937,000	5.3	7.3
Total	1,124,200	4,043,400	7.2	10.0
Total — Recurring (Direct)	3,016,966	8,282,363	19.4	20.5
2. *Recurring (Indirect)*				
Scholarships	628,200	2,416,200	4.0	6.0
3. *Recurring (Direct and Indirect)*	3,645,166	10,698,563	23.4	26.5
4. *Capital*				
Buildings and Equipment	576,855	2,673,186	3.7	6.6
GRAND TOTAL	4,222,021	13,372,049	27.1	33.1

Unit Costs in Higher Education

Considering the importance of unit cost studies in higher education, where the provision of educational facilities is much more expensive than at other levels of education, the Education Commission requested a few universities to investigate the per student expenditure in higher education under their jurisdiction. Accordingly, twelve

TABLE 5.39: Cost Per Student in Universities (University Teaching Departments, Faculties and University Constituent Colleges)

(*Amount in Rs.*)

	Andhra	Anna-malai	Bhagal-pur	Jiwaji	Kuruk-shetra	Nagpur	Osmania	Poona	Rajas-than	Sardar Vallabh	Utkal
Postgraduate Courses											
Arts	998	1,861	490	241	—	736	922	1,684	1,681	1,148	1,226
Commerce	998	—	490	262	—	—	847	—	—	650	1,256
Science	—	1,851	5,011	397 **	2,208	2,589	—	2,752	5,251	3,220	—
Social Sciences	—	—	—	261	1,666	—	—	—	—	—	—
Languages	—	—	—	—	1,776	—	—	—	—	—	—
Vedic Studies	—	—	—	—	2,608	—	—	—	—	—	—
Engineering	—	2,424	—	—	—	—	2,116 *	—	—	—	—
Education	—	8,566	—	—	—	—	—	—	—	—	—
Oriental Studies	—	13,119	—	—	—	—	—	—	—	—	—
Fine Arts	—	—	—	—	—	—	—	—	—	—	—
Agriculture	—	5,432	—	—	—	—	—	—	—	—	—
Law	—	—	—	358	—	—	—	—	966	—	—
Undergraduate Courses											
Arts	—	729	409	219	1,170	—	—	—	552	308	—
Commerce	—	—	—	278	—	—	—	—	—	434	—
Science	—	586	489	—	1,463	—	—	—	599	372	—
Engineering and Technology	—	1,045	—	—	—	—	—	1,525	—	1,574	1,391
Education	—	448	—	—	—	—	—	725	—	—	—
Oriental Studies	—	783	—	—	—	—	—	—	—	—	—
Fine Arts	—	1,229	—	—	—	—	—	—	—	—	—
Agriculture	—	1,183	—	—	—	—	—	—	—	824	—
Law	—	—	—	117	—	—	—	302	—	—	—

* Science and Technology
** Average of science subjects.

universities, namely, Andhra, Annamalai, Bhagalpur, Bombay, Jiwaji, Kurukshetra, Nagpur, Osmania, Poona, Rajasthan, Sardar Vallabhai and Utkal conducted such studies which are being presented in a separate volume.

Being a comparatively new field, where not much systematic work has been done so far in our country, these studies throw up interesting results. These relate to both undergraduate and postgraduate courses in various faculties in general as well as in professional education. The results have been summarised and are given in Tables 5.39 to 5.45. These deal with costs in university teaching departments and university/constituent colleges and affiliated colleges.

A glance at these statements is enough to show how wide the variations in the costs are : While some variation is, no doubt, due to the differences in the methodology and the scope of these studies, a good deal of the variation may be due to the differences in the levels of the facilities and services provided in these institutions which in turn depend on such variable factors as salaries of teachers, student-teacher ratio, library, laboratory and other facilities provided, besides the capital cost.

In order that these studies are more useful it is necessary that these be conducted on a uniform pattern based on agreed concepts and definitions. We feel that the UGC should assist some universities to conduct such investigations periodically on the basis of standardised techniques.

TABLE 5.40: Cost per Student in Postgraduate Departments in Bombay University, 1963-64

(*In Rs.*)

Department	Instruction	Instruction including research
1. Economics	962	1,460
2. Civics and Politics	495	534
3. Business Management	1,294	1.244
4. Sociology	613	688
5. English	1,410	1,394
6. Sanskrit	2,116	2,194
7. Mathematics	1,550	1,519
8. Applied Psychology	1,926	1,816
9. Statistics	1,483	1,470
10. Law	416	436
11. Chemical Technology	2.665	2,569

TABLE 5.41: Cost per Student in Colleges in Bombay University, 1949-50 to 1963-64

(In Rs.)

Year	Commerce	Training	Law	Arts & Science	Science	Engineering	Medicine	Dentistry
1949-50	226	1,060	107	350	1,361	2,092	879	553
1950-51	212	1,063	162	272	1,858	1,000	726	888
1951-52	246	970	146	312	1,333	574	816	897
1952-53	282	972	156	310	1,291	1,077	923	913
1953-54	156	815	122	298	1,192	833	1,037	814
1954-55	171	677	149	297	—	1,260	—	—
1955-56	177	428	160	298	1,384	1,205	1,216	1,591
1956-57	148	540	162	284	1,330	1,203	1,248	1,570
1957-58	168	602	164	302	1,696	1,241	1,342	1,671
1958-59	179	707	162	285	1,603	1,314	1,725	1,485
1959-60	172	787	171	327	1,543	1,190	1,973	1,835
1960-61	253	815	166	351	1,616	1,535	2,033	2,055
1961-62	347	872	173	359	1,453	2,359	1,652	2,281
1962-63	317	744	208	384	1,643	1,316	1,693	2,782
1963-64	307	845	205	431	1,497	1,194	2,155	2,767

TABLE 5.42: Cost per Student in Undergraduate Institutions in Nagpur University, 1964-65

Institution	Cost per student (Rs.)
1. College of Arts (Smt. Binzani M.M. College)	433
2. College of Science (M.M. College of Science)	450
3. Institute of Technology (Laxminarayan Institute of Technology)(a)	1,857
4. College of Arts & Science (Hislop College)(b)	497
5. College of Arts, Science & Commerce (Dhanwate National College)	222

(a) The institute has a very small enrolment for the master's degree, so that practically it may be treated as an undergraduate institution.

(b) This college has only one postgraduate department (Sociology), the expenditure on which has been deducted from the total expenditure. It has been treated as an undergraduate institution combining arts and science.

TABLE 5.43: Cost per Student in College with Undergraduate and Postgraduate Sections in Nagpur University, 1964-65

Institution	Cost per student (Rs.)
1. College of Commerce	
(G.S. College of Commerce and Economics, Nagpur)	
A. Undergraduate Section	281
B. Postgraduate Section	360
2. College of Agriculture	
(Government College of Agriculture, Nagpur)	
A. Undergraduate Section	873
B. Postgraduate Section	1,613

TABLE 5.44: Cost per Student in Colleges in Osmania University, 1963-64

College	Cost per student (Rs.)
(A) *University and Constituent Colleges*	
1. University College of Science	1,027
2. University College of Arts & Commerce	775
3. Evening College, Secunderabad	687
4. Nizam College	681
5. Saifabad Science College	637
6. Women's College	612
7. Arts & Science College, Secunderabad	564
8. City Science College	453
9. Arts and Science College, Warangal	404
10. Hyderabad Evening College	329
(B) *Private Colleges*	
11. Sri Venkateswara Arts & Science College, Palem	757
12. Hindi Mahavidyalaya, Hyderabad	693
13. Arts & Science College, Jadcherla	675
14. Urdu Arts College	659
15. Anwar-U-loom College, Hyderabad	497
16. Badruka College of Commerce (Day)	444
17. Vanitha Mahavidyalaya, Hyderabad	443
18. Arts & Science College, Godwal	440
19. R.B.V.R.R. Women's College	382
20. Nankram Bhagwandas Science College	377
21. Vivek Vardhani College (Day)	364
22. Mumtaz College	358
23. St. Francis College, Secunderabad	337

Contd.

TABLE 5.44 *Contd.*

College	Cost per student (Rs.)
24. New Science College, Hyderabad	284
25. Badruka College (Evening)	221
26. Vivek Vardhani College (Evening)	212
(c) *Government Colleges*	
27. Government Arts & Science College, Adilabad	829
28. Government Nagarjuna College, Nalgonda	587
29. Government Arts & Science College, Siddipet	578
30. Government Giriraj College, Nizamabad	509
31. S.R. & B.G.N.R. Government Arts College, Khammam	457
32. S.R. Government College, Karimnagar	387

TABLE 5.45: Cost per Student in Undergraduate Courses in Poona University

(*In Rs.*)

College	Pre-Degree	3-year degree course	4-year degree course
Arts			
1. Fergusson College, Poona	269	342	319
2. Shri Shahu Mandir College, Poona	203	256	236
3. H.P.T. College, Nasik	348	456	409
4. R.B. Borawake College, Shrirampur	454	587	538
Science			
1 Fergusson College, Poona	352	400	380
2. H.P.T. College, Nasik	448	521	486
3. R.B. Borawake College, Shrirampur	598	814	701
Commerce			
1. B.M. College of Commerce	247	224	232
2. B.Y.K. College of Commerce, Nasik	323	309	314
3. C.D. Jain College, Shrirampur	365	532	444
4. Shri Sahau Mandir College, Poona	222	285	249
Law			
1. Law College, Poona	—	302	—
Education			
1. Tilak College of Education	—	725	—
Engineering			
1. College of Engineering, Poona	—	1,525	—

SUPPLEMENTAL NOTE V

TABLE 5.46: Consolidated Statement showing Anticipated Recurring and Capital Expenditure on Education, 1966-67 to 1985-86

Year	Total	Expenditure on education (Rs. in million)		Percentage to total of	
		Recurring	Capital	Recurring Expenditure	Capital Expenditure
1966-67	6,600	5,909	691	89.5	10.5
1967-68	7,260	6,543	717	90.1	9.9
1968-69	7,986	7,242	744	90.7	9.3
1969-70	8,785	8,013	772	91.2	8.8
1970-71	9,664	8,863	801	91.7	8.3
1971-72	10,630	9,799	831	92.2	7.8
1972-73	11,693	10,830	863	92.6	7.4
1973-74	12,862	11,966	896	93.0	7.0
1974-75	14,148	13,218	930	93.4	6.6
1975-76	15,562	14,596	966	93.8	6.2
1976-77	17,118	16,014	1,104	93.6	6.4
1977-78	18,830	17,568	1,262	93.3	6.7
1978-79	20,713	19,271	1,442	93.0	7.0
1979-80	22,784	21,136	1,648	92.8	7.2
1980-81	25,062	23,178	1,884	92.5	7.5
1981-82	27,568	25,415	2,153	92.2	7.8
1982-83	30,325	27,864	2,461	91.9	8.1
1983-84	33,358	30,545	2,813	91.6	8.4
1984-85	36,694	33,479	3,215	91.2	8.8
1985-86	40,364	36,682	3,682	90.9	9.1
Total	378,006	348,131	29,875	92.1	7.9

N.B.: The capital expenditure is comparatively restricted in the first decade because of the need to upgrade salaries of teachers and to provide adequate scholarships.

6

WORKING PARTY ON EDUCATIONAL PLANNING, ADMINISTRATION AND EVALUATION, 1968*

Introduction

The Planning Commission appointed a Working Party on Educational Planning, Administration and Evaluation vide letter No. 1/32/67 Edn., dated January 24, 1968, to review the position of educational administration and evaluation, suggest long term objectives of development in these sectors and make specific proposals. The working party was left itself to define its detailed terms of reference.

Composition

Chairman

Shri J.P. Naik, Adviser, Ministry of Education, New Delhi.

Members

1. Dr. M.B. Buch, Head of the Department of Educational Administration, NCERT, New Delhi.
2. Dr. D.A. Dabholkar, Chitamanrao College of Commerce, Sangli (Maharashtra).
3. Dr. B. Dutta, Secretary, Education Department, Government of West Bengal, Calcutta.
4. Prof. R.K. Kapur, Executive Director, Asian Institute of

* Planning Commission, New Delhi, 1968.

Educational Planning and Administration.

5. Prof. M.V. Mathur, Director, Asian Institute of Educational Planning and Administration, New Delhi.
6. Dr. S.M. Mehrotra, Deputy Secretary, Education Department, Government of Uttar Pradesh, Lucknow.
7. Shri B. Mehta, Retd. Chief Secretary, Government of Rajasthan.
8. Shri D.P. Nayar, Senior Specialist (Education), Planning Commission, New Delhi.
9. Shri V.V. Satav, Chairman, Works and Education, Committee (Shikshan Samithi) Zila Parishad, Poona.
10. Shri I.C. Saxena, Research Officer, Education Division, Planning Commission, New Delhi.
11. Prof. N. Srinivasan, Vice-Principal and Professor of Public Administration, Indian Institute of Public Administration, New Delhi.
12. Shri N.D. Sundravadivelu, Joint Educational Adviser, Ministry of Education.

Member-Secretary

Dr. S.N. Saraf, Director (Education), Planning Commission, New Delhi.

Terms of Reference

The Working Party adopted the following as its terms of reference:

1. To suggest ways and means of gearing educational administration to developmental needs;
2. To suggest needed improvement in the educational Planning Process;
3. To suggest reforms in educational administration with special reference to making the implementation of educational plans more effective; and
4. To discuss, in some details, the following major areas:
   (a) Administration at the national level;
   (b) Administration at the State level;
   (c) Special problems in educational administration with reference to:

(i) organization,
(ii) procedures, and
(iii) personnel;

(d) Supervision and guidance;
(e) Evaluation;
(f) Broad-based and decentralized planning;
(g) managerial aspects of educational administration; and
(h) Flexibility, dynamism and adaptability among administrators and supervisors.

The Working Party also decided to work out the broad financial implications of its proposals.

Main Recommendations

1. *Comprehensive educational plans:* The plans drawn up, at present, merely indicate financial allocations to selected educational programmes. Instead, comprehensive educational plans should be formulated.

2. *Decentralized system of educational planning:* There is need to adopt a broad-based and decentralized system of educational planning and, to that end, to prepare well coordinated plans at the Institutional, District, State and National levels.

3. *Institutional plan:* The base for this new process of educational planning will be provided by institutional plans.

4. *District as the basic unit of educational planning:* The District should be taken as the basic unit of educational planning, development and administration.

District plans should be introduced on a pilot basis in a few districts in every State with effect from next year. By the end of the Fourth Plan, planning at the District level should become universal.

5. *State plans:* The State plans are very important and the centre of gravity of the entire planning process in education will have to be at the State level.

6. *Removal of regional imbalances:* It is the responsibility of the Central Government to take a long-term and coordinated view of educational development and to ensure that regional imbalances between States are minimized. Special programmes will have to be developed in the National Plan from this point of view.

Planning should also be a two-way process from above as well as from below.

7. *Involvement of teachers:* There is need to involve teachers intimately and effectively in the preparation and implementation of educational plans.

8. *Provision of necessary training:* Necessary training should be provided to persons concerned with formulation and implementation of plans.

9. *Project preparation technique:* The project preparation technique for formulating educational development programmes should be adopted.

10. *Expenditure orientation of programmes:* Expenditure orientation of our educational development programmes should be reduced and efforts should be made to develop and adopt techniques of planning suited for developing countries.

11. *Determination of priority at various levels:* For effective educational planning, it would be necessary to decide priorities at different levels — National, State, District and Institutional.

12. *Better coordination between different agencies of planning:* There is an urgent need for securing better coordination between different agencies concerned with educational planning and for better coordination between the Centre and the States in the work of Plan formulation and Plan implementation.

13. *Developmental educational administration:* The most urgent task in the field of improving the implementation of educational plans is to change the present "Maintenance Administration" to "Developmental Administration".

14. *Reorganization of services:* The new concept of "Developmental Administration" involves considerable reorganization of educational services of the Centre and in the States.

15. *The in-service education of administrators:* The organization of adequate programme of in-service education for educational administrators should receive the highest priority in our Plans. On first appointment to the administrative or supervisory side, every officer should be required to undergo an induction course. The duration and content of such courses will depend upon the level at which the appointment is made and the type of duties he is expected to perform. In addition several different programmes of in-service education need to be developed to keep the departmental officers abreast of the latest developments in the field and the policies and programmes of Government. These may include annual seminars on education and

administrative matters, conduct of journeys, sabbatical leave, visits to other States, etc.

16. *Establishment of National Staff College:* We attach the greatest importance to the Education Commission's recommendation regarding the establishment of a National Staff College for Educational Administrators and recommend that it should be set up immediately and developed to its full stature by the end of the Fourth Plan. The possibilities of developing it as an Indian Wing of the Asian Institute of Educational Planning and Administration should be explored.

17. *Incentive for professional growth:* It is necessary to provide incentive for actual professional growth shown by officers of the Department.

18. *Crash programme for in-service training:* While attempts to develop in-service training programmes should be undertaken in earnest, it is equally essential to supplement them by a crash programme of in-service education in which all officers in educational administration at all levels will be reoriented to the complex and difficult tasks of educational reconstruction. The Centre and the State should fully cooperate in organizing this programme which should be developed at the district, state and national levels for different categories of officers.

19. *Programmes for qualitative improvement:* Appropriate institutional and personal arrangements to look after programmes of qualitative improvement are necessary if educational administration is to be reformed. These will include the NCERT at the national level, the State Institutes of Education at the State level, appropriate organizations at the district level, and the school complexes.

20. *Better supervision and guidance:* Steps will have to be taken to provide better supervision and guidance to schools. This will include, amongst others, an increase in the strength of inspecting officers where necessary and the appointment of subject inspectors. Efforts are also needed to improve the quality of inspection.

21. *Comparative studies of administrative procedures:* The departmental procedure and practices, which at present are very often unsatisfactory and unsuitable to the requirements of developmental administration, should be reformed. Comparative studies of administrative practices will greatly help in this. Attention has also to be paid to such programmes as the adoption of the officer-oriented system, establishment of an O and M organization in each State Education Department, and particularly to securing an adequate delegation

of authority.

22. *Flexible and dynamic administration:* The functioning of the education departments should be made flexible and dynamic.

23. *Evaluation and educational research:* It is suggested that in the years ahead, much greater emphasis should be placed on evaluation and educational research which should be vigorously promoted.

24. *Research studies by the Asian Institute of Educational Planning and Administration:* The Indian wing of the Asian Institute of Educational Planning and Administration should take up research studies in the administrative problems of universities in collaboration with University Grants Commission and arrange appropriate training programmes for the university staff of higher cadres. A special working party should be set up immediately to work out the details of a programme of action.

25. *Strengthening and improving programme of educational planning:* The programmes for reform in educational planning, administration and evaluation need to be developed on a basis of high priority during the Fourth Five-Year Plan. Adequate funds should be provided for strengthening and improving educational administration. A satisfactory norm in this respect would be that expenditure on educational planning, administration and evaluation, including research and in-service education of teacher, headmasters and educational administrators should be of the order of about 5 per cent of the total educational expenditure.

26. *Rs. 22 crores for improvement in educational planning programme:* A provision of Rs. 22 crores is recommended for various schemes relating to improvement of educational planning, administration and evaluation. It will help to watch over the development of programmes relating to educational planning, administration and evaluation, if this expenditure is shown as a separate sector in the Plans.

7

SEMINAR ON INSTITUTIONAL PLANNING, 1968*

Introduction

The National Seminar was organized by the National Council of Educational Research and Training in collaboration with the Ministry of Education, Government of India, and was held at Regional College of Education, Bhopal, from 3–5 November, 1968.

Seventy-four educators which included officers of the Education Departments of various States, Principals and Lecturers of Colleges of Education and Principals and Headmasters of Schools participated in the seminar.

Prominent resource persons, among others, included: Prof. B.D. Nagchaudhuri, Member, Planning Commission; Shri J.P. Naik, Adviser, Ministry of Education; Prof. M.V. Mathur, Director, Asian Institute; Dr. Shri K. Mitra, Joint Director, NCERT.

RECOMMENDATIONS

The recommendations are grouped under three heads:

1. School Principals and Institutional Planning.
2. Institutional Planning and Teachers Colleges.
3. Role of Educational Administrators in Institutional Planning.

I. School Principals and Institutional Planning

In his capacity as the leader of a school, the Principal has to discharge two functions: (i) as an Administrator; (ii) as the Supervisor.

* Regional College of Education, Bhopal, 1968.

To be an effective Leader/Supervisor, the Principal must possess three types of skills:

(i) Technical Skills,
(ii) Personal and Social Skills, and
(iii) Conceptual Sills.

(i) *Technical skills:* The technical skills are acquired from study, experience and research. These technical skills now distinguish him from other learned men in other walks of professional life and make him an acceptable administrator. These technical skills fulfil the criteria of supervisor and for the most part give him the skill to manage the school, its financial, physical and human resources and the academic programme. It is true that the Principal of a school cannot know all there is to know about the various subjects which are taught in the school, but he must have a generalized knowledge of all the subjects which are offered in the school and he must be a proficient scholar at least in one of the subjects offered in the school. As a Principal, he must continue to study and conduct research in his own area of specialization. If he forfeits his scholastic profession in his own area, he will forfeit the very foundation upon which these technical skills are based.

(ii) *Personal and social skills:* The Principal must have personal and social skills and he should utilize these skills to determine the effectiveness of overall development of the school. By social skills, it is meant that he is warm, open minded and a hearty fellow having a thorough knowledge and study of the application of the psychological and sociological principles of being a change agent. He should know each and every member of the staff, their background, their strengths and limitations and should relate them to the needs of the programmes of the institutional development. He should possess the ability to initiate programmes, sustain and evaluate them. It is only a democratic attitude and a democratic approach in administration that will help him to be recognized by the staff as the leader in a programme of institutional planning.

(iii) *Conceptual skills:* The Principal must have conceptual skills. By conceptual skill is meant the ability to see the separate organizational parts of the school; the ability to see the role of each staff member to each to these organizational parts; the ability to see the relationship of each part to the whole; the ability to see the relationship of individual effort to the collective effort and lastly the ability to take his school from the existing professional status to a higher target.

Improvement means change. It is necessary for the Principal to know that the school does not consist of furniture and equipment only. The Principal should realize that the school has a social system and to bring about a change in a social system has its own complexities. As a social system the school has various aspects like goals, established procedures, different subject groups, relationship among the various subject groups and its own norms. An attempt to change one aspect of the school life will influence and disturb the overall school equilibrium.

The first job of the Principal should be to look at the whole school system, assess the strengths and weaknesses of his staff members, and carefully create the ground work for various changes. He will have to proceed in a planned manner.

FIVE STEPS IN INSTITUTIONAL PLANNING

1. *Individual and group conferences:* The first step might be a series of individual conferences with the staff followed by group conference. After this there might be a staff meeting in which the Principal and outside experts may explain the whole purpose and the need for preparing an institutional plan. The Principal shall take a close look at how the discussion in the staff meetings are received by the teachers. In other words, he will evaluate the result of the first staff meeting.

2. *Discussion with teachers and experts and identification of problems:* The second step will be a discussion about undertaking a survey of the needs for improvement and development of the school. This will be a longer process as most teachers find it difficult to identify the real problems. Experts from outside, senior teachers and the Principal himself will have to work with individual teachers and subject teachers groups to have the survey of the real needs felt by the school staff for improvement and development in various areas. It will be necessary for the Principal to arrange the areas requiring improvement in a proper sequence from the view point of available resources and the nature of difficulties involved in implementing the programmes. The Vice-Principal will always encourage teachers to take up such programmes as can be completed by the teachers

without much difficulty. It is the success in the initial programmes that will inspire confidence for undertaking major improvement programmes.

3. *Survey of resources:* The third step will be a survey of the resources available in the school and the community. Here again greater stress will be laid on knowing what already exists in the school.

4. *Preparation of improvement programmes:* The fourth step will be preparation of improvement programmes. Here adequate reading materials, reference materials, expert guidance shall have to be provided to teachers planning improvement programmes. Each improvement programme will take the form of a project and guidelines of preparing projects will be supplied to the teachers by the Principal.

5. *Evaluation of the programme:* The fifth step will be the evaluation of the programmes after they have been implemented and completed. In fact the Principal will carry on periodical evaluation of the various programmes and staff consultative surveys of the teachers in modifying the procedures if need is felt for it.

ESSENTIALS OF INSTITUTIONAL PLANNING

1. *Different levels of improvement programmes:* The principal should realize that all improvement programmes will not go at the same rate. Some programmes will develop at a faster rate than other depending upon the ability of the teachers concerned, and also upon the degree of simplicity or complexity. Whereas some teachers will lead at a faster rate in implementing improvement programmes several other teachers will lag behind. A broken front approach where teacher goes with his own speed should be followed by the Principal. He should neither insist nor expect the same level of development for different improvement approaches.

2. *Each school has its own individuality:* The Principal in no case should try to impose a plan prepared by another school on the staff of his own school. He should realize that each school is different from the other in its resources, problems and pressures. Some schools may be big, some small. Some schools may be full-day schools and some part-time shift schools. It is, therefore, natural that the planning for each school will be different from the other. Within their own limitations, with a systematic and scientific programme, school can certainly effect improvement in many areas of work.

3. *Involvement of all teachers of the school:* In the process of preparing the school plan for improvement and development, the Principal should take care to involve all the teachers of his school. He should also make conscientious effort to involve the community groups as well as the students. It is advisable that the Principal should initiate his staff on the programme of preparing the plan for the school, put the teachers on the right rails and entrust the work of preparing the school plan to a small committee acceptable to all the staff members. A successful Principal should be in a position to delegate the powers and withdraw himself leaving the programme of preparing plans for the school to the teachers committee. He should, however, periodically attend the committee meetings as an observer. In this way, the Principal will be in a position to involve a large number of teachers effectively in the process of planning. Once the plan has been prepared by the teachers committee, the same should be discussed in the meetings of the staff and modified on the basis of suggestions. To do this successfully, it is necessary that the Principal should so arrange the school year that the teachers meet at least a week earlier than the students come to the schools. It should be made a firm principle that the school session will not start unless the school plan has been completed.

4. *Forward looking plan:* While planning for the institution, the experience of the past year should be taken into consideration and the plan should be a forward looking plan aiming at a high ideal, viz., to be the pursuit of excellence. It is worth-while remembering for the Principal that the institutional planning may not be taken up in isolation of the national plan for the improvement of education. Main target of the national plan should be squarely put before the staff members to give them a direction for planning.

MAJOR AREAS OF THE INSTITUTIONAL PLANNING

(i) *Academic programmes:* Here improvement of instructional programmes and enrichment of curriculum should be included to improve the school results both in the home examinations as well as in external examinations by reducing wastage and stagnation, improving the attendance ratio, improving ways of home work assignments, etc.

(ii) *Co-curricular area:* Here a programme of school beautification, creating an environment which can stimulate learning by pupils, physical education programmes, co-curricular programmes, etc., should be included.

(iii) *In-service programmes and professional growth of teachers:* This is an important area for planning. A plan for the professional growth of individual teacher should be prepared. Programmes for the in-service education of teachers and group programmes for the in-service education of the entire school faculty should be prepared in a planned way. Stress should be laid on the in-service needs of the individual teachers.

(iv) *School services:* There is an urgent need to prepare a planned programme for the improvement and utilization of a library service, laboratory service, guidance services, etc. Other services which directly concern the students' welfare like the mid-day meal, drinking water, sanitation and hygiene should also be planned for improvement.

(v) *Maximum utilization of school resources:* This is an area which is the most important for any programme of institutional planning. There are schools which have surplus teachers without adequate work. There are schools which have teachers not fitting into the school curriculum offerings. There are schools which have shortage of teachers. The Institutional Planning should aim at maximum utilization of all available teacher resources. The planning should also aim at utilizing the unutilized teaching aids, the building facilities, the play-grounds, etc. A good Institutional Plan should study this area of human and physical resources and their maximum utilization improvement of the school.

II. Institutional Planning and Teachers Colleges

Main recommendations are as under:

1. As for the improvement of the syllabus, a long-term planning is needed through which we could involve more and more teachers in revising the syllabus and making it more up to date. There should be a better representation of the teachers on the Board of Studies.
2. The major area, which a programme of institutional planning should include, should be how to teach the prescribed syllabus in the best possible manner.
3. Before taking up the work of teachers, meetings of subject teachers should be held. They should discuss the specific objective of

teaching, methods of teaching and evaluation. Such meetings may also be convened at intervals during the session.

4. In these meetings the secondary school teachers should also be involved.

5. Student's reaction to the syllabus should be given due importance.

6. An orientation course for students should be organized in the beginning of the session. They should be given an idea of the total programme and also what expectations the college has from them.

7. All measures should be taken to make teaching practice realistic.

8. Training college should accept its responsibility of serving as a guide to the schools in solving their problems.

9. A research committee in each college or in a group of colleges should be formed. The head of these committees should be a person who has experience in research.

10. The research committee should also have some experienced teachers from schools as its members.

11. Extension work should be based on the felt needs of the schools.

12. The principals have to play a key role in institutional planning. The quality of institutional planning will ultimately depend upon the quality of educational leadership they provide. It would be worthwhile if the Principals themselves periodically examine their own role in promoting institutional planning.

Similarly, all teachers should continually review themselves and their contribution. It is good to remember that:

> A poor teacher tells,
> An average teacher explains,
> A good teacher demonstrates,
> And a great teacher inspires.

III. Role of Educational Administrations in Institutional Planning

Just as the community development programme is the people's programme so is the Institutional Plan, the plan of the school community consisting of the principal, the teachers, the students and the local people for the improvement and development of physical and educational facilities in the institution. The success of the programme depends on the participation of the people concerned with the programme. This is the basis for a sound national plan.

Planning Stage

1. The first step for the District Educational Officer is to create an awareness amongst the heads of institutions for Institutional Planning and its importance by calling a meeting of the heads of schools at the district level.

2. The heads of institutions will be asked to prepare improvement and development plans on the basis of felt needs and availability of resources in consultation with the teachers, students and the local community and fix priorities. Every school will, however, be required to put up a minimum action plan.

3. The plan will be phased according to the extent, need and resources, which should be normally for one academic session, which may be the duration of the plan.

4. The District Educational Officer will have the advisory role to play with regard to the institutional plans and he will be helped by an academic cell which may be created in his office. This cell will consist of subject experts — specialists in guiding research workers who will be associated with the plan at all stages. The cell will provide expert advice from time to time according to the needs of the school.

5. The autonomy of the schools in Institutional Planning of implementation and to a certain extent in evaluation is a must at all stages, it being their own plan.

6. The District Educational Officer will extend help and guidance to the schools promptly when the schools ask for it.

7. The district Educational Officer will ensure recognition of good work at different levels. The directorate will also encourage good workers.

Implementation

1. District Educational Officer will arrange publicity of the State and national plans as far as they relate to and affect the schools and the teachers.

2. He will use his influence and good offices in tapping level resources, different agencies and enlisting community help for the

implementation of the plans.

3. He will provide resource personnel from the district, extension services and from outside.

4. He would arrange for in-service training of teachers in areas of institutional planning.

5. He will encourage inter-school visits for exchange of ideas and provide T.A. and D.A. facilities.

6. He, being a very important link between the schools and the department, will secure financial aid for the schools wherever needed to encourage good work and if the requirements of the plan so demand.

7. He will help in getting the pupils' fund rules liberalized to facilitate utilization of funds by the head of the institution with the help of the school committee set up for the purpose.

8. Due publicity will be arranged for good plans and significant individual work, through School and District Bulletins, departmental journals, conferences and seminars.

Evaluation

1. *Self-evaluation:* The school community will make an appraisal of the entire plan chalked out, targets achieved and difficulties experienced. This will be done frequently and modifications made to make it more practicable and useful.

2. *Supervision and inspection:* The District Educational Officer and the panel inspection team comprising experienced headmasters (including retired personnel) will evaluate the programme at least once a year or more if possible.

3. The evaluation will be done by the team in terms of the extent of contribution of creative ideas in planning, resourcefulness shown in implementation — the depth of their qualities as well as the number of people involved in making their contribution. This should be helpful in judging as to how far the plan has been successful. A scrutiny will be made by examining the process and the produce.

Conclusion

The success of institutional planning, implementation and proper evaluation will depend on the dynamic leadership, initiative and personality of the District Educational Officer. He will be instrumental in encouraging good work by securing special development grants for the schools on the basis of the performance.

8

COMMITTEE ON TEN PLUS TWO PLUS THREE, 1973*

Introduction

In pursuance of the recommendations of the Indian Education Commission, 1964-66, the 10+2+3 structure was incorporated in the National Policy Statement which was issued by the Union Government in 1968. The structure was discussed and endorsed by a number of all-India Forums including the Central Advisory Board of Education, of which every State Education Minister is a member. However, the details of the structure for its implementation needed to be examined carefully. The Government of India, Ministry of Education and Social Welfare, appointed the National Committee to formulate practical measures for introducing the proposed educational structure all over the country and to estimate the expenditure involved.

Terms of Reference

1. To suggest practical steps to be taken for implementation of the uniform pattern of 10+2+3 for the school and college classes in all States and Union Territories of the country.
2. To estimate the cost of implementing the programme.

Chairman

P.D. Shukla, Chairman, Central Board of Secondary Education, New Delhi.

---

* Ministry of Education and Social Welfare, Government of India, New Delhi.

Members

1. Education Secretary, U.P.
2. Education Secretary, Rajasthan.
3. Education Secretary, Delhi.
4. Education Secretary, Tamil Nadu.
5. Education Secretary, West Bengal.
6. Education Secretary, Gujarat.
7. Education Secretary, Assam.
8. Education Secretary, Mysore.
9. Director (Education), Planning Commission, New Delhi.

Member-Secretary

Dr. R.P. Singhal, Secretary, Central Board of Secondary Education, New Delhi.

Recommendations on Financial Implications*

The total expenditure on introducing the new structure during the Fifth Plan is estimated to be as under:

TABLE 8.1: Total Estimated Expenditure on 10+2+3 Structure during Fifth Plan

(*Rs. in crores*)

States where it takes 14 years to obtain the first degree in general education	32.5
States where it takes 15 years to obtain the first degree in general education	17.0
Vocationalization of higher secondary education	10.0
Total	59.5

Earmarking of Funds

In view of the fact that structure of education acts like the foundation of a building, we suggest that the entire development of education should in future be on the basis of the proposed structure and, therefore, the funds in the Fifth Plan to be earmarked for that purpose and they should be outside the plan allocations of the States.

* Original Table Number has been changed to conform to this Chapter number

9

DRAFT NATIONAL POLICY ON EDUCATION, 1979*

Introduction

The first non-Congress (Janata) Government at the Centre headed by Shri Morarji Desai was formed on March 24, 1977. It decided to revamp the system of education in the country and prepared a Draft National Policy on Education in 1979. However, with the fall of the Janata Government on August 22, 1979, action could not be taken on finalising the National Policy on Education. Para 22 of the Draft National Policy, 1979, deals with the resources for education, and *inter alia* includes:

22. Investment in Education**

22.1 Government expenditure on education in the country has steadily grown and is now of the order of 2,800 crore rupees per annum. A larger outlay will be needed to implement the policy . . . However, efforts must be made to realise the objective through exercise of economy, more effective utilization of existing resources, additional outlays and programmes such as "Food for Work".

22.2 Fees may be charged in secondary and higher education stages from those sections of population who are in a position to pay at rates which bear a reasonable relationship to the cost of providing education.

22.3 Support from local communities in cash and kind should also be encouraged on a wider scale than is done at present.

22.4 While financial inputs are an important part of the total ef-

* Ministry of Education, New Delhi, 1979.

** Para number refer to Paras the document.

fort required to implement the policy, even more important will be human element, the intellectual and moral energy dedicated to the task. Without this human contribution, the transformation and expansion of the education system . . . and improvement of its quality will not be possible.

10

NATIONAL COMMISSION ON TEACHERS I (On School Teachers) 1983-85*

Introduction

It was for the first time in the history of independent India that in recognition of the importance of teachers and their role in developing the nation's human and material resources, the Government of India appointed two National Commissions on Teachers, one for the school stage and the other for higher education (including technical education) in February 1983. The Commissions submitted their reports in March 1985. The reports were not made public for almost two years. It is very strange that the reports have received very little attention for the concerned circles except the recommendations regarding pay scales of teachers as suggested by the National Commission on Teachers I, popularly known as Chattopadhaya Commission after the name of its Chairman. Chapter X of the report 'The Teacher and Society', deals with the financial aspects.

Terms of Reference of the National Commission on Teachers I

1. Lay down clear objectives for the teaching profession with reference to the search for excellence, breadth of vision and cultivation of values in keeping with the country's heritage and ideals of democracy, secularism and justice;
2. Identify steps to be taken to give an appropriate status to members of the profession;
3. Suggest measures for fostering dynamism in the profession and responsiveness to development elsewhere in the world;

---

* *Report of the National Commission on Teacher-I, 1983-85,* Controller of Publications, Delhi, 1986.

4. Recommend measures needed for attracting and retaining talented persons in the teaching profession and widening the base for recruitment, particularly of women;
5. Review the existing arrangements for pre-service and in-service training/orientation for teacher and to recommend improvements;
6. Review and recommend the application of improved methods and technology for teaching;
7. Recommend measures to enhance the role of teachers in facilitating, motivating and inspiring students in the acquisition of knowledge, skills and values and promoting through them the spread of scientific temper, secular outlook, environmental consciousness and civic responsibility;
8. Identify the role of teachers in integrating education with development work in the community and home.
9. Study the social requirements of teachers in the field of non-formal and continuing education and to suggest ways and means by which these requirements can be met;
10. Identify the role of teachers' organisations in professional growth and professional consciousness;
11. Look into the feasibility of evolving an acceptable and implementable code of conduct for teachers; and
12. Assess the adequacy of arrangements for promotion of teachers' welfare with special reference to the National Foundation of Teachers' Welfare and to suggest modifications where necessary.

RECOMMENDATIONS

Financial Estimates*

10.55 Of the several recommendations that we have made . . . the ones with large financial implications are the following:

(1) Universalisation of Elementary Education (UEE);
(2) Improvement of salary scales of teachers;

---

* (i) Number of paras refer to paras of Chapter X.
(ii) Original Table numbers have been changed to conform to this Chapter numbers.

(3) Construction of residential quarters for women teachers in rural areas;
(4) Improving infrastructure and other facilities of teacher training institutions;
(5) In-service education of teachers;
(6) National Organisation for Standards in School Education; and
(7) Research and Statistics.

I. Universalisation of Elementry Education

10.56 The estimates of additional enrolments to be reached by 1990 through formal and non-formal channels of elementary education have been provided* . . . To recall the data:

TABLE 10.1: Estimates of Additional Enrolment to be Reached by 1990 through Formal and Non-Formal Channels of Elementary Education

(in lakhs)

	Enrolment through Formal channels	Enrolment through Non-formal channels	Total
Primary	233.00	78.00	311.00
Middle	288.00	32.00	320.00
Total	521.00	110.00	631.00

10.57 We suggest that the cost estimates of the programme be worked out for four levels of projections, namely:

(a) 100 per cent level;
(b) High level (aimed at achieving 75% of the target);
(c) Medium Level (50% of the target); and
(d) Low Level (25%).

The projections for the high, medium and low levels are given in Table 10.2.

We have to make another assumption regarding the distribution of the projected enrolments over the 5 years of the Seventh Five Year

* In para 6.16 of Chapter VI of the document.

Plan period. A simple assumption often made in such exercises nationally and internationally is to provide for 20 per cent of the total additional enrolment every year. By this assumption the proportions of the total enrolment to be reached in the different years of the plan work out as given in Table 10.3.

TABLE 10.2: Projection for High, Medium and Low Levels in Universalization of Elementary Education

	Formal channels	Non-formal channels	Total
High Level Projections (75%)			
Primary	174.75	58.50	233.25
Middle	216.00	24.00	240.00
Total	390.75	82.50	473.25
Medium Level Projections (50%)			
Primary	118.50	39.00	155.50
Middle	144.0	16.00	160.00
Total	260.50	55.0	315.50
Low Level Projections (25%)			
Primary	58.25	19.50	77.75
Middle	72.00	8.00	80.00
Total	130.25	27.50	157.75

TABLE 10.3: Distribution of Projected Enrolment in Elementory Education over Seventh Five Year Plan Period, 1985-86 to 1989-90

1985-86	20% = 20%
1986-87	20% + 20% = 40%
1987-88	20% + 20% + 20% = 60%
1988-89	20% + 20% + 20% + 20% = 80%
1989-90	20% + 20% + 20% + 20% + 20% = 100%

Choice of Per Pupil Cost

10.58 The all-India per primary pupil cost in 1970-71 was Rs. 57.00. By 1977-78 this had risen to Rs. 127.1 indicating a net increase of 122.98 per cent. We do not have any statistics available for a very recent year but if the assumption can be made that a similar increase in the per pupil cost has occurred during 1977-78 to 1984-85, the present figures should be Rs. 283.41. We suggest this per pupil cost be rounded off to Rs. 300.

10.59 The per pupil cost in a middle school in 1970-71 stood at Rs. 84.9. By 1977-78 the figure had risen to Rs. 164.8. Assuming a similar rise (arithmetically) by 1984-85 we get a figure of Rs. 319.89. We suggest that this figure also be rounded off to Rs. 300 per pupil. It is interesting that both our rounded figures come to Rs. 300. This is for the formal channel.

10.60 For the per pupil cost in the non-formal channel, it is suggested that it may be taken at 50 per cent of the cost in the formal channel, that is Rs. 150 per pupil. Except for this we do not propose to make any further differentiation in the calculation of the estimates for the two channels.

10.61 The cost estimates for total plan period for the four levels of projections are now worked out below (Table 10.4):

TABLE 10.4: Cost Estimates for Enrolment Projection in Elementary Education During Seventh Plan Period, 1985-86 to 1989-90

	1st Year of the plan (1985-86)	Last Year of the plan (1989-90) = 5 X (1)	Total Plan Period (1985-90) = 3 X (2)
	1	2	3
100% Enrolment*	37,860	189,300	567,900
High Level (75%)	28,395	141,975	425,925
Medium Level (50%)	18,930	94,650	28,395
Low Level (25.%)	9,465	47,325	141,975

* These estimates have been presented simply to indicate the cost implications of UEE under 4 different assumptions. The necessary allocations for the purpose will continue to be made in the Plan Budget of the State Government as heretofore.

II. Improvement of Salary Scales

10.62 Our expectation regarding the recommendations. . . is that each State Government will determine its own running scale keeping in view the general principles. . . . It was mentioned there that as a result of the new pay fixation approach, . . . we would like to see the secondary teachers of the country have on an average a benefit not less than Rs. 100 per month and the primary teacher not less than Rs. 150 per month.

10.63 We do not know the exact number of teachers in the country but the figures for the last year (1982-83) for which statistics are available are 1,389,956 primary teachers, 856,389 middle schools teachers, and 993,115 secondary teachers. The three figures add up to a total of 3,238,860 teachers. For the present estimates it is suggested that we might use constantly a figure of 25 lakhs for primary and middle school teachers and 10 lakhs for secondary teachers.

10.64 Assuming further the rate of increments for these two categories of teachers to be Rs. 20-30-30-30 and Rs. 30-30-40-40 for primary and secondary teachers for the 2nd, 3rd, 4th and 5th years for the Plan respectively, the estimates work out as follows (Table 10.5):

TABLE 10.5: Financial Implication of the Improvement of Salary Scales of Teachers during Seventh Plan, 1985-86 to 1989-90

	1985-86	86-87	87-88	88-89	89-90
Average benefit for a primary and middle school teacher	150	170	200	230	260
Number of teachers (in lakhs)	25	25	25	25	25
Total benefit (in lakhs) for primary and middle school teachers	3,750	4,250	5,000	5,750	6,500
Average benefit for a secondary teacher	100	130	160	200	240
Number of secondary teachers (in lakhs)	10	10	10	10	10
Total benefit for secondary teachers (in lakhs)	1,000	1,300	1,600	2,000	2,400
Total benefit for school teachers (in lakhs)	4,750	5,550	6,600	7,750	8,900

The total financial implication for the plan period comes to Rs. 33,550 lakhs.

III. Construction of Residential Quarters for Women Teachers in the Rural Areas

10.65 We have suggested the construction of one lakh residential units @Rs. 25,000 each during the Seventh Plan period. The total cost of the proposal comes to Rs. 25,000 lakhs.

IV. Implication of Improved Teacher Training Facilities

(a) *Existing training colleges/university departments of education elementary training schools*

10.66 Two of our important recommendations . . . concern the improvement of infrastructure of the existing training colleges, and the establishment of four-year integrated colleges. We have suggested that each of the 300 training colleges to be selected for the purpose be given a capital grant of Rs. 3.00 lakhs. For 300 institutions, this implies an outlay of Rs. 900 lakhs.

10.67 We have also recommended a non-recurring grant of Rs. 1 lakh each for 500 elementary training schools to improve their physical facilities. The total cost of this programme comes to Rs. 500 lakhs.

(b) *Establishment of four-year integrated colleges*

10.68 We have recommended the establishment of an integrated college for each State. For the country as a whole, it is suggested that this be taken to mean the establishment of 25 four-year institutions. We have further suggested that to meet the need for additional physical facilities, nothing less than Rs. 20 lakhs per institution will be needed. In fact, if the project is not executed expeditiously and suffers from procrastination, a familiar weakness in Indian planning, our fear is that this provision may have to be increased by at least 5 per cent for each year of the postponement.

10.69 For working out the estimates of the recurring costs, we had assumed an enrolment of 100 trainees in the first year and suggested that from the second year* on there should be on an average an addition of 7 staff members every year for three years. This will give us a teacher ratio of 100/7(14.3). As regards emoluments, we have suggested an average salary of Rs. 2,000 per month for the teacher educator.

10.70 On these two assumptions, the recurring costs for a four-year institution for the Plan period work out as in Table 10.6.

The total cost — recurring and capital — for 25 integrated colleges for Seventh Plan period thus comes to Rs. 1,140 lakhs (900 + 240).

---

* We assume that these 25 four-year Integrated Colleges will for the most part be established by converting existing institutions.

TABLE 10.6: Recurring Cost for Four Year Integrated Colleges for Teachers Training During Seventh Plan, 1985-86 to 1989-90

	Per institution				
	Additional enrolment	Total enrolment	Additional Faculty	Cost	Total cost for 25 institutions (in lakhs)
1985-86	0	100	0	0	0
1986-87	100	200	7	1.05	26.25
1987-88	200	300	14	2.10	52.50
1988-89	300	400	21	3.15	78.75
1989-90	300	400	21	3.15	78.75
			Total	9.45	236.25
			or say	9.5	240.00

V. In-service Training

10.71 Our main recommendation on the need for every primary and secondary teacher to be given an opportunity for in-service training at least once every 5 years. . . . We have suggested a provision of Rs. 50 per teacher for this purpose. Though modest, the estimate may serve as a basis for determining the cost implications of this programme. We have nearly 3.5 million primary and secondary teachers in the country. If 1/5th of this are to be covered every year, the cost will come to Rs. 3500 lakhs. For 5 years this bill comes to Rs. 17500 lakhs.

VI. A National Organisation for Standards in School Education

10.72 We have suggested a capital grant of Rs. 50 lakhs for its accommodation, equipment and related facilities, and a recurring provision of Rs. 20 lakhs for the first year of the Plan period which may be progressively raised to stabilise at Rs. 50 lakhs in the penultimate year of the Plan. The recurring provision for 5 years comes to Rs. 20, 30, 40, 50 and 50 lakhs respectively.

10.73 The proposed National Testing Service, when developed fully, could be a source of income, but it is not possible to make any estimates at this stage. Depending upon the income, the Government liability could be suitably adjusted.

10.74 The total cost of the proposal comes to Rs. 50 lakhs capital and 190 lakhs recurring.

VII. Research and Statistical Information

10.75 We have suggested that UGC may consider providing annually at the rate of Rs. 20,000 for 100 selected colleges/university departments of education to promote indigenous action-oriented research. The cost of this programme works out at Rs. 20 lakhs annually, or Rs. 100 lakhs for the plan period.

10.76 At the elementary level we have recommended an annual provision of Rs. 10,000 for each of the 1,000 training schools in the country. This means an annual expenditure of Rs. 100 lakhs, or Rs. 500 lakhs for the plan period.

TABLE 10.7: Summary of Financial Estimates of Universalisation of Elementary Education and Improvement of Teacher's Salaries, etc.

(Rs. in lakhs)

Item	Capital Expenditure	For one year (Average)	For the 7th Plan period
I. UEE:			
(i) 100% Enrolment	—	1,13,580	5,67,900
(ii) 75% Enrolment	—	85,185	4,25,925
(iii) 50% Enrolment	—	56,790	2,83,950
(iv) 25% Enrolment	—	28,395	1,41,975
II. Improvement of Salary Scales	—	6,710	33,550
III. Construction of Residential Quarters	25,000		
IV. Training Colleges:			
(i) Upgrading of 300 Colleges	900		
(ii) Upgrading of 500 Elementary Schools	500		
(iii) Establishment of 25 four-year Integrated Colleges	500	48	240
V. In-service Training	—	3,500	17,500
VI. National Organisation for Standards in School Education	50	38	190
VII. Research and Statistics:			
(i) Elementary Level	—	100	500
(ii) Secondary Level	—	20	100
Total (Excluding I)	26,950	10,416	52,080
Grand Total for 5 years of the 7th Plan (Capital + Recurring)			79,030

11

CHALLENGE OF ACTION: A Policy Perspective, 1985*

Introduction

This document represents an important stage in the process of reviewing and shaping the educational system in the country. The analysis of the development over the last two decades had made it clear that desired improvements had not materialised after the formulation of the education policy adopted in 1968. It was, therefore, desired to have a comprehensive review of the state of education in the country — so as to formulate a new policy on education which could usher a new era. The review as contained in the document pointed out the limitations and constraints as also pointers to the direction of future initiatives, based essentially on the views and suggestions from educational planners, teachers, students, parents, intellectuals and other citizens interested in education. There was a nation-wide debate on the document which ultimately became a basis of the National Policy on Education, 1986.

Chapter 4 of the document incorporates observations on educational planning and financing. These are appended:

Goal Orientation for Educational Planning**

4.6 A recapitulation of the goals of education, emphasised by the Indian Constitution and enunciated, from time to time, by thinkers, planners, policy-makers and educationists, indicates that this basic issue should be considered from three inter-related approaches.

4.7 First of all, it is necessary to define the role of the educational

* Ministry of Education, Government of India, New Delhi, 1985.

** *Note:* Paras numbers refer to paras of Chapter 4 of the document.

system in totality since it has an institutional character of its own which goes beyond its main function of imparting education to pupils. The system is expected to generate new knowledge in all fields within the reach of the human mind. In addition, it has to evolve principles, methodologies and guidelines for the application of knowledge for benefiting society. It is also expected to provide knowledge and skills for solving the problems of development. must also enable the students to develop an understanding and a perspective of the physical and social environment. Research and development and extension, therefore, have to be accepted as essential ingredients of the educational process.

4.8 Secondly, emphasis has to be laid on the socio-economic well-being, competence and creativity of the individual, which encompasses:

(i) physical, intellectual and aesthetic development of personality;
(ii) inculcation of a scientific temper and democratic, moral and spiritual values;
(iii) development of self-confidence to innovate and face unfamiliar situations;
(iv) creation of an awareness of the physical, social, technological, economic and cultural environment;
(v) fostering a healthy attitude to dignity of labour and hard work;
(vi) a commitment to principles of secularism and social justice;
(vii) dedication to uphold the integrity, honour and foster the development of the country; and
(viii) promotion of international understanding.

4.9 In addition to developing the personal attributes listed above, education has to assume the responsibility for imparting knowledge about concepts and facts relating to different subjects and for developing skills in the area of languages and communication, as also interest in hobbies, games and sports.

Financial Constraints

4.49 is hardly necessary to establish the relevance of financial constraints in the context of educational planning. Whether one looks at the question of equity or coverage or quality or diversification, the provision of sizeable financial resources appears inescapable. There is no point in discussing universalisation of elementary education (UEE), vocationalisation of education, removal of illiteracy, qualitative improvement of school and higher, particularly technical education, or of establishment of institutions of excellence unless a system is evolved for allocation of funds on the basis of an objective determination of norms of per unit cost in various streams.

4.50 In addition to facing these issues, it appears necessary that adequate thought should be given to the scope of raising funds for education; by levy of appropriate cess on consumption or imports; earmarking of resources for manpower development in all large projects; and mobilization of private resources. It will also have to be decided as to what should be the proportion between Central and State funding and what steps should be taken for the enforcement of earmarking conditions for various educational programmes. As the major reason for those who are opting out of education at the school level is poverty, it would be unrealistic to expect them to contribute significantly to resources for education. Secondly, now that education is a concurrent subject, the Central share for education will have to be enhanced; otherwise, it will not be possible to establish any correlation between responsibility and performance. Thirdly, except for school and vocational levels, the pricing of education at other levels will have to be reconsidered and quantum and nature of subsidisation will have to be related either to merit or the dictates of social justice.

Approaches to Resource Mobilisation for Education

4.68 Providing these facilities will involve additional expenses. At least for schools and for institutions of excellence, the expenditure will have to be met fully between the State and Central Governments. In the case of other institutions and the general run of students, excepting, of course, the disadvantaged section who have to be brought at par with others, the possibility of rationalising the fee structure may have to be considered. This will, apart from augmenting internal resources, also change the perception about the value of education.

4.69 Other suggestions received in this connection are: requiring development sectors to allocate a percentage of their budgets for education; including manpower development as an item in the cost structure of public sector projects; realisation of at least a part of the real cost of education in professional institutions from those employing their products; levy of cess on imports; encouraging private entrepreneurs to contribute to educational development, particularly in respect of vocational and professional streams, by giving suitable rebates in taxes; and setting up of training institutions in collaboration with public and private enterprises, a surcharge on land revenue and on municipal house-tax.

4.70 The problem of resources for education has already reached the proportions of a crisis for the Central as well as the State Government. Over the years, despite the recognition of its crucial role in human resource development, education has been treated as a residual sector to be taken care of, largely by the States, out of the resources accruing to them through the Finance Commission awards and Central Assistance for plan expenditure under the modified Gadgil formula. Now, however, education is being encouraged to assume its assigned role in the process of development, a new strategy for raising and sharing resources has, therefore, to be devised. If investing in education is costly, not doing is costlier. A possible approach to this could be the setting up of a high powered joint commission of the Centre and States for studying the problem of resources for education and working out a strategy for mobilising these on a long-term basis.

12

NATIONAL POLICY ON EDUCATION, 1986*

Introduction

The then Prime Minister Rajiv Gandhi in his broadcast to the Nation on January 5, 1985, declared that a new education policy would be formulated that would equip the country both scientifically and economically to enter the 21st century. He observed:

> "Education must promote national cohesion and the work ethic. The grandeur of our freedom struggle and its significance for national integration have to be brought home to every student. Our schools and colleges should acquaint the younger generations with India's ancient heritage and culture. The curricula and textbooks should curb parochial and communal interpretations of our composite culture".

He further remarked:

> "I would strongly emphasise education's organic link with the productive forces of society. We shall reorganise vocational education to align it with industry, agriculture, communications and other productive sectors of our economy."

The then Education Minister, K.C. Pant, presented a 'Status Report' on education to the Prime Minister on 20th August, 1985. The same day, it was presented to Parliament. The 'Status Report' is

---

* *National Policy on Education, 1986*, Ministry of Human Resource Development, Department of Education, Government of India, New Delhi, 1986.

entitled *"Challenge of Education: A Policy Perspective"*. The paper was discussed at various levels and in various forms and was revised in the light of the various observations made. The draft was also debated in the Parliament and finally adopted in the Lok Sabha on May 1, 1986, and the Rajya Sabha on May 12, 1986. Thus, the National Policy on Education (NPE), 1986 emerged. With a view to implementing the NPE, a 'Programme of Action' (1986) was chalked out.

Financial observations, which are contained in Part XI of the NPE, are appended.

Resources and Review*

11.1 The Education Commission of 1964-66, the National Education Policy of 1968 and practically all others concerned with education have stressed that the egalitarian goals and the practical, development-oriented objectives of Indian society can be realised only by making investments in education of an order commensurate with the nature and dimensions of the task.

11.2 Resources, to the extent possible, will be raised by mobilising donations, asking the beneficiary communities to maintain school buildings and supplies of some consumables, raising fees at the higher levels of education and effecting some savings by the efficient use of facilities. Institutions involved with research and the development of technical and scientific manpower should also mobilize some funds by levying a cess or charge on the user agencies, including Government departments, and entrepreneurs. All these measures will be taken not only to reduce the burden on State resources but also for creating a greater sense of responsibility within the educational system. However, such measures will contribute only marginally to the total finding. The Government and the community in general will find funds for such programmes as: the universalisation of elementary education; liquidating illiteracy; equality of access to educational opportunities to all sections throughout the country; enhancing the social relevance, quality and functional effectiveness of educational programmes; generating knowledge and developing technologies in scientific fields crucial to self-sustaining economic development; and creating a critical consciousness of the values and

* Para Numbers refer to paras of the document.

imperatives of national survival.

11.3 The deleterious consequences of non-investment or inadequate investment in education are indeed very serious. Similarly, the cost of neglecting vocational and technical education and of research is also unacceptable. Sub-optimal performance in these fields could cause irreparable damage to the Indian economy. The network of institutions set up from time to time since Independence to facilitate the application of science and technology would need to be substantially and expeditiously updated, since they are fast becoming obsolete.

11.4 In view of these imperatives, education will be treated as a crucial area of investment for national development and survival. The National Policy on Education, 1968, had laid down that the investment on education be gradually increased to reach a level of expenditure of 6 per cent of the national income as early as possible. Since the actual level of investment has remained far short of that target, it is important that greater determination be shown now to find the funds for the programmes laid down in this Policy. While the actual requirements will be computed from time to time on the basis of monitoring and review, the outlay on education will be shaped up to the extent essential for policy implementation in the Seventh Plan. It will be ensured that from the Eighth Five Year Plan onwards it will uniformly exceed to 6 per cent of the National income.

13

PROGRAMME OF ACTION : National Policy on Education, 1986*

Introduction

For the first time in history of education in Independent India, the Government of India itself prepared a 'Programme of Action' for the implementation of National Policy on Education (NPE). Twenty-three Task Forces were constituted and each was assigned a specific topic covered by NPE. Eminent educationists; experts, senior bureaucrats and representatives of the Central and State Governments were associated with these Task Forces. The Task Forces projected the necessary action and indicated the broad targets. They submitted their reports in July 1986. The reports were further considered in a series of meetings of the Education Secretaries of the State Governments and the Union Territories and of the Central Advisory Board of Education. The Lok Sabha and the Rajya Sabha discussed and approved POA on August 22 and 23, 1986, respectively.

Chapter XIV of the Programme of Action deals with Management and Planning of Education. This is appended.

Training of Educational Planners, Administrators and Heads of Institutions**

16. Educational planning and management requires separate identity and separate attention; special schemes for research and development in this area will be launched as soon as possible.

17. In addition to specialised institutions at the national and State

* Ministry of Human Resource Development, Department of Education, Government of India, New Delhi, 1986.

** Para Numbers refer to the paras of Chapter XIV of the document.

levels, for the training of educational administrators and heads of institutions, Institutes of Management and other similar organisations will also be motivated and enabled to take up management development and training programme, as well as policy-oriented research in these areas through documentation of case studies of real life situations and action research for institutional development.

18. Training of senior level personnel will be designed to provide some exposure to educational perspective and the role of education in social development and, in addition, include institutional planning and development, curriculum planning and programme evaluation and review techniques.

19. For Heads of Institutions training in financial rules and procedures, legal provisions governing educational activities, personnel management, programme planning and data management and review techniques will be considered essential.

20. Before training is initiated, the objectives of the training programme for various categories of personnel like planners, administrators and heads of institutions will be defined in terms of job profiles of various levels of personnel and the required expertise skill and, institutional development.

21. Pre-induction training will be prescribed as an essential requirement for personnel selected as Heads of Institutions. Further, their confirmation in grades of Heads of Institutions will be subject to satisfactory completion of periods of probation as may be prescribed in the relevant recruitment rules.

Machinery for Implementation at District Level

22. District Boards of Education will be set up with the responsibility for implementation of all educational programmes including, school, non-formal and adult education up to the higher secondary level. The Boards will also be vested with the responsibility for planning which would include inter alia, area development, spatial planning, institutional planning, administrative and financial control and personnel management with respect to primary, middle, secondary and higher secondary schools.

23. The District Boards will be required to formulate development strategies and plan educational activities of these institutions mentioned for the entire district. These plans will, interalia, look into the settlement pattern of the habitations, distribution of educational

institutions, the demographic profile and projections. The District Educational Plans will also go into the levels of participation and retention of boys and girls under different age groups by socio-cultural and economic categories and plan for measures for ensuring not only for physical infrastructure and a more equitable access to all but also for the qualitative aspects of education.

24. The need for ensuring that the decisions at the State level regarding various educational programmes should invariably take into account the plans drawn up and suggestions put forward at the district level would call for special emphasis.

25. Considering the planning and management model envisaged, and their functions, unless the District Boards of Education are vested with appropriate statutory authority, these bodies cannot effectively manage the functions entrusted to them.

26. In such States where administration and management of education already constitute the responsibility of Panchayat Raj bodies, the composition of the District Boards of Education will in consonance with the existing management structure of the Panchayat Raj bodies. In States where Panchayat Raj institutions are not in existence, the composition of the District Boards of Education will take into account the need for representation of educationists, women, youth representative of parents, Scheduled Caste/Scheduled Tribes, minorities and interests of representative institutions in the district if any.

27. In order that the District Boards of Education discharge the functions allotted, it would be necessary to assign State funds for implementation of the various programmes. Provision will also be made while constituting the statutory authority to enable the District Boards of Education to raise their own resources. Some un-earmarked funds will also be placed at the disposal of the District Boards by the State Governments so that District Boards can use these resources for any purpose that may be considered essential by raising matching funds of their own.

28. The relationship of the State Government with the District Boards of Education in terms of administrative and financial control and personnel management vis-a-vis primary, middle, secondary and higher secondary levels will need to be clearly spelt out in appropriate guidelines to be issued by the State Governments. It will also be necessary to spell out clearly the levels of recruitment and structure of cadres of teachers of different categories. The State

Governments will take the measures required to constitute District cadres of elementary school teachers.

29. There will be a Chief Education Officer for the District to look after all levels of education — primary, middle and secondary. Under him there will be a District Education Officer looking after establishment, budgeting, planning and the educational database. In addition there will be district level official of appropriate rank engaged in specific educational programme.

30. Implementation of different educational programmes at the District level, will be supervised and monitored by the District Boards of Education which will oversee all aspects of educational development.

31. Monitoring of all educational programmes for implementation in the district will take place at the State level and relevant indicators to establish inter-district comparison will need to be worked out.The resources to be transferred to the District will be linked to the performance and achievement.

32. For ensuring quality of education in educational institutions at different levels, considerations will be given to appointment of District Inspectors of Education to look after academic functions exclusively. Such functionaries who will be selected with due regard to their understanding of the academic functions to be performed, will be responsible for looking after the academic standards in educational institutions, provide academic leadership and help in better performance of their academic functions by heads of institutions and teachers.

33. The District Institute of Education & Training (DIET) under the District Board will be responsible for making substantive curricular and pedagogic inputs into all programmes of education at the district level and will also be responsible for training of personnel and provision of resource support to programmes including adult education.

Machinery for Implementation at Local Levels

34. Consistent with the important role assigned to the heads of institutions, their selection should be done with due care. It is essential that there should be fixed term of appointment for the head of the institution and transfer should be kept to the minimum to enable the head of the institution to exercise a leadership role and make his con-

tribution to the development of the institution.

35. The head of the institution particularly at the primary/middle school level will be made accountable to the Village Education Committee of which he will be a member in respect of running of his institution.

36. A Village Education Committee comprising not more than 15 members with representatives from parents, Panchayats, cooperatives, women, Scheduled Castes/Scheduled Tribes, minorities and local development functionaries will be constituted to look into the over-all management of all educational programmes at the village level.

37. The State Governments will lay down general guidelines regarding the constitution of the Village Education Committee and establish norms of accountability in respect of head of the institution at the village level to this Committee. Accountability will be established also in respect of programmes like Early Childhood care Education (ECCE), elementary education, ICDS, non-formal education, adult and continuing education.

Promotion of School Complexes

38. School complexes as network of institutions on a flexible pattern will be promoted to provide synergic alliances to encourage professionalism among teachers, ensure observance of norms and conduct and enable the sharing of experiences and facilities. The school complex will serve as the lowest viable unit of area planning and will form a cluster of 8-10 institutions in which different institutions can reinforce each other by exchanging resources, personnel, material, teaching aids etc. and using them on a sharing basis.

39. It is expected that in course of time, school complexes when fully developed, will take over much of the inspection functions. The inspection functions of school complexes will be performed keeping in view the needs to bring in greater cohesion among the participating schools and will include *inter alia*:

> educational mapping, grading of institutions and identifying strength and weakness of individual schools. Inspection to be conducted will invoke a culture of participation and providing correctives rather than the existing practice of finding faults. These inspections will be in addition to the normal routine inspection

functions of District/Block level inspecting authorities.

40. The State Governments may lay down necessary guidelines for qualitative inspections to be undertaken by the school complex and also specify the nature of quantitative data required in respect of each institution and each complex for inspection purposes.

41. Considering that many of the schools which will form part of the complex will be non-governmental institutions, the State Governments may make necessary provision of funds for facilitating the work of school complexes including trains, resource support travel costs as well as allowances for inspection.

42. Immediate preparatory action to implement the above suggestions will require to be taken so that appropriate guidelines for development of school complexes could be issued by the State Governments and the school complexes could become operational in the year 1987.

People's Participation and Involvement of Voluntary Agencies

43. The successful implementation of programmes like elementary education including non-formal education, early childhood care and education (ECCE), adult education, education of the disabled, etc. will require people's involvement and participation in educational programmes at the grass-root level and participation of voluntary agencies and social activist groups on a much larger scale. Considering the need for ensuring relationship of the genuine partnership between the Government and voluntary agencies, Government will take positive steps to promote their wider involvements. Consultations will be held with them from time to time and representation given to them on bodies responsible for making decision in respect of them. They will be assured necessary facilities to participate in implementation of programmes and procedures for selection of voluntary agencies and of financial assistance will be streamlined to enable the voluntary agencies to play optimal role.

Phasing of Requirements and Advance Preparatory Action

Requirement of Resources

44. The Plan of Action relating to Management of Education will require to be prepared at the State and local levels — village, block, and

district. The State Governments will be required to work out these details and issue necessary guidelines for developing a multi-level planning model with decentralisation and autonomy.

45. It is essential that involvement of the local communities in the management of educational institutions in rural areas is ensured and the school complexes should commence from the year 1986-87.

46. Keeping this in view, the State Governments will consider giving necessary powers to the Boards of Secondary Education to earmark funds for developing multi-level planning models for management of education, and development of school complexes.

14

DRAFT APPROACH TO EIGHTH FIVE YEAR PLAN, 1990*

Introduction

The meeting of the National Development Council held on 18-19 June, 1990 discussed the approach paper entitled *'Towards Social Transformation'*, which was prepared when the National Front Government headed by Shri V.P. Singh was in power. Its introduction begins with these words:

> "The people of India have once again shown great democratic awareness. They have signalled their powerful desire for change. Their mandate calls for an alternative model of development within the framework of national planning. . . . There is urgent need to remove the sources of discontent and unrest by attending to unemployment, illiteracy, ill-health and decline in living conditions of the poor and vulnerable sections".

With the fall of the National Front Government, the document also lost its identity.

Paras 58, 59 and 60 of the approach paper dealing with Education are reproduced here:

Education

58. Crucial to the evolution of an equitable and decentralised social order is a thorough revamping of the educational system. This is necessary both for realizing the goal of greater equity and for providing the necessary technical inputs at various levels. We need to make

* Planning Commission, Government of India, New Delhi, May 1990.

education less of a passport to privilege and access to white collar jobs and more as a means to enhance the capabilities of people as citizens and as producers. This calls for two simultaneous emphases. First, there is need to give greater priority to mass literacy and elementary and secondary education, as against the tendency to divert resources to ever higher levels of education which has produced the socially volatile phenomenon of educated unemployed. Second, there is need for greater emphasis on technical and vocational aspects of education in place of the present accent on general education which pushes the educated from rural areas to migrate to the cities. The economy suffers from both a surfeit of the highly educated and major shortages of relevant technical manpower, particularly in rural areas and small towns where transport, servicing of infrastructure and simple things like repair of pumpsets and construction or maintenance of drainage and sanitation system suffer from lack of requisite skills.

59. Beyond these specific reorientations there is the need to move away from thinking of education as an autonomous sector and locating it in the larger agenda of social transformation. The habit of thinking of education only in terms of financial allocations and quantitative expansion should be given up. The focus should instead be on getting the people and the community actively involved in it. One main reason why even minimum objectives like raising literacy levels of both the younger generation and the adult population, and urgent needs like attending to women's education, have not been achieved is that they have not been given the necessary political backing and made an integral part of a larger social movement. The kind of all out effort that has been evident in Ernakulam is what we now need a movement for "education for all" in which all citizens and all major institutions feel involved.

60. There is at present a serious mismatch between the supply of educational resources and institutions and the demand, particularly in rural areas where the rates of absenteeism and dropout are very high. This has resulted among other things in a lot of wastage of resources: more and more schools may get opened but, the response of the people being lukewarm, they only give rise to so much real estate (as with primary health centres) without either teachers or students using them. There is little feeling among the people that these are their schools for their children. Only when this happens will it be possible to keep the "demand" for education in pace with the "supply",

indeed make the former a pressure for more and better education, relevant to people's needs (which very often it is not at present) and of requisite quality (which has been steadily declining). It will also bring about a more balanced distribution of educational resources. The stress will shift to the lower tiers of the educational pyramid from the starting of new colleges and universities as status symbols. What matters are quality and relevance rather than quantitative targets.

15

EDUCATION FOR ALL : Indian Perspective, 1990*

Introduction

Education for All by 2000 is a study of various aspects of basic education in the context of the Indian situation. It attempts to indicate possible directions in which India should move, to achieve this goal and as such not a final plan of action. The study highlights the basic education requirements as one of the survival needs of the country and takes into account socio-economic-cultural milieu and the status of the present position. In this context, it attempts to lay emphasis on the special requirements of different disadvantaged groups such as women, Scheduled Castes and Scheduled Tribes. The process of education including content, evaluation and teacher education are examined and discussed. A broad estimation of resource requirements has also been attempted.

Full text of Chapter 13 entitled *'Resources for Education'* is appended.

Resources for Education[1]

Inadequacy of resources constitutes a major bottleneck in realising

---

* National Institute of Educational Planning and Administration, New Delhi, 1990.

Notes:

1. (i) All figures, including costs and norms, are based on official (published and unpublished) sources of the Ministry of Human Resource Development, Department of Education.
   (ii) Original Table numbers have been changed to conform to this Chapter number.

any plan targets. Elementary education suffered in India, apart from several factors, because of insufficient allocation of financial resources. While finances are an important constraint, they are not the only constraint, but one among many. Resources are a neccssary, although not a sufficient, condition in achieving the educational goals.

A quick glance at the trends in public expenditure on education shows that over the years, it has increased as a proportion of GNP. At the inception of planning (1950-51) India was spending 1.2 per cent of GNP on education, and according to the latest available statistics (1986-87), this increased to approximately 4 per cent. The share of elementary education also increased from an insignificant level of 0.48 per cent of GNP in 1950-51 to 1.7 per cent in 1986-87 (Table 15.1).

TABLE 15.1: Secorwise Share of Education in GNP (Percentage), 1950-51 to 1986-87

	Total	Primary	Upper Primary	Elementary
1950-51	1.2	0.40	0.08	0.48
1960-61	2.5	0.45	0.31	0.76
1970-71	3.1	0.65	0.47	1.12
1980-81	3.1	0.71	0.48	1.19
1984-85*	3.7	—	—	1.77
1985-86@	4.0	—	—	1.87
1986-87+	3.9	—	—	1.68

Notes: * Budget Expenditure (Actual)
@ Budget Expenditure (Revised Estimates)
+ Budget Expenditure (Budget Estimates)

While these increases arc indeed significant, they are much below the actual requirements of the system; and the total educational expenditure as a proportion of GNP is far below the general target of six per cent.

While universalisation of elementary education has been becoming an increasingly tough task, causing repeated postponement of the goal, the relative priority given to elementary education in the total educational expenditures has been gradually declining over the successive five-year plans.

It was only during the First Five Year Plan that elementary education was allocated a sizeable proportion of the total educational outlay: it was 56 per cent. During the subsequent five-year plans this proportion has been constantly declining. In the Seventh Five Year Plan a meagre 29 per cent of the educational outlay was allocated for elementary education (Table 15.2).

TABLE 15.2: Share of Education in Five Year Plan Outlays/Expenditures: (Percentage), First Plan to Seventh Plan.

	Share of Education in Total Plan Expenditure/Outlay (%)	Percentage Share in Total Education Outlay of Ist Plan to 7th Plan	
		Elementary Education	Adult Education
First Five Year Plan	7.86	56	3
Second Five Year Plan	5.83	3	2
Third Five Year Plan	6.87	34	Negl.
Annual Five Year Plan	4.86	24	Negl.
Fourth Five Year Plan	5.04	30	1
Fifth Five Year Plan	3.27	35	2
Sixth Five Year Plan	2.70	30	4
Seventh Five Year Plan	3.55	29	6

These 'plan' outlays are meant for further development of education. On the other hand, 'non-plan' expenditure on education, that is generally meant for maintenance of the system is very substantial. It is not only with respect to the plan outlays, the total, plan plus non-plan, expenditure on elementary education as a proportion of total educational expenditure also declined. The share of elementary (that includes primary and upper primary levels) education in the total (direct/recurring) expenditure on education declined from 48 per cent in 1950-51 to 40 per cent in 1980-81. The share of primary education declined sharply from 40 per cent in 1950-51 to 24 per cent in 1980-81 (Table 15.3).

While the share of upper primary education justifiably increased, the relative increase in the share of upper primary education is not as pronounced as the relative decrease in the share of primary education. It is now recognised that secondary education also did not benefit; it is only higher education that benefited more at the cost of primary education.

TABLE 15.3: Share of Elementary Education in the Total (Direct/Recurring) Expenditure on Education, 1950-51 to 1986-87

(Percentage)

	Primary	Upper Primary	Elementary
1950-51	40	8	48
1960-61	25	17	42
1970-71	2	1	43
1980-81	24	16	40
1984-85*	—	—	40
1985-86@	—	—	47
1986-87+	—	—	47

Notes: * Budget Expenditure (Actual)
@ Budget Expenditure (Revised Estimates)
+ Budget Expenditure (Budget Estimates)

Much of the growth in expenditure on elementary education, as in the case of most other sectors, had been offset by an increase in prices, and a rapid increase in population, student numbers in particular. In real prices, the increase in expenditure on elementary education has been quite modest. Compared to 105 times increase in current prices between 1950-51 and 1986-87, the real increase has been only by 13 times (Table 15.4).

TABLE 15.4: Direct/Recurring Expenditure on Elementary Education, 1950-51 to 1986-87

(Rs. in millions)

	Primary	Upper Primary	Elementary
At Current Prices			
1950-51	366	77	443
1960-61	630	429	1059
1970-71	2365	1709	4074
1980-81	8156	5511	13667
1984-85*	—	—	36601
1985-86@	—	—	43572
1986-87+	—	—	46791
At 1950-51 Prices			
1950-51	366	77	443
1960-61	580	396	976
1970-71	1147	829	1976
1980-81	1613	1090	2703
1984-85*	—	—	5184
1985-86@	—	—	5784
1986-87+	—	—	5899

Notes: * Budget Expenditure (Actual)
@ Budget Expenditure (Revised Estimates)
+ Budget Expenditure (Budget Estimates)

In expenditure per student, the system is managing with more or less the same amount of money in real terms in 1950-51 and 1980-81, years for which comparable figures are readily available. In fact, between 1970-71 and 1980-81 recurring expenditure per student on primary education declined from Rs. 27 to Rs. 20 (at 1950-51 prices), and so also, on elementary education from Rs. 31 to Rs. 27, suggesting that we spent in 1980-81 much less money per pupil on elementary education than in 1970-71 (Table 15.5). The trends in the 1980s indicate that they are likely to be reversed.

TABLE 15.5: Direct/Recurring Expenditure Per Student, 1950-51 to 1986-87

(in Rupees)

	Primary	Upper Primary	Elementary
At Current Prices			
1950-51	19.9	37.1	21.6
1960-61	27.6	40.5	31.7
1970-71	57.0	84.9	66.1
1980-81	110.5	266.0	144.6
1984-85	—	—	333.9
1985-86	—	—	380.2
1986-87	—	—	394.3
At 1950-51 Prices			
1950-51	19.9	37.1	21.6
1960-61	23.8	34.9	27.3
1970-71	27.0	40.3	31.4
1980-81	20.4	49.2	26.7
1984-85*	—	—	46.9
1985-86@	—	—	50.5
1986-87+	—	—	49.7

Notes: * Budget Expenditure (Actual)
@ Budget Expenditure (Revised Estimates)
+ Budget Expenditure (Budget Estimates)

But the negative or insignificant positive growth of real expenditure must have affected educational inputs both quantitatively and qualitatively. This should be of very serious concern.

All this implies that there is need to step up the level of total resources to be allocated for education, even to maintain the present levels of quality of education.

FUTURE REQUIREMENTS

Elementary Education

According to population projections, the target population for elementary education, i.e., of the age group 6-14, will be 163 million in A.D. 2000; 102 million of the age group 6-11 and 61million of the age group 11-14. How much would it cost to provide primary education to 95 per cent of children of the age group 6-11 and upper primary education to 80 per cent of children of the 11-14 age group, as pragmatically suggested in this document? It is proposed that 70 per cent of the children will be provided formal education and the remaining 30 per cent will have to be covered by non-formal education. Further, it is felt that the number of over- and underage children in elementary education would come down gradually, to levels of 25 per cent in primary education and 15 per cent in upper primary education.

In the absence of recent estimates on expenditure per student, we shall consider here the salary of teachers in estimating the requirement of resources. After all, teachers' salaries constitute about 95 per cent of the total recurring expenditure. The average salary of teachers in primary school is found to be Rs. 24,000 per annum and in the upper primary school Rs. 36,000 per annum. Assuming teacher-pupil ratios of 40 and 35 in primary and upper primary schools respectively, the total number of teachers required in A.D. 2000 is estimated at 2.1 million in primary and 1.1 million in upper primary schools. Accordingly the teacher costs worked out to Rs. 91.2 thousand million – Rs. 50.9 thousand million in primary schools and Rs. 40.3 thousand million in upper primary schools. To this, we add 5 per cent non-teaching recurring cost, i.e., Rs. 0.46 thousand million. Thus the total recurring cost amounts to Rs. 91.7 thousand million.

Now, this is only recurring expenditure, and it does not cover expenditure on capital items; it also does not make any allowance for improvement in the quality of education. This is the level of resources required.for elementary education by A.D. 2000.

One may briefly note that the additional resources required, in the context of several measures of improvement in quality as suggested in the present document, would be quite substantial. The Working Group on Resources for Education for the Eighth Five Year Plan (1990-95) has estimated the requirements for a few such items. The Group estimated the indirect expenditure on administration and supervision, quality improvement, stipends, scholarship and other incentives, at Rs. 2,067 million, the cost of construction of classroom for additional children at Rs. 11,095 million, and the cost of construction of the backlog of schools, based on the Fifth All India Educational Survey, at Rs. 38,561 million. In addition, for Operation Black-board, an additional amount of Rs. 15,139 million was estimated as the requirement, and in all Rs. 88 thousand million. It is assumed that during 1995-2000 an additional amount of Rs. 23 thousand million would be required. Thus on an average, Rs. 11.2 thousand million would be required for formal elementary education as non-recurring expenditure every year during 1990-2000. These estimates exclude normal recurring expenditure in the form of teacher cost etc., that we have estimated separately.

Thus in all, putting recurring and non-recurring expenditures together, elementary education requires about Rs. 800 thousand million during the next ten years; in other words the total expenditure should gradually increase to Rs. 103 thousand million in A.D. 2000 at 1989-90 prices.

Non-formal Education

It is being planned that 30 per cent of the children of the age group 6-14 would be provided education through the non-formal channel.

We believe that the non-formal system of education should be comparable with formal system as far as the quality and content are concerned. Then only vertical mobility of the students into the formal system of education would be possible. This obviously requires ore resources.

At present it is estimated by the Ministry of Human Resource Development (Department of Education), that a centre for non-formal education costs about Rs. 12,000 per year and it provides education to 20 students. Within two yeas of non-formal education, one is expected to have acquired an education equivalent to compulsory elementary education. The unit cost of non-formal education for two years per student works out to Rs. 1,200 (at current 1989-90 prices). Accordingly it is estimated that non-formal education will require Rs. 52.6 thousand million in A.D. 2000 at 1989-90 prices. It amounts to about Rs. 500 thousand million for the 10 yeas until A.D. 2000.

In all, the requirements of elementary education, including non-formal education, in A.D. 2000 would be of the order of Rs. 156 thousand million at 1989-90 prices. Given the earlier trends, it seems to be a gigantic task. Between 1960-61 and 1970-71, the real expenditure on elementary education was nearly doubled; and between 1970-71 and 1980-81 it increased by about 40%. The present estimates suggest that these trends would be substantially reversed : the total expenditure should be doubled by the turn of the century.

Adult Education

The 15-35 age group constitutes the most productive work force. Constrained by resources made available to the education sector, adult education programmes have been confined to this age group only. On the basis of the projections of population, we had in 1986, 259 million adults (15-35 age group) among whom 151 million were literates, and 108 million illiterates. By 2000 the total population in this age group is likely to increase to 364 million. They need to be made literate through adult education programmes.

In the absence of reliable estimates of costs per head, it is assumed, as suggested by the Ministry of Human Resource Development (Department of Education), that an amount of Rs. 200 will have to be invested per head to make one person functionally literate, which means that on average, each year, we would require Rs. 4,200 million at 1989-90 prices to provide literacy to about 21 million persons each year.

It might be necessary to provide organised post-literacy education to the newly turned literates, lest they relapse into illiteracy. However, this is not being explicitly planned here, except marginally through the *Jana Shikshan Nilayams,* discussed below. Thus, our estimates on literacy programmes form a bare minimum level of resources required.

Continuing Education

It is proposed in this document that all literates should be provided with opportunities to improve their skills. *Jana Shikshan Nilayams,* and public libraries, along with extensive use of the media are proposed in this context. It is felt that every 50 villages should have a *Jana Shikshan Nilayam,* and that at least every block should have a good public library that will provide learning materials to the people. This means that during the next ten years 10,000 *Jana Shikshan Nilayams* and 5,000 public libraries have to be created. According to the estimates of the Ministry of Human Resource Development (Department of Education), a *Jana Shikshan Nilayam* would cost Rs. 7,000 per year as recurring expenditure, besides Rs. 7,000 as non-recurring expenditure. Similarly, a public library would cost Rs. 50,000 as non-recurring expenditure, and Rs. 25,000 every year as recurring expenditure. Accordingly the total resources required are estimated at about Rs. 1.4 thousand million.

Thus the requirement of resources for a few major programmes is estimated here. It should also be noted that the estimates are based on crude and quick calculations. More importantly, these estimates allow for mere enrolment in the system by A.D. 2000. Hence they should be viewed as the minimum level of resources required.

It is clear that, the estimates made here do not cover several programmes and policies suggested in this document, such as training of teachers, administrators, voluntary agencies, mothers, community leaders, public provision of incentives to school children, particularly of the weaker sections, establishment of special organisations like National Testing Service at Central, State, and district levels, district boards of education, village education committees, school complexes, and mechanisms of monitoring, etc. These are only illustrative. If one were to cost each item, assuming that reliable estimates of unit costs of the items are available, it is likely that the actual level of requirement of resources would be of a very high order.

While every effort should be made to generate additional resources for education, it is also required that non-conventional strategies need to be devised in mobilising and effectively utilising monetary, physical, and human resources. As an example, a few strategies relating to human resources are outlined below. However, it may be noted that these strategies do not necessarily mean that the level of resources required for education could be substantially lowered.

Human Resources

The stupendous task of Education for All will require massive human resources. For this, we will have to diversify the sources. Some of them are as follows:

The local community is a tremendous fund of human resources, if imaginatively used. Our present approach to looking towards outside sources will have to change to enable us to properly identify and utilise the local human resources. The teachers and instructors for NFE and adult education can be drawn from the community. They will have a grater motivation and involvement. Volunteers from the community can be identified and their assistance obtained. Persons in the community with special skills and expertise can be identified and used as resource persons for development of those specified skills.

The concept of Village Education Committee also reflects the utilisation of local human resources for management and supervision, which the existing hierarchical and bureaucratic system is unable to perform satisfactorily. In framing curriculum and preparation of textual materials, we are adopting a decentralised approach and also desire that the local needs and environment should be properly linked.

The support of voluntary organisations and social action groups may be enlisted for motivating and enabling the community to get fully involved in EFA, working as a catalyst for changing the culture of educational management in which community and teachers will have a more central role and to identify, promote, and encourage more voluntary groups and social activists in areas where they are required. A well-designed policy to approach the human resources in colleges, universities, research institutions, and other institutions of higher learning, national laboratories, etc., and to motivate them to spare their free time and knowledge for elementary education is required. There is a number of other important sources from which valuable human resources can be drawn for educational effort, including educated people.

CONCLUDING OBSERVATIONS

It will be against the spirit of the Constitution to allow elementary education to suffer from inadequacy of resources. As far as funding elementary education and literacy programmes is concerned, it should be viewed in the framework of the Constitution. It is not just the Department of Education, but all the government departments which should be made to allocate substantial resources for elementary education, as no sector can develop significantly with illiterate masses. In fact, the whole nation should feel responsible for the development of education in the country.

In the system of central planning we are used to in this country, only the resources required from the government or public sector agencies are taken into account. However, for an activity like education, there are considerable costs borne by the children and their parents. Individuals have to spend on books, stationery, uniform, transport, etc. These costs are not included in the financial implications presented here, except for the provision of incentives like books and uniforms to the weaker sections. The Constitution has directed that education for children in primary and upper primary levels of education should be free. This has been so far taken, in practice, to mean that schools should not charge any fees. The cost incurred by parents for education of their children has been ignored and has not been considered as a violation of the directive of free education. In view of the paucity of resources, it may be pragmatic to continue this approach and let the parents bear costs of this nature, while underscoring that ideally these costs should be borne by public funds.

We may also have to move from the concept of exclusive responsibility of the government for education to shared responsibility between the government and the community. This would not be difficult, keeping in view the tradition in India of community support to education from ancient times. This will also be consistent with the general approach of decentralisation, community involvement, and people's participation, which we have strongly advocated in this document. While community support will take a variety of forms, in different States and parts of the country, some areas where the role of the community would be most significant are construction and maintenance of school buildings based on local design and local material, supply of local material for preparation of teaching-aids, locally made educational toys and other learning material, and the running of early childhood care and education centres with the help of local women, and using the primary school building or any other public building or appropriate place provided by the community. The scope for better utilisation of non-financial resources available within and outside the education system should be explored, and the provision for meeting the cost to utilise them, which would obviously be small, should be made.

Serious efforts should be initiated to encourage individuals and organisations through tax incentives and other measures to make large endowments and donations to the education sector. However, given the earlier experience, mobilisation of cheap local resources, revision of the fee structure in higher education, and voluntary donations and endowments, etc., should be viewed only as peripheral sources of mobilisation of additional resources for marginal improvements in the system. After all, they cannot become primary and reliable sources of revenue for large scale improvements in the system. The government cannot but continue taking more responsibility for elementary education.

For safeguarding democracy and strengthening the foundations of the integrated nation, it is necessary not to compromise with the requirements of these basic needs in education. It should be noted that without adequate resources, financial, physical, and human, our target of Education for All will remain unachieved even by the turn of the century. If we have to enter the twenty-first century without the burden of the unfulfilled goals originally proposed by the Constitution-makers of India, substantial resources should be allocated to elementary and adult education programmes.

16

COMMITTEE TO REVIEW THE NATIONAL POLICY ON EDUCATION (1986), 1991*

The National Front Government formed in 1989 decided to review the implementation of the National Policy on Education, in terms of its election manifesto. It, therefore, appointed on May 7, 1990, a committee with Acharya Ramamurti as its Chairman. The Committee submitted its report entitled 'Towards an Enlightened and Humane Society' to the Minister of State in the Ministry of Human Resource Development on December 26, 1990. The report was tabled in Parliament on January 9, 1991. Among other observations and recommendations, the Committee went into the different aspects of resources for education. Action could not be taken on the report as the National Front Government was very short-lived.

Terms of Reference

The terms of reference were:

- To review the National Policy on Education, 1986, and its implementation;
- to make recommendations regarding the revision of the Policy; and
- to recommend action necessary for implementation of the revised policy within a time frame.

Extracts from Government of India Resolution No. F.1-6/90-PN (D.I.) dated 7th May, 1990, regarding appointment of the Committee if reproduced below.

---

* *Towards an Enlightened and Humane Society: NPE, 1986, A Review*, Part I (1990). Committee for Review of National Policy on Education, Government of India, New Delhi, 1991.

"Despite efforts at social and economic development since attainment of Independence, a majority of our people continue to remain deprived of education, which is one of the basic needs for human development. It is also a matter of grave concern that our people comprise 50 per cent of the world's illiterate, and large sections of children have to go without acceptable level of primary education. Government accords the highest priority to education -- both as a human right and as the means for bringing about a transformation towards a more humane and enlightened society. There is need to make education an effective instrument for securing a status of equality for women, and persons belonging to the backward classes and minorities. Moreover, it is essential to give a work and employment orientation to education and to exclude from it the elitist aberrations which have become the glaring characteristic of the educational scene. Educational institutions are increasingly being influenced by casteism, communalism and obscurantism and it is necessary to lay special emphasis on struggle against this phenomenon and to move towards a genuinely egalitarian and secular social order. The National Policy on Education, 1986 (NPE), needs to be reviewed to evolve a framework which would enable the country to move towards this perspective of education."

RESOURCES FOR EDUCATION[1]

Background

15.1.0 Education has tended to be given comparatively lower priority in the matter of sectoral allocation of resources. Allocation for education cannot be wholly treated either as investment outlay or as consumption outlay. Gestation period for investment in education to yield results is also too long. Difficulties are encountered in accurately estimating or quantifying the returns on investment in education. Reason is that the functional relationship between inputs and outputs in education is indeterminate. The net result is that, in India also as in other developing economies, education is treated as a social service sector and often gets for itself only the residual

1. (i) Para Numbers refer to the paras of the document.
(ii) Original Table Numbers have seen changed to conform to this Chapter number.

resources after allocations to the so-called productive sectors.

15.2.0 Though education has been in the Concurrent List in the Constitution since 1976, it remains primarily a State activity. Bulk of the investments is made by the State Governments. Free and compulsory education is expected to be provided by the States for all children up to 14 years of age. In most States education is free in the entire school stage. Up to class XII education is free for girls in all the States. The fee structure for higher education in the colleges and universities has virtually remained unchanged for many years. The pattern of educational development has, consequently, come to be dependent on the availability of public resources for education. On account of increasing resource crunch, however, share of Education in plan allocations has been declining over the years. Allocations have come to be sub-optimal. Table 16.3 below may be seen for share of Education in Five Year Plan outlays/expenditures.

Present Picture regarding Funding of Education in India

15.3.1 Education is now funded by various sources – Central and State Governments, local bodies and private contributions. Data on source-wise contribution of finance to Education in India (as far as they are available) are furnished in Table 16.1 below:

TABLE 16.1: Source-wise Contribution of Finances to Education, 1950-51 to 1980-81

(Percentage)

	1950-51	1960-61	1970-71	1980-81
Government Sector				
Central and State Governments	57.10	68.00	75.60	80.00
Local Governments (Zilla Parishads, Municipalities, Panchayats)	10.90	6.50	5.70	5.00
Private Sector				
Fees	20.40	11.20	12.80	12.00
Endowments etc.	11.60	8.30	5.90	3.00
Total	100.00 (114.00)	100.00 (344.40)	100.00 (1118.30)	100.00 (4687.50)

Note: Figures in brackets – in crores of rupees.
Source: *NIEPA Journal*, July-October, 1987.

15.3.2 It may be seen from Table 16.1 that the Central and State Governments account for the bulk of the funding of Education in India. The share of the private sector is quite small and that of local bodies almost negligible.

15.4.1 Presented in the following Table (Table 16.2) is the picture regarding Central and State share in Plan expenditure:

TABLE 16.2: Contribution of Centre and the States to Plan Expenditure on Education (Percentage) First Plan to Seventh Plan

Five Year Plan	Central Govt.	State Govt.	Total
First	25	75	100 (153)
Second	25	75	100 (273)
Third	26	74	100 (589)
Fourth	33	67	100 (823)
Fifth	30	70	100 (930)
Sixth	30	70	100 (2945)
Seventh	37	63	100 (6383)

Note: Figures in parentheses are in crores of rupees.
Source: Five Year Plans.

15.4.2 Table 16.2 would show that during the Fifth and Sixth Plans, Central share came down from the level of the Fourth Plan. Of course, during the Seventh Plan, the share has increased.

15.5.0 More often, Plan expenditure is lesser than the original outlays as may be seen from the following Table 16.3.

15.6.1 Table 16.4 brings out the position regarding Centre-State partnership in financing non-plan expenditure on Education:

15.6.2 Table 16.4 would show that the share of the Central Government in non-plan expenditure has come down to 6 per cent during the Sixth Five Year Plan, State Governments' share having gone up to 94 per cent.

15.7.0 While the share of Education in the revenue budget is reasonably high, on the Capital side its share is almost negligible. The share of Education in Central budget as a percentage of Revenue and Capital expenditure is only 1.7 per cent. In the budgets of States and UTs, the share is 18.9 per cent. In this context, Table 16.5 may be seen.

TABLE 16.3: Differences* between Plan Outlays and Expenditure in Education: First Plan to Seventh Plan

(Rupees in crores)

Five Year Plan	Outlay	Expenditure	Column (2) - (3)	Column (4) as % of (2)
1	2	3	4	5
First	170 (17.2)	153 (7.9)	-17	-10.00
Second	177 (6.2)	273 (5.8)	+96	+54.23
Third	560 (7.5)	589 (6.9)	+29	+15.20
Fourth	822 (5.2)	786 (5.0)	-36	-4.40
Fifth	1284 (3.3)	930 (3.2)	-354	-27.60
Sixth	2524 (2.6)	2835 (2.6)	+311	+12.30
Seventh	3230 (3.9)	2998 (3.6)	-232	-7.20

Note: ( ) % to total plan outlay/expenditure.

* Difference occurred on account of more or less resources made available through the annual plans during the Plan periods and also on account of actual performance.

Source: *A Handbook of Education and Allied Statistics: Economic Survey 1984-85*, Ministry of Human Resource Development, Department of Education, Government of India.

TABLE 16.4: Centre-State Partnership in Financing Non-Plan Expenditure on Education, Second Plan to Seventh Plan

(per cent)

Five Year Plan	Central Govt.	State Govt.	Total
Second	14	86	100 (577)
Third	16	84	100 (1056)
Fourth	4	96	100 (4820)
Fifth	6	94	100 (8009)
Sixth	6	94	100 (23434)
Seventh	6	94	100 (44913)

Note: Figures in parentheses are in crores of rupees.

Source: Department of Education, Ministry of Human Resource Development, Government of India.

TABLE 16.5: Budget Expenditure (Actual) on Education by Education and other Departments, 1985-86

	Expenditure (Rs. in crores)	Total expenditure on all sectors (Rs. in crores)	% of total Budget
Centre			
Revenue	528.50	33384.00	1.6
Capital	—	8899.60	—
Loans and advances	2.93	13807.15	—
Total	531.43	56090.75	0.9
State & Union Territories			
Revenue	6928.47	33707.41	20.6
Capital	114.24	5064.30	2.3
Loans and advances	11.83	3711.29	0.3
Total	7054.54	42483.00	16.6
Total			
Revenue	7456.97	67091.41	11.1
Capital	114.24	13963.90	0.8
Loans and advances	14.76	17518.44	0.1
Total	7585.97	98573.75	7.7

Source: *Analysis of budgeted expenditure on education, 1985-86*, Ministry of Human Resource Development, Department of Education, Government of India, New Delhi.

15.8.1 The total Central and State Plan expenditure has also been falling. It was only 3.55 per cent for the seventh plan. Table 16.6 may be seen for data on intra-sectoral resource allocation for Education during the various plans.

The Picture reflected by the Table 16.6 is:

15.8.2 The share of Elementary Education has come down from the level of 56 per cent in First Plan to 29 per cent in the Seventh Plan. The share of Secondary Education has remained somewhat stable with marginal differences – between 13 per cent and 18 per cent. Higher (College and University Education) has expanded over the years – from 9% during the First Plan to 22% in the Fifth Plan. (Of course, share of Higher Education as a percentage of outlay during the Sixth and Seventh Plans has come down to the levels of 19% and 12% respectively.)

15.9.1 The status of household expenditure on Education in India is reflected in Table 16.7.

TABLE 16.6: Intra-Sectoral Resource Allocation for Education in the Five Year Plans in Centre and States of First Plan to Seventh Plan

(Figures in crores of rupees) — (Figures in brackets are in%)

	Expenditure						Outlay	
	1st Plan	2nd Plan	3rd Plan	Plan Holiday	4th Plan	5th Plan	6th Plan	7th Plan +
Elementary*	85	95	201	75	239	317	906	1830
	(56)	(35)	(34)	(24)	(30)	(35)	(36)	(29)
Secondary**	20	51	103	53	140	156	398	1000
	(13)	(19)	(18)	(16)	(18)	(17)	(16)	(16)
University	14	48	87	77	195	205	486	750
	(9)	(18)	(15)	(24)	(25)	(22)	(919)	(12)
Other General	14	30	73	37	106	127	457	2121
	(9)	(10)	(12)	(11)	(14)	(14)	(18)	(33)
Total General	133	224	464	241	680	805	2247	5710
	(87)	(82)	(79)	(75)	(87)	(88)	(890)	(89)
Technical	20	49	125	81	106	107	278	682
	(13)	(18)	(21)	(25)	(13)	(12)	(11)	(11)
Grand Total	153	273	589	322	786	912	2524	6383
	(100)	(100)	(100)	(100)	(100)	(100)	(100)	(100)
% to total Plan outlay	7.86	5.83	6.87	4.86	5.04	3.27	2.59	3.55

Note: * includes pre-school education
** includes teacher education, social education (youth survey)
+ Draft

Source:(i) *A Handbook of Education and Allied Statistics.*
(ii) *Seventh Five Year Plan.*

TABLE 16.7: Household Expenditure on Education, 1970-71 to 1982-83.

	Expenditure (in Rs. Crores)		Per Capita Expenditure in Rs.		Total as percentage of GNP
	At current prices	At 1970-71 prices	At current prices	At 1970-71 prices	
1970-71	896	896	16.6	16.6	2.05
1976	1253	844	20.6	13.9	1.9
1981	1928	817	28.4	12.0	2.1
1982-83	2568	896	36.2	12.6	2.1
Rate of Growth %	9.2	0	6.7	-2.4	

Source: *National Accounts Statistics*, Central Statistical Organisation, New Delhi.

15.9.2 Table 16.7 shows that at constant prices, growth of household expenditure between 1970-71 and 1982-83 has been nil. Per capita household expenditure has, in fact, had a negative rate of growth.

Resources for Education as envisaged in the National Policy on Education, 1986

15.10.1 The National Policy on Education, 1986, spells out the approach to mobilisation of resources for Education as follows:

> "The Education Committee of 1964-66, the National Education Policy of 1968 and practically all others concerned with education have stressed that the egalitarian goals and the practical, development printed objectives of Indian society can be realised only by making investments in education of an order commensurate with the nature and dimensions of the task.
>
> Resources, to the extent possible, will be raised by mobilising donations, asking the beneficiary communities to maintain school buildings and supplies of some consumables, raising fees at the higher levels of education and effecting some savings by the research and the development of technical and scientific manpower should also mobilize some funds by levying a cess or charge on the user agencies, including Government departments, and entrepreneurs. All these measures will be taken not only to reduce the burden on State resources but also for creating a greater sense of responsibility within the educational system. However, such measures will contribute only marginally to the total funding. The Government and the community in general will find funds for such programmes as the universalisation of elementary education; liquidating illiteracy, equality of access to educational opportunities to all sections throughout the country; enhancing the social relevance, quality and functional effectiveness of educational programmes; generating knowledge and developing technologies in scientific fields crucial to self-sustaining economic development; and creating a critical consciousness of the values and imperatives of national survival.
>
> The deliterious consequences of non-investment or inadequate investment in education are indeed very serious.

Similarly, the cost of neglecting vocational and technical education and of research is also unacceptable. Sub-optimal performance in these fields could cause irreparable damage to the Indian economy. The network of institutions set up from time to time since Independence to facilitate the application of science and technology would need to be substantially and expeditiously updated, since they are fast becoming obsolete.

In view of these imperatives, education will be treated as a crucial area of investment for national development and survival. The National Policy on Education, 1968, had laid down that the investment on education be gradually increased to reach a level of expenditure of 6 per cent of the national income as early as possible. Since the actual level of investment has remained far short of that target, it is important that greater determination be shown now to find the funds for the programmes laid down in this policy. While the actual requirements will be computed from time to time on the basis of monitoring and review, the outlay on education will be stepped up to the extent essential for policy implementation in the Seventh Plan. It will be ensured that from the Eighth Five Year Plan onwards, it will uniformly exceed 6 per cent of the National Income."

National Policy on Education, 1986 and Centre-State Partnership in Education

15.10.2 In the following words, the National Policy on Education, 1986, calls for a "Meaningful" partnership between the Centre and the States in regard to Education:

"The constitutional Amendment of 1976, which included Education in the Concurrent List, was a far-reaching step whose implications – substantive, financial and administrative – require a new sharing of responsibility between the Union Government and the States in respect of this vital area of national life. While the role and responsibility of the States in regard to education will remain essentially unchanged, the Union Government would accept a larger responsibility to reinforce the national and integrative character of education, to maintain quality and standards (including those of the teaching profession at all levels), to study and monitor the educational requirements of the country as a whole in regard to manpower for development, to cater to the needs of research and advanced study, to look after the international aspects of education, culture, and Human Resource Development and, in general, to promote excellence at all levels of the educational pyramid throughout the country. Concurrency signifies a partnership which is at once meaningful and challenging; the National Policy will be oriented towards giving effect to it in letter and spirit."

Funding for Education According to Envisaged Perspective and Strategies

15.11.1 The perspective for Education, as for other Sectors, has been presented up to the year 2000 A.D. by the Seventh Plan document under the chapter on "Development Perspective: Towards the Year 2000", as follows:

> "By the year 2000, illiteracy would be eliminated and universal elementary education would have been provided for all children up to the age of 14. It is expected that drop-outs in the age group 6-14 would be reduced to negligible levels. Extensive provision would be made for continuing and recurrent education and use of modern communication technology. There will be substantial vocationalisation of secondary education by the turn of the century. Non-formal education using a variety of means and methods, including video technology and computers, would play a significant role."

15.11.2 The Seventh Plan document lays down the strategy and pattern of growth of Education as follows:

> "Enrolment in elementary education (Class I-VIII) is expected to increase by 25 million and cover 92 per cent of the population in the age-group 6-14 years by 1989-90. In addition, non-formal systems will be used to bring closer the objective of universalisation of elementary education. Secondary school enrolment is expected to go up by 5 million partly through better utilisation of existing schools, and with a special emphasis on vocationalisation. Special efforts will be made to improve the

quality of education. As part of this drive, model schools will be set up in each district to impart quality education to promising children, particularly those coming from rural areas. Adult literacy programmes will be pursued with the objective of covering all illiterates in the age-group 15-35 by 1990. In higher education and technical education, the emphasis will be on consolidation and improvements in quality."

Recommendations of the Eighth Finance Commission

15.12.1 Though Education is conventionally treated as a developmental sector, the Eighth Finance Commission considered it as a non-developmental sector which deserved to be upgraded. For the purpose of upgradation, physical norms were followed by that Commission.

15.12.2 The State Governments gave requests to the Eighth Finance Commission aggregating to nearly Rs. 4,000 crores – for appointment of additional teachers, provision of furniture and equipment, construction of buildings, provision of mid-day meals etc. The then Ministry of Education also emphasized the need for clearing the backlog of *pucca* buildings for primary and middle schools, conversion of single teacher schools into two-teacher schools, provision of adequate inspecting staff and administration facilities. The Ministry also assessed the financial requirements for this purpose as over Rs. 3,000 crores. The Eighth Finance Commission disposed of the matter as follows:

"It seems to us that lack of *pucca* buildings for the primary schools and the existence of single-teacher primary schools constitute two basic weaknesses in the education system. Presently, 185,666 primary schools accounting for 40.88 per cent of total number of primary schools in all the 22 States are functioning in thatched huts, tents, etc. We have decided that the States in which the percentage of primary schools without pucca buildings exceeds 40 per cent, should be helped with upgradation outlays to bring down the percentage of such primary schools to the all-India average, i.e. 40 per cent. We have assumed a unit cost of Rs. 40,000 for a school building of two class-rooms. We have added 30 per cent to the unit cost for the hill States. We have thus allocated Rs. 164.39 crores for the construction of 38,946 additional school buildings in 11 States to bring them to the all-India average of 60 per cent building satisfaction in respect of primary schools.

Another facet of the education sector, which caused us concern, was the preponderance of single-teacher primary schools in some States. Out of the 454,213 primary schools in the 22 States, 165,848 schools function as single-teacher schools. Thus, they form 36.5 per cent of the total number of primary schools. We have decided to extend our support to those States where the proportion of single-teacher schools exceeds 35 per cent, which is the all-India average. The States wherein the proportion of single-teacher primary schools exceeds 35 per cent are Andhra Pradesh, Gujarat, Himachal Pradesh, Jammu & Kashmir, Karnataka, Madhya Pradesh, Maharashtra, Meghalaya, Orissa, Rajasthan and Tripura. We have provided outlays for the appointment of 45,255 additional teachers to bring these States to the all-India level. In the computation of upgradation outlays, we have adopted State specific emolument – levels for each of the 11 States. We have thus provided Rs. 122.01 crores. With this provision, it should be possible to raise the number of primary schools with two teachers or more, in the 11 States, to 65 per cent which is the all-India average. We have provided a total sum of Rs. 286.40 crores for upgradation of the education sector."

15.12.3 The upgradation grants were also to be monitored, as per the recommendation of the Eighth Finance Commission. The monitoring mechanisms suggested were State-level and Central level empowered committees of inter-departmental/inter-Ministerial nature, the former headed by chief Secretaries of States and the latter being convened by the Finance Ministry. The Central level Empowered Committee was also given flexibility in terms of transfer of grants from one scheme to another within each sector, alter physical targets depending upon escalation in prices or alternations in physical norms etc. Release of money was designed to be 10 per cent as initial on account advance; 30 per cent after receipt of intimation regarding institutional arrangements; and the balance according to actual Physical progress.

15.12.4 Upgradation assistance provided to the State Governments as per the recommendations of the Eighth Finance Commission has been confined to four years commencing from 1985-86. A detailed statement of release of assistance to the State Governments for upgradation in terms of provision of school buildings and teachers may be seen in Table 16.8.

ꞁBLE 16.8: Statement of Release of Assistance for Upgradation of Schools based on Recommendations of the Eighth Finance Commission, 1985-8€ to 1987-88

(Rs. lakhs)

	1985-86 Capital	1986-87				1987-88				For completed works
	1985-86 on A/C	Revenue		Capital		Revenue		Capital		
		P	F	P	F	P	F	P	F	
									On A/C	
1. Andhra Fradesh	299.20	3900	232.00	148	44.40	6000	522.00	327	385.08	65.40
2. Assam	576.10	—	—	—	—	—	—	—	806.08	—
3. Bihar	986.80	—	—	802	304.36	—	—	—	1214.29	—
4. Goa	—	—	—	—	—	—	—	—	48.00	—
5. Himachal Pradesh	175.35	—	—	—	—	—	—	—	245.49	—
6. Jammu & Kashmir	174.18	—	—	—	—	—	—	—	243.85	—
7. Madhya Pradesh	—	7000	110.15	—	—	7000	449.85	—	—	—
8. Manipur	208.54	—	—	—	—	—	—	—	291.95	—
9. Meghalaya	168.11	300	5.00	—	—	—	—	—	235.35	—
10. Nagaland	61.23	—	—	—	—	—	—	70	72.99	27.30
11. Orissa	398.30	1600	115.68	—	409.72	1600	16.08	—	311.79	—
12. Rajasthan	—	—	—	—	—	2812	294.14	—	—	—
13. Tripura	98.67	—	—	—	—	21	2.25	—	138.14	—
14. West Bengal	775.90	—	—	920	291.44	—	—	905	921.25	181.00
Total al States	3904.38	12800	162.83	1870	1049.92	17433	1284.32	1302	4914.72	273.70

ꞁurce: Finan•e Commission Wing, Ministry of Finance, Government of India, New Delhi.

P = Physical Unit - Buildings/Teachers in numbers
F = Financial - Amounts released in lakhs of rupees

A summary of actual release of assistance is furnished in the Table 16.9.

TABLE 16.9: Upgradation Assistance for Education based on Recommendations of Eighth Finance Commission, 1985-86 to 1987-88.

(Rupees in crores)

	1985-86	1986-87	1987-88	Total for 1985-86 to 1987-88
Capital	39.04	10.50	49.14	98.68
Revenue	—	1.63	12.84	14.47
Total	39.04	12.13	61.98	113.15 @

Source: Finance Commission Division, Ministry of Finance, Government of India, New Delhi.

@ includes on account payments.

15.12.5 It may be seen from the Table 16.9 that over the three-year period from 1985-86 to 1987-88 the total release of upgradation assistance under both Capital and Revenue account has been only of the order of Rs. 119 crores including on account payments. In physical terms the States were helped, during the three-year period, to provide over 30,000 teachers and over 3,000 school buildings as may be seen from Table 16.10.

TABLE 16.10: Number of teachers and buildings provided under upgradation assistance for Education based on recommendations of the Eighth Finance Commission, 1985-86 to 1987-88.

(Units in numbers)

	1985-86	1986-87	1987-88	Total for 1985-86 to 1987-88
Teachers	—	12800	17433	30233
Buildings	—	1870	1302	3172

Source: Finance Commission Division, Ministry of Finance, Government of India, New Delhi.

15.12.6 As has been brought out earlier, the Eighth Finance Commission had recommended upgradation assistance for putting up school buildings based on an estimate of Rs. 40,000 per school building. Subsequently, in the three-year period from 1985-86 to

1987-88 there was cost escalation. The Empowered Committee in the Ministry of Finance itself – in two spells – allowed an escalation of costs for putting up school buildings to the extent of 50 per cent (30% initially in 1985-86 and 20% later in March 1988). Consequent on this, the number of buildings that could be provided with upgradation assistance over these three years came down from the level originally envisaged when the Eighth Finance Commission gave its recommendations.

Recommendations of the Ninth Finance Commission in its first report (1989-90) and second report (1990-95)

15.12.7 The cost of upgradation of standards of administration so far as it concerns education as per the proposals furnished by the States to the Ninth Finance Commission was of the order of Rs. 1723.21 crores. In its first report the Commission indicated that it was making available to the States grants for completion of the task which was likely to remain unfulfilled by 1988-89 out of that charted by the Eighth Finance Commission for the five years 1984-89. The Commission found that the physical targets as regards upgradation of capital works having been escalated to the extent of 30 per cent for the three year period 1985-88 and 50 per cent for the year 1988-89. On this basis the Ninth Finance Commission recommended in its first report a financial provision for the year 1989-90 for upgradation of standards of administration in the area of education to the extent of Rs. 41.92 crores. Over and above this the Ninth Finance Commission in its first report also recommended a financial provision of Rs. 200 crores for equalisation of social and community services for elementary education – specifically considering that provision of school buildings under Operation Black Board from the NREP and RLEGP resources to be inadequate.

15.12.8 In its second report (for 1990-95) the Ninth Finance Commission has followed the normative approach according to which needs and capacities of different governments are assessed normatively and such normative assessments are taken as the basis far determining the volume and pattern of federal transfers. So for as education is concerned the factors that have been taken into consideration for the purpose of assessing expenditure are the following:

Primary Education

- Expenditure per child in the age group of 6-10 (taken as a dependent variable).
- Proportion of enrolment in primary stage to the population in the age group 6-10.
- Students-teacher ratio in primary state.
- Differences in the average salaries of primary school teachers across the States.

Secondary Education

- The expenditure on secondary education per child in the age group of 11-18 (taken as a dependent variable).
- Enrolment in secondary stage as a proportion of children in the age group of 11-18.
- Proportion of private unaided secondary schools to total number of schools.
- Salary differences of trained graduate teachers in the States.
- Student-teacher ratio in the States.

Higher Education

- Per capita expenditure on higher education.
- Proportion of enrolment in higher stages of education to total population.
- Student-teacher ratio.
- Difference in price levels amongst States.
- Population density and proportion of enrolment in private college to total enrolment.

15.12.9 Based on the above parameters, econometric formulae have been worked out, normative expenditures assessed with reference to them and built into the overall requirements of the states. Upgradation grants as per previous practices have not been specifically recommended.

15.12.10 The direct consequence of this is that allocation for Education from out of the grants-in-aid recommended by the Finance Commission would be dependent on the priority for Education assigned by the respective States. States may or may not assign adequate priority. If adequate priority is not assigned, from the point of view of Education there would be retrogression from the earlier practice of allowing specific upgradation grants tied to Education. In fact, Shri Justice A.S. Qureshi, Member of the Ninth Finance Commission, in his dissenting note, has made the following valid observations:

> "In our first Report, we had given the upgradation grants for improvement of certain beneficial services. We had also given grants for the special problems of the States. Those grants were separate and identifiable. The advantage of such grants is that they could be tied grants for specific purposes. It was possible to insist upon the performance relatable to the grants from the concerned States. In the present Report, we have departed from that practice and instead of giving upgradation grants or special problem grants they have been built in the requirements of the States in this regard which is assessed on normative basis by the use of econometric models and algebric formulae. In my opinion, this is not correct. We should have followed the same method as we followed in our first Report and should have recommended grants for special problems and upgradation of services, so as to make abundantly how is given, for what purpose and to ascertain the compliance of the objectives of the grants."

Strategies for Raising Resources

15.13.1 As brought our elsewhere (Table 16.6) intra-sectorally, allocations have shown a marked preference for Higher Education in spite of low rate of literacy, though over the sixth and seventh plans, a comparatively lesser priority has been shown for Higher Education. Primary Education is yet to reach the level attained during the first plan. This pattern is not consistent with the Constitutional mandate for achieving universalisation of Elementary Education. Nor is it consistent with the need for providing a meaningful vocational bias for School Education. Continued high levels of investment in Higher Education is contradictory to the results of studies on returns from investment in Education which have brought out that lower levels of education have a higher average rate of return. Research findings are also to the effect that investment in lower levels of education contributes more to income distribution and reduction of poverty, besides to economic growth.

15.13.2 It is in the above background of ever increasing involvement of the Government in educational financing and distortions in terms of intra-sectoral priorities that mobilisation of resources and their deployment should be considered.

15.13.3 Public expenditure on Education as a proportion of GNP, over the years, has been as indicated in Table 1.3 which shows that while it has increased, as of 1986-87, it fell far short of 6%.

15.13.4 The Central Statistical Organisation has recently released the quick estimates of National Income (GNP) for the year 1988-89 which has been placed at Rs. 3,06,822 crores at current prices on the basis of which the plan and non-plan budget of Education Departments at the Centre and the States as a percentage of national income comes to 4.2 per cent for the years 1989-90.

15.13.5 India ranks 115th in the world in terms of investment in Education as a percentage of GNP. Amongst the countries with a population of 10 crores and above, India is at the very bottom, barring Bangladesh. That India's educational expenditure as a proportion of GNP compares very unfavourably *vis-a-vis* world-wide expenditure on Education is brought out by Table 16.11:

TABLE 16.11: Comparative Expenditure on Education as Percentage of GNP in various countries.

Country Groups	*1982*	
Africa	4.9	Development Nations 6.2
America	6.4	Developing Nations 4.3
Asia	5.1	
Europe (incl USSR)	5.6	
Oceania	5.8	

Recommendations

(i) The first step, therefore, should be to provide for at least six per cent of the GNP for Education which has not so far been provided, through this has been repeatedly urged for over quarter of a century. (The figure of 6 per cent of GNP was suggested by the Education Commission 1964-66 on the basis that, that was the level of investment which had already been reached even by certain developing countries of Asia. As estimate of investment required for implementing the recommendations of the report of Education Commission 1964-66 was made. Coincidentally, it was noted that this amount approximated to six per cent of GNP. It had also been noted that the economic growth rate per annum for 20 years since then was envisaged at six per cent. A quarter of a century has since passed by considerable changes have come about in the economy. Therefore, in the changed context, there is need for reviewing the proportion of GNP that should go into Education as on date). Even providing six per cent of GNP means substantially larger allocations for Education in the budgets of the Central and State Governments. (In this context, Table 16.12 which speaks for itself may be seen).

TABLE 16.12 Share of Education in Five Year Plan Outlays/Expenditures (%), First Plan to Seventh Plan

Plans	Share of Education in Total Plan Outlays/Expenditure (%)
First Five Year Plan	7.86
Second Five Year Plan	5.83
Third Five Year Plan	6.87
Annual Five Year Plan	4.86
Fourth Five Year Plan	5.04
Fifth Five Year Plan	3.27
Sixth Five Year Plan	2.70
Seventh Five Year Plan	3.55

(ii) All technical and Professional education should made self-financing, education being viewed as involving the use of resources (inputs) that should be necessarily paid fir by the beneficiaries as it confers on them greater employability (output).

Other than public funding, the alternative methods of funding Higher Education are:

(i) Graduate taxes
(ii) Increase in fees and
(iii) Student loans

Graduate taxes, if any, are to be imposed upon the beneficiaries i.e., the users of services of graduates, namely, employers. However, the employers are likely to resist imposition of such taxes on grounds of economic viability of their own operations getting adversely affected. This is also likely to result in discouragement of employment of the qualified.

The tuition fees now prevalent in educational institutions, by and large, are those fixed many years ago. In 1950-51, income from fees accounted for 20 per cent of the total expenditure on education. This proportion has now come down to five per cent. Table 16.13 brings out the picture regarding low levels of fees charged in the University System.

TABLE 16.13 Levels of fees charged in the University System

Type of Higher Education Institution	Nature of courses	Fee charged per annum
Central Universities	Under-graduate level general courses	Between Rs. 120 in Banaras Hindu University and Vishwa Bharati and Rs. 180 in Delhi University.
Central Universities	Post-graduate level general courses	Between Rs. 144 in Vishwa Bharati and Rs. 300 to Rs. 400 in the North Eastern Hill University.
Central Universities	Professional courses like B.Ed., LL.B. etc.	Between Rs. 120 in Vishwa Bharati and Rs. 1,440 in Delhi University.
State Universities	Under-graduate level general courses	Between Rs. 40 to Rs. 180 in Rajasthan University and Rs. 400 in Gujarat, Bombay & Nagpur Universities.
State Universities	Post-graduate level general courses	Between Rs. 100 to Rs. 200 in Rajasthan University and Rs. 500 to Rs. 600 in Bombay University.
State Universities	Under-graduate Professional courses like B.Ed., LL.B. etc.	Between Rs. 100 to Rs. 200 in Rajasthan University and Rs. 500 in Bombay University.
State Universities	Engineering courses	An average of Rs. 533.

The disparity between the cost of Higher Education and fees is also rather high. To give an example, in Engineering Colleges, the annual recurring expenditure alone comes to Rs. 2,000.

(iii) In the circumstances, a justifiable strategy is bringing about an appropriate increase in the fees payable by students going in for Higher Education. This increase should be appropriately linked to at least the cost of recurring expenditure and levels of income of the parents of the beneficiaries. The richest quartile of the people can bear 75 per cent of the cost of the education; the next richest quartile 50 per cent of the cost; and the next richest quartile 25%. The last quartile of the economically weak (to be appropriately defined) need not bear any part of the cost.

(iv) Besides tuition fees, fees charged for specific purposes in the Higher Educational Institutions like laboratory fees, library fees, building fees, magazine fees, games fees etc. also have to be increased on a rational basis with reference to the costs of providing the relevant facilities/services.

(v) With the ever increasing number of examinees, examination fees can also be an important means of raising internal resources to meet the cost of Higher Education.

While student loans have the advantage of bringing down government investment in Higher Education, they do involve certain problems. They are: Psychologically, people are against loans. Credit market are not developed. There are difficulties in securing repayment of loans even as the government experience of operating loan scholarship shows. (Reference has been made to this later.) The poor could face difficulties in having access to loans.

(v) However, institutional loans as a strategy for releasing the pressure on government resources and as a means of putting resources in possession of those aspiring for Higher Education is indispensable. Problems in administration of loans should not result in the easy solution of opting out of them.

Nationalised banks and financial institutions, as a rule of practice, generally concentrate on industrial financing and financing of commercially viable activities. However, there are examples like the State Banks of India advancing loans for Higher Education.

(vii) Therefore, there is need for a committed programme of the nationalised banks for providing loans for recipients of Higher Education.

(viii) Term lending institution like the Industrial Development Bank of India (IDBI), Industrial Finance Corporation of India (IFCI) and Industrial Credit and Investment Corporation of India (ICICI) should launch programmes for promoting research in universities. This could ease the burden on the University Grants Commission which, in turn, is provided funds by the government of India. The IDBI has to its credit several promotional activities with a view to helping the process of industrialisation. It has, for example, set up the Entrepreneurship Development Institute of India. It has also provided assistance to voluntary agencies engaged in imparting production and vocational training. Assistance has also been provided to the National Association for the Blind to set up a polytechnic at Bombay. The IDBI and ICICI have had chairs instituted for specific projects in various universities. This activity could be expanded in an organised way with reference to the merits of individual programmes of the respective Higher Educational Institutions.

An analysis of institutional costs of education reveals that educational infrastructure development, and consequently quality of education, has suffered, as brought out Table 16.14.

TABLE 16.14: Institutional Costs of Education (1970-79)

Item	Recurring	Non-recurring	Total
Salaries	85.8	—	80.6
Buildings	1.3	36.8	3.5
Furniture & Equipments	0.8	27.3	2.4
Consumables	1.3	—	1.2
Libraries	0.5	9.2	1.0
Hostels	0.5	—	0.5
Stipends/Fellowships and Concessions	2.9	—	2.7
Games & Sports	0.4	—	0.4
Miscellaneous	6.7	26.7	7.7
Total	100.0	100.0	100.0

On the other hand, it has been estimated that about 46 per cent of the total non-recurring institutional expenditure on Education is required for fixed assets like buildings, libraries etc. (An analysis of expenditure by levels of Education also reveals that the share of salary goes down as the level of education rises. Share of costs of capital assets also increases with increase in the level of education. The proportion of non-recurring costs to the total institutional costs of education is less than five per cent at the primary level and about 11 per cent for higher levels).

(ix) Institutional finance for infrastructure needs to be raised in the circumstances. Housing Finance Institutions, therefore, could take up programmes for creation of capital assets in the educational sector i.e. for buildings for schools, colleges, universities as also hostels for the students, staff and teachers. Repayment of loans may have to be guaranteed by the appropriate Governments. (It is worthy of mention, in this context, that Housing Development Finance Corporation (HDFC) has already finance schemes for construction of staff quarters and ownership houses for University staff in Gulbarga, Karnataka. The Universities and Educational Societies, on their part, could consider investment of their provident fund money in the bonds of Housing Finance Institutions approved under Section 36(i) (viii) of the Incometax Act.

The contribution of Life Insurance Corporation to housing efforts has been quite significant. At present, the annual average accretion to the total investible funds of the LIC approximately Rs. 3,000 crores. The current pattern of the allocation of LIC's investments between the sub-sectors of the socially oriented sector brings out that housing component is receiving about 21 per cent of its total plan allocations, the rate of return ranging from 10.5 per cent to 13.5 per cent. In the non-plan investment of the LIC in the socially oriented sector, 97 per cent (with a rate of return ranging from 12 per cent to 14 per cent) goes for housing schemes.

(x) There is a strong case for LIC's investment in the area of housing going for hostel facilities for the students, staff and teachers in the educational institutions. However, diversion of these resources for the education sector would mean doing so at the expense of other development schemes, 90 per cent of the accretions of the LIC already being committed to socially oriented sectors. Therefore, this is a matter on which the Government as well as Planning Commission will have to take a conscious decision regarding the reallocation; of the LIC's investible resources with substantive priority for the Education sector.

(xi) Economically weaker sections of the people going for Higher Education who cannot afford the enhanced fees or loans from financial institutions could be provided appropriate scholarships.

(xii) Funds provided in the Central sector for scholarships during the Seventh Plan period was of the order of Rs. 22.26 crores. This would have to be considerably enhanced for the benefit of the economically weaker sections in the interest of equity and providing access to Higher Education for them. There is also need for rationalisation of the whole programme of awarding scholarships. The National Loan Scholarship Scheme, for example, has not been capable of proper implementation. States to which funds for provision of these scholarship are provided by Central Government have not been repaying the dues to the Government of India promptly. Out of a total of Rs. 84.36 crores provided to the States under this Scheme since 1963-64, an amount of Rs. 69.4 crores is still outstanding repayment.

(xiii) The Government of India scheme of scholarships in approved residential secondary schools benefit only a small number of 500 students per annum in the whole country. Serious malpractices in the selection of scholars have also reportedly come to the notice of the Government, the benefits, of late, being cornered apparently by manipulations on the part of those hailing from a very few centres in India. This scheme could as well be discontinued and the number of scholarships enhanced for meaningful programmes like for upgradation of merit of SC/ST students.

(xiv) One of the modalities for securing better implementation of scholarship schemes with more direct and responsible involvement on the part of the States, no doubt, would be for the administration of the scholarships being left totally to the states themselves necessary outlays being provided to the states as part of the State Plan Outlays on an earmarked basis.

(xv) Certain other means of raising resources for education are presented below:

- A sustained programme to be implemented every year right down to the Panchayat levels for raising community contribution (Rules for grants-in-aid provided to the educational institutions could be modified to provide for built-in incentives such that Government assistance is related to contributions raised from the community on matching basis. In the course of interactions with the Ministers and Secretaries of Sates a suggestion was made that there could be funds created for educational development. Like relief funds created in the names of Prime Minister of India and the State Chief Ministers, there could be Prime Minister's and Chief Minister's Educational Funds into which the community contributions, educational cess (about which reference is made later) etc. could be credited. These funds could be operated for the purpose of building up infrastructure for educational institutions up to the elementary levels).
- Institution of innovative programmes like the Savatribhai Phune Foster Parent Scheme of Maharashtra for promoting primary education of girls under which registered foster parents pay Rs. 25 p.m. in cash or kind to the needy girls from weaker sections.
- Removal of restrictions on the investment of surplus income of educational institutions like the stipulation that such income should be invested in low yielding Government securities/bonds etc.
- Collection of educational cess related to revenue sources such as land revenue, excise duties, charges on cash drops, charges on buildings in urban areas etc. (The sources on which cess could be charged naturally will be quite diversified and different for different States. It would be for the respective States to identify the sources on which cess is to be levied).

SECTION II

FIVE YEAR PLANS IN INDIA : Outlays for Education

17

OVERVIEW OF FIVE YEAR PLANS

Education ranks as an important impact of creating a social order founded on the values of freedom, social justice and equal opportunity. Accordingly, it has had to be assigned a pivotal role in the developmental process through the Plan periods. Rapid expansion of educational facilities from one Plan to another has been a characteristic feature of educational planning in India.

First Five Year Plan (1951-56) took note of the recommendations of the University Education Commission (1948-49) and the Constitutional Provisions of Universal Elementary Education. Accordingly it emphasised the expansion of elementary education.

Second Five Year Plan (1956-61) laid great stress on basic education. The Assessment Committee on Basic Education (1956) appointed by the Government of India became the basis of the expansion and reform in basic education. In the field of secondary education, it was guided by the recommendations of the Secondary Education Commission (1952-53).

Third Five Year Plan (1961-66) emphasised the requirement of trained manpower for the major determinant of the measures of advance which could be achieved in different directions.

There were three *One-Year Plans* (1966 to 1969).

Fourth Five Year Plan (1969-74) took into account the recommendations of the Education Commission (1964-66) and the Resolution on National Policy on Education (1966) passed by the Government of India. The chapter on education was entitled 'Education and Manpower'.

Fifth Five Year Plan (1974-79) provided modest outlays for education during the first three years of the Plan. The rule of two Governments by different political parties, i.e., the Congress up to 1977 and thereafter the Janata Government running in different directions was not very conducive to development.

Sixth Five Year Plan (1980-85) perceived education, broadly as a seamless continuum of life-long learning and essential for human resource development. The emphasis in the development of education in the Sixth Plan was on the optimum utilisation of existing facilities, qualitative improvement of system and making available the educational services to the socially deprived sections of the community. While it was recognised that financial outputs were important and necessary to create additional infrastructure, it was equally important to bring about changes and improvements in the system through increased attention to non-monetary inputs.

Seventh Five Year Plan (1985-90). The development of education during this period was marked by the formulation of the National Policy on Education (NPE) (1986) and the Programme of Action (POA) (1986). The Seventh Plan provided for reorientation of the education system so as to prepare the country to meet the challenges of the 21st century. Launching of Operation Black Board (OB) for the improvement of elementary education and opening of Navodaya Vidayalayas at the secondary stage of education in the rural areas providing free education were the two important characteristics of the development programmes in the field of education during the Seventh Five Year Plan. Vocationalisation of education, especially at the senior secondary stage, was yet another thrust area.

Eighth Five Year Plan (1992-97). Quite a large number of educational plans like plans in other sectors could not be implemented in the way as envisaged by its formulators on account of rapid changes in the Central Government. The formulation of the Eighth Five Year Plan was also delayed. The main objectives in the Eighth Plan, according to available indications, would be universalisation of elementary education and complete eradication of illiteracy among the 15-35 age-group.

18

FIRST FIVE YEAR PLAN*

Introduction

In the post-independence period problems of educational reconstruction, expansion, qualitative improvement and financial implications thereof were reviewed by several Commissions and Committees, notably the Scientific Manpower Committee (1947), the University Education Commission (1948-49) and the Secondary Education Commission (1952-53). The recommendations of these reports together with the constitutional provisions became the basis for priority determination in the First Five Year Plan. The Basic system of education as propounded by Gandhiji was another source of determining priority at the primary stage of education.

In view of the limited resources at the disposal of the Central and State Governments for education, it was envisaged that a large share of responsibility in this area would have to be borne by the people themselves. The plan also visualised that private agencies would be encouraged by the States to take up the work of educating the people in a big way. As regards priorities, it was recommended that improvement and remodelling of existing institutions on right lines should receive the utmost consideration. The plan emphasised that in view of the poor return from primary education, the tendency to open new primary schools should not be encouraged and as far as possible, resources should be concentrated on basic education. In the field of secondary education, economic activities like agriculture, cottage industries, small scale industries, etc., were assigned an important place. The recommendation of the University Education Commission (1948-49) for the setting of a University Grants Commission was

* Planning Commission, Government of India, New Delhi 1952; *Review of the First Five Year Plan*, Planning Commission, Government of India, New Delhi, 1957.

reiterated. It was stipulated that social education should be woven round the overall national priorities like the organisation of cooperatives, agricultural extension work, and cooperative farming, etc.

1. General[1]

The Planning Commission is mainly concerned with viewing education as a part of the total national effort, establishing and strengthening its links with other aspects of national life and assigning priorities for the various educational programmes awaiting implementation.

Assessment of the Present Position: The needs of the present situation are:

(1) Re-orientation of the educational system and integration of its different stages and branches;

(2) Expansion in various fields, especially in those of basic and social education, remodelled secondary education and technical and vocational education;

(3) Consolidation of existing secondary and university education and the devising of a system of higher education suited to the needs of the rural areas;

(4) Expansion of facilities for women's education, especially in the rural areas;

(5) Training of teachers, especially women teachers and teachers for basic schools, and improvement in their pay-scales and conditions of service; and

(6) Helping backward States by giving preferential treatment to them in the matter of grants.

Resources: The Five Year Plan makes a provision of Rs. 151.66 crores (35.02 crores for the Centre and Rs. 116.64 crores for the States) for educational development or of Rs. 30.33 crores per annum. . . . The inadequacy of this provision is all too obvious. . . . In the context of prevailing conditions a larger share of responsibility for social services will have to be borne by the people themselves.

Priorities: A serious attempt should be made to achieve the fol-

---

1. (i) Chapter XXXIII of the document.
   (ii) Original Table Numbers have been changed to conform to this Chapter number.

lowing broad targets:

(1) At the conclusion of the Five Year Plan, educational facilities should be provided for at least 60 per cent of all the children of the school-going age within the age group 6-11.
(2) At the secondary stage, the target should be to bring 15 per cent of the children of the relevant age-group into educational institutions.
(3) In the field of social education . . . at least 30 per cent of the people (and 10% of women) within the age group of 14 to 40 receive the benefit of social education.

2. Pre-School Education

In view of the shortage of funds Government can accept only limited responsibility in this field, confined to research in evolving methods suited to our needs, training of teachers, helping private agencies who take up this work in the rural areas by grants-in-aid and running a few model balwadis or nursery schools in each State.

3. Primary (including Basic) Education

The provision of free and compulsory primary education is the first necessary step towards establishing equality of opportunity for every citizen.

A most important development in the field of education in recent years has been the acceptance of basic education by the country as the pattern for the education of children of the age group 6–14. . . . The foremost task in the field of basic education is the improvement of technique and the development of methods, by which it can be passed on to the vast majority of teachers of rather low educational qualifications and average ability.

We would recommend that all States should run, wherever conditions permit, eight-year full-fledged basic schools instead of five-year schools.

As regards the question of ordinary primary education, we feel that, in view of the poor return from it, the tendency to open new primary schools should not be encouraged and, as far as possible, resources should be concentrated on basic education and the improvement and remodelling of existing primary schools on basic lines, as far as that can be done with the personnel available.

4. Secondary Education

In the first place, secondary education must be closely related to the psychological needs of the adolescents for whom it is being designed. Secondly, it should be vitally related to the existing socio-economic situation, to the directive principles of State policy laid down in the Constitution and the approved schemes for social and economic reconstruction. In order to equip the youth adequately for the needs of the existing socio-economic situation, it is necessary to give secondary education a vocational bias. . . . Thirdly, secondary education would grow from the education that is being given at the primary stage, i.e., it should be closely integrated with the basic education and its essential underlying principles.

5. University Education

The problem of the re-organisation of university education is really three-fold: the reform of the existing system to enable it to yield the best results it is capable of yielding, the building up of a new system (or systems) more suited to our national needs and the working out of the relationship of the various systems, while they exist side by side. In spite of their grave defects, the existing universities are the only repositories we have of the tradition of organised knowledge and the course of wisdom is to improve their working while we attempt to build a system or systems better suited to our needs.

Another very important problem is the serious overcrowding in most of the colleges, which makes individual attention, so necessary at this stage, simply impossible. We must develop and apply selective tests on a large scale so that nobody is allowed to go up for higher education who is not fit to profit by it.

6. Social Education

The concept of adult education, while was mostly confined to literacy, was found to be too narrow to be able to meet the various needs of the adults. It was, therefore, widened to include, in addition to literacy, the health, recreation and home life of the adults, their economic life and citizenship training; and to denote this new concept the term 'social education' was coined. Social education implies an all-comprehensive programme of community uplift through community action.

In rural areas the point at which the social education programme in a locality can begin will of course depend on the condition prevailing in the given area. Attempt should, however, be made at the earliest opportunity to organise an economic activity on co-operative basis. . . . Similarly, programmes of health education and health services should also be organised on co-operative lines.

7. Professional Education

Organisation of facilities for professional education cannot be strictly related to the existing opportunities for employment but should take into account the developments planned in the various other spheres of national activity which require technical personnel. It is also necessary to turn out youngmen with initiative and grit in excess of the numbers indicated by the normal employment position in order that new ideas may be developed and small scale ventures might receive an impetus.

The greatest need for expansion of training facilities is at the level of artisans and craftsmen. Institutions run by the Ministry of Labour, trade schools, industrial schools, production-cum-training centres should be opened on an extensive scale, so that the skills of the large numbers of people, engaged in production or likely to be so engaged, are developed.

8. Women's Education

The general purpose and objective of women's education cannot, of course, be different from the purpose and objective of men's education. There are, however, vital differences in the way in which this purpose has to be realised.

The problem of women's education in India is above all the problem of the education of grown-up women. Generally, women cannot always be educated in the same continuous fashion as men. Unlike boys, girls are forced to suspend their studies in the early teens due to a variety of reasons and take up wider responsibilities of the home. Arrangements should, therefore, be made to facilitate resumption of studies by women at a time when they have leisure.

The total allotment for educational development proposed in the Plan is Rs. 151.66 crores for the five-year period or an average annual expenditure of Rs. 30.33 crores.

The expenditure provided under the head 'Education' does not include the sum of Rs. 55.28 crores, during the five-year period or Rs. 11.06 crores annually on an average, proposed to be spent on a number of schemes of training, education and research, which are shown under other heads such as Agriculture, Medical, Industries, Labour, etc.

The distribution of the total expenditure visualised over the five years of the Plan among the various sub-heads will be according to the schemes submitted by the Central Ministry and the States (Table 18.1).

In the field of primary education the number of primary schools will increase by 17 per cent and the number of pupils by 25 per cent. The corresponding increase in the junior basic schools would be 22 per cent and 81 per cent. Taking the primary and junior basic schools together, we find that whereas in 1950-51 only 44.5 per cent of the children of the age group 6–11 were being provided for, the percentage is estimated to rise to 55.7 per cent in 1955-56. this result is estimated only on the basis of the State resources. We feel that it can be considerably improved if local resources are properly developed and tapped for the purpose of education. Though firm estimates are impossible at this stage it should not be difficult to reach the target of 60 per cent (Table 18.2).

In the field of secondary education while secondary schools are estimated to increase by 18 per cent during the period of the Plan the number of pupils would increase by 32 per cent. The percentage of the age-group 11–17 being provided for will increase from 10.8 per cent in 1950-51 to 13.3 per cent in 1955-56.

As regards teachers' training, facilities expand differently at different levels. While the number trained during the year increases only by 15 per cent in the case of primary teachers, it increases by 54 per cent in the case of secondary schools and 162 per cent in the case of basic teachers. The low percentage increase in the case of primary teachers is explained by the fact that with the policy of ultimately converting all primary schools into basic schools most of the States are taking steps to convert their primary teachers' training colleges into basic training colleges.

TABLE 18.1: Distribution of Total Expenditure Visualised over Five Years of the Plan among Various Sub-heads, 1951-1956

(*Rs. in lakhs*)

State/Ministry	Adminis-tration	Primary Education	Secondary Education	University Education	Technical and Vocational Education	Social Education	Other Schemes	Total
States	75.7	74,52.8	8,30.4	9,25.1	9,90.4	7,60.0	5,84.1	1,16,18.5
Central Government	—	12,50.0	—	2,47.0	11,55.0	7,50.0	1,00.0	35,02.0
Total (1951-1956)	75.7 (0.5%)	87,028 (57.6%)	8,30.4 (5.5%)	11,72.1 (7.8%)	21,45.4 (14.2%)	15,10.0 (10.0%)	6,84.1 (4.5%)	1,51,20.5* (100%)

* Figures do not include Rs. 46 lakhs, earmarked for Jammu and Kashmir State, as break-up of this amount into sub-heads is not available.

TABLE 18.2 Number of Institutions, Pupils and Teachers in Primary (Ordinary), Junior Basic and Secondary Education, 1950-51 and 1955-56

(*Rs. in lakhs*)

Year	Primary Ordinary			Junior Basic			Secondary		
	No. of Institutions	No. of Pupils	No. of Teachers	No. of Institutions	No. of Pupils	No. of Teachers	No. of Institutions	No. of Pupils	No. of Teachers
1950-51	1,72,779	1,51,10,316	3,86,169	35,002	29,00,322	77,013	16,387	43,87,657	1,63,575
1955-56	2,02,141	1,87,88,750	4,60,324	42,833	52,76,278	1,11,893	19,262	57,79,395	2,06,856
Percentage of Increase	17	25	19.2	22	81	45	18	32	26

19

SECOND FIVE YEAR PLAN*

Introduction

Chapter XXIII on Education highlights the role of education in the development of the economy. It begins with these remarks:

"The system of education has a determining influence on the rate at which economic progress is achieved and the benefits which can be derived from it. Economic development naturally makes growing demands on human resources and in a democratic set up it calls for values and attitudes in the building of which the quality of education is on important element."

Again in the concluding part of this chapter it is stated:

"For economic development to make its full contribution to the well-being of the mass of the people, programmes of education should be ahead of economic plans. Means must, therefore, be found to overcome current limitations upon efforts in the field of education."

The role of education in developing requisite skills for accelerating economic development has been clearly appreciated in these words:

"Modern economic development calls for a wide diffusion of the scientific temper of mind, a sense of dignity in labour and discipline in service, and a readiness to adapt new techniques and new knowledge to the needs of the people. These values and at-

---

* Planning Commission Government of India, New Delhi 1958.

titudes will be realised in everyday life in the measure in which they are expressed through educational ideals and practices."

The main thrusts in the Plan were on popularising and expanding basic education, checking wastage and stagnation diversification of secondary education in the light of the recommendations of the Secondary Education Commission (1952-53), improvement of standards of college and university education, emphasis on social education rather than literacy, austere school buildings and improvement in the condition of teachers.

EDUCATION[1]

Introduction

The system of education has a determining influence on the rate at which economic progress is achieved and the benefits which can be derived from it. Economic development naturally makes growing demands on human resources and in a democratic set-up it calls for values and attitudes in the building up of which the quality of education is an important element. The socialist pattern of society assumes widespread participation of the people in all activities and constructive leadership at various levels. In a period of intensive development, however, the resources to be allocated for education and the targets to be achieved are among the difficult issues which have to be faced in drawing up a plan of economic and social development. In recent years, there has been a great deal of re-examination of the pattern of education, and on several issues the opinion of educationists has crystallised into fairly specific proposals for change, as indicated in the recommendations of the University Education Commission, the Secondary Education Commission and a number of committees which have inquired into educational problems. The progress achieved in different branches of education has been reviewed by the Central and State Governments with a view to formulating programmes for the second five year plan. The main features of the programmes which have been drawn up are indicated in

1. (i) Para Numbers refer to paras of Chapter XXIII of the document.
   (ii) Original Table Numbers have been changed to conform to this chapter number.

this chapter.

2. The second five year plan provides for a larger emphasis on basic education, expansion of elementary education, diversification of secondary education, improvement of standards of college and university education, extension of facilities for technical and vocational education and the implementation of social education and cultural development programmes. In the first five year plan about Rs. 169 crores were provided for the development of education—Rs. 44 crores at the Centre and Rs. 125 crores in the States. In the second five year plan, Rs. 307 crores have been provided – Rs. 95 crores at the Centre and Rs. 212 crores in the States. The distribution of outlay between different fields of education in the first and second plans is set out below (Table 19.1):

TABLE 19.1: Distribution of Outlay between Different Fields of Education in the First and Second Plans

	First Plan	Second Plan
	(Rs. in crores)	
Elementary Education	93	89
Secondary Education	22	51
University Education	15	57
Technical and Vocational Education	23	48
Social Education	5	5
Administration and Miscellaneous	11	57
Total	169	307

A proportion of the outlay provided for in the first plan related to the continuance of scheme of educational development which had been introduced prior to the plan; for the second plan, however, expenditure on educational institutions which have come into existence in the course of the first plan has been taken as committed expenditure and the plan outlay pertains to proposals for new institutions or for the expansion or development of existing ones. In addition to the provisions mentioned above, the allotment made in the second five year plan for national extension and community projects includes about Rs. 12 crores for general education and about Rs. 10 crores for social education. Programmes in different sectors of development, such as, agriculture, health, welfare of backward classes, rehabilitation of displaced persons and others, also provide considerable sums for the expansion of educational facilities.

3. In the summary statement given below (Table 19.2) the progress achieved in different fields of education during the first plan and the targets proposed for the second are set out. The progress in each direction is reviewed separately in the sections that follow.

TABLE 19.2: Progress Achieved in Different Fields of Education during the First Plan and Targets Proposed for the Second Plan, 1950-51, 1955-56, 1960-61

	Unit	1950-51	1955-56	1960-61
I. *Facilities of schooling for Children in different age groups*				
(a) 6-11	Pupils	1,86,80,000	2,48,12,000	3,25,40,000
Percentage of the age group		42.0	51.0	62.7
(b) 11-14	Pupils	33,70,000	50,95,000	63,87,000
Percentage of the age group		13.9	19.2	22.5
(c) 14-17	Pupils	14,50,000	23,03,000	30,70,000
Percentage of the age group		6.4	9.4	11.7
II. *Institutions*				
(a) Primary/Junior Basic	Schools	2,09,671	2,74,038	3,26,800
(b) Junior Basic	Schools	1,400	8,360	33,800
(c) Middle/Senior Basic	Schools	13,596	19,270	22,725
(d) Senior Basic	Schools	351	1,645	4,571
(e) High/Higher Secondary	Schools	7,288	10,600	12,125
(f) Multipurpose Schools	Schools	..	250	1,187
(g) High School to be upgraded to Higher Secondary Schools		..	47	1,197
(h) Universities		26	31	38
III. *Engineering*				
(a) Institutions—				
(i) Degree level		41	45	54
(ii) Diploma level		64	83	104
(b) Output—				
(i) Degree holders		1,700	3,000	5,480
(ii) Diplomates		2,146	3,560	8,000
IV. *Technology*				
(a) Institutions—				
(i) Degree level		25	25	28
(ii) Diploma level		36	36	37
(b) Output—				
(i) Degree holders		498	700	800
(ii) Diplomates		332	430	450

4. The statement above suggests that the efforts made during the first plan and those envisaged in the second plan are by no means small. They have, however, to be seen against the background of the magnitude of the total problem. In several fields distinct advances have been made in recent years. Nevertheless, there are enormous tasks to be carried out. For instance, a directive in the Constitution laid down that the State shall endeavour within a period of ten years from the commencement of the Constitution to provide free and compulsory education for all children until they complete the age of 14 years. The proportion of children in the age group 6-14 years at school has risen from from 32 per cent before the first plan to 40 per cent at the end of the first plan and is likely to increase to 49 per cent only by the end of the plan.

Elementary Education

5. The problems of education at the elementary level are mainly two: the expansion of existing facilities and the reorientation of the system of education on basic lines. Both are equally urgent tasks and vital to social and economic development.

6. As regard expansion, the progress made in the first plan and the targets set for the second are indicated in Table 19.3.

TABLE 19.3: Progress of Elementary Education Made in the First Plan and the Targets set for the Second Plan, 1950-51, 1955-56 and 1960-61

Stage	Number of pupils as percentage of number of children in corresponding age-groups								
	1950-51			1955-56 Estimates			1960-61 Targets		
	Boys	Girls	Total	Boys	Girls	Total	Boys	Girls	Total
1. Primary (6-11)	59	25	42	69	33	51	86	40	63
2. Middle (11-14)	22	5	14	30	8	19	36	10	23
Elementary (6-14)	46	17	32	57	23	40	70	28	49

It will be seen that the goal set in the Constitution about free, compulsory and universal education is yet far away. The statement above gives all-India figures, but the position varies considerably between States and in many States the averages are much lower than those for all India. It is, however, necessary to make every possible effort to fulfil the directive of the Constitution with in the next ten to fifteen years.

7. The problem of expanding educational facilities is a complex one and its different aspects have to be considered. It will be seen that while the progress in regard to boys of the age-group 6-11 years is satisfactory, the advanced in respect of boys of the age group 11-14 years has been relatively meagre. In both the age-groups the education of girls has lagged far behind. An aspect of the situation which causes concern is the 'wastage' which exceeds 50 per cent at the primary stage. Thus, out of 100 pupils who join the first class at school scarcely 50 reach the fourth class, the rest dropping out before completing four years at school, which is regarded as the minimum period for providing permanent literacy. The wastage is greater in the case of girls. Closely allied to the problem of wastage is that of stagnation, that is, a pupil continues in the same class for more than the normal period. The problems of expansion of educational facilities may differ considerably as between States and different parts of the same State. It is, therefore, necessary in each area to undertake detailed educational surveys to determine the measures needed. Such surveys are being initiated by the Ministry of Education in collaboration with State Governments. On a broad consideration of the facts certain general suggestions may be made for improving the situation.

8. To prevent wastage the introduction of compulsion is essential. Its enforcement may be easier if busy agricultural seasons coincide with school holidays as far as possible. Further, especially in rural conditions, effort should be made to give a practical bias to education as far as possible. The principal remedy for stagnation lies in improving the quality of teachers and teaching techniques, including understanding of human relations and personality problems.

9. A most urgent problem is that of girls' education. Public opinion in every part of the country is not equally alive to the importance of girls' education. Special efforts at educating parents, combined with efforts to make education more closely related to the needs of girls, are needed. The situation in each area will need to be studied separately. Where there are difficulties in the acceptance of co-education, other methods will need to be explored. In some areas there may be no alternative to separate schools. In others, it may be

possible to adopt a shift system as an interim measure—one shift working for boys and the second for girls.

A major obstacle in the way of promoting girls' education is the dearth of women teachers. In 1953-54 women teachers accounted for about 17 per cent of the total number of teachers employed in primary and secondary schools. The task of training women teachers has to be approached as a matter of urgency, especially when it is remembered that in the third five year plan the problem of expanding primary education will to a large extent concern girls' education. The provision of housing facilities for women teachers in villages would be an important step to take. Opportunities for part-time employment may draw educated married women into the teaching profession.

10. In regard to children in the age-group 11-14 years who contribute to family income, continuation schools could help keep up the education of large numbers of children at schools.

11. There is also considerable need for making more effective use of available buildings and other facilities. In this connection the introduction of shift system in both basic and non-basic schools has been recommended by the Central Advisory Board of Education at their last meeting in 1956. This step will need to be accompanied by considerable propaganda for increasing enrolment in schools with a view to the gradual introduction of compulsion, which is necessary for taking full advantage of this scheme. The shift system has been tried only in Tranvancore-Cochin and Bombay, but for the rest of the country, it is a new experiment.It is suggested that it may be introduced, to begin with, in the first two classes only, and the experience gained should be reviewed at intervals. The shift system is recommended, not as an ideal method, but to meet certain practical difficulties. The reduced school hours will call for rationalisation of the curriculum and careful planning of work, both inside and outside the school.

12. As regards school buildings, it is inevitable that at the present stage austere standards should be adopted. Much of the work may be done out of doors, while the minimum covered accommodation needed is provided by the local community with some assistance from public authorities. Experiments in cheap designs for schools need to be carried out. The starting of a school in a village need not be contingent on certain prescribed standards being observed. A school could be started under whatever arrangements are immediately pos-

sible in a locality, and common buildings like village temples and 'panchayat ghars' could also be used. Once a school is actually functioning, the provision of a building can be taken in hand as soon as circumstances are favourable and local contributions are forthcoming.

13. If the directive of the Constitution in favour of free and compulsory education up to the age of 14 years is to be fulfilled, Government's resources will have to be supplemented in increasing measure by local community effort. In many countries the principal responsibility for providing elementary education rests with the local community. The State authorities encourage local effort by providing adequate grants-in-aid. Even in India for centuries the tradition was that most of the expenditure on education was met by the community. In recent years also local communities have come forward to make generous contributions in land, labour and money for the provision of school buildings. What is now required is, in addition, a contribution towards the cost of maintenance of schools, which will be steady and recurring, not merely sporadic or occasional. To enable local communities to shoulder in some measure the continuing responsibility which this implies, it is recommended that each State should consider enacting legislation to enable local authorities (including village panchayats), to levy a cess for education. The advantage of bringing in this cess as a local measure would be that the responsibility and initiative of individual communities would be specially stressed and the people would know that whatever they contributed would be used for their benefit. A degree of flexibility in detail could be provided in the legislation, so that the example of communities which are progressive and forward looking may stimulate others to similar action. The education cess could be related to appropriate State and local taxes such as land revenue,property taxes, etc., so as to enable different sections of the community to make their contribution.

Basic Education

14. The importance of basic education for a country which seeks to develop rapidly is now well recognised. In the first five year plan basic education programmes began to be implemented effectively for the first time. The progress made in basic education and the targets set for the second plan are indicated in Table 19.4.

TABLE 19.4: Progress made in Basic Education in the First Plan and the Targets Set for the Second Plan, 1950-51, 1955-56 and 1960-61

	1950-51	1955-56	1960-61
Schools	1,751	10,000	38,400
Enrlomcnt	1,85,000	11,00,000	42,24,000
Training Schools	114	449	729

The position varies considerably in different States. Taken as a whole, the relative advance seems fairly rapid, but considering that the whole of elementary education has to be reoriented on basic lines, the process has not advanced very far yet. In 1950-51 the number of children going to basic schools accounted for less than 1 per cent of the total number of children in the elementary stage; the proportion increased to nearly 4 per cent by the end of first plan and is expected to rise to 11 per cent. by 1960-61. There has been greater progress in providing facilities for training basic teachers. In order to prepare schools for conversion to the basic system, crafts and other student activities are being introduced in an increasing measure.

15. In the spread of basic education certain administrative problems have to be considered. On the administrative side, it is essential that those concerned with educational administration should be fully acquainted with the new programme and the conditions necessary for its fulfilment. Existing personnel should be trained. The aim should be that new entrants into educational services have had training in basic education. Administrative procedures will have to be revised so as to give the maximum initiative to the school and to the local community.

16. In organising training for basic teachers it is important to ensure the observance of high standards of teaching. Seminars, refresher courses and schemes of in-service training should also be organised. Further, post-graduate basic training colleges need to be affiliated to the universities so that those who are trained there are able to go up for higher professional training. Negotiation for the purpose with the various universities will need to be taken up. Production of literature for basic institutions and research in various problems affecting basic education are also essential. National Institute of Basic Education which has been established recently will give attention to these aspects.

17. In the spread of basic education a difficulty which often arises

is cost relatively to that of education in other elementary schools. On the basis of experience during recent years a few suggestions may not be out of place. In any new programme the need for economy is obvious. The productive aspect of basic education, consistent with the requirements of education has to be recognised and encouraged as an essential part of the scheme of basic education. From the limited experience available, it would appear that where reasonably satisfactory conditions have been provided, the results of basic education have been encouraging. There is, however, a consensus of opinion that the best results will be obtained with full-fledged eight-year basic schools—or with a number of five-year basic schools feeding a central eight-year school—instead of the five-year schools now common in most States. A number of measures calculated to improve attendance at school will need to be taken. In obtaining land and equipment for the school the contribution of the local community should be drawn upon to the maximum extent. Frequently, when agricultural holdings are consolidated or cooperative farming units formed or when land comes into the possession of the village community from any source, it should be possible to allot an area to the village school both for its activities and for providing it with a regular source of supplementary income. Special emphasis should be placed on the quality of the articles produced. This will also facilitate their disposal. Assistance of local co-operatives should be sought for disposing of surplus goods not consumed by the school or by the community. So far as possible students should participate in making the craft equipment.

The practical value of basic education and even its financial return can be increased by linking it up with allied programmes like-agriculture, village and small-industries, cooperation, development and national extension service, etc., and thereby giving a definite place to institutions impairing basic education in the scheme of development in each district and each block. This will itself help to keep basic education in step with the needs of development in other fields. To facilitate such coordination, advisory committees for basic education should include persons representing different branches of development work.

18. The village schools and specially those which are run on basic lines have an important role in community development. Thus, new ideas worked out in the school pass into the life of the community through the normal contact of teachers with children. Villagers, who visit the local school and see good work being done there, pick up

new suggestions. To enhance the value of the contribution which the school can make to the progress of the village community it is suggested that all senior basic schools should have a farm and a workshop attached to them. As a rule the people are willing to support such activities with generous contributions.

19. It will be clear from what has been said above that elementary education is an area of fundamental importance in which it will be necessary for a considerable period to experiment with new ideas, undertake pilot studies, evaluate results, and develop speedy methods of applying proven methods on a large-scale. Large innovations will be called for, for instance, in administrative procedures, recruitment rules, promotion methods, etc. To undertake these and other tasks referred to in this chapter, the Ministry of Education have under consideration a proposal to set up a Council for Basic and Elementary Education.

Secondary Education

20. Problems of secondary education were reviewed by the Secondary Education Commission whose report was presented in 1953. The Commission considered the basic shortcomings of the present secondary schools and observed that the curricula now followed and the traditional methods of teaching did not give students sufficient insight into the every day world in which they lived and failed to train the whole personality of the pupil. In the past excessive emphasis on the study of the English language led to neglect of many other subject. With the increase in the size of classes the personal contact of teachers and students diminished and discipline and character were not sufficiently inculcated. While piecemeal reforms were introduced from time to time, there was need for new re-orientation in the system of secondary education as a whole. The Secondary Education Commission, therefore, made proposals for bringing about a greater diversity and comprehensiveness in educational courses and providing more comprehensive courses which would include both general and vocational subjects. They did not contemplate any artificial division between "general or "cultural" education and "practical" or "vocational" or "technical" education. In the new organisational pattern which the Commission recommended it was visualised that following the four or five year period of primary or junior basic education, there would be a middle or senior basic or junior secondary

stage of three years and a higher secondary stage of four years. The first degree course would then be of three years duration. The Commission recommended the establishment of multipurpose schools, of technical schools either separately or as part of multi-purpose schools and of special facilities for agricultural education in rural schools. The provision in all secondary schools for courses in Languages, General Science, Social Studies and a Craft as a common core was also proposed for general adoption. These recommendations form the basis of programmes adopted by the Centre and the States for the second five year plan. A sound system of secondary education, which offers openings in a large number of different directions, is an essential foundation for economic development on modern lines. With the expansion of elementary education, an increasing number of students will reach the secondary stage. Already partly because of the 'unilinear' character of secondary education in the past, the problem of unemployment has been accentuated among matriculates, arts colleges have tended to be overcrowded and often neither the community nor the individual profited adequately from the system.

21. Programmes in the second five year plan require for their implementation large numbers of skilled workers, technicians and specialists with a background of elementary or secondary education followed by technical and vocational training in specific vocations. Thus, the requirements of teachers, workers in national extension and community project areas, cooperative personnel, revenue administrators, technical and supervisory personnel in industry, agriculture and other fields of development have to be met mainly from the age group 14—17 years. In this group, there is at present considerable wastage and mis-direction as may be seen from the fact that over 50 per cent or more of the students who take matriculation or equivalent examinations fail to qualify. It is common ground that at the secondary stage of education, there should be increasing diversification of courses, so that students could be guided and directed to secure training in courses according to their aptitudes and capacities. This object is proposed to be attained through introduction of crafts and diversified courses, better facilities for science teaching, establishment of multi-purpose schools and junior technical schools as well as upgrading of the high schools to higher secondary schools.

22. Steps to implement the pattern of re-organisations for secondary education recommended by the Secondary Education Commis-

sion have been initiated during the past two years. With the provision of Rs. 51 crores in the second plan as against Rs. 22 crores in the first, it is hoped that the re-orientation of secondary education will be carried a stage further. Among other programmes, a proportion of the existing high schools are to be converted into higher secondary schools and multi-purpose schools. In the first plan about 250 multi-purpose schools were established; during the second plan the number of multi-purpose schools is to be increased to 1,187. The number of high and higher secondary schools (which generally include middle classes) will increase from 10,600 to 12,000 at the end of the second plan. About 1,150 high schools are also expected to be converted into higher secondary schools over the period of the second plan, thus bringing the total number of higher secondary schools to about 2,800. In order to develop agriculture education at the secondary stage in rural areas, it is proposed to provide additional 200 agricultural courses in rural secondary schools. In the course of the second plan the numbers at school in the secondary stage will increase from 2.3 million to 3.1 million.

To enable students to enter an occupation at the end of the secondary course as semi-skilled workers or for setting up small businesses of their own, the second five year plan provides for the setting up of 90 junior technical schools. In these institutions general and technical education and workshop training will be provided for a period of three years to boys of the age-group 14-17 years.

23. At the end of the first plan, about 60 per cent of the staff of secondary schools consisted of trained teachers. According to the plans of States in the next five years, the proportion of trained teachers is expected to increase to 68 per cent. The training of secondary teachers for vocational courses will need a great deal of attention. The teaching of crafts in elementary and secondary schools is one of the essential features in the reconstruction of the system of education, but progress in providing such courses is slow because of lack of trained teachers. The Ministry of Education have a programme for training 500 degree teachers and 1,000 diploma teachers for multi-purpose and junior technical schools. Plans of States provide Rs. 46 crores for the re-orientation of secondary education and include programmes for upgrading high schools into higher secondary schools, improving laboratories and libraries, training teachers and improving technical standards, improving teachers' salaries and providing educational and vocational guidance.

24. At the secondary stage, the education of girls lags seriously behind. At present, out of the total population of 12 million girls in the age-group 14—17 years, about 3 per cent are attending schools. Plans of States do not provide in sufficient measure for the education of girls, for, the number of high schools for girls is expected to increase from 1,500 to 1,700 only by the end of second plan. To enable girls to take up careers for which openings exist and are likely to increase (such as gram sevikas, nurses, health visitors, teachers, etc.) special schemes are recommended. Girls' education at this stage requires special encouragement.

25. A question at the secondary stage of education which is now being studied by a Committee of the Central Advisory Boards of Education concerns the manner in which basic education and the scheme of reform for secondary education should be related to each other. The programme of conversion of primary into basic schools is already under way. As it proceeds, the senior basic and the middle school which represent the next stage, will come closer together in their methods and approach. It is being visualised that the senior basic stage should be followed by a post-basic stage. The number of institutions imparting post-basic training is still very small. On this account the Ministry of Education have made a financial provision for assisting the development of post-basic schools. As the programme for the re-orientation of secondary education is carried out in the States, it would be desirable to devise ways of bringing about closer correlation between post-basic education and the structure of secondary education which is now being evolved.

26. With the re-organisation of the system of education, which is now in progress, at the secondary stage of education the study of Hindi and other regional languages assumes greater importance. In this connection, a question which has received attention is the provision of facilities for the study of Hindi in non-Hindi speaking areas and for the study of languages other than Hindi in Hindi-speaking areas. The main difficulty here is the lack of teachers trained in particular languages. To meet this deficiency the Minister of Education have provided funds for providing Hindi teachers in secondary schools in non-Hindi speaking areas and teachers in languages other than Hindi in secondary schools in Hindi-speaking areas.

University Education

27. During recent years the rapid increase in the number of students

in universities and colleges has affected the standards of education. At the end of the first plan the total enrolment is estimated to be 720,000 as compared to 420,000 five years ago. The number of students qualifying each year in degree and higher examinations in arts and science has risen during this period from 41,000 to 58,000. For improving the quality of university and college education and for reducing wastage and stagnation of students who are unable to qualify, a number of measures are being taken by the University Grants Commission. These include the institution of three-year degree courses, organisation of tutorials and seminars, improvement of buildings, laboratories and libraries, provision of hostel facilities, stipends for meritorious students, scholarships for research and increase in salaries of university teachers. In the course of the second five year plan, seven new universities are to be established.

28. There are a number of important problems affecting university education which are being considered. Two of these may be specially mentioned. The introduction of diversified courses at the secondary level may succeed to some extent in checking the rush of students to Arts colleges. The questions whether and to what extent possession of degrees can be dispensed with for the purpose of recruitment to public services has been under examination by a committee appointed by the Central Government. Affiliated colleges, in many of which the prevailing standards are unsatisfactory, constitute another problem which is now receiving attention. It is essential that by action at the secondary as well as at the university stages and through appropriate changes in the conditions and methods of recruitment to public services, university education should acquire greater purpose and direction and fit more closely into plans of economic and social development.

29. The total provision for university education in the second five year plan is about Rs. 57 crores, of which Rs. 22.5 crores are provided in the State plans and Rs. 34.4 crores at the Centre, the latter provision including an allotment of Rs. 27 crores for the University Grants Commission. The greater part of the expenditure will be on consolidation and increased provision for technical and scientific education in the universities. In addition to this, the programme of technical education provides Rs. 13 crores for engineering and technology at the university and higher stages and Rs. 10 crores for scholarships. Further, Rs. 4.6 crores have been provided for agricultural education and Rs. 10 crores for health education at the university and higher

stages under programmes in these fields, besides Rs. 20 crores provided for scientific and industrial research in the programme of the Council of Scientific and Industrial Research and other associated programmes.

Technical Education

30. In each sector of development technical personnel are needed in rapidly increasing numbers. Steps which are proposed to be taken to augment the existing training facilities for doctors, agricultural and veterinary specialists and others have been explained in the appropriate chapters. Despite the advances made in the first plan, the requirements for engineering and technological personnel will be on a scale exceeding the capacity of existing institutions. This is the main problem in the development of technical education in the second plan.

31. In the field of technical education long-term planning has to be undertaken. During the first five year plan significant progress was made in developing technical education. The Indian Institute of Technology, Kharagpur, was established as the first of the four higher technological institutes recommended by the All India Council for Technical Education, a few years ago. The Institute has been planned ultimately to provide under-graduate courses for 1,200 students, post-graduate courses and research for 600 students. It offers facilities for training in a wide range of subjects, some of which for instance, Naval Architecture and Marine Engineering, Fuel and Combustion Engineering, Production Technology, Mechanical Handling of Materials, Agricultural Engineering, Geophysics, Town and Regional planning and Architecture are designed to requirements for technical personnel which are relatively new. The Indian Institute of Science, Bangalore, has been developed for technological studies and research in Aeronautical Engineering, Power Engineering, Internal Combustion Engineering, Metallurgy and Electrical Communications Engineering. A large number of technical institutions all over the country have been developed for degree and diploma courses; and new institutions have been established to meet the needs of different States. The following statement (Table 19.5) summarises the position of technical education at the beginning and end of the First Plan.

TABLE 19.5: Engineering and Technology Education at the Beginning and End of the First Plan

	1949-50			1955-56		
	Number of Institutions	Intake	Out-turn	Number of institutions	Intake	Out-turn
Post-graduate courses and research facilities	8	136	91	18	270	190
Degree or equivalent courses	53	4,120	2,200	60	6,050	3,700
Diploma courses	81	5,900	2,480	108	8,700	3,900

32. It will be seen that admissions to institutions and the out-turn of graduates and diploma holders show a 50 per cent increase since 1949-50; compared to the position in 1947 the increase has been as much as three-fold. On the basis of the present admission an out-turn of 4,600 graduates and 5,220 diploma holders is expected from 1958-59 onwards. These numbers represent a doubling of the out-put figures of 1950. Besides expansion in numbers, qualitative improvement of the standards of instructions has also been kept in view. The crux of the problem of quality in education is better staff, better equipment and better accommodations in the technical institutions. The All-India Council for Technical Education and its Regional Committees have carried out comprehensive studies of the state of various institutions in the country, their deficiencies, courses offered, standards and the improvements needed. On the basis of the reports of the Council, the Central Government has given substantial grants to individual institutions.

33. Particular attention has been given to the development of facilities in special fields. A scheme of Management Education and Training, covering Industrial Engineering, Industrial Administration and Business Management, has been implemented in seven selected centres and a Board of Management Studies has been set up for bringing about coordinated development of facilities for training in these subjects in association with industry and commerce. Proposals for the establishment of an administrative Staff College at

Hyderabad and an organisation for the promotion of Scientific Management are in an advanced stage. Four Regional Schools of Printing are being established at Madras, Calcutta, Bombay and Allahabad, and a fifth is planned for Delhi. A School of Town and Country Planning is being established in Delhi in association with the Institute of Town Planners. A scheme for giving interest-free loans to institutions for the construction of hostels for students has also been implemented. On completion this will provide hostels accommodation for about 7,000 students. Over 500 research scholarships of Rs 200 per mensem have been instituted for students who wish to undertake research in science, engineering or technology. A scheme for research fellowships for encouraging advanced scientific research has also been introduced.

34. Despite the steps taken during the first five year plan, on account of the large demand for technical personnel which will arise in the coming years, considerable expansion of technical education is now imperative. During past two or three years increasing attention has been given to planning for manpower. Generally, it will be beyond the capacity of the majority of existing institutions to admit a much larger number of students for training than they do at present and at the same time maintain proper standards.

In the second five year plan, a provision of about Rs 48 crores has been made for technical eduction. Part of this provision is for completing schemes initiated during the first plan, the rest being earmarked for the establishment of new institutions and courses. In the course of the second plan the Indian Institute of Technology, Kharagpur, will be fully developed for under-graduate and post-graduate studies. Post-graduate courses and research in engineering and technology at other selected centres will also be organised. The scheme relating to the improvement of existing institutions for first degree and diploma courses initiated a few years ago will be completed.

New schemes to be undertaken in the second plan include Higher Technological Institutes established in a phased programme of these in the Western, Northern and Southern Regions in the country. Two of these will be located at Bombay and Kanpur; the location of the third Institute is under consideration. Each Institute when fully developed will provide for a total student body of 1,200 for undergraduate courses and 600 for post-graduate courses and research.

35. Training facilities at the Delhi Polytechnic are to be expanded in respect of a wide range of subjects. For the provision of adequate

facilities for the first degree and diploma courses in engineering and technology in different parts of the country, 9 institutions of the degree level and 21 institutions of the diploma level are proposed to be established. A scheme for training foremen which provides for periods of training alternating with periods of work is to be implemented in cooperation with industry. Reference has already been made to the programme for opening 90 junior technical schools. For the qualitative improvement of technical education at all levels, refresher and other courses for technical teachers are proposed to be organised. The number of scholarships will be increased from 633 to 800, and substantial provision has been made for scholarships and free places for technical studies. Additional hostel accommodation for about 13,000 technical students and 3,300 students in junior technical schools will be constructed. A Central Institute for Printing Technology has also been planned and the Indian School of Mines and Applied Geology, Dhanbad, will be expanded to provide additional facilities for training in Mining Engineering and related fields. As a result of the development programmes described above admissions to technical courses at different levels will increase as shown below (Table 19.6) :

TABLE 19.6: Estimated Admissions to Technical Courses at Different Levels by 1960-61

Post-graduate courses and research work	570
First degree courses	7,550
Diploma courses, including courses for Foreman	11,300
Junior Technical Schools	5,400

These figures represent a total annual out-turn of graduates and diploma holders after 1960-61 of about 5700 and 6,800 respectively, that is, twice as many graduates and three times as many diploma holders as at the end of the first plan.

36. Whether the increase in training facilities proposed above will prove sufficient has been examined by the Engineering Personnel Committee set up by the Planning Commission whose recommendations have been recently received. The conclusion reached by the Committee is that even with the expansion of facilities for engineering education proposed in the second plan, it would be necessary to provide for additional training facilities for additional engineering graduates for service in civil, mechanical, electrical, telecommunica-

tion, metallurgical and mining engineering fields and 6,225 diploma-holders in civil, mechanical and electrical engineering fields. Unless special measures are taken, the shortage of personnel are likely to be intensified in the later years of the second plan and in the third plan. The Committee has recommended that the capacity of existing institutions should be increased by 20 per cent for graduate training and by 25 per cent for the training of diploma holders. It has also suggested that steps should be taken to establish 18 more engineering colleges and 62 more engineering schools in different parts of the country. These suggestions which will involve a total outlay of about Rs 10 crores, are under consideration.

37. Increasing demands for skilled workers and foremen and other supervisory personnel will need to be met during the second plan. The Ministry of Labour has a programmes for increasing the output of craftsmen by about 20,000 per annum and two institutions are being set up for training craft instructors. Apprenticeship training facilities have to be developed on a larger scale and in this field an important duty is cast upon the managements of the better organised enterprises in the private sector as well as on public enterprises. The Ministry of Iron and Steel has set up a directorate of training to coordinate the personnel requirements of steel plants and to arrange for the necessary training facilities. In view of the large programmes which it has to undertake, the Ministry of Railways also proposes to establish a number of new technical schools.

Social Education

38. The Census of 1951 showed that only 16.6 per cent of the population were literate and even if children below 10 years are excluded the proportion rises to 20 per cent only. Apart from the low percentage of literacy there is serious disparity in literacy between men (24.9%) and women (7.9%) and between the urban population (34.6%) and the rural population (12.1%). Rapid social and economic progress along democratic lines and widespread illiteracy are scarcely compatible with each other.

39. As essential reforms proposed in the system of education are carried out, facilities for continuation classes and social education classes at various levels should be developed. Plans of States provide for the opening of literacy and social education centres, training of social education workers and organisers, libraries, publication of

literature, audio-visual education and establishment of janata colleges. The total allotment in the plan for social education is about Rs 15 crores, including about Rs 10 crores in the national extension and community development programmes. The Ministry of Education propose to establish a fundamental education centre for training social education organisers and for continuing study and research in problem relating to social and basic education.

While literacy is undoubtedly important, it should be recognised that it is one element in a wider concept of social education. Social education embodies a comprehensive approach to the solution of the problems of the community, primarily through community action. Besides literacy, it includes health, recreation and home life, economic activities and citizenship training. The entire national extension and community development programme, social welfare extension projects, rural programmes undertaken by Government agencies in cooperation with the people, programmes of voluntary organisations like the Sarva Seva Sangh, the Bharat Sevak Samaj and others, the cooperative movement, village panchayats etc. are all facets of the nation-wide effort towards social education and rural improvement which is now in progress in the country. From this aspect the range of social education work is not to be judged merely by the financial provisions made specifically under this description. However, as an organised and systematic activity directed to specific purposes, social education is a new field of work. A large number of development agencies are engaged in some form or other of social education. Their work has to be supplemented by suitable specialised agencies. The beginning made in this direction in national extension and community project areas has, therefore, much significance. A period of careful evaluation will help to determine the nature of specialised agencies and methods and techniques needed in this field, both in rural and in urban areas.

Higher Rural Education

40. A number of far-reaching proposals for the development of rural education at the higher levels were made by the University Education Commission which reported a few years ago. The subject has been examined afresh recently by the Higher Rural Education Committee which recommended the establishment of Rural Institutes. These institutes are intended to perform, a variety of functions for the rural

community and, more especially to provide (a) facilities for higher studies to students who complete their post-basic or higher secondary courses, (b) certificate courses in subjects such as rural hygiene, agriculture and rural engineering and also shorter courses, and (c) comprehensive teaching-cum-research-cum-extension programmes. It is visualised that Rural Institutes will function as cultural and training centres and as centres for development planning in rural areas. The Ministry of Education propose to establish 10 Rural Institutes in the second five year plan and have made a provision of Rs 2 crores for this purpose. For locating these Institutes leading centres already engaged in rural work have been selected. For following up the programmes the Central Government have recently constituted a Council for Rural Higher Education.

Teachers

41. At all times the teacher is the pivot in the system of education. This is specially the case in a basic change and re-orientation. There is general agreement that the teaching profession fails to attract a sufficient number of persons who adopt teaching as a vocation and that far too many persons work as teachers for short periods and then move on to other occupations. Improvement in the conditions of teachers, is, therefore, an important desideratum of progress in education. Measures which are necessary, whether by way of better training or better salaries and conditions of service, may be held back because of the large number of teachers involved in any reform. Thus, the number of teachers has risen from 7.3 lakhs before the first plan to 10.24 lakhs in 1955-56 and is expected to increase to 13.56 lakhs in 1960-61.

42. Before the first five year plan 59 per cent of teachers in primary schools and 54 per cent of teachers in secondary schools were trained teachers. These proportions have risen to 64 and 56 per cent respectively by the end of the first plan. In the second plan Rs. 17 crores have been provided for increasing training facilities for teachers and, besides expanding existing institutions, it is proposed to establish 231 training schools and 30 training colleges. At the end of the second plan it is expected that the proportion of trained teachers will increase to 79 and 68 per cent in primary schools and secondary schools respectively. The number of basic training colleges is to be increased from 33 to 71 and basic training schools from 449 to 729. A

National Institute of Basic Education is also being established as a research centre.

43. The question of improving the salaries of teachers has been under consideration for some time past. It is generally recognised that the provision of satisfactory services for teachers is a measure essential for the effective reorganisation of the system of education. In many States steps to improve teachers' salaries have been taken during the past few years. In the nature of things teachers' salaries have to be fixed at levels consistent with the local pay structure, at which suitably qualified persons can be attracted and retained in the teaching profession. The problem in different States is, therefore, by no means identical. While recognising the importance of the question of improving salary scales of teachers, the Central Government have taken the view that responsibility for meeting additional expenditure on this account belongs to State Governments. As a temporary measure, until the next Finance Commission makes its proposals, the Central Government have, however, agreed to assist States to the extent of 50 per cent of additional expenditure which may be involved in raising salary scales of primary teachers suitably consistent with local conditions. They have further suggested that in order to meet the additional cost involved in raising the salary scales of primary teachers, State should explore the possibility of reducing expenditure as far as they can on the construction of school buildings. They have also proposed that a special educational cess may be levied by States to enable them to meet expenditure on the improvement of salary scales.

44. As regards conditions of service, the fact that teachers are employed by various authorities, such as State Governments, Municipalities, District Boards and private bodies, is an important element in variations in salaries, standards, working conditions and prospects of teachers which may be found within the same State. It is recommended that each State may consider bringing elementary school teachers in the State into its own service in appropriate cadres. When the services of teachers are placed at the disposal of local bodies or of private institutions, according to the cadres to which they belong, their terms of appointment would be maintained. This would enable State Governments to extend to teachers adequate benefits of security, pension, provident fund contributions, promotion and opportunities to qualify for higher grades and also provide them appropriate amenities.

Scholarships

45. With a view to providing greater equality of opportunity in the field of education and making available educational facilities to deserving students, a number of scholarship schemes were introduced during the first plan. About Rs. 12 crores for scholarships are being provided in the second five year plan; these are besides continuing schemes for scholarships which do not form part of the plan. Scholarships are provided, amongst others, for students from scheduled tribes, scheduled castes and other backward classes. The programmes also includes post-matriculation scholarships, research scholarships, overseas scholarships and cultural scholarships for Asian, African and other foreign students for study in India.

46. The main categories of scholarships provided are as follows (Table 19.7):

TABLE 19.7: Main Categories of Scholarships

	Number of scholarships, stipends, etc.
(a) *Central Government—Continuing Schemes*:	
1. For scheduled castes, scheduled tribes and other backward classes	155,000
2. For study abroad	361
3. For foreign students for study in India	2,580
4. Others	359
(b) *Central Government—under the second five year plan* :	
1. For scheduled castes, scheduled tribes and other backward classes	74,500
2. For research in humanities	500
3. For young artists in different fields	500
4. For study abroad	465
5. For foreign students for study in India	610
6. Others	1,560
(c) *State Governments—under the second five year plan in in addition to continuing schemes*):	
1. At elementary stage	2,500
2. At secondary stage	12,000
3. At university stage (humanities)	6,600
4. Technical education	1,200
5. Others	16,000

47. Stipends for vocational and industrial education have been in-

cluded in schemes sponsored by the Labour and Industries Departments in the States and by the Ministry of Labour at the Centre. Stipends for higher scientific and technological research are given by the Ministry of Natural Resources and Scientific Research, for agricultural research by the Ministry of Agriculture, and for medical research by the Ministry of Health. It would be correct to say that under the second plan a fair proportion of students, with ability and aptitude, who wish to undertake higher studies and research, will be able to do so with practical support from the State.

Cultural and Other Programmes

48. The Ministry of Education have a number of important programmes of value for cultural development and integration which may be briefly stated.

(a) The plan provides for the development of Hindi and of regional languages. The programmes relating to Hindi includes the preparation of a Hindi encyclopaedia, standard text-books and elementary readers, grants to organisations engaged in the study and development of the Hindi language, and scholarships for higher studies in Hindi to candidates from non-Hindi speaking areas. Besides provisions at the Centre, State plans include schemes for the development of regional languages and also provide for the dissemination of the Hindi language. The Akadami of Letters will also have schemes for developing the various languages and literatures of the country. A National Book Trust is being constituted for promoting the publication of good books in all languages at low prices through Indianm publishers with a view to making them available on as large a scale as possible. A beginning in this direction has been made through the setting up of the South India Book Trust. The plan also provides for the establishment of a Sanskrit University at Kurukshetra and Banaras, and it is proposed to appoint a Commission to enquire into the present state of Sanskrit education in the country and to suggest measures for its further development.

(b) For the development of arts, the Akadami of Letters, the Akadami of Dance, Drama and Music and the Akadami of Fine Arts have programmes for which provision is made in the plan. The plan provides for the construction of a building for the National Theatre, for re-organisation and development of museums including a National Children's Museum, development of the National Gallery of

Modern Art, establishment of a Bal Bhavan (children centre), for development of the National Library, Calcutta, establishment of a Central Reference Library in Delhi and the publication of a National Bibliography.

(c) Provision has been made for the development of the Department of Archaeology, the National Archives of India and the Department of Anthropology. A Central Institute of Indology is also to be established. Gazetteers for various States and districts are to be revised. Work on the preparation of the History of the Freedom Movement is to be completed during the plan period.

(d) The plan provides for the Research Centre for Southern Asia on the Social Implications of Industrialisation which has been recently established by UNESCO in co-operation with the Government of India.

49. Our survey of programmes of education during the second five year plan has shown that in every field tasks of great significance for the future of the nation have to be accomplished. If larger resources can be made available for education by public authorities as well as by each local community, greater progress can be achieved and goals, which still seem distant, can be reached earlier. For economic development to make its full contribution to the well-being of the mass of the people programmes of education should be ahead of economic plans. Means must, therefore, be found to overcome current limitations upon efforts in the field of education. The problem of re-organisation of the system of education may be viewed as comprising a series of practical objectives, such as expansion in the numbers for whom educational facilities are available, provision of larger opportunities for girls and for women generally, diversification of education at the secondary stage, replacement of the traditional primary education by education along basic lines, development of social education, adequate provision for technical and vocational education, and improvement of education in the universities. Behind these tasks lie more fundamental aims. With so much lost ground to recover, to advance rapidly the nation needs unity, co-operation in all fields, and a high spirit of endeavour. Modern economic development calls for a wide diffusion of the scientific temper of mind, a sense of dignity in labour and discipline in service, and a readiness to adapt new techniques and new knowledge to the needs of the people. These values and attitudes will be realised in every day life in the measure in which they are expressed through educational ideals and practice.

20

THIRD FIVE YEAR PLAN*

Introduction

The Third Plan noted that education must become the focal point of planned development. And as such the Chapter XXIX on Education is sub-titled 'Education and National Development'. Education has been considered as the most important single factor not only in achieving rapid economic development and technological progress but also in creating a social order founded on the values of freedom, social justice and equal opportunity. The plan aimed at developing both skill and knowledge and a creative outlook, a feeling of national unity which stands above region, caste and language and an understanding of common interests and obligations The emphasis was laid on the provision of facilities for the education of all children in the age group 6-11, orientation of all elementary schools to the basic pattern, establishment of basic schools in urban areas, to link up basic education with the development activities of each local community, provision of diversified courses in secondary schools, development of multipurpose schools, expansion and improvement of facilities for the teaching of science, provision of educational and vocational guidance, enlargement of facilities for vocational education, training of teachers for basic schools, inclusion of craft as one of the core subjects, extension and improvement of the teaching of science at the secondary and university stage, increase in scholarships, freeships and other assistance, and concentration on the education of girls. The plan also stressed that the school programme should be designed to awaken in the pupils an awareness of national oneness and for this purpose educational institutions should include community living based on cooperative self-help and democratic principles.

---

* Planning Commission, Government of India, New Delhi 1961.

EDUCATION[1]

Education and National Development

Education is the most important single factor in achieving rapid economic development and technological progress and in creating a social order founded on the values of freedom, social justice and equal opportunity. Programmes of education lie at the base of the effort to forge the bounds of common citizenship, to harness the energies of the people, and to develop the natural and human resources of every part of the country. Developments of the past decade have created a momentum for economic growth; yet, there are large deficiencies in the sphere of education, which must be removed speedily if progress is to be sustained and enduring. It is one of the major aims of the Third Plan to expand and intensify the educational effort and to bring every home within its fold, so that from now on, in all branches of national life, education becomes the focal point of planned development.

2. In the field of general education, as distinguished from technical education, the main emphasis in the Third Plan will be on the provision of facilities for the education of all children in the age group 6-11, extension and improvement of the teaching of science at the secondary and university stages, development of vocational and technical education at all levels, expansion and improvement of facilities for the training of teachers for each stage of education, and increase in scholarships, freeships and other assistance. There will be special concentration on the education of girls, and the existing disparities in levels of development in education between boys and girls will be substantially reduced. All elementary schools will be oriented to the basic pattern. Reorganisation of university education along the lines of the three-year degree course will be completed, and facilities for post-graduate studies and research work will be further expanded and improved. At all stages of education, the aim must be to develop both skill and knowledge and a creative outlook, a feeling of national unity which stands above region, caste and language, and an understanding of common interests and obligations.

1. (i) Paras refer to paras of Chapter XXIX of the document.
   (ii) Original Table Numbers have been changed to conform to this chapter number.

Achievements and Targets

3. Over the decade 1951-61, the number of students increased from 23.5 million to 43.5 million. The increase in the number of pupils in the age-group 6-11 was 79 per cent, in the age-group 11-14, 102 per cent, and in the age-group 14-17, 139 per cent. The proportion of children in these groups attending schools rose respectively from 43 to 61 per cent, 13 to 23 per cent and 5 to 12 per cent. In the course of the Third Plan, the total number of pupils at school is expected to increase by 20-4 million, 15.3 million in the age-group 6-11, 3.5 million in the age-group 11-14 and 1.6 million in the age-group 14-17. Table 20.1 shows the progress during the first two Plans and the likely increase in the Third Plan.

TABLE 20.1: Number of Students at School: Progress during First Plan and Second Plan and Estimated increase during Third Plan, 1950-51, 1955-56, 1960-61, 1965-66

(lakhs)

Stage and age-group	1950-51	1955-56	1960-61 (likely achievement)	1965-66 (targets)
Primary (6-11)				
enrolment	191.5	251.7	343.4	496.4
percentage of the age-group	42.6	52.9	61.1	76.4
Middle (11-14)				
enrolment	31.2	42.9	62.9	97.5
percentage of the age-group	12.7	16.5	22.8	28.6
Secondary (14-17)				
enrolment	12.2	18.8	29.1	45.6
percentage of the age-group	5.3	7.8	11.5	15.6
Total (6-17)				
enrolment	234.9	313.4	435.4	639.5
percentage of the age-group	25.4	32.1	39.9	50.1

4. During the first two Plans, the number of schools increased by 73 per cent from 230,555 to 398,200, increase in the number of primary schools being 63 per cent, in middle schools 191 per cent, and in high schools 128 per cent. Progress in basic education at the elementary level is reflected in the increase in the proportion of junior basic schools and senior basic schools from 16 per cent to 29 per cent and from 3 per cent to 30 per cent respectively. Reorganisa-

tion of secondary education has mainly taken the form of conversion of high schools into higher secondary schools, establishment of multipurpose schools providing for a variety of courses, and expansion of teaching facilities both for general science and science as an elective subject. The All-India Educational Survey, which was undertaken during 1957-59, revealed important gaps in the distribution of educational institutions. Thus, for the country as a whole, in 1957, about 29 per cent of rural habitations and about 17 per cent of the rural population were not served by any school. In some States these proportions were very much higher.

Progress in establishing new schools during the first two Plans was relatively greater in respect of middle and high schools than in the case of primary schools. With the provision of educational facilities for the entire population in the age-group 6-11, this trend will be corrected to a considerable extent in the course of the Third Plan. The Plan envisages increase in the number of primary schools by 73,000, of middle schools by 18,100 and of high schools by 5,200. The total number of schools in the country will go up by about 24 per cent to about 494,500. Table 20.2 shows the progress realised in setting up new schools during the first two Plans and the programme for the Third Plan.

TABLE 20.2: Progress in setting up New Schools during First Plan and Second Plan and Programme for the Third Plan, 1950-51, 1955-56, 1960-61, 1965-66

Item	1950-51	1955-56	1960-61 (likely achievement)	1965-66 (targets)
Primary schools (including Junior basic)	209671	278135	342000	415000
junior basic schools	33379	42971	100000	153000
Middle schools (including Senior basic)	13596	21730	39600	57700
senior basic schools	351	4842	11940	16700
High and higher secondary schools	7288	10838	16600	21800
higher secondary schools	47	503	3121	6390
multipurpose schools	..	255	2115	2446
secondary schools with elective science	..	..	4625	9579

5. The proportion of trained teachers has increased during the period 1951-61 from 59 to 65 per cent in primary schools, from 53 to

65 per cent in middle schools, and from 54 to 68 per cent in high schools. These figures suggest that progress in providing trained teachers has not been on an adequate scale. As a result of the more intensive programmes proposed for the Third Plan, the proportion of trained teachers in each category is expected to rise to about 75 per cent. Increase in the number of training institutions and in the number of trained teachers may be seen from the Table 20.3.

TABLE 20.3: Trained Teachers and Training Institutions: Progress during First Plan and Second Plan and Estimated Increase during Third Plan, 1950-51, 1955-56, 1960-61, 1965-66.

Item	1950-51	1955-56	1960-61 (likely achievement)	1965-66 (targets)
Training institutions				
training schools	782	930	1307	1424
training colleges	53	107	236	312
Teachers:				
Primary schools				
teachers	537918	691249	910000	1266000
trained teachers	316124	423192	591500	949500
percentage of trained teachers	58.8	61.2	65.0	75.0
middle schools:				
teachers	854996	148394	230000	360000
trained teachers	45569	86810	149500	270000
percentage of trained teachers	53.3	58.5	65.0	75.0
high/higher secondary schools:				
teachers	126504	189794	229000	290000
trained teachers	68059	113307	155720	217500
percentage of trained teachers	53.8	59.7	68.0	75.0

It is considered that the targets in respect of trained teachers at present formulated by States should be regarded as provisional and every effort made to improve upon them.

6. There has been a large increase in the number of students in universities and colleges, the total enrolment for arts, science and commerce courses being 360,000 in 1950-51, 634,000 in 1955-56 and about 900,000 in 1960-61. During the Second Plan, for the country as a whole, the proportion of students taking science courses increased from 33 per cent to about 36 per cent. In some States progress was specially marked, but there are others where there are still considerable lags. The Third Plan envisages that of the increase of

400,000 students at the university stage, about 60 per cent should be in respect of science classes, bringing the proportion of students taking science courses to over 42 per cent. Development in university education in relation to arts, science and commerce during the first two Plans and the proposals for the Third Plan are summarised in the Table 20.4.

TABLE 20.4: Enrolment and Institutions: Development during First and Second Plan and Proposals for Third Plan, 1950-51, 1955-57, 1960-61, 1965-66

(in thousands)

Item	1950-51	1955-56	1960-61 (likely achievement)	1965-66 (targets)
University stage, age-group 17-23:				
enrolment	360	634	900	1300
percentage of age-group	0.0	1.5	1.9	2.4
Enrolment in science classes	202	222	323	353
Enrolment in science classes as % of total enrolment	38.1	33.0	35.8	42.5
Institutions:				
arts, science and commerce college (numbers)	542	772	1050	1400
Universities (numbers)	27	32	45	58

Outlays

7. The total outlay on education, including engineering and technological education, was Rs. 153 crores in the First Plan and Rs. 256 crores in the Second Plan. Programmes included in the Third Plan entail a total outlay of Rs. 560 crores. For programmes, other than those relating to engineering and technological education set out . . . outlay during the First Plan was Rs. 133 crores, and during the Second Plan Rs. 208 crores, while programmes for the Third Plan involve a total expenditure of Rs. 418 crores including a provision of Rs. 10 crores for cultural programmes.

Table 20.5 shows the distribution of outlay on scheme of general education under the First, Second and Third Plans.

In addition to provisions under the head 'Education', resources to the extent of Rs. 87 crores are expected to be available under the community development programme and of about Rs. 42 crores under the programme for the welfare of backward classes, thus bringing the total provision for general education in the Third Plan to Rs. 497 crores, as against Rs. 250 crores during the Second Plan.

TABLE 20.5: Distribution of Outlay on Schemes of General Education under First, Second and Third Plans

Sub-head	amount (Rs. crores)			percentage		
	First Plan	Second Plan	Third Plan	First Plan	Second Plan	Third Plan
Elementary education	85	87	209	63.9	41.9	50.0
Secondary education	20	48	88	15.1	23.1	21.1
University education	14	45	82	10.5	21.6	19.6
Other programmes:						
social education		4	6		1.9	1.4
physical education and youth welfare	14	10	12	10.5	4.8	2.9
others		10	11	..	4.8	2.6
Total	133	204	408	100.0	98.1	97.6
Cultural programmes	*	4	10	..	1.9	2.4
Grand total	133	208	418	100.0	100.0	100.0

* The outlay on cultural programmes in the First Plan was included under other programmes.

8. Provisions in each Plan for education, as in other fields, are in addition to resources provided for 'maintaining' institutions established up to the end of the preceding Plan, as well as to contributions from non-government sources. It is estimated that during the Third Plan period maintenance of educational institutions will involve a total expenditure of about Rs. 700 crores as against Rs. 375 crores in the Second Plan. The contribution from non-government sources is difficult to estimate precisely. Over the past decade this contribution has increased from about Rs. 50 to crores to about Rs. 90 crores per year. In the course of the Third Plan on account of the transfer of responsibility for elementary education to panchayats and panchayat samitis and greater effort on the part of corporations and municipalities, this contribution is likely to increase to about Rs. 120-130 crores per annum.

Pre-school Education

9. The need for expanding facilities for pre-school education is

being increasingly stressed. In the past progress in this direction has depended mainly on the work of voluntary organisations and the establishment of a number of balwadis. The number of children enrolled in pre-school classes rose from 28,000 in 1950-51 to 75,000 in 1955-56, and is now estimated at about 300,000. There are at present about 5,000 balwadis; of these about 2,500 are assisted by the Central and State Social Welfare Boards. The existing balwadis need to be improved and provided with trained child welfare workers (bal sevikas). The Third Plan provides for setting up of six training centres for Bal Sevikas. In the programme for education Rs. 3 crores have been allotted for child welfare and allied schemes at the Centre and about Rs. 1 crore in the State in addition to resources available under the community development and social welfare programmes. Schemes for child welfare now being formulated by the Ministry of Education include improvement of existing balwadis, opening of new balwadis, expansion of the training programmes for bal sevikas and a number of pilot projects for child welfare in which education, health and welfare services will be organised in an integrated manner. Schemes for children, specially the setting up of balwadis, will continue to be an important part of the programmes undertaken for women and children in community development blocks and in welfare extension projects.

Elementary Education

10. The Constitution envisaged the provision of free, universal and compulsory education for children up to the age of 14 years. In view of the magnitude of the task, it was agreed early in the Second Plan that as a first step facilities should be created for the education of all children in the age-group 6-11. This is one of the central aims of the Third Plan, to be followed by extension of education for the entire age-group 11-14 during the Fourth and Fifth Plans. The principal problems in providing facilities for the entire age-group 6-11 in the course of the Third Plan period arise from the following factors:

(a) difficulties of bringing girls to school in sufficient numbers;
(b) extreme backwardness of certain areas and certain sections of the population in the matter of education; and
(c) 'wastage' due to parents taking away children from school as soon as they are able to add to the family income so that more

than one-half of the children do not reach class IV, thus failing to gain permanent literacy.

11. A very large gap still exists between the proportion of boys and girls attending school. In 1960-61, about 80.5 per cent of the boys were in school as against about 40.4 per cent of the girls. Among States in which the proportion of girls falls much below the average for the country as a whole, are Rajasthan (15%), Uttar Pradesh (20%), Jammu and Kashmir (21%), Madhya Pradesh (19%). Bihar (27%), Orissa (24%) and Punjab (36%). The National Council for Women's Education carefully considered the special measures needed for promoting the education of girls at the primary, middle and secondary stages and made a series of recommendations.These include the provision of quarters for women teachers, special allowances to women teachers working in rural areas, condensed educational courses for adult women so as to enlarge the supply of women teachers, stipends for women teacher trainees, attending prizes and scholarships, appointment of school-mothers in co-educational institutions and provision of the necessary amenities. To some extent proposals on these lines have been embodied in the plans of States. It is suggested that the various provisions which have been made in these plans should be reviewed afresh at an early date and, from the second year of the Plan, additional steps should be taken to expand specially those facilities which aim at enlarging the supply of women teachers and attracting them to service in the rural areas.

12. The problem of providing educational facilities in backward areas is in part one of ensuring that the institutions are so located that almost every child can go to a school within easy walking distance from his home. The findings of the Educational Survey, referred to earlier, will assist States in planning and locating of new schools from this aspect. Scattered habitations, such as hilly tracts, present certain obvious difficulties, in these, it will be necessary to provide additional facilities, even though these will be relatively more expensive.

13. Apart from the poverty of parents, the circumstances which lead to wastage are lack of properly qualified and trained teachers, defective curricula and insufficient appreciation of the value of education by parents. Closely allied to 'wastage' is 'stagnation' which occurs in the case of children who continue in the same class for

more than a year. Introduction of compulsion, appointment of trained and qualified teachers, improvement in the methods of teaching, greater understanding on the part of parents of the desirability of letting their children remain at school, and the planning of school holidays, so that they coincide with the harvesting and sowing seasons, are among the steps to be taken to reduce the incidence of 'stagnation' and 'wastage'.

14. The programme for extending education to all children in the age-group 6-11 is of such crucial importance that financial considerations as such should not be allowed to come in the way of its successful execution in any State. There may, however, be other limitations which may be more difficult to overcome in a short period for instance, the measure in which some of the poorer or more backward sections of the population or the more backward areas respond to the drive for education, the time needed to persuade all parents to send their daughters to school, the extent of participation and eagerness on the part of the local community, the ability on the part of education authorities to obtain a sufficient number of teachers, both men and women, who will identify themselves with the communities in which they work and, finally, the practical steps taken to provide reasonable conditions and prospects to the vast body of teachers working in primary schools. Taking all these factors into account, it is at present estimated that by the end of the Third Plan about 90 per cent of the boys and about 62 per cent of the girls will be at school, the overall percentage for the age-group 6-11 being 76. Table 20.6 shows, in the course of the Third Plan, about 15.3 million additional children will come into schools, of whom 8.6 million are likely to be girls.

TABLE 20.6 Pupils in Age-Group 6-11, 1950-51 to 1965-66

Year	Enrolment in classes I-V (lakhs)			Percentage of population in age-group 6-11		
	boys	girls	total	boys	girls	total
1950-51	137.7	53.8	191.5	59.8	24.6	42.6
1955-56	175.3	76.4	251.7	70.3	32.4	52.9
1960-61	233.8	109.6	343.4	80.5	40.4	61.1
1965-66	301.2	195.2	496.4	90.4	61.6	76.4

Differences in levels of development between States will be narrowed to some extent, but they will still be quite considerable. This may be seen from the targets indicated by different States which are set out in Annexure I to this chapter.

15. *Middle school education* (11-14 *years*).—During the decade 1951-61, the number of children in the age-group 11-14 doubled, while the number of girls increased nearly three-fold. Nevertheless, at the end of the period, as compared to 34 per cent of the boys only about 11 per cent of the girls were at school. The Third Plan envisages almost a doubling of the number of girls at school as against the total increase for the age-group of about 54 per cent. The disparity between boys and girls will, however, be still a marked feature, for, against 40 per cent of the boys at schools from this age-group the proportion of girls is likely to be less than 17 per cent. Table 20.7 shows the enrolment of boys and girls in classes VI-VIII during the First, Second and Third Plans.

TABLE 20.7: Pupils in Age-Group 11-14: 1950-51 to 1965-66

Year	Enrolment in classes VI-VIII (lakhs)			Percentage of population in age-group 11-14		
	boys	girls	total	boys	girls	total
1950-51	25.9	5.3	31.2	20.7	4.5	12.7
1955-56	34.2	8.7	42.9	25.5	6.9	16.5
1960-61	48.2	14.7	62.9	34.3	10.8	22.8
1965-66	70.0	27.5	97.5	39.9	16.5	28.6

16. The main problems which arise in the expansion of facilities for children in the age-group 6-11 are found in a more accentuated form in the next age-group 11-14, specially in rural areas.

There are large differences in the extent of development in different States as may be seen in Annexure II to this chapter. The difficulties of providing schooling facilities for backward areas and for scattered populations are even greater in the case of middle school education than in that of primary education.

In the more backward areas and among the more backward sections of the population, rapid development of middle school education can take place only after the necessary foundations at the primary level have been laid. Accordingly, in the Third Plan, for these areas, it will be necessary to concentrate on the expansion of primary education for these groups.

The question of providing facilities on a part-time basis for training in suitable vocations or by way of continuation classes is at present being studied. It should be possible to organise such courses to an increasing extent at middle schools, basic schools, junior technical schools and other centres. The possibility of organising vocational training on a full-time basis for children in the age-group 11-14 should also be examined.

For expanding facilities for the education of girls, the various recommendations of the National Council for Women's Education should be considered further on the lines suggested earlier for primary education.

17. For practical and administrative reasons, the programme of education for the age-group 6-14 visualised in the Constitution has been divided into two stages, 6-11 and 11-14. If the entire age-group 6-14 is considered together, it will be seen from the table below that over the past ten years the number of children at school has gone up from 22.3 million to 40.6 million, the proportion of the total population in the age-group rising from about 32 to 49 per cent. In the case of boys the proportion has risen from 46 to 65 per cent, and in the case of girls from 18 to 31 per cent.

TABLE 20.8: Pupils in Age-group 6-14, 1950-51 to 1965-66

Year	Enrolment in classes I-VIII (lakhs)			Percentage of population in age-group 6-14		
	boys	girls	total	boys	girls	total
1950-51	163.6	59.1	222.7	45.9	17.5	32.1
1955-56	209.5	85.1	294.6	54.6	23.5	40.0
1960-61	282.0	124.3	406.3	65.4	30.6	48.5
1965-66	371.2	222.7	593.9	73.0	46.1	59.5

The Third Plan postulates an increase in the number of children in the age-group 6-14 about equal to that achieved during the preceding decade. For girls the proportion in the age-group should go up to about 46 per cent and for boys to about 73 per cent, the overall proportion increasing to nearly 60 per cent. These figures provide a measure of the task that remains to be carried out during the Fourth and Fifth Plans.

Basic Education

18. Reorganisation of school education along basic lines has been a key programme since the First Plan. During the Third Plan it is proposed to convert about 57,760 schools into basic schools, to orient the remaining schools to the basic pattern, to remodel all training institutions along basic lines, to establish basic schools in urban areas, and to link up basic education with the development activities of each local community.

19. Progress towards fully developed basic schools will inevitably be spread over a long period, since the number of elementary schools involved is large and the majority of the existing teachers have yet to be trained in the techniques of basic education. By way of preparation for conversion into basic schools, a programme for orienting all existing schools to the basic pattern was initiated during the Second Plan. This aims at the adoption of a common syllabus in all basic and non-basic schools and the introduction of simple crafts and activities like social service, community living, and cultural and recreational programmes, which do not involve much expenditure or require teachers fully trained in basic education. With a view to completing the process of orientation during the earlier phase of the Third Plan, it is proposed that schools should be given simple equipment needed for the purpose and teachers who have not been trained in basic education should be given short orientation courses.

Trained Teachers for Basic and Other Schools

20. Perhaps the most important measure for the expansion of basic education is the provision of larger facilities for the training of teachers for basic schools and the reorganisation of existing training centres along basic lines. At the end of the Second Plan, elementary school teachers were being trained in 1,307 institutions, of which about 70 per cent were already organised on the basic pattern. By the end of the Third Plan, the number of training institutions will increase to 1,424 and all of them will impart training on basic lines, the number of pupil-teachers on rolls being about 200,000 as compared to 135,000 in 1960-61. For teachers who have not been trained in basic education, short-term courses of training in the simpler aspects of basic education are to be provided.

In most States the period of training for elementary school

teachers is proposed to be extended to two years with a view to ensuring a greater measure of thoroughness both in regard to courses and methods. In a number of training schools extension departments will be established for improving the quality of teaching in schools in the neighbourhood. Towards the end of the Second Plan, 276 new training institutions were set up in preparation for the introduction of universal primary education during the Third Plan. The State schemes provide for equipment, buildings and other facilities for these and other institutions.

A factor limiting the expansion of basic education is that it has been largely confined to rural areas. A number of experimental basic schools are, therefore, proposed to be set up in urban areas, so that the problems of basic schools in urban areas can be clearly identified and solutions found for them in cooperation with training colleges.

Community Effort

21. Provisions made in the plans of States need to be supplemented by local community effort in programmes such as organisation of enrolment drives, persuading parents to send girls to schools, construction of school buildings, and provision of additional equipment and furniture to schools and of mid-day meals and free clothing for the poorer children. In several States encouraging results have been achieved in the mobilisation of local resources, and it is expected that local support will be forth coming in even greater measure as Panchayati Raj institutions are established in different States.

Several States have provided in their plans for mid-day meals for children attending schools, notably, Madras, Kerala, Andhra Pradesh, Mysore and Orissa. In Madras, which has the largest programme in this field, one million children are expected to benefit in addition to about a million already being served by the programme. About 40 per cent of the expenditure is being met by the local community. The movement for mid-day meals provides a special opportunity for each urban or rural community not only to participate in the educational effort, but also to improve nutrition and health in the schools and to assist the poorer students. Although the programme is at present somewhat limited on account of financial considerations, it is suggested that State Governments should endeavour to provide for it, at any rate, wherever local communities come forward to take their due share in it.

Secondary Education

22. Development of the economy and the large increase in the number of secondary schools and in the number of students of the age-group 14-17 enrolled in them have altered the character of the demands which secondary education is called upon to meet. New social groups are seeking education and are coming within its influence. Expansion has brought into secondary schools a larger range of abilities and aptitudes. Secondary schools have to be so reorganised that they provide diversified educational service to pupils according to their needs. In the middle and lower grades of many branches of economic life, in administration, rural development, commerce, industry and the professions, the requirements of trained manpower have to be met after the necessary training, by products of secondary schools.

The programme for the reorganisation and improvement of secondary education, which was taken up following the report of the Secondary Education Commission, has proceeded along several lines and is designed both to enlarge the content of secondary education and to make it a self-contained unit within the educational process. The measures envisaged are the conversion of high schools into higher secondary schools, development of multipurpose schools with provision of a number of elective subjects along with and in addition to the academic course, expansion and improvement of facilities for the teaching of science, provision of educational and vocational guidance, improvement of the examination and evaluation system, enlargement of facilities for vocational education, increased facilities for the education of girls and the backward classes and encouragement to merit through scholarships.

23. Reconstruction along these lines involves a major revision of the secondary school curriculum and the introduction of new techniques and procedure. Subject such as general science and social studies and the various elective courses are relatively new concepts in the secondary school curriculum and call for a new orientation on the part of the secondary school teacher. In turn, this has necessitated a country wide programme of in-service teacher education organised by State Education Departments as well as special extension services.

Secondary school teachers have to be thoroughly prepared for handling the new subjects efficiently. The teachers education programme at the pre-service level has also to be reorganised in line with the changes that have taken place at the secondary level. The standard of science education has to be raised to a level which will effectively support the future scientific advance of the nation. Shortcomings which have been observed in the working of the multipurpose schools have to be remedied and the scheme placed on a stable footing. Educational and vocational guidance programmes have to be extended to reach as many schools and pupils as possible. Several other measures have also to be taken to strengthen the entire programme of the secondary school reorganisation, such as improvement in craft teaching, organisation of school libraries, the better use of audio-visual techniques, etc. Special emphasis is, therefore, to be given in the Third Plan to the consolidation and improvement of quality in all aspects of secondary education reorganisation.

24. *Enrolment*—In the first two Plans the number of secondary schools increased from 7,288 in 1950-51 to nearly 16,600 at the end of 1960-61. The number of children enrolled in classes IX to XI increased from about 1.2 million to 2.9 million. Although the number of girls in these classes increased from 200,000 to 520,000 during this period, girls constituted less than one-fifth of the total number attending secondary schools. As the following table shows, at the end of the Second Plan only about 4.2 per cent of girls availed of high school education as compared to about 18.4 per cent of boys of the age-group 14-17. There is thus serious disparity between enrolment in the two groups which, in turn, affects the number of women available for filling such positions as teachers, nurses, village level workers, social workers and others. In the Third Plan the number of girls in schools will be nearly doubled, but their proportion in the age-group as a whole will remain low, being about 7 per cent as compared to about 24 per cent in the case of boys.

TABLE 20.9: Pupils in age-group 14-17, 1950-51 to 1965-66

Year	Enrolment in classes IX-XI (lakhs)			Percentage of population in age-group 14-17		
	boys	girls	total	boys	girls	total
1950-51	10.2	2.0	12.2	8.7	1.8	5.3
1955-56	15.8	3.0	18.8	12.8	2.6	7.8
1960-61	23.9	5.2	29.1	18.4	4.2	11.5
1965-66	35.7	9.9	45.6	23.7	6.9	15.6

The Statewise position in regard to the enrolment at this stage is given in Annexure III to this chapter.

25. *Higher secondary schools*—One of the principal recommendations of the Secondary Education Commission was that high schools should be upgraded to higher secondary schools so as to make the curriculum more broad-based than in the past and to provide better standard of education by providing an additional year in school. This would make secondary education a terminal point for a large proportion of students who have to enter life directly at the end of the secondary school. During the first two Plans 3,121 higher secondary schools were established in different States. This number is expected to rise to 6,390 by the end of the Third Plan.

26. *Science education*—The Second Plan gave high priority to the expansion and improvement of science education at the secondary stage. The Secondary Education Commission had recommended that every secondary school pupil should study general science as a compulsory subject, so that he gains a basic quantum of scientific knowledge as part of his general education. In addition, provision was to be made for science as an elective subject for those students who wished to pursue higher studies. By the end of the Second Plan a programme of general or elementary science has been introduced in almost all secondary schools, while science of an elective standard has been provided in about 4,625 schools. However, a considerable proportion of schools lacks the basic minimum requirements in respect of laboratories and equipment and also suitable text-books and handbooks. Teachers have to be prepared in the integrated approach which is required in the teaching of general science. It is also necessary to encourage students in creative and original activity in science. This was sought to be done during the Second Plan by establishing science clubs in selected secondary schools and training colleges. About 450 such science clubs were established during this period.

In the Third Plan, in addition to providing general science in all the secondary school as s compulsory subject, more than 9,500 out of 21,800 secondary schools will also have science of an elective standard. The completion of this programme is expected to provide a more satisfactory foundation than at present for the further expansion of science education at the university stage during the Third and subsequent Plan periods. A number of supporting measures are also proposed to be taken to improve and strengthen the teaching of science. The existing science syllabi in force in different State will be reviewed and modified where necessary, with a view to integrating them with the science syllabi at the earlier and later stages of education. A programme of preparation of teachers' handbooks, students' manuals, science text-books and supplementary reading material in science will also be undertaken. The present shortage of science teachers will be made up to as large in extent as possible by increasing facilities of science education at the university stage and by providing various types of in-service training in content and methodology for the existing science teachers. The training of laboratory assistants in the techniques of handling laboratory apparatus will also be taken up during this period. In addition, steps will be taken to standardise designs of science apparatus and to get them manufactured in the country itself. In order to coordinate, guide and direct the entire programme of science teaching as well as the training of key personnel, a central organisation for science education is proposed to be set up in the Third Plan. A scheme of science talent search is to be introduced with a view to identifying promising talent at the secondary stage and providing opportunities for its development.

27. *Multipurpose schools*—One of the main defects in the secondary education system was its unilateral character, only one type of academic course being provided for all students irrespective of their individual aptitudes and abilities. The Secondary Education Commission, therefore, recommended the setting up of multipurpose schools, which would offer a number of practical courses along with the academic stream, so as to present the pupil with a variety of courses, out of which he could make his choice according to his special interests. During the first two Plans 2,115 multipurpose schools were established. These offer one or more practical courses in Technology, Agriculture, Commerce, Home Science and Fine Arts in addition to humanities and science. Although the concept of the multipurpose school has been readily accepted and the scheme has expanded rapidly, certain difficulties have been encountered, such as the lack of teachers trained to teach the practical subjects, insufficient teaching material, specially text-books and handbooks, limited range of elective courses and inadequacy of educational and vocational guidance facilities. During the Third Plan, therefore, it is proposed to concentrate on the consolidation of the scheme by strengthening the institutions already established, the programme of expansion being

limited to about 331 new schools. An integrated teacher training programme for the multipurpose schools is to be undertaken, and for this purpose four regional training colleges will be established which will prepare teachers for the multipurpose schools through in-service and pre-service training programmes both in the practical and the scientific subjects. Steps will also be taken to stimulate greater experimental work in multipurpose schools for providing courses of study suited to different levels of ability, including special programmes of education for gifted students.

28. *Education and vocational guidance*—The successful organisation of secondary education requires the provision of a well-planned programme of educational and vocational guidance which will help parents and pupils in selecting the most suitable educational courses and most satisfying vocational pursuits. The lack of such an organised programme of guidance has been one of the handicaps in the working of the multipurpose schools in the past. During the Second Plan, in addition to setting up of a Central Bureau of Educational and vocational Guidance. State Bureaux of Educational and Vocational Guidance were established in 12 States. These bureaux have been carrying out a programme of training of career masters and counsellors, test construction and guidance services to schools. The guidance movement, however, has not yet made a significant impact on secondary schools. It is, therefore, proposed in the Third Plan to strengthen the State Bureaux in such a manner as to help them to carry the guidance programme farther into the field and also to ensure a minimum programme of career information service in as many secondary schools as possible.

29. *Teaching of crafts*—The reorganised curriculum of secondary schools includes crafts as one of the core subjects. The problem of securing craft teachers in sufficient numbers and improving the teaching of crafts is one of great importance both for secondary education and for vocational education. A special study of the problem, is therefore, being undertaken by the Ministry of Education, and the findings of the study will be utilised to formulate a programme for craft and vocational education.

30. *School libraries*—Another aspect of secondary education which needs particular attention is the organisation of school libraries. Steps were taken in the First and the Second Plans for the improvement of school libraries but much remains to be done in the way of ensuring better utilisation of library facilities and improving

the reading habits of pupils. Use of library resources has to be an integral part of class teaching. During the Third Plan it is proposed to set up a few model school libraries in the demonstration schools attached to selected training colleges to serve both as models for the organisation and running of libraries as well as training centres for teacher librarians. A study is already under way of the existing organisation of the secondary school libraries and the directions in which improvement should be undertaken.

31. *Post-basic schools*—In some States post-basic schools were started by way of continuation at the secondary stage of senior basic schools. There are at present about 66 such schools. The relationship between post-basic schools and higher secondary schools has been recently considered by a committee, and it is proposed that these schools should be assisted to improve their standards of curriculum, instruction, equipment, laboratory and staff, so as to place them at par with the higher secondary and multi-purpose schools. Until these steps have been taken, the school final examination of the post-basic schools may be regarded as equivalent to certificates awarded to student of higher secondary schools for employment and other purposes.

32. *Training of teachers*—The number of training colleges has risen from 53 in 1950-51 to 236 in 1960-61. In the Third Plan the number of training colleges is expected to increase to 312. The existing training colleges will also be strengthened and expanded to increase the supply of trained teachers. While these measures take care of the numerical supply of trained graduate teachers, steps will also have to be taken to reorganise and strengthen the training college programme in order to align it with the current needs of the secondary school. Special emphasis in this matter will be given to pre-service training of teachers in science and social studies, introduction of new techniques of evaluation, provision of a variety of special subjects, such as guidance and audio-visual education and the organisation of research.

To provide in-service training facilities for secondary school teachers, extension centres were established during the Second Plan at 54 selected training colleges. These centres have been carrying out a comprehensive programme of in-service training, covering seminars, workshops and conferences, audio-visual, library and guidance services and publications. Each centre provides extension service to a number of schools in the area allotted to it (the number varying from

100 schools to over 300 schools), and intensive training for a group of selected schools (about 20) in the immediate neighbourhood. The extension service programmes has been found to be a valuable medium for continuous in-service training and as a means of keeping the training colleges and the secondary schools in close touch with each other. It is proposed to extend the scheme to a larger number of training colleges during the Third Plan with the ultimate object of making extension service an integral part of the work of every training college.

University Education

33. With the expanding base at the elementary and secondary education, the demand for higher education has greatly increased over the past decade. The number of universities has increased from 27 in 1950-51 to 32 in 1955-56 and to 46 in 1960-61, and about a dozen more universities are likely to be added during the Third Plan. The number of colleges (exclusive of intermediate colleges) rose from 772 in 1955-56 to 1,050 in 1960-61. During the Third Plan about 70 to 80 colleges will be added every year. The rapid expansion in the numbers of universities and colleges in recent years has led to a number of problems. These have been reviewed in the report of the University Grants Commission for 1959-60.

The Commission has stressed that if deterioration is to be avoided, increase in the number of students should be accompanied by corresponding expansion of physical and other teaching facilities. In the Third Plan larger facilities are being provided for diverting students to vocational and technological education. However, the problem is one of large dimensions and, even after taking into account these facilities, the number of those seeing admissions to the courses of higher education in arts, science and commerce will be large and suitable criteria for selection have to be adopted. In addition to the provision in the Plan for expansion of facilities for higher education, proposals for evening colleges, correspondence courses and the award of external degrees are at the present under consideration.

34. *Science education*—The programme for expanding facilities for science education during the Third Plan has been described earlier. This will involve larger provision of scientific equipment as well as appointment of more science teachers. It is proposed to prepare

standard lists for scientific equipment for the guidance of educational authorities. Schemes will also be initiated for the manufacture and supply of such equipment at low cost. A large number of scholarships will be provided to the meritorious science students. A continuing review of standards of teaching and examination in science and technology, at all levels, will also be carried out and preparation and publication of standard textbooks for use in the education programmes will be undertaken.

35. *Post-graduate studies and research*—Post-graduate studies and research in science and humanities will be further expanded in the Third Plan. Assistance was made available to universities during the Second Plan for additional accommodation, laboratory equipment and library facilities. Measures taken by the University Grants Commission during the Second Plan related to the development of new departments in universities in specialised fields of scientific study such as geophysics, astronomy, astrophysics, applied geology, oceanography, applied physics and animal genetics. In humanities, departments of Buddhistic and African studies and institutes or departments were developed for studies in Hindi, linguistics and social sciences, and for archaeology, museology, music, etc. The University Grants Commission also initiated a scheme during the Second Plan for awarding post-graduate and research scholarships and fellowships. Programmes initiated during the Second Plan will be continued and further developed during the Third Plan. The University Grants Commission will assist universities and post-graduate departments of colleges in the development of post-graduate studies and research, special emphasis being placed on scinece education. The number of students expected to undertake post-graduade studies in science courses is expected to increase by about 7,000 for post-graduate studies and 1,000 for research. In all, there will be an increase of about 70 per cent in the enrolment of science students at the post-degree level. The number of additional arts students will be 7,000 and 2,000 respectively.

36. *Women's education*—Shortages of educated women available for taking up various occupations point to the need for increasing the proportion of women students in colleges and universities. The proportion of women students to the total enrolment in Indian universities was about 13 per cent in 1955-56 and about 17 per cent in 1960-61, and is expected to be about 21 per cent in 1965-66. Apart from providing facilities for the increasing numbers of women stu-

dents, during the Second Plan, courses of special interest to women were initiated, such as Home Science, Music, Drawing, Painting, Nursing, etc. These facilities will have to be further expanded. During the Second Plan, the University Grants Commission provided liberal assistance for women's colleges and women's hostels. This will be continued in the Third Plan. Further, in order to encourage women students, special scholarships will continue to be provided. A proposal for setting up an institute for training women in organisation, administration and management is at present under examination.

37. *Rural institutes*—Eleven Rural Institutes were established in the Second Plan with the object of providing higher education after the secondary stage to the rural students in their own setting for developing rural leadership, and for stimulating active participation of the rural population in welfare and community development programmes. The Institutes were intended to train rural youth for specialised jobs in fields like rural development, cooperation, social welfare, social education and small-scale industries. Diploma courses in rural services, rural civil engineering, agricultural and health services were offered in the rural institutes. The enrolment of the Institutes by the end of the Second Plan was over 2,300 and the annual output in various courses was over 500.

This scheme is still in an experimental stage and will be continued in the Third Plan, so that the Institutes can develop their activities fully. The working of a few rural institutes was assessed by special committees and measures for improvement have been taken in the light of their recommendations. In the Third Plan, it will be necessary to examine the full potentialities of these Institutes and their contribution towards meeting the manpower requirements for rural development as as to equip them fully to the development needs of rural communities.

38. *Three-year degree course*—With a view to bringing about qualitative improvement in higher education, in most of the universities, the three-year degree course in arts, science and commerce following the higher secondary school examination or a year's course at the pre-university stage after the present matriculation or equivalent examination, has been already introduced. The three-year degree course also includes other reforms such as improvement in the teacher-pupil ratio, introduction of tutorial system, general education, improvement of libraries, laboratories and instructional build-

ings. Periodical conferences, seminars, summer schools and refresher course will continue to be organised as in the Second Plan for teachers in different subjects. Teachers will also obtain special grants for visiting centres of research for short periods. Among additional amenities for students are the provision of hostels, hobby workshops, non-resident students' centres, health centres, counselling and student aid funds. These will continue in the Third Plan.

Girls' Education

39. Some aspects of the problem of girls' education at different stages have been touched upon earlier in the discussion of elementary, secondary and university education. There are a few broader aspects of the subject which need further consideration. Over the past decade, while the additional number of boys enrolled in schools was 13.2 million, in the case of girls the additional enrolment was only 6.8 million. The census of 1961 has shown that, as against a literacy rate of 34 per cent for men, only about 13 per cent of the women are literate. Consequently, by far the most important objective in the field of education during the Third Plan must be to expand facilities for the education of girls at various stages. According to the programmes which have been formulated, taking age-group 6-14, the proportion of girls at schools should increase to 46 per cent, compared to 73 per cent for boys. Out of about 20.4 million additional children to be enrolled in schools during the Third Plan in the various age-groups, about 10.3 million are expected to be girls, their proportion in the lowest age-group being 56 per cent. At the end of the Third Plan, the disparity between boys and girls, although somewhat reduced, will still the considerable. Even to achieve the estimates mentioned above, a massive effort will be needed throughout the country and, more especially, in those States where the education of girls has seriously lagged behind.

40. It is estimated that of the resources available under the Plan for the development of education about Rs. 175 crores will be devoted to the education of girls, of which about Rs. 114 crores are for education at the primary and middle schools stages. As stated earlier, some provision has also been made for special schemes intended to support the general programme for girls' education. It is suggested that in implementing the various provisions made for girls' education in their plans, State should keep in view detailed recom-

mendations contained in the Report of the National Committee on Women's Education. As has been pointed out, special emphasis must be laid on creating suitable conditions for encouraging parents to send their daughters to schools, educating public opinion, increasing the number of women from rural areas who will take up the vocation of teaching and inducing women from urban areas to accept post of teachers in rural schools. It is proposed to evaluate carefully from year to year the progress made in implementing the programme for girls' education and to take such further measures as may be needed for realising the targets set for the Third Plan. In the field of girls' education, it is specially necessary to study closely such successful method as may be evolved in different parts of the country and to make such experience available generally. In drawing up annual plans also, care should be taken to see that the programme for girls' education is not held back for lack of financial resources and that the social and organisational limitations which impede progress at present are eliminated as early as possible.

Scholarships

41. Expenditure on scholarship programmes rose from about Rs. 3.5 crores in 1950-51 to over Rs. 8 crores in 1955-56 and to about Rs. 11 crores in 1957-58. It is expected to increase to about Rs. 18 crores by 1960-61. The number of scholarship-holders rose from 3.6 lakhs in 1950-51 to 8.8 lakhs in 1956-57. Of the latter about 7.8 lakhs were in schools and about 1 lakh in colleges and universities. In addition to this, by 1956-57 free studentships and other financial concessions were available to about 50 lakhs of students—1.5 lakhs in colleges and universities and 48.5 lakhs in schools. The proportion of students in colleges and universities receiving scholarships and stipends was 9 per cent in 1950-51, and is at present estimated to be about 16 per cent. These scholarships will be continued in the Third Plan.

An important scheme for scholarships is that relating to post-matriculation scholarships for scheduled tribes, scheduled castes and other backward classes which was taken up several years ago and now benefits over 50,000 students at an annual cost of Rs. 2.7 crores. At the pre-matriculation stage, 4 to 5 million children belonging to these groups received scholarships and other concessions in 1960-61, and the expenditure incurred under this head during the Second Plan was Rs. 12 crores.

42. In the Third Plan, provisions for new scholarships in different fields are given in Table 20.10.

TABLE 20.10: Provisions for New Scholarships in Different Fields in the Third Plan

Education programme	
pre-university stage	4.0
university stage	6.0
Programme for the welfare of backward classes	
pre-university stage	11.0
university stage	6.0
Technical and vocational education	
engineering and technology	8.0
craftsmen	2.0
total	37.0

Besides the provision mentioned above, there are research scholarships and fellowships provided by the University Grants Commission and scholarship schemes in fields such as agriculture, health, scientific research, etc.

43. State plans provide for extension of the existing schemes for scholarships. Among schemes undertaken by the Ministry of Education reference may be made to national scholarships for outstanding students at the post-matriculation stage, scholarships for overseas studies and a wide range of scholarships offered to Indian students by foreign countries and by international agencies. Under the programme for the welfare of backward classes, it is expected that the number of scholarships-holders in the school stage will increase to about 7 million. In the field of technical education, it is expected that as against about 6,000 students now receiving scholarships or other assistance, the number will rise to about 32,000 or 18 per cent of the total enrolment.

44. In view of the importance attached to scholarships in the Third Plan, it is suggested that State Governments and the Central Ministries concerned should review their existing schemes with the object of ensuring that, subject to continued good performance, the rules under which scholarships are given do in fact enable promising students in need of assistance to complete their education and that ordinarily help is not discontinued at intermediate stages. For such students there should be adequate provision not only at the post-matriculation stage, but also in the secondary classes. In the case of

students drawn from the economically backward sections, the aim should be to ensure adequate provisions for the numbers forthcoming and also for assisting an increasing proportion to reach the higher stages in education. It has been observed that because a sufficient number of qualified candidates are not forthcoming, administrative regulations regarding reservation of posts for this section of the population are not always fully implemented. Finally, there are some categories of personnel required in large numbers for which, in the ordinary course, there would be inadequate supply of candidates, for instance, science teachers, women teachers, nurses, etc. Such categories should be carefully identified in each State and an attempt made to select promising students at the post-matriculation stage and assist them with scholarships and stipends through the entire period of training. They should given the prospect of assured employment and should, in return, be under obligation to serve for prescribed periods.

Teachers' Salary Scales and Conditions of Service

45. The problem of raising the salary scales of teachers received special attention towards the end of the First Plan. During the Second Plan considerable progress was made and expenditure of about Rs. 30 crores is estimated to have been incurred on increasing the salaries of school teachers. As a result, the basic salaries of elementary teachers and, to some extent, of secondary teachers, were improved in almost all the States. In addition, expenditure was incurred on raising the salary scales of university teachers. In the Third Plan provision has been made by some of the States for improving the salaries and allowances of teachers.

Attempts will continue to be made during the Third Plan to improve the social and economic status of teachers. The institution in 1958 of national awards for outstanding work in the field of teaching is a usefuli nnovation. The number of these awards is to be increased in the Third Plan. The Plan also provides for merit scholarships for the children of elementary and secondary schools teachers.

Educational Research and Training of Key Personnel

46. Any system of education requires for its growth a vigorous programme of research in educational objectives, methods and tech-

niques. It is especially important in Indian today where the whole system is being modified to suit the changing needs of a rapidly developing society. During the first two Plans, a number of research institutions were set up. The National Institute of Basic Education has conducted a series of investigations into various problems connected with basic education and has organised short-term training courses and seminars for key personnel in the States and published a number of valuable studies on various problems. The National Fundamental Education Centre has studied problems of social education and trained a number of batches of District Social Education Organisers. The National Institute of Audio-visual Education carries out research in various media of mass communication—both ancient and modern – and has organised a number of seminars for key personnel working in this field. The Central Bureau of Educational and Vocational Guidance has built up a number of objective tests for conducting examinations in different subjects and for assessing the special abilities and aptitudes of students with a view to guiding them in their choice of courses and careers. The Bureau organises seminars and short-term courses for guidance personnel in the States. In addition to the development of vocational and educational guidance, these measures will facilitate the introduction of mental health services in schools and colleges, including counselling for personal and emotional problems of students. The Ministry of Education has assisted in the setting up of similar units also in the States. The Central Bureau of Text-book Research studies text-books adopted in various States from the point of view of their content as well as the procedures followed in their selection. Criteria for evaluating text-books have also been worked out, and workshops for training writers in the preparation of text-books are also arranged.

47. Training colleges were assisted during the Second Plan in carrying out investigations into problems of secondary education. The Directorate of Extension Programmes for Secondary Education has studied various problems pertaining to secondary education such as examination reform, syllabi for new subjects for reorganised secondary schools, problems of science education, diversification of courses and others.

48. During the Third Plan research activities described above will be continued and expanded. With a view to developing at the national level a centre of training and research, it is proposed to establish National Institute of Educational and Training in which will be merged

the existing Central Institute of Education and other Central Institutes and agencies referred to above. It is proposed that the National Institute of Educational Research and Training should be an autonomous organisation and that its functions should cover different areas of educational research, including elementary, secondary, social and audio-visual education, as also the training of key personnel in these and other fields. The programme of extension services through the training institutions will be coordinated and guided by the National Institute.

Extension departments will be started in 120 elementary teacher training institutions, which will take up research in selected areas and provide in service training for elementary schools teachers.

Text-Books

49. The problem of text-books has been assuming greater urgency in recent years. The main aspects to be considered in a text-book are its content, method of presentation, printing, get-up and price. The procedure for selection of text-books is another important question. To overcome difficulties experienced in respect of text-books, State Governments have started, on an experimental basis, 'nationalisation' of text-books. The experiment is too brief to warrant definite conclusions being drawn from it. Steps will have to be taken to select, train and encourage writers and illustrators, to increase the supply of paper and to provide suitable printing machinery. The Centre and the States will need to coordinate their efforts in large scale production of text-books with a view to reducing costs as well as keeping certain national objectives uniformly in view. To bring down the price of foreign books, on which inevitably considerable reliance has to be placed at the university stage, arrangements for getting them printed in India are under examination. The interest of Indian writers must, of course, be fully safeguarded. The problem of translation of standard text-books into various languages and the writing of original books in these languages have become important in view of their greater use in the universities.

Examination Reform

50. The existing examination system has become inadequate for the needs of secondary education which has expanded in the scope and

variety of its objectives. It has come in for considerable criticism in recent years. The Secondary Education Commission laid special emphasis on the need for improvement of the examination system. A programme of examination reform was, therefore, taken up towards the end of the Second Plan when an Evaluation Unit was set up in the Directorate of Extension Programmes for Secondary Education. The programme envisages the reform of examination techniques in gradual stages and is designed for the following purposes:

(i) identifying and defining the specific educational objectives underlying the study of various school subjects;
(ii) aligning the techniques of external examinations to these objectives, so that the examination questions and other tests may measure the attainments with reference to them;
(iii) making corresponding changes in internal examinations;
(iv) giving increasing weightage to internal assessment; and
(v) introducing improvements in teaching techniques and curricula in the light of the educational objectives indicated for each subject.

The programme so far accomplished has helped to introduce a large body of teachers to the new concepts and techniques through seminars and workshops and to make training colleges, secondary school boards and others familiar with the problems of the examination reform. Considerable preparatory work has also been in progress. Work along the lines mentioned above will be intensified during the Third Plan. It is a also proposed to set up State evaluation units which will work in coordination with the Central unit in implementing the programme. The University Grants Commission has assisted the establishment of examination research units in three universities. Further research work will also be organised and evaluation personnel trained in large numbers. Research and evaluation units will be set up income of the universities.

51. *Development of Hindi and Sanskrit*—For the development of Hindi, during the first two Plans schemes were initiated for the evolution of Hindi terminology, production of dictionaries and original literature, translation of books of university level into Hindi and regional languages, and publication of popular books in Hindi through private publishers. Financial assistance was given to voluntary institutions engaged in the propagation of Hindi. Books were

distributed as 'free gifts' to school libraries and other educational institutions in the non-Hindi speaking areas. Grants were given to certain States for the expansion of facilities for the training of Hindi teachers and for setting up Hindi teachers' training colleges. Funds were also provided for the appointment of Hindi teachers in secondary schools in non-Hindi speaking States as well as for revising their pay scales. The programmes and schemes started during the First and Second Plans will be continued and expanded in the Third Five Year Plan.

52. In order to consider the question of the state of Sanskrit education in the country in all its aspects and recommend measures for its development, the Ministry of Education appointed the Sanskrit Commission, which made its recommendations in 1957. Implementation of these recommendations commenced during the Second Plan. The Central Sanskrit Board was set up in 1959 with a view to advising the Government of India on matters relating to propagation and development of Sanskrit and some steps have been taken in consultation with it. Programmes for the Third Plan will include production of literature, research scholarships, development of Gurukulas, modernising Sanskrit pathashalas, preparation of dictionaries and establishment of Central Sanskrit Institute for training teachers. Some States have also provided for programmes along these lines.

53. *Education of the handicapped*—During the Second Plan several schemes for the education and training of the handicapped were initiated. These will be continued in the Third Plan. The National Centre for the Blind will be strengthened and a national Braille library started. A training centre for the adult deaf and a school for the mentally deficient children will also be established. The scheme of scholarships under which assistance is given for higher education and also for technical and professional education to the handicapped students will be further expanded. Emphasis will be laid on the development of services for the handicapped through voluntary agencies and on the provision of special employment exchanges for the physically handicapped.

Physical Education, Sports and Youth Welfare Activities

54. Among the significant developments in this field during the Second Plan reference may be made to the establishment of the National College of Physical Education at Gwalior (which was the first

degree college of its kind in the country), the setting up of Bal Bhavans to cater to the recreational needs of children, the launching of a national physical efficiency drive on the basis of carefully graded physical tests and the organisation of youth groups in rural areas as part of the community development programme. Towards the end of the Second Plan the National Institute of Sports was set up for training high grade coaches in different games and sports. In the sphere of youth activities, grants were given for the construction of stadia, swimming pools, open-air theatres, etc. Steps were also taken for the promotion of the activities of the National Cadet Crops, Auxiliary Cadet Corps, Bharat Scouts and Guides and the National Discipline Scheme.

During the Third Plan period all these programmes will be continued. The National Institute of Sports will be developed so as to provide for all the major games. With the help of coaches trained at the Institute, a national coaching scheme providing for widespread coaching facilities will be introduced so that the standard of sports can be steadily raised. The national physical efficiency drive will be further intensified so that it has greater impact. A National Children's Museum is also proposed to be established as a complement to the Bal Bhavan.

Social Education and Adult Literacy

55. As was stated in the First Plan, social education implies 'an all-comprehensive programme of community uplift through community action'. Social education, thus, comprises literacy, health, recreation and home life of adults, training in citizenship and guidance in improving economic efficiency. In the last analysis, in the setting of democracy, the success of planned development, which encompasses the needs of millions of people, depends on the spread of social education and a progressive outlook and the growth of a sense of shared citizenship. Yet, the educational aims of agriculture, community development, health and other welfare programmes are among the most difficult to realise. Over the past decade, in several directions there has been a measure of progress, as in the development of community centres, reading rooms in villages, organisation of youth groups and mahila mandals, and the revitalisation of village panchayats and the cooperative movement. One aspect of social education, and in some ways the most important, has however,

caused concern. Between 1951 and 1961, literacy has increased only from about 17 to about 24 per cent. The introduction of Panchayati Raj at the district and block levels and the important role assigned to village panchayats render it imperative that in as short a period as possible a substantial proportion of the adult population should become capable of reading and writing. This is essential in their own interest as in that of the community as a whole. As sufficient progress has not been achieved so far in this direction, the problem is now being studied afresh with a view to working out means for the rapid As the followexpansion of adult literacy.

56. Programmes of the Ministry of Education provide for the further development of the National Fundamental Education Centre as a part of the National Institute of Education, production of literature for neo-literates, assistance for voluntary organisations in the field of social education and expansion of library facilities. The educational plans of States provide for libraries and continuation classes and, to a limited extent, for adult schools and other schemes for promoting adult literacy. The main provisions for social education are made under the community development programme through the schematic budget. Altogether, in the Third Plan, about Rs. 25 crores are expected at present to be available for social education.

57. Any large-scale and effective programme for adult literacy must be based on the closest possible cooperation at every level of personnel engaged in education and in community development. It will call for a pooling of the available resources in men and money, mobilisation of voluntary workers and organisations and development of adult education and literacy work at the block and village levels, and in every city and town, so that it takes the character more and more of a popular movement. Social education and adult literacy have to be developed as extension activities undertaken by educational institutions, specially village schools, in collaboration with panchayats and cooperatives and voluntary organisations. The broad aim should be that wherever a group of persons sufficient to constitute a class desires to attain literacy, the requisite facilities by way of teachers and teaching materials should be made readily available. Every educational institutions should be involved in this effort, and individual teachers participating in it should be given suitable honoraria. At the same time, the village panchayat and other agencies should make their due contribution towards the effort. While Social Education Organisers, Block Education Officers and

individual educational institutions should work closely together to place the facilities needed at the service of local communities, it will be primarily for Panchayat Samitis, village panchayats and voluntary organisations to create and maintain popular enthusiasm and develop adult education and literacy on a continuing basis in a manner related organically to their own needs and conditions. At every step the local leadership, the teachers and the voluntary workers should be drawn into the movement for the expansion of literacy both among men and among women. Proposals for a large-scale programme of adult literacy on these lines are being drawn up by the Ministry of Education in consultation with the Ministry of Community Development and Co-operation, and it is hoped that appreciable progress will be realised during the Third Plan.

58. *Libraries*—An adequate system of libraries is an essential part of any well-organised system of education. The Library Committee which reported in 1959, set up by the Government of India indicated the large gaps between the present position and the demands of an adequate system of libraries. These can, however, only be filled through a long term and properly phased programme. During the Third Plan, steps will be taken to set up or develop all the four National Libraries at Delhi, Calcutta, Bombay and Madras. There are provisions also for strengthening libraries at the State headquarters and for increasing the number of libraries at the district and taluka levels. Besides these, educational institutions have libraries of their own. These will be improved and strengthened during the Third Plan. An Institute of Library Science was set up during the Second Plan to train key library personnel. This will be further developed during the Third Plan. Other universities also have facilities for research in library science and facilities for training library personnel.

Cultural Programmes

59. India's exceptional heritage in art, literature, dance, drama and music has to be further developed in response to the urges of a new generation. Archaeological monuments and ancient art are to be preserved and re-interpreted for communicating India's underlying cultural unity. Among important steps already taken are the establishment of the Lalit Kala Akademy (academy of fine arts), the Sahitya Akademy (academy of letters) and the Sangeet Natak Akademy (academy of dance, drama and music), the National

Museum and the National Gallery of Modern Art. The other schemes carried out in the Second Plan were the reorganisation and development of museums and libraries and preparation of gazetteers which will be developed through the Third Plan.

Work of revision of District and Indian Gazetteers initiated during the Second Plan will be carried further. A scheme for the publishing of ancient manuscripts, cataloguing and preserving them and building up a microfilm library of rare manuscripts and for the acquisition of such manuscripts forms part of the Plan.

60. Along with Hindi and Sanskrit, it is of the utmost importance to develop modern Indian languages. It is proposed to undertake the preparation of bi-lingual dictionaries, award prizes for translations, arrange for the preparation of encyclopaedias in the various regional languages, and of English-Indian language dictionaries, and publish old manuscripts and rare books as well as catalogues and bibliographies. The Plan also provides for the linguistic survey of India.

Contemporary Indian literature has been surveyed recently by the Sahitya Akademy. The National Book Trust is taking steps to encourage the production of good literature and to make such books available at moderate prices for libraries, educational institutions,and the public in general. The National Book Trust also aims at translation of well known books from foreign languages and of standards books from one Indian language into another.

In the development of India's cultural unity, considerable importance must be attached to the propagation of Indian languages and their literatures in different parts of the country. This aspect has been emphasised by the Central Advisory Board of Education which has recommended the study at the secondary stage by every students of an Indian language other than his own mother-tongue. Facilities for the study of Indian languages are being provided at some universities. In the context of the Third Plan they need to be established on a much wider basis.

61. Reorganisation and development of museums will be undertaken on the lines recommended by the Expert Museum Survey Committee, 1955, and on the advice of the Central Advisory Board on Museums which has been established for this purpose. A project for the acquisition of art collections for the National Gallery of Modern Art is included in the Plan, and committees have been set up to advise the Government. The Salar Jung Museum at Hyderabad has been taken over by the Central Government and will be

developed as a National Museum for the South India.

62. The Department of Archaeology has schemes like assessment of Monuments, copying of ancient paintings and survey of antiquities which will be continued in the Third Plan along with the strengthening of the Excavations Branch. A National Trust will be established to look after places of historical interest and national beauty which do not fall within the purview of the Department of archaeology.

63. The Third Plan provides for research in the field of Anthropology and Ethnogaphy.

Trained personnel required for the various schemes will be made available and creative talent encouraged through scholarships for students and young workers in different cultural fields. Along with these, a few overseas scholarships have also been included.

64. Cultural relations with other countries will continue to be encouraged during the Third Plan. Among schemes subserving this objective are the development of the Indian Council for Cultural Relations, construction of the International Students' Home in the Delhi University and re-productions of paintings, sculptures and Indian Art for the use of cultural organisations in foreign countries.

The scheme for establishing Buddha Jayanti monument in Delhi which started in the Second Plan will be completed in the Third Plan. Existing institutions of higher learning and research will be further developed.

65. Among other programmes are the setting up of a National Theatre and also a large open-air theatre in Delhi.

In the Second Plan an expenditure of Rs. 4 crores was incurred on various cultural programmes, Rs. 2.6 crores at the Centre and Rs. 1.4 crores in the States. The Third Plan allocation is Rs. 10 crores—Rs. 6 crores at the Centre and Rs. 4 crores in the States.

National Integration

66. The success of economic planning in India will largely depend upon our capacity to hold together as a nation in the midst of diversity of language, region, caste and religion. Unity in a democracy must be based on the consciousness of a common cultural heritage and commonly accepted future goals and on a constant effort to realise them. India has a rich and composite culture to which every sections of the community has contributed and of which it has every reason to be proud. The essentials of this culture are broad-

mindedness and mutual tolerance, balance between the material and the spiritual, and the cooperative way of life in which various individuals in a group are bound together by commonly accepted rights and obligations. India's future goals are embodied in the Constitution and her development plans are among the principal means for realising them.

67. Educational institutions have a vital role to play in bringing about national integration and social cohesion among the younger generation. The school programme should be designed to awaken in the pupils an awareness of national oneness and for this purpose, includes community living based on cooperative self-help and democratic principles, the study of India's history and culture in the curriculum at various stages of education and suitable textbooks to inculcate moral and social values among students. The school programme has to be supplemented by other activities such as programmes for bringing students together on a common platform and enabling them to gain first-hand knowledge of the diversified culture of the country through educational tours, the development of modern Indian and classical languages and making their rich storehouse of literature available to larger numbers in different parts of the country through translations and the revival and development of India is composite cultural heritage through fine arts. dance, drama, music and literature. Various steps taken to create more widespread understanding of the Plan among students are intended to strengthen the forces of integration and national unity in a positive and constructive manner. One State Government has recently approved a scheme of 100 scholarships a year to be given to graduate and post-graduate students from different States with provision for residential facilities. Proposals on these lines can be of great value in promoting national integration.

The question of achieving emotional integration and promoting national consciousness is at present being studied by a special committee, with reference to the system of education and educational polices and programmes will need to be reviewed further in the light of such recommendations as it may offer.

ANNEXURE I

TABLE 20.11: Schooling Facilities for Children in the Age-Group 6-11, (1960-61 and 1965-66)

Name of the State	enrolment in classes I-V						percentage of the population in the age-group 6-11 (estimated)					
	1960-61			1965-66			1960-61			1965-66		
	total	boys	girls	total	boys	girls	total	boys	girls	total	boys	girls
			(lakhs)									
Andhra Pradesh	28.20	17.50	10.70	44.20	25.40	18.80	60.3	74.0	46.2	84.5	96.1	72.7
Assam	10.68	6.79	3.89	15.08	8.99	6.09	61.7	73.7	48.0	77.4	86.6	66.9
Bihar	32.00	24.00	8.00	48.00	30.00	18.00	53.5	80.0	26.9	72.6	90.4	54.7
Gujarat	20.00	12.30	7.70	26.63	15.62	11.01	72.0	85.9	57.3	84.2	95.8	71.9
Jammu & Kashmir	1.97	1.54	0.43	3.02	2.24	0.78	45.0	66.1	21.0	62.3	87.2	34.2
Kerala	23.44	12.58	10.86	26.61	14.28	12.33	108.8	118.0	99.7	108.7	117.8	99.7
Madhya Pradesh	20.00	16.00	4.00	30.00	20.00	10.00	47.0	73.5	19.3	64.0	83.3	43.8
Madras	33.50	21.26	12.24	47.50	25.50	22.00	78.9	99.7	58.0	100.0	106.8	93.1
Maharashtra	39.00	24.47	14.53	54.00	32.30	21.70	73.3	89.0	56.6	90.5	104.8	75.3
Mysore	21.44	13.64	7.80	31.44	16.08	15.36	67.4	84.0	50.1	88.2	88.4	88.1
Orissa	10.00	7.50	2.50	16.00	10.50	5.50	47.8	71.6	23.9	64.6	85.0	44.3
Punjab	16.86	12.26	4.60	22.86	15.00	7.86	61.8	84.0	36.3	74.6	91.4	55.2
Rajasthan	11.51	9.51	2.00	21.00	13.90	7.10	42.0	66.2	15.3	68.2	86.2	48.4
Uttar Pradesh	40.43	32.00	8.43	66.50	45.00	21.50	45.4	68.6	19.9	61.7	79.5	41.9
West Bengal	28.52	18.67	9.85	35.02	21.50	13.52	65.6	80.8	48.4	73.4	84.5	60.7
Delhi	2.91	1.68	1.23	4.08	2.21	1.87	86.6	89.3	83.1	99.5	104.2	94.4
Himachal Pradesh	0.80	0.63	0.17	1.14	0.71	0.43	48.8	73.3	21.8	69.5	83.5	54.4
Pondicherry	0.35	0.20	0.15	0.47	0.25	0.22	72.9	83.3	62.5	87.0	92.6	81.5
Other Union Territories	1.79	1.23	0.56	2.80	1.68	1.12	62.6	84.2	40.0	78.2	91.8	64.0
Total	343.40	233.76	109.64	496.35	301.16	195.19	61.1	80.5	40.4	76.4	90.4	61.6

ANNEXURE II

TABLE 20.12: Schooling Facilities for Children in the Age-Group 11-14, 1960-61 and 1965-66

Name of the State	enrolment in classes VI-VIII						percentage of the population in the age-group 11-14 (estimated)					
	1960-61			1965-66			1960-61			1965-66		
	total	boys	girls	total	boys	girls	total	boys	girls	total	boys	girls
			(lakhs)									
Andhra Pradesh	3.55	2.74	0.31	6.13	4.68	1.45	15.6	23.9	7.2	21.9	33.1	10.4
Assam	2.05	1.49	0.56	3.25	2.20	1.05	27.4	37.4	16.0	35.3	44.8	24.5
Bihar	5.50	4.90	0.50	9.25	7.40	1.85	19.4	34.3	4.2	26.7	42.6	10.7
Gujarat	3.56	2.67	0.39	5.77	3.56	2.21	26.8	39.0	13.8	34.9	41.8	27.6
Jammu & Kashmir	0.60	0.51	0.09	0.88	0.72	0.16	27.8	44.0	9.0	33.5	51.4	13.0
Kerala	5.44	3.18	2.26	6.19	3.61	2.58	50.3	59.4	41.3	45.3	53.4	37.3
Madhya Pradesh	3.27	2.73	0.54	4.96	4.16	0.80	16.3	26.6	5.5	20.3	33.3	6.7
Madras	6.36	4.44	1.92	9.36	6.57	2.79	30.1	41.8	18.3	35.9	50.1	21.5
Maharashtra	7.25	5.35	1.90	11.47	8.22	3.25	28.5	40.7	15.5	36.2	50.2	21.2
Mysore	3.64	2.66	0.98	5.64	3.66	1.98	23.8	34.1	13.1	29.5	37.5	21.2
Orissa	0.85	0.74	0.11	1.70	1.36	0.34	7.9	13.8	2.0	13.1	21.0	5.2
Punjab	3.75	2.75	1.00	5.55	3.54	2.01	28.3	38.8	16.3	33.8	40.3	26.4
Rajasthan	1.91	1.66	0.25	3.85	3.10	0.75	14.8	24.5	4.1	23.9	36.7	9.8
Uttar Pradesh	8.60	7.50	1.10	11.60	10.00	1.60	18.6	30.9	5.0	20.5	33.7	5.9
West Bengal	4.72	3.60	1.12	9.02	5.30	3.72	21.1	30.3	10.7	33.3	36.7	29.4
Delhi	1.02	0.70	0.32	1.65	1.06	0.59	60.4	73.7	43.2	67.3	84.1	49.6
Himachal Pradesh	0.20	0.17	0.03	0.30	0.25	0.05	28.6	45.9	9.1	36.6	59.5	12.5
Pondicherry	0.08	0.06	0.02	0.10	0.07	0.03	33.3	50.0	16.7	35.7	51.0	21.4
Other Union Territories	0.53	0.37	0.16	0.81	0.54	0.27	38.1	52.9	23.2	43.5	58.1	29.0
Total	62.88	48.22	14.66	97.48	70.00	27.48	22.8	34.3	10.8	28.6	39.9	16.5

ANNEXURE III

TABLE 20.13: Schooling Facilities for Children in the age-group 14-17 (1960-61 and 1965-66)

Name of the State	enrolment in classes IX-XI						percentage of the population in the age-group 11-14 (estimated)					
	1960-61			1965-66			1960-61			1965-66		
	total	boys	girls	total	boys	girls	total	boys	girls	total	boys	girls
			(lakhs)									
Andhra Pradesh	1.86	1.62	0.24	2.36	1.94	0.42	8.8	15.1	2.3	9.6	15.7	3.5
Assam	1.10	0.87	0.23	1.71	1.31	0.40	17.5	26.0	7.8	22.9	32.9	11.5
Bihar	3.10	2.90	0.20	5.00	4.40	0.60	12.4	23.0	1.5	17.3	30.3	4.2
Gujarat	1.48	1.14	0.34	2.26	1.53	0.73	12.2	18.2	5.8	15.9	20.8	10.6
Jammu & Kashmir	0.20	0.17	0.03	0.27	0.23	0.04	9.9	15.9	3.2	11.8	18.9	3.7
Kerala	2.25	1.39	0.86	2.95	1.80	1.15	21.6	27.0	16.3	24.2	30.0	18.7
Madhya Pradesh	0.78	0.67	0.11	1.10	0.95	0.15	4.3	7.3	1.3	5.3	9.0	1.5
Madras	2.66	1.98	0.68	3.97	2.71	1.26	13.4	19.9	6.9	17.3	23.4	11.0
Maharashtra	3.15	2.42	0.73	4.97	3.78	1.19	13.6	20.1	6.5	18.2	26.8	9.0
Mysore	1.47	1.16	0.31	2.05	1.44	0.61	10.4	16.6	4.5	12.3	16.9	7.5
Orissa	0.40	0.36	0.04	0.80	0.67	0.13	4.2	7.5	0.8	7.4	12.4	2.4
Punjab	1.45	1.25	0.20	2.25	1.82	0.43	12.0	19.3	3.6	16.1	24.4	6.6
Rajasthan	0.86	0.79	0.07	1.53	1.33	0.20	7.4	13.0	1.3	11.2	18.6	3.1
Uttar Pradesh	5.12	4.60	0.52	7.40	6.60	0.80	12.2	20.9	2.6	15.3	26.1	3.5
West Bengal	2.38	2.00	0.38	5.30	4.00	1.30	11.2	17.6	3.8	21.9	31.1	11.5
Delhi	0.54	0.40	0.14	1.19	0.90	0.29	32.5	43.0	19.2	60.1	88.2	30.2
Himachal Pradesh	0.06	0.05	0.01	0.08	0.06	0.02	10.02	16.1	3.6	9.8	14.3	5.0
Pondicherry	0.03	0.02	0.01	0.06	0.04	0.02	13.6	18.2	9.1	23.1	30.8	15.4
Other Union Territories	0.19	0.12	0.07	0.31	0.20	0.11	12.8	16.0	9.6	16.4	21.1	11.7
Total	29.08	23.91	5.17	45.56	35.71	9.85	11.5	18.4	4.2	15.6	23.7	6.9

21

FOURTH FIVE YEAR PLAN*

Introduction

The most important feature of the Fourth Five Year Plan for education was its thrust on manpower planning. It was, therefore, not without reason that the chapter on education was titled 'Education and Manpower'. The Plan recognised that educational development at the higher level should be broadly related to the pattern of jobs and the estimates of demand in the country for educated manpower. It was realised that as manpower was not homogeneous, manpower planning had to concern itself with different categories, such as doctors, nurses, engineers, agricultural graduates and craftsmen each having its own level of education and specialisation. It was emphasised that a suitably oriented system of education could facilitate and promote social change and contribute to economic growth by training skilled manpower for specific task of development. As regards elementary education, the Fourth Plan recognised that facilities for elementary education were a pre-requisite for equality of opportunity and keeping this fact in view the provision of facilities for girls and for backward areas was accorded the first priority. Efforts were directed to remove the imbalances within States. It was expected that the new pattern of secondary education as recommended by the Education Commission (1964-66) would be implemented in many States during the Fourth Plan. The main teacher education programmes needed attention were: improving the quality of teacher education through in-service education, training of more women teachers and teachers from the tribal communities and training of mathematics and science teachers. In the field of higher education it was proposed to extend correspondence courses to science dis-

* Planning Commission, Government of India, New Delhi 1970.

ciplines also. The Plan cautioned that proposals to set up new universities would be carefully examined by the University Grants Commission. Mobilisation of voluntary effort and local community resources was considered very vital for spreading adult literacy.

Keeping in view the large scale unemployment of engineers the main emphasis in technical education in the Fourth Plan was on improving its quality and standards.

EDUCATION AND MANPOWER[1]

Education

A suitably oriented system of education can facilitate and promote social change and contribute to economic growth, not only by training skilled manpowers for specific tasks of development but, what is perhaps even more important, by creating the requisite attitudes and climate. Facilities for universal elementary education are a prerequisite for equality of opportunity.

16.2 There has been expansion at all levels of education during the last eight years (Annexures I to IV). The enrolment in classes I-V increased from 35 million in 1960-61 to 55.5 million in 1968-69; in classes VI-VIII from 6.7 million to 12.3 million; in classes IX-XI from 3 million to 6.6 million; and at the university stage (for arts, science and commerce faculties) from 0.74 million to 1.69 million. The admission capacity in engineering and technological institutions increased from 13,824 to 25,000 at the degree level and from 25,800 to 48,600 at the diploma level. Considerable thought has also been given to the reform of the education system. The recommendations of the Education Commission (1964-66) form the basis of the National Policy on Education and provide the framework for the formulation of the Plan programmes. Some efforts have been made in the States and at the Centre to enrich curricula and improve text-books and teaching methods. Steps have been taken to provide educational and vocational guidance, and develop facilities for science education and post-graduate education and research. The number of scholarships, stipends and freeships have considerably increased, especially for the

1. (i) Para Numbers refer to paras of Chapter 16 of the document
   (ii) Original Table Numbers have been changed to conform to this chapter number.

backward sections of the community. Salary scales and service conditions of teachers have been improved. Expenditure on education from all sources[2] is estimated to have increased from Rs. 344 crores in 1960-61 to Rs. 850 crores in 1968-69. During the same period, expenditure from Government sources increased from Rs. 234 crores, or 68 per cent of the total expenditure in 1960-61, to an estimated sum Rs. 640 crores or 75 per cent in 1968-69.

16.3. The unfulfilled tasks are many. Much delay has already occurred in complying with the Constitutional Directive which enjoins on the State to "endeavour to provide, within a period of ten years from the commencement of this Constitution, for free and compulsory education for all children until they complete the age of fourteen years". By 1968-69, only 62 per cent of the children in the age-group 6-14 were going to schools. The percentage of the children in the age group 6-11 was 77 and that of the 11-14 age-group 32. The corresponding percentages for girls were 59 and 19 respectively. The percentage of children going to school in rural areas in still much lower than that in the urban areas, though the gap has steadily narrowed. In spite of the rapid increase in the number of children at school from the Scheduled Castes, Scheduled Tribes and other backward classes, the percentage of their enrolment remains much below the national average. The position of facilities available or utilised differs from State to State and district to district. The State-wise data in Annexures II, III and V, reveal serious disparities. The problem of enrolling girls and children of the Scheduled Castes and Scheduled Tribes assumes serious dimensions in some States. Mention may also be made of the considerable delays in putting up buildings and in the supply of equipment, particularly at the primary and secondary levels.

16.4. The rapid expansion in numbers has put a severe strain on the physical facilities and teaching personnel of educational institutions. At the primary level there is considerable wastage and stagnation. The proportion of failures at the secondary and university levels is high. The quality of post-graduate education and research and science education needs to be improved. Insufficient attention has been paid to vocational education. In technical education, coordination between institutions and industry has not been effective.

---

2. Government and non-Government (Local bodies fees, and endowments, etc.) on all types of educational institutions.

APPROACH

16.5 Priority will be given to the expansion of elementary education and the emphasis will be on the provision of facilities for backward areas and communities and for girls. A survey of the deficiencies in respect of buildings and equipment of educational institutions will be made with a view to removing them according to a phased programme. Other programmes of importance will be: improvement of teacher education, expansion and improvement of science education; raising standards of post-graduate education and research; development of Indian languages and book production, especially text-books, and the consolidation of technical education including reorganisation of polytechnic education and its closer linking with the needs of industry and its orientation towards self-employment. Increased efforts will be made to involve people in educational programmes and to mobilise public support. Youth services will be developed. It is proposed to effect economies by utilisation of existing facilities to the maximum possible extent, streamlining of the planning, implementing and evaluating machinery, increasing the use of educational technologies – part-time and correspondence courses, modern media of communication, optimum size of institutions – which promote expansion and development with minimum investment and without lowering standards; and undertaking new tasks only after careful preparation through pilot projects. Activities like improvement of curricular and text-books, in-service education of teachers and research in methods of teaching, which do not require large funds but have a wide impact will be encouraged. Educational programmes will be increasingly related to social and economic objectives. This will require, among other things, coordination with development programmes in other sectors and the drawing up of a perspective plan on the basis of manpower needs, social demand, and the likely availability of financial, material and human resources.

16.6 *Pre-school Education* – In the field of pre-school education, Government effort will be confined mainly to certain strategic areas such as training of teachers, evolving suitable teaching techniques, production of teaching materials and teachers' guides. In the Social Welfare sector, however, there is a small provision for the opening of balwadis in rural and urban areas.

16.7 *Elementary Education* – The targets of elementary education are set out in Table 21.1.

The State-wise position of enrolment is indicated in Annexures II, III and V. Bihar, Madhya Pradesh, Rajasthan and Orissa have the problem of low enrolment of girls and of children of Scheduled Castes and Scheduled Tribes whose numbers in these States are quite sizable. Efforts will be made to remove the imbalances within States in regard to the provision of educational facilities at the elementary stage. Some States are considering the adoption of double shift in classes I and II, which between them account for 60 per cent of the enrolment in classes I-V. It is proposed to make a study of the system as it has operated in Kerala so as to facilitate its introduction elsewhere.

16.8 In regard to the age-group 11-14, the problem is much more difficult as a large majority of the parents in rural areas withdraw their children from schools. The problem needs special attention in Bihar, Madhya Pradesh, Orissa, Rajasthan and Uttar Pradesh. A possible remedy is to provide part-time education on a large-scale to children of this age-group and provision has accordingly been made for pilot projects, which will facilitate large-scale development later on. Setting up of schools within the reach of every child is the first necessary step towards universality of enrolment. To achieve this at minimum cost detailed district plans will be drawn up. Each State will formulate a phased programme for the introduction of universal education for all children in the age-group 6-14.

16.9 *Secondary Education*: In the Fourth Plan, it is expected to enrol 3.1 million additional pupils in classes IX-XI. The trend of expansion of facilities at the secondary stage is shown in Table 21.2.

The location of new schools will be determined according to the requirements of each area as spelt out in detailed district plans. The main effort in the Fourth Plan will be to enrich the content and improve the quality of secondary education. A few States have taken preliminary steps to adopt the new pattern of secondary education, recommended by the Education Commission, and propose to complete the change over during the Fourth Plan.

16.10 A major task in the field of post-elementary education is to provide a large variety of vocational courses for children who do not intend to continue their general education beyond the elementary stage. These courses have to be of varying durations, depending upon the trades and vocations proposed to be learnt. The industrial training institutes will meet a part of this demand. To prepare students to take up employment after the secondary stage, a number of voca-

TABLE 21.1: Expansion of Elementary Education, 1960-61 to 1973-74

(enrolment in million)

Sl. No.	Stage (age-group)	1960-61		1965-66		1968-69		1973-74	
		Enrolment	Percentage of age-group	Enrolment	Percentage of age-group	Enrolment	Percentage of age-group	Enrolment	Percentage of age-group
0	1	2	3	4	5	6	7	8	9
	Primary (6-11) classes *I-V*								
1.	Total	34.99	62.4	50.47	76.7	55.49	77.3	68.58	85.3
2.	Boys	23.59	82.6	32.18	96.3	34.92	95.2	41.25	99.6
3.	Girls	11.40	41.4	18.29	56.5	20.57	58.5	27.33	70.1
	Middle (11-14) classes *VI-VIII*								
4.	Total	6.70	22.5	10.53	30.9	12.27	32.3	18.10	41.3
5.	Boys	5.07	33.2	7.68	44.2	8.76	45.4	12.19	54.3
6.	Girls	1.63	11.3	2.85	17.0	3.51	18.8	5.91	27.7
	Elementary (6-14) classes *I-VIII*								
7.	Total	41.69	48.7	61.00	61.0	67.76	61.7	86.68	69.8
8.	Boys	28.66	65.2	39.86	78.5	43.68	78.0	53.44	83.7
9.	Girls	13.03	30.9	21.14	43.0	24.08	44.7	33.24	55.1

tional courses are being provided after class X in industrial training institutes, polytechnics, schools for nursing, and agricultural schools. It will also be necessary to devise a number of additional courses in response to new demands. Provision is being made for pilot projects for the purpose.

TABLE 21.2: Expansion of Secondary Education, 1960-61 to 1973-74

Year	Enrolment (in million)			Percentage of age-group (14-17)		
	Boys	Girls	Total	Boys	Girls	Total
1	2	3	4	5	6	7
1960-61	2.47	0.56	3.03	17.5	4.3	11.1
1965-66	4.08	1.20	5.28	25.6	7.9	17.0
1968-69	4.95	1.63	6.58	28.5	9.8	19.3
1973-74 (target)	7.00	2.69	9.69	34.3	13.7	24.2

16.11 *Girls' Education* – Sustained efforts to extend education among girls have been made from the First Plan period. Girl students, as a percentage of their population in the relevant age-group, increased from 25 in 1950-51 to 59 in 1968-69 in classes I-V, 5 to 19 in classes VI-VIII and 2 to 10 in classes IX-XI. The gap between the enrolment of boys and girls is still considerable. During the Fourth Plan, the enrolment of girls will be further increased through the organisation of special programmes, the nature of which will vary from State to State. The position is shown in Table 21.3.

Among the special programmes to be undertaken for encouraging girls' education stress will be laid on providing sanitary facilities for girls.

16.12 *Teacher Education* – At the elementary stage, the number of teachers is estimated to have increased from about 1.09 million in 1960-61 to about 1.60 million in 1968-69. There has been correspondingly a steady expansion of teacher training facilities so that the number of elementary trained teachers during the period increased from about 0.71 million to about 1.24 million, raising the percentage of trained teachers from 65 to 77. Further, during the period 1966-69, owing to financial stringency, some of the States were unable to employ all the teachers who passed out of the training institutions. This has led to considerable unemployment among trained teachers

TABLE 21.3: Expansion of Girls' Education, 1950-51 to 1973-74

(enrolment in million)

Year	Enrolment I-V			Enrolment VI-VIII			Enrolment IX-XI		
	Total	Girls	col (3) as percentage of col. (2)	Total	Girls	col (6) as percentage of col. (5)	Total	Girls	col (9) as percentage of col. (8)
1	2	3	4	5	6	7	8	9	10
1950-51	19.15	5.38	28.1	3.12	0.53	17.0	1.26	0.17	13.5
1960-61	34.99	11.40	32.6	6.70	1.63	24.3	3.03	0.56	18.5
1965-66	50.47	18.29	36.2	10.53	2.85	27.1	5.28	1.20	22.7
1968-69	55.48	20.56	37.1	12.27	3.51	28.6	6.58	1.63	24.8
1973-74 (target)	68.58	27.33	39.9	18.10	5.91	32.7	9.69	2.69	27.8

in some States. Faced with this situation, a few States have closed down some of the training institutions. Also taking advantage of the larger availability of trained teachers, some States have raised the period of training to two years. At present, the problem of untrained teachers is confined largely to the States and Union Territories in the eastern region. The programmes which need special attention are: improving the quality of teacher education, training of more women teachers and teachers from the tribal communities, training of mathematics and science teachers for the middle classes and in-service training. Wherever necessary, correspondence courses will be organised for untrained teachers now working in schools. The State Institutes of Education will cooperate in the implementation of these programmes.

16.13 At the secondary stage, the number of teachers in 1968-69 was estimated at 0.525 million of whom 0.381 million or 73% were trained. The training facilities available, at present at this stage are considered adequate and can be easily expanded if the need arises. The correspondence courses organised by the Central Institute of Education, Delhi and the four Regional Colleges of Education are helping to speed up the training of untrained teachers. The main programmes during the Fourth Plan will be to improve standards of teacher education at this level and to organise a large in-service education programme especially for mathematics and science teachers. Funds will be placed at the disposal of the University Grants Commission to improve the physical facilities of the departments of education in universities and secondary training colleges and upgrade the professional competence of the teacher educators working in them. These programmes will be coordinated with those of the National Council of Educational Research and Training, State Institutes of Education and State Institutes of Science Education.

16.14 *National Council of Educational Research and Training and State Institutes of Education* – To work out the programmes of qualitative improvement at the school stage, greater coordination will be effected between the National Council of Education Research and Training (NCERT) and the State Institutes of Education. Most of the States propose to bring under the State Institutes of Education the various institutions set up to guide the programmes of school improvement. During the Fourth Plan, the programmes already initiated in the fields of evaluation and guidance, curriculum construction, extension, text-book production, educational research and science education will be expanded. A number of pilot projects will be worked out and evaluated through these organisations. An important area of investigation and experimentation will be the reduction of wastage and stagnation at the primary stage. Training programmes for teacher educators will also be continued. A Committee was appointed to review and evaluate the activities and programmes of NCERT. In the light of its recommendations, the departments of the National Institute of Education have been reorganised. Also suitable changes are being made in the working of the Regional Colleges of Education so that they may provide leadership in the field of teacher education.

16.15. *Higher Education* – The enrolment in Arts, Science, Commerce and Law courses in universities and colleges increased by 0.2 million during each of the First and Second Plans and by 0.5 million in the Third Plan. The additional enrolment in the Fourth Plan is estimated to be about one million. Of this, 0.15 million students will be provided education through correspondence courses, evening colleges and part-time classes. In providing for the additional enrolment, emphasis will be on rational location of institutions and on optimum institutional size. So far, the correspondence courses have been confined to humanities only. It is proposed to extend them to other disciplines as well. The estimates of university enrolment are set out in Table 21.4.

TABLE 21.4: Expansion of University Education, 1960-61 to 1973-74

Sl. No.	State (age-group)	1960-61	1965-66	1968-69	1973-74
1	2	3	4	5	6
	University/collegiate (age-group 17-23)				
1.	Total enrolment* (million)	0.74	1.24	1.69	2.66
2.	Percentage of age-group	1.5	2.3	2.9	3.8
3.	Enrolment in science courses (million)	0.19	0.51	0.68	1.19
4.	Enrolment in science courses percentage of total enrolment	25.7	41.1	40.2	44.7

* Arts, science and commerce subjects excluding intermediate students of the U.P. Board but including the pre-university classes run by the universities.

16.16. During the Fourth Plan, the main emphasis will be on consolidation and improvement of higher education through the strengthening of staff and library and laboratory facilities. Affiliated colleges with provide education to more than 88 per cent of the university students will be helped. Assistance for fuller development will be given to a few colleges selected on the basis of their achievements, existing facilities and potentialities.

16.17 Post-graduate courses occupy a key position in the university system. Facilities for post-graduate education and research will be increased and their quality improved. The centres of advanced study, which are intended to encourage the pursuit of excellence, will be developed. It is also proposed to assist a few other promising university departments to grow as advanced centres. In order to develop intra-disciplinary research, clusters of advanced centres will be set-up in related subject. The Indian Council of Social Science Research has been established to promote research in social sciences.

16.18 Proposals to set up new universities will be carefully examined by the University Grants Commission and the Ministry of Education. The requirements of increased facilities for post-graduate studies will be met by establishing university centres in cities with a number of colleges and a large student population. These centres will have adequate library and laboratory facilities and a nucleus of university teachers.

16.19 The other programmes for higher education include provision for hostels, student study homes and other facilities. The programmes of improving the quality of teaching personnel include provision of summer schools, seminars, and staff quarters. The rural institutes will be more effectively linked with the needs of rural areas.

16.20 *Scholarships and Fellowships* – The present schemes of scholarships administered by the Central Government like the National Scholarships Scheme, the National Loan Scholarships Scheme, National Scholarships for the Children of School Teachers and Merit Scholarships in Residential Schools will be stepped up. The University Grants Commission will also continue to provide fellowships for postgraduate education and research. The number of post-matric scholarships under the scheme for assisting students from the backward classes will increase from 145,000 in 1968-69 to about 200,000 in 1973-74. Scholarships will also be awarded for medical and agricultural education and scientific and industrial research.

16.21 *Science Education* – Enrolment in science subjects which was about 26 per cent of the total enrolment at the university stage (including pre-university classes) in 1960-61, rose to about 40 per cent in 1968-69 and is estimated to rise further to 45 per cent in 1973-74. Science education will be expanded and improved at elementary, secondary and university stages. With this end in view, programmes of pre-service and in-service training of teachers will be strengthened, the curricula in science upgraded and laboratory facilities provided. The administration and supervision of science programmes will be strengthened and informal activities encouraged through science clubs and science fairs.

16.22. *Adult Literacy* – Efforts will be made to spread literacy amongst adults through mobilisation of voluntary effort and local community resources. Pilot projects will be initiated in selected districts to begin with and the programme will be extended to other areas in the light of experience. For the development of the programme, assistance will be sought from industry, from the students working under the National Service Scheme, and from voluntary organisations which will be assisted financially and given technical guidance. The programme of Farmers' Education and Functional Literacy in the high-yielding variety areas, already mentioned under Agriculture, will be extended to 100 districts and will cover one million adult farmers. Adult education will continue to be an integral part of the community development programme. The University Departments of Adult Education will be helped to take up pilot projects, to conduct research and organise extension and extra-mural lectures. The National Board of Adult Education has been set up to advise Government on the development programmes and for enlisting the cooperation of the interests and agencies concerned. The further development of television and the experiments with satellite communications, which are to begin from 1972-73, may have significance for education, especially adult education.

16.23 *Language Development and Book Production* – The Official Languages (Amendment) Act, 1967 and the Government Resolution thereon, enjoin on the Government of India to prepare and implement a comprehensive programme for the spread and development of Hindi as well as the other modern Indian languages mentioned in the Constitution. The three-language formula will be progressively implemented. The Institute of Languages has been set up by the Central Government for inter-linguistic research, training of translators and encouraging the production of appropriate literature. The State Governments will also set up similar institutes at the State level. It is also proposed to set up four regional institutes for the training of teachers in modern Indian languages so as to enable the Hindi speaking States to introduce the teaching of modern Indian languages, other than Hindi, under the three-language formula. The work of the Scientific and Technical Terminology Commission will be continued. The schemes for the development of Sanskrit will be continued and their scope expanded.

16.24 Two important programmes as contemplated for book production are: the production of books in modern Indian languages, with a view to their adoption as media of instruction at the university stage, and the indigenous production of books in English, with a view to reducing our dependence on imported books. These programmes will be taken up by the Central Government in collaboration with the University Grants Commission and the State Governments. Programmes of production of cheap text-books for the university stage will continue. At the school stage, intensive efforts will to made to improve the quality of text-books, to produce ancillary teaching materials and to make proper arrangements for the distribution and sale of text-books. Three modern printing presses will be set up to print school text-books. A number of State Governments propose to set up autonomous book production corporations. As recommended by the National Integration Council, a National Board of School Text-Books has been set up to coordinate the programmes of books production at the Central and State levels. Emphasis will also be placed on the production of children's books to promote national integration and develop their interest in science.

16.25 *Cultural Programmes* – The existing programmes for the development of the three national Akademics, the Archaeological Survey of India and the National and other museums will be stepped up. In addition, replicas and prints of museum and archaeological objects will be supplied to selected institutions to increase the awareness of our cultural heritage among students. The work relating to the compilation of the Indian and district gazetteers will be continued.

16.26 *Youth Services* – Youth services will be developed, both for students and non-students, to meet their needs in respect of personal development, idealistic yearnings and channelisation of energies – intellectual, emotional and physical. For students, the programmes will include improvement in curricula and methods of teaching and evaluation, provision of amenities such as hostels, reading seats and libraries including text-book libraries, strengthening of guidance, counselling and health services and increased provision for physical education, games and sports. Programmes of community or social service will be developed at the school stage as an integral part of the curriculum. At the university stage, the NCC will continue on an optional basis and, in addition, the National Service Corps Programme will be implemented on a selective basis, in the first instance, with a view to involving students in programmes of national or social service, including the conduct of literacy classes for adults. For non-students, the programme will include wider opportunities for further education and vocational or professional advancement through part-time or correspondence courses; development of facilities for physical education, games and sports and cultural activities; and provision of guidance and counselling. Special attention will be paid to the needs of rural youth and training of youth leadership. Provision has been made for setting up and assisting Planning Forums in colleges and universities. Efforts will be made to develop, both among student and non-student youth, a wider national outlook by bringing them together from different parts of the country for studies, social service and recreation. Efforts will be made to stimulate voluntary organisations to participate in and develop these programmes. It is proposed to set up a National Youth Organisation to advise Government on the development of youth services.

16.27 *Employment* – Job opportunities will increase as the development programmes visualised in the Plan get implemented. In addition, special efforts will be made to increase opportunities for self-employment. Apart from changes in curricula and methods of teaching oriented to this end at different stages of education, assistance will be provided in the form of technical guidance and, to the the extent possible, loans for establishing small enterprises. Also, programmes of vocational guidance and counselling will be stepped up, by strengthening the University Employment Information and Guidance Bureaux and bringing them into closer contact with employing agencies. At the school stage, provision for vocational guidance will be stepped up, by the Employment Service in collaboration with the educational authorities. For non-student youth, the programmes of guidance and counselling and supply of employment market information through the employment exchanges will be strengthened and expanded. These will require an expansion of the Employment Service both in the urban and rural areas, more studies and surveys to supplement the current employment market information programme and sustained publicity to ensure maximum utilisation of these services by employers as well as workers. To ensure a uniform development of these programmes throughout the country and to build up a National Employment Service, more frequent and intensive evaluation will be necessary.

16.28 *Technical Education* – Technical institutions have been planned for an annual admission capacity of 25,000 students at the degree level and 48,600 students at the diploma level. In view of the present unemployment among engineers, the actual admission in 1968-69 were about 18,000 in degree and 27,000 in diploma courses. It is proposed to keep the enrolment targets under review in the light of the assessed demand of engineering personnel in the Fifth and subsequent Plans. The main emphasis in technical education, during the Fourth Plan, will be on improving quality and standards. The improvement programmes would relate to pre-service and in-service training and training in industry of teachers, the reorganisation of diploma courses in order to diversify them functionally to the needs of industry, expansion and improvement of postgraduate engineering studies and research, curriculum development and preparation of instructional materials including laboratory equipment. The number of places for practical training in industry which was increased from 2,000 in 1967-68 to 11,000 in 1968-69 will be maintained at about the same level during the Fourth Plan. The Apprentices Act is proposed to be amended to include graduates and diploma holders. Centres of advanced study will be developed in aeronautics at Bombay, in material sciences at Kharagpur and in electronics and automation at Bangalore. Steps will be taken to improve the part-time degree and diploma courses. Management studies at the Institutes of Management at Calcutta and Ahmedabad and in the universities will be further developed. Support will be given for development of the Indian Institute of Science, Bangalore, the National Institute of Training in Industrial Engineering, Bombay, the National Institute of Forge and Foundry, Ranchi and other institutions. An attempt will be made for the closer linking of science and technology. The activities of technical institutions in fabricating equipment will be developed.

16.29 *Planning, Administration and Evaluation Machinery* – To implement educational programmes effectively, the administrative machinery will be streamlined. The strength of the cadres, their recruitment and training policies and the incentives provided to them at various levels as well as the remedial measures required will be reviewed. The work-load of supervisors will be examined and the concept of supervision broadened to include professional guidance to teachers. Provision will be made for the training and re-training of administrative cadres. Research will be carried out in procedures and practices in different States as well as in other countries. The State Directorates of Education will carry out periodic reviews to reform the administrative machinery in response to the changing needs of education programmes and policies. The task of detailed planning will be progressively shifted to the district level and individual institutions will be encouraged to plan and implement their own programmes of development.

OUTLAYS

16.30 Rs. 822.66 crores have been provided in addition to an average annual non-Plan expenditure of Rs. 550 crores. Of the Plan outlay, Rs. 551.66 crores (67 per cent) will be in the State sector, Rs. 32.40 crores (4.0 per cent) in the Centrally sponsored sector and Rs. 238.60 crores (29.0 per cent) in the Central sector. Sub-headwise break-up of the total outlay is given in Table 21.5. State-wise allocations for education are given in Annexure VI. According to the existing trends, about Rs. 150 crores are likely to be available from non-Government sources, which include fees, contributions by local bodies and endowments. In addition, education cess could be levied for elementary education and local resources mobilised for school buildings, school improvement, and mid-day meals.

II

Manpower

16.31 Ideally educational development at the higher level should be broadly related to the pattern of jobs and the estimates of demand in the economy for educated manpower. This is important both for the individual and the society. The individual is enabled to take decisions about future careers with the assurance that his training will be put to proper use and he would be productively employed. The gain to

TABLE 21.5: Sub-headwise Distribution of Outlay for Education in Fourth Plan: Centre, States and Union Territories

Sl. No.	Sub-head	Outlay (Rs. crores)				Percentage distribution of the outlay			
		Central and centrally sponsored	States	Union Territories	Total	Central and centrally sponsored	States	Union Territories	Total
0	1	2	3	4	5	6	7	8	9
1.	Elementary education	5.56	214.84	14.34	234.74	2.0	43.0	27.7	28.5
2.	Secondary education	0.27	104.25	13.80	118.32	0.1	20.8	26.6	14.4
3.	University education	103.99	76.06	3.47	183.52	38.4	15.2	6.7	22.3
4.	Teacher training	8.00[1]	12.20	0.97	21.17	3.0	2.4	1.9	2.6
5.	Social education	3.57[1]	3.91	0.82	8.30	1.3	0.8	1.6	1.0
6.	Other programmes	75.37[2]	30.88	12.51	118.75	27.8	6.2	24.2	14.5
7.	Cultural programmes	7.26	4.87	0.36	12.49	2.7	1.0	0.7	1.5
8.	Total: general education	204.01	447.01	46.27	697.29	75.3	89.4	89.4	84.8
9.	Technical education	66.99[1]	52.88	5.50	125.37	24.7	10.6	10.6	15.2
10.	Total education	271.00[3]	499.89	51.77	822.66	100.0	100.0	100.0	100.0

1. Rs. 8 crores allocated for teacher training, Rs. 0.5 crore for adult education and Rs. 10.6 crores for technical education will be administered by University Grants Commission.
2. Includes Rs. 8.30 crores for National Council of Educational Research and Training which besides other programmes has departments of Teacher Education and Adult Education.
3. Includes Rs. 32.4 crores (Rs. 19.4 crores in general education and Rs. 13 crores in technical education) in the Centrally sponsored sector.

society flows from the fact that a timely view of educated manpower required to achieve the varied tasks of economic development makes it possible to provide adequately, yet not excessively, for the scale and pattern of educational development which will best serve the purpose. There are uncertainties inherent in the task. Long term forecast of the growth of the economy has to be made and in order to provide guidance for educational planning it must be not only sufficiently detailed but fairly authoritative. Even when this condition is broadly realised, it is not easy to work out the implications for employment and the corresponding requirement of phased output from the educational system.

16.32 As new facts emerge and better methods of analysis are evolved, fresh estimates will need to be made. Manpower planning, based on the needs of an economy postulated to grow at a certain pace will create problems of maladjustment if the pace of growth slackens significantly over protracted periods. On the other hand, if such planning is, from the beginning, predicated on an overcautious approach regarding the future tempo of development, there will be the certainty of exposing the economy to severe constraints imposed by a shortage of trained personnel at various levels when other conditions favour faster growth. There are greater risks of loss when such avoidable shortages arise than when there is a marginal surplus of trained manpower.

16.33 As manpower is not homogeneous, manpower planning has to concern itself with different categories, such as doctors, nurses, engineers, agricultural graduates and craftsmen, each having its own level of education and specialisation. The provision of educational facilities to meet the estimated manpower requirements of some of the important categories is discussed below.

16.34 *Medical Personnel* – Expansion in admissions and outturn of doctors during the Third Plan period, the three subsequent years and as planned for the last year of the Fourth Plan are shown in Table 21.6.

16.35 By the end of the Fourth Plan, the number of medical colleges is expected to increase to 103, with an admission capacity of 13,000. To meet the requirement of teachers in medical colleges, specialists and research workers, existing facilities for post-graduate education will be expanded.

16.36 To stock of doctors increased from an estimated 70,000 in 1960-61 to 86,000 in 1965-66 and to 102,000 in 1968-69. It is estimated that it will increase to 138,000 in 1973-74. The doctor-population ratio in 1968-69 was approximately 1 : 5200. It is expected that by the end of Fourth Plan a doctor-population ratio of 1 : 4300 will be reached and five years later 1 : 3700.

TABLE 21.6: Admission and Out-turn of Medical Graduates, 1961 to 1973

(Numbers)

Year	Colleges	Annual admission	Annual out-turn
1	2	3	4
1961	66	7008	4068
1962	71	7348	3992
1963	79	9667	4179
1964	81	10227	4415
1965	87	10520	5135
1966	89	11079	6159
1967	91	11106	7407
1968	93	11500 [1]	10804 [1]
1973	103	13000 [1]	10300 [1]

[1] Provisional estimates.

16.37 The training of nurses and para-medical personnel takes less time and adjustments of supply and demand can be made within a shorter span of time. The programme of expansion of facilities for the training of nurses and para-medical personnel will be related broadly to the requirements of these categories of personnel in connection with medical, public health and family planning programmes. The expected increase in their number is as as given in Table 21.7.

TABLE 21.7: Stock of Para-Medical Personnel, 1965, 1968-69 and 1973-1974

(Numbers)

Sl. No.	Category	1965-66	1968-69 (anticipated)	1973-74 (targets)
0	1	2	3	4
1.	Nurses	45000	61000	88000
2.	Auxiliary nurse-midwives	22000	34000	54000
3.	Health/sanitary inspectors	18000	20000	32000
4.	Pharmacists	48000	51000	66000
5.	Radiographers	700	1300	11300
6.	Laboratory technicians	2000	3200	8600

16.38 *Agricultural Personnel* – There has been a rapid expansion of facilities for the training of agricultural and veterinary graduates to meet the requirements of trained manpower for agricultural development.

16.39 The stock of agricultural and veterinary graduates has increased from about 14,000 and 5,000 in 1960-61 to 32,000 and 9,300 respectively in 1965-66. On the basis of the present intake the stock of agricultural and veterinary graduates should increase to 65,000 and 15,500 respectively in 1973-74. It is expected that the requirements will be adequately met.

TABLE 21.8: Training Facilities for Agriculture and Veterinary Graduates, 1960-61 to 1967-68

(Numbers)

Years	Colleges	Annual admission	Annual out-turn
1	2	3	4
Agricultural graduates			
1960-61	51	5634	2090
1965-66	70	10049	5259
1966-67	70	8883	4734
1967-68	71	8400 [1]	5900 [1]
Veterinary graduates			
1960-61	17	1301	831
1965-66	20	1599	1070
1966-67	20	1425	1086
1967-68	20	1425 [1]	1000 [1]

[1] Provisional

16.40 Provision is being made to create suitable training facilities to meet the requirements for agricultural technicians such as tractor operators and mechanics.

16.41 *Engineering Personnel* – During the Third Plan there was a considerable expansion of facilities for engineering education both at the degree and diploma levels. The admission targets set originally in the Third Plan were 19,100 for the degree courses and 37,400 for diploma courses. The position was reviewed in 1962 after the Chinese aggression and the declaration of a state of emergency. It was decided to accelerate the expansion of facilities for engineering education to meet the urgent additional requirements arising from the new developments. In the event, the targets set for the end of the Third Plan were exceeded by 1963-64. The actual levels are Table 21.9.

16.42 There was virtually, no increase in sanctioned intake in the degree and diploma levels of engineering education after 1965, but admissions dropped in 1967-68 and much more steeply in 1968-69 – 33 per cent below the level of previous year.

16.43 The stock of graduate engineers is estimated to have increased from 58,000 in 1960-61 to 134,000 in 1968-69, and of diploma holders from 75,000 in 1960-61 to 198,000 in 1968-69.

16.44 A decline and later the stagnation in the tempo of industrial development, the slowing down of the rate of investment, the severe control on Government expenditure -- these features of the years 1966-67 and 1967-68 restricted the opportunities for employment of engineers, while new output continued on the basis of admissions 3 to 5 years earlier. While long-term solution was recognised to lie in the accelerated pace of economic development and in particular on rapid industrial advance, a number of short-term measures were approved by Government to create employment opportunities for engineers, and seek a balance in supply and demand. As many institutions had expanded in a hurry, it was recommended that admissions be restricted to the number with which the institutions could adequately cope so that standards could be maintained. The out-turn of graduates and diploma holders during the Fourth Plan is, except to a marginal extent, pre-determined by the admissions which have already taken place. The existing facilities for engineering education should be sufficient to meet the Fourth and Fifth Plan requirements. No shortages are expected. The problem will be primarily of effective deployment and better utilisation of persons trained. There is need for studies to be undertaken both industry-wise and region-wise in order to ensure that regional or inter-speciality imbalances do not develop between supply and demand of broad categories of personnel.

TABLE 21.9: Expansion of Engineering Education, 1960-61 to 1968-69.

(Numbers)

Year	Degree level				Diploma level			
	No. of institutions	Sanctioned intake	Actual intake	Out-turn	No. of institutions	Sanctioned intake	Actual intake	Out-turn
1	2	3	4	5	6	7	8	9
1960-61	102	13824	13692	5703	195	25801	23736	7969
1961-62	111	15850	15497	7026	209	27701	26525	10349
1962-63	114	17074	17669	8436	231	30826	29924	12046
1963-64	118	21040	20744	9120	248	39712	37822	12938
1964-65	131	23757	22214	9456	264	46243	41645	15202
1965-66	133	24695	23315	10282	274	48048	43984	17699
1966-67	137	25000	24934	13051	284	48579	46461	22260
1967-68	138	25000	24237	13873	284	48580	42935	22476
1968-69	138	25000[2]	17890	14593[1]	284	48600[2]	27255	23224[1]

[1] Provisional estimates.
[2] Admission capacity.

ANNEXURE I

TABLE 21.10: Growth of Enrolment in Schools and Colleges: 1960-61 to 1973-74

Stage/age-group	Unit	Boys/ Girls	1960-61	1965-66	1968-69	1973-74 (Targets)
1	2	3	4	5	6	7
Primary (6-11)						
classes I-V	million	total	34.99	50.47	55.49	68.58
			(62.4)	(76.7)	(77.3)	(85.3)
	million	boys	23.59	32.18	34.92	41.25
			(82.6)	(96.3)	(95.2)	(99.6)
	million	girls	11.40	18.29	20.57	27.33
			(41.4)	(56.5)	(58.5)	(70.1)
Middle (11-14)						
classes VI-VIII	million	total	6.70	10.53	12.27	18.10
			(22.5)	(30.9)	(32.3)	(41.3)
	million	boys	5.07	7.68	8.76	12.19
			(33.2)	(44.2)	(45.4)	(54.3)
	million	girls	1.63	2.85	3.51	5.91
			(11.3)	(17.0)	(18.8)	(27.7)
Secondary (14-17)						
classes XI-XI[1]	million	total	3.03	5.28	6.58	9.69
			(11.1)	(17.0)	(19.3)	(24.2)
	million	boys	2.47	4.08	4.95	7.00
			(17.5)	(25.6)	(28.5)	(34.3)
	million	girls	0.56	1.20	1.63	2.69
			(4.3)	(7.9)	(9.8)	(13.7)
University education (17-23) (arts, science and commerce)	million	total	0.74	1.24	1.69	2.66
			(1.5)	(2.3)	(2.9)	(3.8)
Technical education (admission capacity)						
diploma	Number	Total	25801	48048	48600[2]	48600
degree	Number	Total	13824	24695	25000[2]	25000

[1] Includes enrolment in classes IX to XII in case of Uttar Pradesh which the State Government regard as part of school education.

[2] The actual admissions were 27255 and 17890 respectively for diploma and degree courses.

Note: Figures in parentheses indicate percentage of enrolment to the population in the corresponding age-group.

ANNEXURE II

TABLE 21.11: Provision of Schooling Facilities: Classes I-V, 1960-61 1965-66 and 1968-69

(Enrolment in thousands)

Sl. No.	State/Union Territory	1960-61		1965-66		1968-69	
		Enrolment	Percentage of the age-group	Enrolment	Percentage of the age-group	Enrolment	Percentage of the age-group
1	2	3	4	5	6	7	8
	States						
1.	Andhra Pradesh	2976	68	3769	77	3839	72
2.	Assam	1126	68	1443	73	1566	71
3.	Bihar	3184	51	3961	54	4414	57
4.	Gujarat	2030	65	2665	82	2988	83
5.	Haryana	included under Punjab		804	67	855	63
6.	Jammu and Kashmir	210	47	297	63	331	66
7.	Kerala	2391	108	2869	116	3219	120
8.	Madhya Pradesh	2011	49	2849	56	3142	57
9.	Maharashtra	3949	77	5194	89	5876	91
10.	Mysore	2168	74	3136	90	3279	85
11.	Nagaland	43	83	58	109	67	117
12.	Orissa	1411	64	1749	70	1899	70
13.	Punjab	1440 [1]	51 [1]	1334	75	1362	69
14.	Rajasthan	1115	41	1618	50	2013	56
15.	Tamil Nadu	3333	85	4511	102	4927	105
16.	Uttar Pradesh	4093	45	9018	84	9935	84
17.	West Bengal	2902	65	3950	74	4367	73
	Union Territories						
18.	Andaman and Nicobar Islands	4	64	8	90	10.7	103
19.	Chandigarh	Included under Punjab		17.2	89	22.3	105
20.	Dadra & Nagar Haveli	n.a.	n.a.	5	56	6.6	67
21.	Delhi	286	83	399	93	447	87
22.	Goa, Daman and Diu	n.a.	n.a.	95	117	109.6	129
23.	Himachal Pradesh	84	51	358	86	378	82
24.	Laccadive, Minicoy & Amindivi Islands	3	102	3.9	111	4.7	127
25.	Manipur	117	98	163	120	171	111
26.	N.E.F.A.	n.a.	n.a.	13.1	27	16.8	32
27.	Pondicherry	31	75	48	100	54	105
28.	Tripura	87	55	134	71	156	73
29.	Total	34994	62	50469	77	55486	77

[1] Includes Haryana and Chandigarh.

Source: Ministry of Education for the years 1960-61 and 1965-66 and State Governments/Union Territories for the year 1968-69.

ANNEXURE III

TABLE 21.12: Provision of Schooling Facilities: Classes VI-VIII, 1960-61 1965-66 and 1968-69

(enrolment in thousands)

Sl. No.	State/Union Territory	1960-61		1965-66		1968-69	
		Enrolment	Percentage of the age-group	Enrolment	Percentage of the age-group	Enrolment	Percentage of the age-group
1	2	3	4	5	6	7	8
	States						
1.	Andhra Pradesh	408	17	651	25	526[1]	27[1]
2.	Assam	220	26	327	32	360	32
3.	Bihar	535	17	716	19	821	20
4.	Gujarat	387	29	597	35	727	40
5.	Haryana	included under Punjab		206	32	308	46
6.	Jammu and Kashmir	59	25	87	34	117	45
7.	Kerala	695	58	865	65	984	69
8.	Madhya Pradesh	317	16	564	22	712	24
9.	Maharashtra	748	28	1223	39	1527	46
10.	Mysore	363	23	578	33	647	32
11.	Nagaland	7	25	12.2	43	17.2	56
12.	Orissa	108	9	251	19	305	21
13.	Punjab	439	29[2]	326	34	427	44
14.	Rajasthan	207	15	330	20	425	23
15.	Tamil Nadu	691	32	1066	46	1273	49
16.	Uttar Pradesh	824	17	1514	27	1659	27
17.	West Bengal	518	22	854	32	990	32
	Union Territories						
18.	Andaman and Nicobar Island	0.5	14	1.5	35	2.2	43
19.	Chandigarh	Included under Punjab		7.5	74	10	95
20.	Dadra & Nagar Haveli	n.a.	n.a.	0.5	12	0.9	20
21.	Delhi	112	62	183	78	205	78
22.	Goa, Daman and Diu	n.a.	n.a.	18	41	30	65
23.	Himachal Pradesh	20	23	86	39	112	49
24.	Laccadive, Minicoy & Amindivi Islands	0.3	18	0.7	38	0.9	47
25.	Manipur	23	43	25	37	29	37
26.	N.E.F.A.	0.8	6	2.6	10	3	11
27.	Pondicherry	7	32	11	45	14	51
28.	Tripura	15	20	29	33	37.9	38
29.	Total	6705	23	10532	31	12270	32

[1] Enrolment in classes VI-VII only. [2] Includes Haryana and Chandigarh.

Source: Ministry of Education for the years 1960-61 and 1965-66 and State Governments/Union Territories for the year 1968-69.

ANNEXURE IV

TABLE 21.13: Provision of Schooling Facilities: Classes IX-XI, 1960-61 1965-66 and 1968-69

(Enrolment in thousands)

Sl. No.	State/Union Territory	1960-61		1965-66		1968-69	
		Enrolment	Percentage of the age-group	Enrolment	Percentage of the age-group	Enrolment	Percentage of the age-group
1	2	3	4	5	6	7	8
	States						
1.	Andhra Pradesh	196	9	342	14	542[1]	15[1]
2.	Assam	126	13	207	18	225	17
3.	Bihar	328	12	450	13	502	13
4.	Gujarat	171	15	311	20	416	25
5.	Haryana	included under Punjab		85	14	111	17
6.	Jammu and Kashmir	23	10	42	17	59	24
7.	Kerala	179	16	369	30	412	31
8.	Madhya Pradesh	140	8	270	12	331	13
9.	Maharashtra	339	14	617	22	803	26
10.	Mysore	169	11	288	18	263	15
11.	Nagaland	2	8	5.2	15	7.7	21
12.	Orissa	45	4	101	8	147	11
13.	Punjab	170[2]	13	151	17	175	19
14.	Rajasthan	77	6	139	9	183[3]	11
15.	Tamil Nadu	268	13	551	25	690	30
16.	Uttar Pradesh[4]	501	8	795	12	930	13
17.	West Bengal	218	10	377	15	535	20
	Union Territories						
18.	Andaman and Nicobar Island	0.2	6	0.5	12	1	20
19.	Chandigarh	Included under Punjab		5.2	56	6.2	61
20.	Dadra & Nagar Haveli	n.a.	n.a.	0.2	6	0.33	8
21.	Delhi	52	31	99.5	45	132	52
22.	Goa, Daman and Diu	n.a.	n.a.	9	22	15	36
23.	Himachal Pradesh	5	7	33	16.6	45	20
24.	Laccadive, Minicoy & Amindivi Islands	n.a.	n.a.	0.23	14	0.34	19
25.	Manipur	14	29	13.6	23	16.6	24
26.	N.E.F.A.	0.3	n.a.	1.6	5	1.7	5
27.	Pondicherry	3	13	6.6	29	8.3	34
28.	Tripura	5	8	12.5	16	17.9	21
29.	Total	3031	11	5282	17	6576	19

[1] Enrolment relates classes VIII to XI.
[2] Includes Haryana and Chandigarh.
[3] Includes Pre-University Class.
[4] Enrolment relates to classes IX to XII.

ANNEXURE V

TABLE 21.14: Statewise and Sexwise Enrolment at School, 1968-69

Sl. No.	State/union territory	Classes I-V					
		Enrolment			Percentage of the corresponding age-group		
		Boys	Girls	Total	Boys	Girls	Total
0	1	2	3	4	5	6	7
	States						
1.	Andhra Pradesh[1]	2283	1556	3839	84	59	72
2.	Assam[2]	953	613	1566	86	56	71
3.	Bihar	3310	1134	4444	85	30	57
4.	Gujarat	1883	1105	2988	102	64	83
5.	Haryana	612	243	855	86	38	63
6.	Jammu and Kashmir	238	93	331	92	38	66
7.	Kerala	1700	1519	3219	123	116	120
8.	Madhya Pradesh	2236	906	3142	79	33	57
9.	Maharashtra	3540	2336	5876	108	74	91
10.	Mysore	1884	1395	3279	96	74	85
11.	Nagaland[2]	43	24	67	149	85	117
12.	Orissa	1245	654	1899	91	48	70
13.	Punjab	815	547	1362	77	59	69
14.	Rajasthan[3]	1469	544	2013	79	32	56
15.	Tamil Nadu	2830	2097	4927	119	91	105
16.	Uttar Pradesh[4]	6290	3645	9935	102	64	84
17.	West Bengal	2771	1596	4367	92	53	73
	Union Territories						
18.	Andaman & Nicobar Islands	6.2	4.5	10.7	115	91	103
19.	Chandigarh	12.1	10.2	22.3	93	123	105
20.	Dadra and Nagar Haveli	4.7	1.9	6.6	96	39	67
21.	Delhi	247	200	447	90	84	87
22.	Goa, Daman and Diu	63.3	46.3	109.6	148	109	129
23.	Himachal Pradesh	238	140	378	102	61	82
24.	Laccadive, Minicoy and Amindivi Islands	2.8	1.9	4.7	140	112	127
25.	Manipur	105.5	65.5	171	136	85	111
26.	N.E.F.A.[2]	15	1.8	16.8	56	7	32
27.	Pondicherry	31	23	54	120	90	105
28.	Tripura	92	64	156	85	61	73
29.	Total	34920	20566	55486	95	59	77

Contd.

ANNEXURE V (contd.)

Sl. No.	State/Union Territory	Classes VI-VIII					
		Enrolment			Percentage of the corresponding age-group		
		Boys	Girls	Total	Boys	Girls	Total
0	1	8	9	10	11	12	13
	States						
1.	Andhra Pradesh[1]	374	152	526	39	16	27
2.	Assam[2]	242	118	360	43	21	32
3.	Bihar	694	127	821	33	6	20
4.	Gujarat	478	249	727	50	28	40
5.	Haryana	242	66	308	69	21	46
6.	Jammu and Kashmir	90	27	117	66	22	45
7.	Kerala	536	448	984	74	64	69
8.	Madhya Pradesh	548	164	712	37	11	24
9.	Maharashtra	1067	460	1527	63	28	46
10.	Mysore	438	209	647	43	21	32
11.	Nagaland[2]	11.7	5.5	17.2	79	35	56
12.	Orissa	243	62	305	35	8	21
13.	Punjab	297	130	427	57	29	44
14.	Rajasthan[3]	352	73	425	37	8	23
15.	Tamil Nadu	834	439	1273	64	34	49
16.	Uttar Pradesh	1340	319	1659	41	11	27
17.	West Bengal	683	307	990	45	20	32
	Union Territories						
18.	Andaman & Nicobar Islands	1.4	0.8	2.2	53	33	43
19.	Chandigarh	5.6	4.4	10	86	110	95
20.	Dadra and Nagar Haveli	0.63	0.25	0.88	29	10	20
21.	Delhi	120	85	205	85	71	78
22.	Goa, Daman and Diu	19	11	30	84	47	65
23.	Himachal Pradesh	87	25	112	76	22	49
24.	Laccadive, Minicoy and Amindivi Islands	0.67	0.24	0.91	66	26	47
25.	Manipur	20	9	29	53	22	37
26.	N.E.F.A.[2]	2	1	3	14	7	11
27.	Pondicherry	9	5	14	66	37	51
28.	Tripura	23.3	14.6	37.9	47	29	38
29.	Total	8758	3512	12270	45	19	32

Contd.

ANNEXURE V *(Contd.)*

Sl. No.	State/Union Territory	Classes IX-XI					
		Enrolment			Percentage of the corresponding age-group		
		Boys	Girls	Total	Boys	Girls	Total
0	1	14	15	16	17	18	19
	States						
1.	Andhra Pradesh [1]	416	126	542	24	7	15
2.	Assam [2]	161	64	225	24	10	17
3.	Bihar	454	48	502	24	3	13
4.	Gujarat	279	137	416	32	17	25
5.	Haryana	88	23	111	26	8	17
6.	Jammu and Kashmir	48	11	59	37	9	24
7.	Kerala	222	190	412	33	29	31
8.	Madhya Pradesh	273	58	331	21	5	13
9.	Maharashtra	600	203	803	38	14	26
10.	Mysore	188	75	263	21	9	15
11.	Nagaland [2]	5.6	2.1	7.7	31	11	21
12.	Orissa	127	20	147	20	3	11
13.	Punjab	121	54	175	24	12	19
14.	Rajasthan [3]	156	27	183	18	3	11
15.	Tamil Nadu	475	215	690	40	19	30
16.	Uttar Pradesh	771	159	930	21	5	13
17.	West Bengal	404	131	535	30	10	20
	Union Territories						
18.	Andaman & Nicobar Islands	0.7	0.3	1	25	14	20
19.	Chandigarh	3.6	2.6	6.2	57	68	61
20.	Dadra and Nagar Haveli	0.25	0.08	0.33	13	4	8
21.	Delhi	78	54	132	56	47	52
22.	Goa, Daman and Diu	9.5	5.5	15	46	26	36
23.	Himachal Pradesh	36	9	45	32	8	20
24.	Laccadive, Minicoy and Amindivi Islands	0.28	0.06	0.34	31	7	19
25.	Manipur	11.3	5.3	16.6	35	15	24
26.	N.E.F.A.	1.3	0.4	1.7	8	2	5
27.	Pondicherry	5.9	2.4	8.3	47	20	34
28.	Tripura	12.1	5.8	17.9	30	13	21
29.	Total	4948	1628	6576	29	10	19

[1] Columns (8) to (13) relate to classes VI and VII and columns (14) to (19) relate to classes VIII to XI.

[2] Columns (2) to (7) relate to classes A, B, I, II and III; columns (8) to (13) relate to classes IV to VI and columns (14) to (19) relate to classes VII to X.

[3] Columns (14) to (19) relate to classes IX, X and Pre-University.

[4] Columns (14) to (19) relate to classes IX to XII.

Source: State Governments/Union Territories

ANNEXURE VI

TABLE 21.15: State-wise Allocation for Education in the Fourth Plan

(Rs. lakhs)

Sl. No.	State/Union Territory	General education[1]	Technical education	Total
1	2	3	4	5
	States			
1.	Andhra Pradesh	3520.00	300.00	3820.00
2.	Assam	2326.00	301.00	2627.00
3.	Bihar	3838.00	310.00	4148.00
4.	Gujarat	2644.00	256.00	2900.00
5.	Haryana	1303.00	155.00	1458.00
6.	Jammu and Kashmir	704.00	90.00	794.00
7.	Kerala	1700.00	225.00	1925.00
8.	Madhya Pradesh	1850.00	300.00	2150.00
9.	Maharashtra	5522.00	950.00	6472.00
10.	Mysore	1300.00	200.00	1500.00
11.	Nagaland	493.30	45.00	538.30
12.	Orissa	1465.00	116.00	1581.00
13.	Punjab	2100.00	85.00	2185.00
14.	Rajasthan	1726.00	34.00	1760.00
15.	Tamil Nadu	5040.00	503.00	5543.00
16.	Uttar Pradesh	5895.00	1048.00	6943.00
17.	West Bengal	3275.00	370.00	3645.00
	Union Territories			
18.	Andaman & Nicobar Islands	105.00	—	105.00
19.	Chandigarh	50.00	30.00	80.00
20.	Dadra and Nagar Haveli	23.35	—	23.35
21.	Delhi	2309.00	251.00	25.60
22.	Goa, Daman and Diu	310.00	84.10	394.10
23.	Himachal Pradesh	661.00	50.00	711.00
24.	Laccadive, Minicoy and Amindivi Islands	36.29	—	36.29
25.	Manipur	389.00	20.00	409.00
26.	N.E.F.A.	205.18	—	205.18
27.	Pondicherry	217.00	20.00	237.00
28.	Tripura	320.70	95.00	415.70
29.	Total	49327.82	5838.10	55165.92

[1] Includes cultural programmes.

22

FIFTH YEAR PLAN*

Introduction[1]

The Fifth Five Year Plan was prematurely abandoned by the Janata Party Government at the Centre. In general terms the Fifth Plan paid emphasis on ensuring equality of opportunities as part of the over-all plan of ensuring social justice. From July 1975, programme of non-formal education was introduced by the government of India to cover children and also younger group who did not have opportunity for formal schooling or left school for one reason or the other. The major categories of population which received priority were (i) children in the age group of 6-14, (ii) uneducated youth in the age group of 15-35; and (iii) specific groups of men and women engaged in development activities or having common occupational or social and cultural identity. In the secondary education sector, efforts were made to implement the new pattern of education, i.e. 10+2. The main emphasis in university education was on consolidation and improvement. In order to reduce the rush in the universities, the facilities of higher education were planned to be provided through evening colleges, correspondence courses and private study.

EDUCATION[1]

5.136 Plan outlays for education during the first three years of the Plan have been somewhat modest because of the economic situation but the growth in the total governmental expenditure on education, both plan and non-plan, must be considered substantial. The total

---

* Planning Commission, Government of India, New Delhi 1976.

1. (i) Para Numbers refer to paras of the document.
   (ii) Original Table Numbers have been changed to conform to this chapter number.

expenditure is estimated to rise from Rs. 1,450 crores in 1974-75 to about Rs. 2,287 crores in 1976-77.

5.137 *Elementary Education:* Very high priority has been given to this programme. Adequate provision has been made for additional enrolment in terms of teaching personnel and construction of class-rooms, especially in backward areas.

5.138 Table 22.1 below indicates the additional enrolments, which are likely to be achieved by the end of the Fifth Plan.

TABLE 22.1: Growth of Enrolment, by the End of Fifth Plan

(figures in lakhs)

	Classes I-V			Classes VI-VIII		
	boys	girls	total	boys	girls	total
(0)	(1)	(2)	(3)	(4)	(5)	(6)
1. 1973-74 (position)*	396 (100)	245 (66)	641 (84)	107 (48)	46 (22)	153 (36)
2. 1974-77 (additional achievement)	37	33	70	17	12	29
3. 1977-79 (proposed additional target)	30	30	60	16	13	29
4. 1974-79 (additional achievement line 2+3)	67	63	130	33	25	58
5. 1978-79 (likely position)	463 (111)	308 (79)	771 (96)	140 (59)	71 (32)	211 (46)

* These figures are taken from Draft Fifth Plan. The Third Education Survey, however, indicated that the enrolments in classes I-V and VI-VII in 1973-74 were 611 lakhs (80%) and 141 lakhs (33%) respectively. Assuming the Survey enrolments as the base figures, the total enrolment in 1978-79 in these two groups would be 741 lakhs (92%) and 199 lakhs (43%) Figures in parenthesis indicate the proportion of children of respective age groups enrolled in Classes I-V and VI-VII.

5.139 In addition to the expansion of educational facilities, provision has been made for curricular re-orientation, work experience and strengthening of educational institutions for teachers.

5.140 *Secondary Education:* The existing trend in the increase of enrolment has been kept in view. Against the additional enrolment of 15 lakhs likely to be achieved in the first three years, an enrolment target of another 15 lakh in classes IX-XI/XII has been proposed for

1977-79. The percentage of children of the age-group 14-17/18, enrolled in classes IX-XI/XII will increase from 20 in 1973-74 to 25 in 1978-79. While making provisions, note has been taken of the requirements on account of the introduction of the new pattern of education.

5.141 After detailed preparatory work, vocationalisation at the secondary stage will be initiated in selected areas during the next two years so that well-conceived and fully thought-out programmes are implemented.

5.142 *University Education:* The main emphasis in university education is on consolidation and improvement. Provision is, however, being made to provide additional educational facilities to weaker sections of society and in the backward areas. Facilities through evening colleges, correspondence courses and private study will be expanded. Post-graduate education and research will continue to be strengthened through the development of centres of advanced study, science service centres, common computer facilities and regional instrumentation workshops. Programmes of faculty development, like summer institutes, seminars and orientation courses will be stepped up.

5.143 *Non-Formal Education:* With the strengthening of existing programmes of non-formal education, about 16 lakh participants are expected to be covered under these programmes. The existing programmes as intended to be reviewed.

5.144 *Scholarships:* 12,000 awards are being given every year from 1974-75 onwards, from the non-plan budget. The number of annual awards under the National Scholarship Scheme was 3,000 in each of the first two years of the Plan and 5,000 in 1976-77. Provision has been made to increase the number to 7,000 in 1977-78 and to 10,000 in 1978-79. Provision has also been made for continuing 20,000 yearly national loan scholarship awards during the Fifth Plan period. The number of national scholarships for talented children from rural areas, which was 10,000 each year during 1974-77, will be increased to 15,000 per year during 1977-79; thus increasing the number of scholarships per community development block from 2 to 3. Other programmes of scholarships will be continued.

5.145 *Language Development:* Provision has been made for the appointment of 2,000 additional Hindi teachers in middle and secondary schools during 1977-79, in non-Hindi speaking States. These are in addition to 4,000 teachers appointed during 1974-77. This programme will be reviewed with a view to determining its benefits. The Central Institute of Indian Languages (Mysore), the Kendriya Hindi Sansthan (Agra), the Rashtriya Sanskrit Sansthan (New Delhi) and the Central Institute of English and Foreign Languages (Hyderabad) will be further developed.

5.146 *Other Programmes:* Provision has been made for strengthening the existing Nehru Yuvak Kendras and for setting up some more Kendras at approved places. While the coverage of the National Service Scheme will be expanded, National Service Volunteers Scheme is expected to be launched on a pilot basis. Facilities for games and sports, coaching camps and rural sports will be expanded. Provision has been made for the development of Central Libraries.

5.147 *Technical Education:* Generally, the emphasis is on consolidation and quality improvement in terms of faculty development, replacement of obsolete equipment and diversification of courses. Centres of studies in material science, cryogenic engineering, energy studies and ocean engineering are expected to be established in close collaboration with user agencies. Provision has been made for augmenting physical facilities at the existing Institutes of Management, and preparatory work will be started for establishment of the fourth Institute at Lucknow. Regional Engineering Colleges and the Engineering Departments in the universities will be further developed.

5.148 *Cultural Programmes:* Provision has been made, inter alia, for further development of the three national academies of Sahitya, Sangeet Natak and Lalit Kala, propagation of culture among college and school students, revision of district gazetteers and development of various activities of the Archaeological Survey of India.

5.149 *20-Point-Socio-Economic Programmes:* Three components of this programme are provision of books and stationery to students at cheaper rates, supply of essential commodities to hostel students at subsidised prices and expansion of apprenticeship training programme. The capacity of the text-book printing presses is being developed further. Book banks will continue to be established in educational institutions. The coverage of apprenticeship scheme is being expanded.

5.150 *Outlays:* For completing the various tasks related to educational development, an outlay of Rs. 1,285 crores has been provided for different sectors as indicated in Table 22.2.

TABLE 22.2: Outlay Provided for Different Sectors during Fifth Plan

(Rs. crores)

Sub-head	Likely expenditure 1974-77	Proposed 1977-79	Proposed Fifth Plan outlay
(0)	(1)	(2)	(3)
1. elementary education	180	230	410
2. secondary education	111	139	250
3. university education	140	152	292
4. special education	9	9	18
5. other programmes	57	65	122
6. total (general education)	497	595	1092
7. technical education	75	81	156
8. art and culture	16	21	37
9. *total education*	*588*	*697*	*1285*

In relation to the first three years, the proposed outlay in the next two years marks a considerable step-up.

23

SIXTH FIVE YEAR PLAN*

Introduction

The Sixth Plan (1979-83) initiated by the Janata Party Government was abandoned by the Congress Party after it was voted back to power in 1980. The Congress Party changed the years of the Plan from 1978-79 — 1984-85 to 1980-85. The emphasis in the development of education in the Sixth Plan was on the optimum utilisation of existing facilities, qualitative improvement of system and making available the educational services to the socially deprived sections of the community. It was highlighted that while financial outlays were important and necessary to create additional infrastructure, it was equally important to bring about changes and improvements in the system through increased attention to non-monetary inputs, i.e., environment conducive to growth and development, participatory management techniques involving the teachers' and the student skills, development of a relevant academic ethos opportunities for learning by doing and appropriate consideration to the problems of education of the first generation planners.

The plan proposed a ten-year strategy to realise the Constitutional Directive of providing free and compulsory education to all children up to the age of 14—an objective which should have been achieved in 1960, i.e., ten years after the commencement of the Constitution. The Sixth Plan proposed universalisation of primary education for the age group 6-11 to be achieved by the end of the Plan in 1985 and universalisation of middle level (class VI to VIII and group 11-14) by 1990.

The Sixth Plan launched by the Janata Party Government had virtually declared a freeze of higher education. The Congress Party

---

* Planning Commission, Government of India, New Delhi 1981.

which was also aware of the undesirable growth of general higher education and that especially at the undergraduate level, emphasised the scope for and possibility of greater use of the infrastructural physical facilities and resources which might need minimum additional support to make them critically viable.

In the designing of strategy of adult education, it was observed that the lot of the weaker sections like women, Scheduled Castes, Scheduled Tribes and agricultural labourers as well as slum dwellers would be given priority.

EDUCATION[1]

Education, broadly perceived as a seamless continuum of life long learning, is essential for human resource development at every age level. In a package of development inputs available to the community, education should form an effective means to improve the status and character of living patterns of the people, help intellectual, social and emotional development of the individuals and to enable them to meet their basic needs of daily life. The long range goal of educational planning is then to make available diverse net-works of facilities and programmes for education, combining formal and non-formal modes of learning. It should enable all citizens to acquire literacy, numeracy, computational skills, basic understanding of the surrounding world and functional skills of relevance to daily life and to local environment. The emphasis in our planning efforts would thus shift from provision of inputs and expansion of facilities in general terms to result to be achieved and tasks to be performed with specific reference to target groups of population, particularly the socially disadvantaged.

21.2 Programmes of human resource development have a fourfold perspective: (i) to prepare individuals for assuming their role as responsible citizens; (ii) to develop in them scientific outlook, awareness of their rights and responsibility as well as a consciousness of the processes of development, (iii) to sensitise them to ethical, social and cultural values which go to make an enlightened nation; and (iv) to impart to them knowledge, skills and attitudes which would enable

1. (i) Para numbers refer to the paras in Chapter 21 of the document.
   (ii) Original Table Numbers have been changed to conform to this chapter number.

them to contribute to the productive programmes in the national development. In the realisation of this, educational system and programmes have to be directed towards a set of goals and tasks. Among these would be the following:

(i) to guarantee to all equality of opportunity for education for improving the quality of life and their participation in the tasks of promoting the general well-being of the society;

(ii) to afford to all young people and adults, irrespective of age, the means for ample self-fulfilment within the framework of harmonious development which reflects the needs of the community to which they belong;

(iii) to provide for a continuous process of life-long education for physical, intellectual and cultural development of people and for inculcating in them capabilities to cope with and influence social change;

(iv) to establish dynamic and beneficial linkages between education, employment and development with due regard for the economic and social aims of the community;

(v) to promote respect for, and belief in values of national integration, secularism, democracy and dignity of labour;

(vi) to sensitise academic communities to the problems of poverty, illiteracy and environmental degradation through extension services and organised participation in poverty reduction and environment improvement programmes;

(vii) to facilitate development, mobilisation, organisation and utilisation of the youth to involve and participate in the process of national development; and

(viii) to support the growth of arts, music, poetry, dance, and drama, including folk art, as instruments of culture, education and national integration.

21.3 The approach to achieve these objectives will be characterised by flexibility and diversity to suit varying needs and circumstances and by a stress on coordination of efforts, resources and programmes of the different sectors and agencies. The need to maintain high quality of education, aiming at academic excellence, and its relevance to national development objectives would be articulated throughout the system.

Review

21.4 Despite a network of over 6.5 lakhs schools and colleges, the employment of over 3 million teachers and an annual budget of the order of Rs. 3,000 crores, it has not been possible so far for the education system to achieve the goal of universal education of all children up to the age of 14 years as enshrined in the Directive Principles of the Constitution. The total enrolment in elementary education has increased from 223 lakhs in classes I-VIII in 1950-51 to around 905 lakhs during 1979-80. Nevertheless, for every three children enrolled in primary and middle schools, one other eligible child is left behind. Over 80 per cent of the children not enrolled so far are confined to a dozen States who have not been in a position to allocate the necessary economic resources to achieve the goal of universalisation according to the present system of elementary education.

21.5 There are also socially disadvantaged groups, such as the economically poor, scheduled castes and scheduled tribes, whose children are on the periphery of the schooling system. About 38 per cent of the scheduled caste children (20 per cent of the boys and 56 per cent of the girls) and 56 per cent of the scheduled tribe children (49 per cent of the boys and 70 per cent of the girls) are yet to receive elementary education. As revealed by the Fourth Educational Survey, the non-availability of schools is not a major constraint in this regard. But socio-economic compulsions in families, particularly in rural areas and among the weaker sections, not-too-relevant nature of curricular programmes and lack of essential facilities in schools seem to be some of the more important factors contributing to the slow progress. Even the existing facilities for elementary education are not optimally utilised, overaged and underaged children account for around 20 per cent of the enrolment and nearly 64 per cent of the children who are enrolled in class I, drop out by the time they complete class V. This represents economic loss in resource utilisation, educational inefficiency and low productivity, not to mention the long-term social loss to the individual child and the family on account of the incomplete development of the former's educational career.

21.6 In the areas of secondary and higher education, facilities have been expanded during the last three decades. Nonetheless, the reforms for qualitative improvement and system reorganisation, as envisaged in the National Policy on Education (1968), are yet to be completed effectively. This is particularly so for the integration of practical aspects in the educational programmes and for planned growth of programmes directed towards gainful employment to be implemented in close cooperation with all the developmental agencies. Inter-sectoral linkages are yet to be brought about and coordination established between work places, schools and development activities for fostering appropriate manpower development programmes.

This has resulted, among other things in an undesirable growth of facilities for general higher education, specially at the under-graduate stage in arts, commerce and humanities, and in the consequent increase in incidence of unemployment among the educated. It has also not been possible to evolve systems approach to educational planning and development aiming, *inter alia,* at flexibility and mobility among different types and levels of education and at maximisation of benefits from educational investment for rapid progress in the different sectors of national economy. This has undermined the role and capability of the higher education system to promote and maintain excellence and high standards in academic programmes, encourage pure scholarship and extend the frontiers of knowledge as well as to participate in national S&T activities and develop national scientific and technical manpower.

Approach

21.7 It may, no doubt, be necessary to create additional infrastructure to ensure the future growth of the educational system but this would have to be appropriate to the needs of, and based on a careful scrutiny in, specific areas and sectors and for identified target groups, particularly those which are in the danger of getting left behind because of their special circumstances. The existing institutions and programmes need to be consolidated and put to optimum use to serve the goals of development in the community as a whole. Provision of suitable educational facilities in backward areas and for the deprived groups and promotion of non-formal programmes at all levels incorporating plurality of models and diversity of patterns are equally important. The organisation of new facilities must also be linked to the actual needs and made relevant to local environment and learning requirements, taking note of the specific characteristics of the prospective beneficiaries.

21.8 The importance of educational planning and management at all levels has to be emphasised in this context and capabilities built for these tasks. Educational planning must effectively be coordinated with manpower planning at all stages and aspects of skill development. Adequate attention has to be given to optimisation of benefits from the existing investments and facilities. The failure to achieve a larger measure of equalisation of educational opportunities both in regard to access and achievement, is an aspect which requires closer attention. Concerted efforts and called for to reach the socially handicapped and economically weaker sections of the society such as, women, scheduled castes, scheduled tribes, landless labourers etc. The imbalances which have developed in the system between the rich and urban level on the one hand and the poor and rural level on the other have to be rectified so that enrolment rates in elementary education of the socially deprived groups and the general population are brought on par at least by the end of the Sixth Plan. It is essential also to transform the system of education qualitatively in terms of its value content, standards and relevance to life. The role of education to promote humanistic outlook, sense of brotherhood and a commitment to ethical and cultural values needs to be re-emphasised.

21.9 The import of educational technology has to be adequately provided for greater efficiency and effectiveness and wider reach of the educational programmes. This would be made possible with the launching of the INSAT. The possibility of using modern technology to take education, especially at the elementary stage, to all sections of population in a shorter frame of time has to be capitalised for achieving minimum basic education of all people within a decade. All these will require the strengthening, reorientation and integration of non-formal and formal programmes of educational development and bringing about inter-sectoral and inter-agency co-ordination at different levels for furtherance of specific aims of human resource development.

Programmes

Early Childhood Education

21.10 From the stand point of priorities within the field of education, importance should be attached, in terms of coverage, to the young child, children in the school going age-groups and those among the socially under-privileged groups. Attention should be paid to all young children during their crucial development years up to 5 years. This early childhood stage is the period of maximum learning and intellectual development of the child and hence of great potential educational significance. The present pre-school child care programmes are limited to the distribution of food supplements and routine health cover; these contribute very little to the personality development of the child, especially to its intellectual, social and emotional growth. The concept of learning and development through play and joyful activities should be articulated, across age-group, through an all round programme which should be comprehensive in scope, integrated in nature and reinforced over long time. Organisation of a creche for children in the 0-3 age-group and/or a balwadi for 3-6 age group, with provision for educational toys, play equipment, learning materials and books for children's reading etc., would be appropriate for this purpose. The educational component of such a package of services would no doubt be significant.

21.11 The approach in the Sixth Plan is characterised by a concern for the all round development of children, especially those from underprivileged sections and poverty groups who may suffer serious consequences in the future because of negligence at the present stage of life. Such a preparatory programme would, additionally, contribute towards universalisation of enrolment and retention of children in elementary education in due course. The programme is envisaged initially to serve the needs of children in the rural and the urban slum areas, based on economic means and social and educational backwardness of the population groups. The target for the Sixth Plan would be at least one early childhood education centre in every community development block. It would be advantageous to develop these centres as adjuncts to village primary schools wherever possible. The resources and inputs of programmes under health, nutrition, social welfare, integrated rural development and education, which are presently devoted to child, family and community welfare would be coordinated for this purpose, with flexibility and freedom built in by allowing various agencies to undertake programmes within a common framework. The services of suitable persons from the community, especially women and the educated unemployed youth, could be used to support them. Necessary pre-deployment training of the workers in the field would be arranged on a selective basis through existing teachers training institutions. The approach at this stage of education would be entirely non-formal and stress laid on the inculcation of sense perceptions among the children, through innovative use of locally available resources in the community and the environment. The National Council of Educational Research and Training, in collaboration with similar agencies in the States would help in developing the learning materials and aids both for teacher training and for programme implementation.

Elementary Education

21.12 It is proposed that the programme of universalisation of elementary education would be given serious consideration, especially in the educationally backward States and for reaching the socially disadvantaged who constitute the bulk of the non-attending children and of the drop-outs. The Sixth Plan assigns the highest priority to this programme which would continue to be a part of the minimum needs programme. While many States have reached 100 per cent enrolment of boys at the primary stage (classes I-V), some are lagging in respect of boys and many in regard to girls. Although the objective is to attain the universalisation up to the age of 14, operationally a strategy needs to be worked out to achieve this is in two distinct stages over a ten year period. Accordingly, the approach in the Sixth Plan is for all the States, which are yet to universalise the primary education, to reach universalisation of primary education (classes I-V), up to the age of 11 years, in the next five years, and, in case of other States, to achieve a substantial increase in the enrolment at the middle stage (classes VI-VIII of children up to 14 years so as to move towards the goal as fast as possible.

21.13 The approach to universalisation of elementary education will cover (i) intensified use of existing facilities, including the adjustment of schooling hours, which would not be more than 3 hours a day, according to local conditions, (ii) provision of new facilities which would be economically viable and educationally relevant, and (iii) promotion of non-formal system of learning. Programmes for non-formal learning would be organised and oriented towards target groups and decentralised in regard to their contents, course duration, placc and hours of learning and pattern of instructions. However, there would be a basic minimum package of inputs identified by the public educational authorities which would have correspondence to the formal system of education. In both formal and non-formal system, the emphasis would be on the retention of students and effective delivery of services to children. It is also essential to ensure appropriate incentives like free midday meals, supply of uniforms and learning materials, and compensation to the families of scheduled caste girls towards the opportunity cost involved. Efforts should be made by the State Governments to introduce measures with a view to eliminate wastage and reduce drop-out in elementary education.

21.14 As part of the efforts to retain children and promote the internal efficiency of the system as well as achieve equalisation of educational opportunities, measures for improvement in the quality of education become very important. The curriculum would be developed with the goal of imparting necessary levels of literacy, numeracy, comprehension and functional skills related to local socio-economic factors and environment needs. It would suit flexible models, with provision of diversification and dexterous balance between common basic goal and varying methodology. The basic objective would stress curriculum as an instrument for inculcating humanistic values, capacity for tolerance, promotion of national integration, scientific attitude and temper and individual capability for learning from the surrounding world.

21.15 Keeping in view the progress already made in the different States in expanding elementary education and the feasibility limits of accelerated growth in the educationally backward States, it is proposed to lay down specific targets Statewise for the Sixth Plan. It is estimated that universalisation of the primary stage of education would imply additional enrolment of about 170 lakh children in classes I-V over the next five years on an average annual rate of enrolment of 34 lakh children. In recent years, however, the rate of enrolment has approximately been of 20 lakhs annually and if the above targets are to be achieved, the educationally backward States of Assam, Bihar, Madhya Pradesh, Rajasthan, Uttar Pradesh and West Bengal would have to step up their present rates of enrolment considerably, in some cases more than double if not three-fold. It is, therefore, proposed that the additional targets should be projected realistically in individually States and Union Territories consistent with the ultimate object of completing the universalisation programme by 1990.

21.16 In the middle stage of elementary education for children in the age-group 11-14, the population to be covered to achieve a target of 50 per cent in the Sixth Plan would be about 63 lakhs or an annual enrolment of 13 lakhs on an average. The achievements so far has been at the rate of 7 lakhs per annum. Those States which have already attained 100 per cent enrolment in the primary classes would have to endeavour in the Sixth Plan to reach higher rates of enrolment in the 11-14 year age groups but, even then, it would require the doubling of the present enrolment rates. This, however, needs to be accepted as a desirable objective and challenge during the Sixth Plan, without which the goal of universal elementary education cannot be attained even by the end of the century.

21.17 Taking the proposals for primary and middle stages together, the additional enrolment in full time elementary education during 1984-85 is given in Table 23.1.

TABLE 23.1: Expension of Full Time Education: Enrolment Targets for 1984-85

Age Group/Classes	Enrolment (in lakhs)		Enrolment as % of Age Group	
	1979-80	1984-85 (Target)	1978-80	1984-85
1	2	3	4	5
6—11/I-V				
Boys	438	485	100.2	108.1
Girls	272	342	65.9	81.5
Total	710	827	83.6	95.2
11—14/VI-VII				
Boys	130	166	52.0	63.1
Girls	65	92	27.7	36.8
Total	195	258	40.2	50.3
6—14/I-VIII				
Boys	568	651	82.3	91.7
Girls	337	434	52.2	65.0
Total	905	1085	67.8	78.8

21.18 Non-formal education programmes have been initiated in the States recently and these would need to be developed and expanded, in the light of experience gained, to cover all those children who would require, and benefit only by, such modes of learning. It would be unrealistic to lay down any specific target for this purpose but it is expected that about 80 lakh children would be covered during the Sixth Plan.

21.19 The provision of non-formal education requires considerable imagination and innovation. The State Institutes of Education, in collaboration with the National Council of Educational Research and Training, would draw up feasible programmes for this purpose outlining the curriculum, syllabus and reading material for these courses and for the training of teaching personnel. The Centrally sponsored scheme to help the educationally backward States with financial assistance for programmes of non-formal elementary education would be continued.

21.20 It is proposed to establish special monitoring arrangements at the Centre and the State level to review progress of elementary education, particularly of the target groups, which are yet to be provided with universal elementary education. Their educational needs would be looked into according to a larger perspective of the families, socio-economic conditions and problems and, whenever necessary, a family approach would be adopted in conjunction with welfare schemes of other sectors and agencies. Apart from providing schooling facilities, they would be supplied with mid-day meals, free books, uniforms and stationery as well as attendance scholarships, as incentives, which would be coordinated and extended with a focus on their human resource development including education. These children would also be given remedial coaching programmes to enable them to overcome their environmental handicaps and educational backwardness. Programmes such as those designed to promote learning while earning, would also be promoted to overcome economic reasons hampering their educational development. It would be the specific responsibility of educational administration and planning to ensure that these groups are brought into the fold of national educational apparatus as soon as possible through appropriately designed strategies and disaggregated and relevant programmes.

21.21 Provision is made for construction of satisfactory primary and middle school buildings and class-rooms, supply of physical facilities and kits, enhancing the teachers' competence and for the updating and extensive use of educational technique for higher efficiency and greater effectiveness. Keeping in view, however, the large magnitude of the problem of school buildings the Plan provides only a modest outlay in the State sector; it envisages continuous efforts to achieve economy in construction costs, among other things, by increasing use of locally available building materials and functionally suitable designs.

Adult Education

21.22 The Sixth Plan lays emphasis on minimum essential education to all citizens, irrespective of their age, sex and residence. The approach to achieve this objective would be characterised by flexibility, inter-sectoral cooperation and inter-agency coordination. Technocracy would be adopted as the major instrument for the spread of literacy, numeracy and practical skills relevant to the economic activities of the people concerned. It would be supported by post-literacy, continuing education through a network of rural libraries as well as instructional programmes through mass communication media, particularly after the INSAT is launched to its orbit.

21.23 Non-formal education for adults, particularly in the productive age-group 15-35 years, would receive priority in the Sixth Plan, in view of its potential for immediate impact in raising the level of productivity in the economy. The programmes of adult education, which had been initiated in the previous Plans and which form part of the minimum needs programme of elementary education would be made more effective and extended in cooperation with the other developmental activities and the employment agencies. The programmes would aim at extending appropriate educational support to the concerned groups of individuals and development departments through carefully designed group-specific and work-based curricula which would be integrated as part of development activity. They would also take advantage of the cultural and other group characteristics in the process of involving the learner groups to participate in, and benefit from, adult education programmes.

21.24 While designing this programme, the lot of the weaker sections like women, scheduled castes, scheduled tribes and agricultural labourers as well as slum dwellers would be given priority. The strategy in these cases would be the development of methods and contents suited to the varied needs and situations, thus promoting flexibility in the programme and in the means of delivery of education. It would also help to involve voluntary agencies of established repute; such agencies have shown a great capacity to innovate effectively and their involvement will be useful where culture-specific improvisations are required.

Secondary Education

21.25 Secondary and higher secondary education are important terminal stages in the system of general education and provide a first stage for linking education with the world of work. It is at this point that options are exercised by the youth to enter the world of employment or to go for technical training or to pursue higher education. With the expansion of the base of education at the lementary stage, increasing number of students, including a large number of first generation learners, would reach secondary education. Facilities have to be provided for their education since such education is the only means of social mobility and economic independence, particularly among the socially disadvantaged. Care has to be taken to ensure that secondary education also prepares them for a long-term career as part of the stock of national man power. Keeping these in view, facilities for secondary education would have to be extended to rural and backward areas and access provided to the weaker and more backward sections of the people, particularly the first generation learners.

21.26 The importance of secondary education to prepare manpower for economic development would stress the need to pay special attention to the quality of education at this stage. This would cover, apart from improving the internal efficiency of the system and enhancing the employability of its products, updating the curriculum and syllabus, production of better text-books and instructional material and creating in the young generation an awareness of the emerging development perspective and associated technologies in fields such as, energy conservation, population stabilisation and environment protection. At the same time, they should not be alienated emotionally or culturally from the society.

21.27 Science teaching would be strengthened and laboratory equipment provided, both for experimentation and demonstration. The programme for supply of science kits at the primary and middle stages would be expanded and an appropriate kit for secondary education designed, produced and supplied to high and higher secondary schools. The curriculum in science and mathematics would continue to be reviewed and upgraded and pre-service as well as in-service training of teachers in all subjects promoted on an extensive scale. The educational system would also recognise the needs of the exceptionally talented children in the society and give them opportunities for taking up special courses or programmes of studies suited to their talent and thus nurture the valuable latent talent as a national resource.

21.28 One of the important links between education and development is provided by manpower development through vocationalisation of secondary education related to employment. This has to be carefully designed, based on detailed surveys of existing and potential work opportunities and of available educational and training facilities. It should also keep in view the specific roles and responsibilities of the different agencies and ensure coordination at the operational level between the developmental programmes and the educational system. Such a differentiation would normally commence after the secondary stage and may cover varying periods depending upon the vocational area, groups of occupations and the nature and level of skills needed. It envisages deepening of practical bias in the school education to be supplemented by appropriate apprenticeship in actual field, farm or factory situations. It is not necessary to follow a rigid sequence in the order of acquiring the several skills and it should be possible to supplement exclusive vocational training courses with necessary educational component. In this way, suitable linkages need to be established within a system for occupational mobility and career development over one's employment/working life. For the provision of relevant practical skills, agencies like Krishi Udyog and Van Vikas Kendras and other vocational training centres would be utilised, particularly for learning by doing. Similarly, experienced craftsmen and practitioners of the arts would be used for imparting operational skills without undue insistence on pedagogic certificates. Wherever new facilities are to be created, they would be located, to the maximum extent possible, in the rural areas.

Higher Education

21.29 Extensive and widespread facilities have already been created for higher education and the main thrust in the Sixth Plan would be to coordinate them and maximise their utilisation. There is sufficient scope for and possibility of, greater use of the infrastructural physical facilities and resources which might need minimum additional support to make them critically viable. The existing imbalances in the level of development of universities among themselves as well as in relation to colleges would have to be examined for suitable remedial programmes and selective support in keeping with their requirements, potential and scope. The problem of non-viable institutions, with low enrolments and inadequate provision of facilities, as well as proliferation of such institutions, offering general academic courses, would need to be tackled with determination, both in order to avoid increasing unemployment among the graduates as well as to make better use of the available economic resources for educational development. At the same time, the problems of first generation learners, particularly the socially disadvantaged sections, for whom higher education provides a transition, opportunity and challenge in terms of life perspectives and socio-economic aspirations of the community would need to be harmonised into the academic pattern. Personalised guidance and higher education would be required for them keeping in view their emphasis on human resource development as well as in order to enable them to avail of employment opportunities specifically earmarked in the several sectors.

21.30 The improvement of quality of higher education would receive special consideration. The redesigning of under-graduate courses and their restructuring to improve employment orientation would be extended during the Sixth Plan. In the area of post-graduate education and research emphasis would be placed on promoting the research and development capability of the university system and on inter-disciplinary studies, particularly in new emerging areas of knowledge, relevant to national development objectives. Research within the university system would be coordinated with the national science and technology efforts according to which areas to which research funds are to be channalised would be clearly identified and close collaboration realised on a structured basis among universities, national laboratories and other research organisations. The necessary infrastructural facilities such as sophisticated instrumentation services, computers and libraries would be made available to the universities on a regional basis.

21.31 The institutions of higher learning would be encouraged and enabled to involve themselves with the development activities in the community and provide requisite support through extension services of students and faculties. Such extension work would be considered as part of the normal academic work of the students and teachers, and not as social service. Universities would not only extend frontiers of knowledge but also supply such knowledge to solve problems of the community on whom they depend.

21.32 The Sixth Plan realises the importance of education to development and envisages concerted effort to forge beneficial links among education, employment and economic development. A committee of experts has already been set up by Planning Commission to examine the several aspects of the issues involved in detail. According to them, it is necessary that educational programmes are related to manpower profiles, existing and needed, in the development and occupational areas/sectors and provide for adequate levels and scope of pre-employment knowledge and skills, as also for continuing education for those who are already employed. The entire educational system must, in fact, respond to this important aspect of human resource development as one of the major purposes of education is to prepare the students for a gainful working life with a capability of learning to match new job requirements. There are, no doubt, deeper reasons for unemployment among the educated but, to some extent, the mis-match between education and employment is due to the kind of education and training which students get in traditional courses, The introduction of work experience and deepening of practical bias, in secondary schools, as proposed, are no doubt, programmes in the desired direction. The higher education has also a major responsibility in this regard which would require (a) restructuring of under-graduate courses to make them purposeful and also terminal for those who would seek employment, (b) provision for vocational courses leading to employment and structured for certificate or diploma, rather than an academic degree and (c) promotion at post-graduate level research on practical problems of local and regional relevance as well as on fundamental research. The minimum objective of such a programme would be to make the first degree courses more relevant and responsive to the development needs of the community and link education with work/field/practical experience and productivity by introducing students to relevant application areas of the subjects of their study. These will have the advantage of achieving a greater sensitisation of the academic community to the problem of poverty, illiteracy and environmental degradation.

21.33 It would be necessary to formulate specific work plans to develop these programme areas and guidelines are being prepared for this purpose by the above committee of experts. These would be considered for implementation in the Sixth Plan by the universities and other appropriate authorities and necessary modifications made in their statues to enable them do so.

21.34 To ensure effective linkages as envisaged, it would be necessary to set up an institutional framework within the university system. One of the ways to achieve this would be the establishment, in every university, of a statutory authority, say, a research (or education) and development council with representation from the university, community and users. Such a council would plan relevant activities and monitor them; it could also be effective for contact and communication with Government Departments, public sector undertakings, and trade and industry. The guidance and counselling services to facilitate proper selection of subjects at the time of entry and of remedial courses would be provided, particularly for the benefit of the first generation learners from weaker and socially handicapped sections of the society. To meet the special needs of women, who may have interruption in their studies; universities would ensure that facilities are provided to enable them to continue their education at the stage they left and complete the same for the final academic awards.

21.35 The various innovative educational programmes which are intended to aid developmental activities would require close coordination and joint action between the educational system and the developmental departments and sectors. For example, the work experience programme would require the secondment of students to places of work which come within the purview of agencies other than educational. The vocationalisation programmes at the higher secondary stage require coordinated action of all educational and training facilities and the services of developmental agencies for suitable placement for apprenticeship and/or employment of students. It is expected that the district level employment generation councils and district development centres, envisaged in the Sixth Plan, would provide a suitable forum to channelise the requirements of the minimum needs programme and the health for all schemes towards the capabilities and facilities of the universities and the higher education system. By virtue of its far reaching social significance, this should deserve to be taken up for implementation jointly by educational institutions and the concerned agencies.

21.36 Beyond the district and sub-regional levels, it would be conducive for the forging of effective linkage if, at the State level, an appropriate forum is set up to ensure close coordination among education, planning and executive efforts. It would be desirable also to set up an inter-university council or board to bring together all the universities located within a State and the governmental agencies to involve them collectively in respect of programmes which could be planned and activated in a complementary manner. There is also a need for continuous feed back from the users of the products of the university system, particularly regarding results of research, relevance and matching of manpower skills and knowledge in actual field conditions and context. Such an interaction would enable the university system to acquire the necessary information and data base about the needs of the community, public undertakings, trade and industry, and the governmental agencies. Problem-oriented research and investigations of immediate application to social progress could be tackled through such cooperative endeavours. Inter-sectoral coordination between education and related sectors of health, food and nutrition, employment, housing and environment is indeed necessary. As stated earlier, education in respect of health and other basic needs of society should become an integral part of the general education system and all forms of formal, incidental and non-formal learning should support these programmes according to a scientific system.

Youth Development

21.37 Youth in the country constitutes a vast human resource which is characterised by idealism and zeal, active habits, positive attitude towards service to others, an urge to be self-reliant and a willingness to explore newer and non-conformist approaches to societal problems. If properly harnessed and utilised, the youth could therefore be a powerful instrument of social, cultural and economic change. There are four major aspects of the youth to be considered in a coordinated manner, viz., development, mobilisation, organisation and utilisation, to promote their involvement and participation in the nation building activities. The general approach to, and details of, an integrated strategy for youth programmes need to be considered in a wider perspective than the educational system because the problems of youth relate to more profound and broader issues like personality development, transition from childhood into adulthood, gainful employment, suitable development of their spirit for adventure and opportunities for community service.

21.38 It is, no doubt, important that the several programmes, which are in operation under the different agencies, need to be coordinated among themselves and at different levels into an integrated conceptual framework. This would help ensuring better coverage, enlargement of targets, and a multiplier effect of the ongoing programmes. It is also important that the tasks to be assigned to the youth are made discreet and tangible and the youth given appropriate training in selected institutions before they are deplayed on these tasks. The details of these aspects would need to be gone into harmonised and a strategy evolved in the form of a National Youth Policy. The guiding principles in this regard should be (a) to provide greater equality of opportunity to all among the youth, (b) to liberate their talent which is now lost to the society, (c) to ensure a higher average level of relevant basic skills and education through work and service, (d) to enable a smooth transition of the youth from childhood through adolescence to adulthood, as well from schools to the world of work and service, and (e) to channellise their energies, idealism and healthy aspirations towards developmental tasks, projects and programmes.

21.39 Insofar as the programmes of educational agencies are concerned, they need to be strengthened and extended in scope and operation. Institutions like the Nehru Yuvak Kendras, Yuvak Mandals and similar bodies linked to the Gram Sabhas would be utilised as the base of operations at the district level and provided with professional inputs and support for the tasks to be done. They would also have an inbuilt mechanism for feed back, assimilation of new concepts and ideas and to extend activities in keeping with the changing area development perspectives. The National Service Scheme for the student youth would be reviewed in order to make provision for real participation of students in development programmes, availing of the proposed non-formal manning structures envisaged in the Sixth Plan. These would also be coalesced with programmes of other departments and agencies and the progress monitored with reference to specific benefits and targets pertaining to the participating youth. There is also a need to decentralise the efforts and to set them in the context of local environmental conditions and needs as perceived by, and acceptable to the community in general and the youth in particular.

Sports

21.40 The objectives of development of sports, games including indigenous games and physical education would be to enlarge the mass base for improving national physical well-being and to promote excellence in competitive events. These will require suitable programme for augmenting physical facilities, training of personnel, and spotting and nurturing of talent. The existing programmes for training of coaches and physical education teachers would be strengthened to improve the sources available with educational institutions, sports federations and others. It is necessary also to strengthen the existing schemes of spotting promising talent in different sports disciplines at a very young age for nurturing it into levels of excellence. For this purpose consideration would be given to the creation of special facilities in selected institutions for promoting sports talent along with normal requirement of general education. At the village and rural area level, full utilisation would be made of existing facilities and institutions and indigenous games supported with a view to build up sporting attitude qualities and talent starting with the village children. Full use would be made of the mass media for the promotion of physical fitness which is so fundamental for the well-being of the nation as a whole.

Technical Education

21.41 The Sixth Plan takes into account the extensive infrastructure of facilities that has been created for technical education at diploma, degree and post-graduate levels as well as for supporting services like teacher education and curriculum development. The emphasis during the Plan will be on (a) consolidation and optimum utilisation of these facilities, (b) identification of critical areas and creation of necessary facilities for education in emerging technologies in the light of proper assessment of future technological manpower requirements, (c) improvement of quality of technical education at all levels and (d) furtherance of national efforts to develop and apply science and technology as an instrument of the country's socio-economic progress.

21.42 Efforts towards consolidation would seek to ensure that the development schemes initiated in the earlier Plans would be completed in all their aspects and the facilities would be modernised in keeping with the state of art in the technology area as incorporated in the national economic sectors. These would help increase the efficiency of the system, reduce the wastage and bring up the present courses beyond the critical level for optimum utilisation. The present approach to develop technical education facilities according to a manpower requirement approach would be continued in the Sixth Plan. These requirements would be assessed for the next ten yeas, separately for States and type of specialisation, so that, taking into account the lead time involved, educational efforts required to be initiated immediately could be specified and taken up. Suitable mechanism for this purpose would need to be established for the collection, storage, updating and processing of manpower and related data to assist technical education planning.

21.43 In the light of studies already made, facilities would be developed for manpower training in areas like computer science, product development, maintenance engineering instrumentation, and bio-sciences. Centres for advance studies and research would also be set up in selected institutions in emerging technologies like bio-conversion, laser technology, micro-processors development and application, fibre optics and optical communication remote sensing technology, energy systems, reliability engineering and atmospheric sciences.

21.44 The programmes of improvement of quality of teaching and of maintenance of standards would be continued and strengthened. Wherever possible engineering projects and contracts at the campuses of engineering colleges would be undertaken by the students and the faculties themselves and suitable stipends paid for this work which would supplement practical learning. The development of an institutional network between well-established institutions/departments and the developing ones, through an internal technical assistance programme, would be given necessary support. Structured linkages would be evolved for industry/institutional interaction. The facilities of technical institutions in the form of faculty, students and laboratories/workshops would be fully utilised to assist the spread of science and technology to the neighbourhood areas and, through effective and productive interaction, to evolve solutions of societal development problems of immediate and future relevance.

Culture

21.45 The Sixth Plan seeks to initiate serious efforts to recognise culture as a basic concept to be integrated with all activities of development and, particularly, the educational efforts at all levels. They would aim at democratising culture and making it part of the programme of human resource development. Proposals have been made in the Sixth Plan to incorporate cultural elements at all levels and into formal and non-formal systems of education, because such an integration of culture elements may be the best means of making education relevant and meaningful. It would also enable the educational system to draw upon the valuable sources available in the community for personality development and help the pupils develop attitudes without getting alienated from their socio-cultural environment. The process would ultimately make culture a way of life for the people and identify their role in the promotion of our national value system.

21.46 Planning for the integration of culture elements would, no doubt, take into account the cultural diversity and pluralism in the country and the need to promote a national outlook and integration. The linking of educational institutions at all levels with various specialised institutions and agencies which have come up in the area of cultural activities and the rich sources of heritage which have considerable educational value would be a very significant aspect of educational development in the Sixth Plan. Besides, the schemes for the preservation of cultural heritage such as, monuments, manuscripts, oral traditions, folk arts, ancient form of arts and crafts etc. would be strengthened. The growth of arts, music, poetry, dance and drama would be supported as instruments of culture, education and national integration. The main objective would be to promote national pride and cultural identity and foster greater understanding between and among the different groups and people of India.

Non-Monetary Inputs to Quality Improvement

21.47 The emphasis in the development of education in the Sixth Plan is on the optimum utilisation of existing facilities, qualitative improvement of system and making available the educational services to the socially deprived sections of the community. While financial outlays are important and necessary to create additional infrastructure, it is equally important to bring about changes and improvements in the system through increased attention to non-monetary inputs. These refer to an environment conducive to growth and development of education, participatory management techniques involving the teachers and the students alike, development of a relevant academic ethos, opportunities for learning by doing and appropriate consideration to the problems of education of the first generation learners.

21.48 Many of the complex problems in the field of education would require, for their solution, a proper blend of professional skill and political will. Such an environment needs to be evolved at all levels through cooperation among all relevant agencies and organisations. This would also help the educational institutions to make progress according to their genius and potential. In respect of management practices, there is no gainsaying the fact that it holds the key to get the best return out of the available resources and investments. Good management leading to promoting harmony among the participants in the system, would produce more durable and sustained results which would exceed the sum total of the individual inputs. For this purpose, there should be an appropriate system of communication among faculty members themselves and between them and the students as well as with parents and local community at large. Development of these programmes is accorded high priority in keeping with the emphasis in the Sixth Plan on enhancement of the productivity level in the economy. Teaching and learning as part of the educational process have become specialised in character, and this needs to be articulated by the academic community both in curricular and extra curricular activities so that the general academic ethos could be related, in a variety of ways to the different levels of the heterogeneous groups of students entering the system and makes a distinct impact on the value system of the faculty and students.

21.49 A common reason for the inability to promote learning through work and service is the absence of adequate facilities in educational institutions for practical training. Improvisations and innovative approaches are seldom promoted. The Sixth Plan envisages that practical training would be organised in real life situations, wherever possible under the several development departments and projects as well as in the natural environment surrounding the educational institutions. This would need a new approach to learning by doing apart from promoting programmes designed for learning while earning. The main programme thrust in the development of education, particularly of higher education, is to provide for the human resource development of those belonging to the socially disadvantaged sections and poverty groups most of whom would be first generation learners. The socio-economic and cultural constraints, handicaps and strengths of the first generation learners would be analysed and understood so as to formulate measures aimed at overcoming the deficiencies. In practical implementation of these measures it may be necessary to evolve different forms and variations of educational programmes to differentiate the structured system of course combination from a more flexible system suited to the learning needs of these students.

Outlays

21.50 The Sixth Plan provides an outlay of Rs. 2,524 crores for development of education and culture. Its distribution among the Centre and State Plans as well as among the several sub-heads is shown in Table 23.2. This is apart from provisions made separately for Hill Area Development Plan as well as under the relevant sectors of Agriculture, for education in agriculture and allied sciences, and Health for education in medicine and related fields.

TABLE 23.2: Sixth Plan Outlay for Education and Culture

(Rs.in crores)

Sl. No.	Sub-Head	States and Union Territories	Centre	Total
(0)	(1)	(2)	(3)	(4)
1.	Early childhood and Elementary Education	851.07	54.30	905.37
2.	Secondary Education	370.00	28.01	398.01
3.	Teacher Education	22.00	*	22.00
4.	University & Higher Education	197.00	288.75	485.75
5.	Adult Education	68.00	60.00	128.00
6.	Physical Education, Sports and	69.00	24.54	93.54
	Games and Youth Welfare	69.41	60.15	129.56
7.	Other Programmes			
	Sub-total General Education	1646.48	515.75	2162.23
8.	Art and Culture	32.90	51.00	83.90
9.	Technical Education	109.61	168.00	277.61
	Total	1788.99	734.75	2523.74

* Included under Secondary Education.

ANNEXURE I

TABLE 23.3: Statewise Enrolment in Classes I—V, 1979-80

Sl. No.	States/U.Ts.	Enrolment (in 000's)			Enrolment as % of age-group 6-11		
		Boys	Girls	Total	Boys	Girls	Total
(0)	(1)	(2)	(3)	(4)	(5)	(6)	(7)
A. *States*							
1.	Andhra Pradesh	3057	2125	5182	93.8	67.7	81.0
2.	Assam*	1013	718	1731	90.0	67.1	78.8
3.	Bihar	4632	1980	6612	104.2	47.4	76.7
4.	Gujarat	2480	1658	4138	118.7	84.6	102.2
5.	Haryana	783	381	1164	91.0	48.8	71.0
6.	Himachal Pradesh	298	214	512	126.8	85.6	105.6
7.	Jammu & Kashmir	333	185	518	93.3	51.7	72.4
8.	Karnataka	2076	1612	3688	89.1	73.3	81.4
9.	Kerala	1664	1564	3228	103.4	102.2	102.8
10.	Madhya Pradesh	3234	1529	4763	84.9	43.2	64.8
11.	Maharashtra	4687	3502	8189	124.4	97.5	111.4
12.	Manipur	85	66	151	97.7	73.3	85.3
13.	Meghalaya	99	96	195	120.7	115.7	118.2
14.	Nagaland	55	46	101	137.5	117.9	127.8
15.	Orissa	1622	1058	2680	96.5	66.9	82.2
16.	Punjab	1157	963	2120	118.1	107.6	113.0
17.	Rajasthan	2059	663	2722	88.0	30.4	60.2
18.	Sikkim	24	16	40	150.0	100.0	125.0
19.	Tamil Nadu	3428	2800	6228	121.1	103.3	112.2
20.	Tripura	126	91	217	94.7	66.9	80.7
21.	Uttar Pradesh	6372	2945	9317	91.0	45.1	68.9
22.	West Bengal	3903	2496	6399	104.4	69.7	87.4
	Total (States)	43187	26708	69895	100.2	65.6	83.4
B. *Union Territories*							
23.	A & N Islands	14	12	26	140.0	120.0	130.0
24.	Arunachal Pradesh	37	18	55	102.8	51.4	77.5
25.	Chandigarh	23	17	40	95.8	73.9	85.1
26.	Dadra & Nagar Haveli	10	6	16	166.6	100.0	133.3
27.	Delhi	346	298	644	104.8	91.7	98.3
28.	Goa, Daman & Diu	67	58	125	104.7	90.6	97.7
29.	Lakhshadweep	4	3	7	154.6	128.6	141.9
30.	Mizoram	34	31	65	90.0	89.9	90.0
31.	Pondicherry	41	35	76	120.6	100.0	110.0
	Total (UTs)	576	478	1054	108.5	91.2	99.0
	Total (States & UTs)	43763	27186	70949	100.2	65.9	83.6

* Classes I—IV.

ANNEXURE II

TABLE 23.4: Statewise Enrolment in Classes I—V : Targets for 1984-85

Sl. No.	States/U.Ts.	Enrolment (in 000's)			Enrolment as % of age-group 6-11		
		Boys	Girls	Total	Boys	Girls	Total
(0)	(1)	(2)	(3)	(4)	(5)	(6)	(7)
A. *States*							
1.	Andhra Pradesh	3463	2672	6135	108.2	88.8	98.8
2.	Assam	1288	993	2281	100.0	82.7	91.2
3.	Bihar	5070	3174	8244	109.9	73.5	92.3
4.	Gujarat	2497	2153	4850	114.3	105.3	109.9
5.	Haryana	803	605	1408	93.4	74.4	84.3
6.	Himachal Pradesh	325	240	565	141.3	92.3	115.3
7.	Jammu & Kashmir	463	300	763	125.1	80.2	102.6
8.	Karnataka	2069	1716	3785	86.2	75.9	81.2
9.	Kerala	1679	1579	3258	101.1	101.2	101.2
10.	Madhya Pradesh	4016	1898	5914	102.2	52.1	78.1
11.	Maharashtra	5200	3900	9100	142.1	113.4	128.2
12.	Manipur	108	109	217	108.0	107.9	103.3
13.	Meghalaya	132	128	260	143.5	137.6	140.5
14.	Nagaland	61	53	114	132.6	117.8	125.3
15.	Orissa	2083	1310	3393	117.7	79.4	99.2
16.	Punjab	1064	907	1971	109.7	100.2	105.1
17.	Rajasthan	2349	1023	3372	94.3	43.2	69.4
18.	Sikkim	30	26	56	166.7	144.4	155.5
19.	Tamil Nadu	3528	3200	6728	130.7	126.0	128.4
20.	Tripura	149	108	257	102.8	73.5	88.0
21.	Uttar Pradesh	7092	4025	11117	97.0	58.4	78.3
22.	West Bengal	4313	3417	7730	107.6	91.1	99.6
	Total (States)	47782	33536	81318	108.0	81.1	95.0
B. *Union Territories*							
23.	A & N Islands	21	18	39	156.1	131.8	144.2
24.	Arunachal Pradesh	49	24	73	122.5	61.5	92.4
25.	Chandigarh	34	29	63	113.3	93.5	103.3
26.	Dadra & Nagar Haveli	7	6	13	140.0	100.0	118.2
27.	Delhi	387	410	797	107.5	107.9	107.7
28.	Goa, Daman & Diu	85	70	155	130.8	107.7	119.2
29.	Lakhshadweep	4	3	7	200.0	150.0	175.0
30.	Mizoram	46	40	86	106.0	104.0	105.0
31.	Pondicherry	42	40	82	123.5	114.3	118.8
	Total (UTs)	675	640	1315	117.4	107.4	112.3
	Total (States & Uts)	48457	34176	82633	108.1	81.5	95.2

ANNEXURE III

TABLE 23.5: Statewise Enrolment in Classes VI–VIII, 1979-80

Sl. No.	States/U.Ts.	Enrolment (in 000's)			Enrolment as % of age-group 11-14		
		Boys	Girls	Total	Boys	Girls	Total
(0)	(1)	(2)	(3)	(4)	(5)	(6)	(7)
A. *States*							
1.	Andhra Pradesh	537	275	812	27.8	14.8	21.4
2.	Assam*	368	240	608	48.6	32.7	40.7
3.	Bihar	1019	321	1340	41.0	13.8	27.8
4.	Gujarat	699	403	1102	57.9	35.4	46.9
5.	Haryana	320	110	430	62.7	24.4	44.8
6.	Himachal Pradesh	122	54	176	87.8	37.8	62.4
7.	Jammu & Kashmir	113	54	167	57.0	27.4	42.2
8.	Karnataka	731	441	1172	55.2	34.7	45.2
9.	Kerala	839	752	1591	91.8	85.3	88.6
10.	Madhya Pradesh	937	299	1236	45.0	15.5	30.8
11.	Maharashtra	1316	727	2043	58.8	33.7	46.5
12.	Manipur	21	12	33	44.7	23.1	33.3
13.	Meghalaya	19	17	36	44.2	36.9	40.4
14.	Nagaland	23	18	41	100.0	78.3	89.1
15.	Orissa	371	172	543	39.0	18.9	29.2
16.	Punjab	407	254	661	68.4	48.4	59.0
17.	Rajasthan	579	135	714	44.5	11.4	28.7
18.	Sikkim	4	2	6	44.4	22.2	33.3
19.	Tamil Nadu	1100	667	1767	64.9	41.2	53.3
20.	Tripura	32	32	64	45.1	39.0	41.8
21.	Uttar Pradesh	2120	672	2792	53.3	18.7	36.8
22.	West Bengal	1010	674	1684	49.4	33.8	41.7
	Total (States)	12687	6331	19018	51.5	27.2	39.7
B. *Union Territories*							
23.	A & N Islands	5	3	8	90.9	51.7	70.8
24.	Arunachal Pradesh	6	2	8	35.3	11.8	23.5
25.	Chandigarh	11	8	19	73.3	61.5	67.8
26.	Dadra & Nagar Haveli	1.2	0.6	1.8	40.0	17.1	27.7
27.	Delhi	175	128	303	90.7	67.4	79.1
28.	Goa, Daman & Diu	38	29	67	97.4	70.7	83.7
29.	Lakhshadweep	1.5	0.9	2.4	125.0	75.0	100.0
30.	Mizoram	13	11	24	76.4	61.1	68.5
31.	Pondicherry	18	14	32	90.0	66.7	78.0
	Total (UTs)	268	197	465	82.2	63.3	74.9
	Total (States & UTs)	12955	6528	19483	52.0	27.7	40.2

* The break up between boys and girls estimated.

ANNEXURE IV

TABLE 23.6: Statewise Enrolment in Classes VI—VIII : Targets for 1984-85

Sl. No.	States/U.Ts.	Enrolment (in 000's)			Enrolment as % of age-group 11-14		
		Boys	Girls	Total	Boys	Girls	Total
(0)	(1)	(2)	(3)	(4)	(5)	(6)	(7)
A. *States*							
1.	Andhra Pradesh	790	470	1260	40.7	25.5	33.3
2.	Assam	493	365	858	58.7	43.9	51.3
3.	Bihar	1319	521	1840	49.7	20.4	35.3
4.	Gujarat'	1050	663	1713	83.3	54.3	69.1
5.	Haryana	380	170	550	75.2	36.4	56.6
6.	Himachal Pradesh	150	80	230	107.9	56.3	81.8
7.	Jammu & Kashmir	150	99	249	74.3	47.6	60.7
8.	Karnataka	911	565	1476	64.6	42.5	53.9
9.	Kerala	894	797	1691	89.4	85.7	87.6
10.	Madhya Pradesh	1261	387	1648	54.8	18.1	37.1
11.	Maharashtra	1600	880	2480	71.7	41.5	57.0
12.	Manipur	40	43	83	72.7	72.9	72.8
13.	Meghalaya	41	37	78	84.5	72.5	78.8
14.	Nagaland	32	25	57	118.5	92.6	105.5
15.	Orissa	507	271	778	50.2	28.5	39.7
16.	Punjab	561	349	910	96.7	36.7	81.8
17.	Rajasthan	804	235	1039	57.4	17.9	38.3
18.	Sikkim	9	5	14	90.0	55.6	73.7
19.	Tamil Nadu	1350	917	2267	79.4	57.7	68.9
20.	Tripura	44	36	80	50.6	40.0	45.2
21.	Uttar Pradesh	2540	1132	3672	60.9	28.8	45.3
22.	West Bengal	1350	900	2250	58.3	41.1	49.9
	Total (States)	16276	8947	25223	62.6	36.3	49.8
B. *Union Territories*							
23.	A & N Islands	8	6	14	109.9	100.0	105.6
24.	Arunachal Pradesh	9	6	15	45.0	30.0	37.5
25.	Chandigarh	17	15	32	94.4	83.3	88.8
26.	Dadra & Nagar Haveli	2.5	1.5	4.0	83.3	50.0	66.6
27.	Delhi	214	155	369	97.3	70.8	84.0
28.	Goa, Daman & Diu	51	36	87	127.5	87.8	107.4
29.	Lakhshadweep	1.5	0.9	2.4	150.0	90.0	120.0
30.	Mizoram	23	20	43	102.0	98.0	100.0
31.	Pondicherry	23	23	46	109.5	104.5	118.6
	Total (UTs)	349	263	612	100.5	75.1	87.8
	Total (States & UTs)	16625	9210	25835	63.1	36.8	50.3

24

SEVENTH FIVE YEAR PLAN*

Introduction

Educational policies and programmes during the Seventh Plan were undertaken in the light of the directions contained in the National Policy of Education formulated in 1986. For the first time a Programme of Action was chalked out for the implementation of the National Policy. Attempts were made to revamp the system of education so as to prepare the country for meeting the challenges of the 21st century. School education included important programmes of 'Operation Blackboard' (OB) for the improvement of elementary education, opening of Navodaya Vidyalayas at the Secondary Stage of education in the rural areas providing for free education and vocationalisation of education. Curriculum and textbooks were also revised. At the higher education stage, thrust was put on programmes for qualitative improvement.

EDUCATION, CULTURE AND SPORTS[1]

10.1. Human resource development has necessarily to be assigned a key role in any development strategy, particularly in a country with a large population. Trained and educated on sound lines, a large population can itself become an asset in accelerating economic growth and in ensuring social change in desired directions. Education develops basic skills and abilities and fosters a value system conducive to, in support of, national development goals, both long-term and immediate. In a world where knowledge is increasing at an ex-

* Planning Commission, Government of India, New Delhi.

1. (i) Para Numbers relate to the paras in Chapter 10 of the document.
   (ii) Original Table Numbers have been changed to confirm to this Chapter number.

ponential rate, the task of education in the diffusion of new knowledge and, at the same time, in the preservation and promotion of what is basic to India's culture and ethos, is both complex and challenging. It is, therefore, appropriate that the commencement of the Seventh Plan coincides with a comprehensive review of the education policy.

10.2. The resolution on the National Policy on Education adopted in 1968 pointed out that the great leaders of the Indian freedom movement realised the fundamental role of education and, throughout the nation's struggle for independence, stressed the unique significance of education for national development. The resolution further declared that the radical reconstruction of education as envisaged involved (i) a transformation of the system to relate it more closely to the life of the people; (ii) a continuous effort to expand educational opportunity; (iii) a sustained and intensive effort to raise the quality of education at all stages; (iv) an emphasis on the development of science and technology; and (v) the cultivation of moral and social values. According to the resolution, the educational system must produce young men and women of character and ability, committed to national service and development.

10.3. There has been a great deal of accomplishment in the field of education since 1947. Any number which may be picked up as a parameter to define growth in education will show the magnitude of the massive quantitative expansion that has taken place. The number of recognised institutions has increased from 2,31,000 in 1951 to nearly 7,55,000 in 1984-85. The total enrolment over the same period in these institutions increased from 24 million to nearly 132 million. The national stock of educated manpower is estimated to have increased from less than 4 million to about 48 million the annual increment to the stock now being of the order of 35 million. It is significant to note that facilities have not only increased but also diversified at all levels and in different subjects. The enrolment for post-graduate studies, for instance has grown from a mere 20,000 in 1951 to over 3,00,000 by 1984-85 while that in science subjects is estimated to have increased from 4,400 to about 73,000. Extensive facilities are available for education in a variety of branches of engineering and technology. The output of this system has contributed significantly to our achievements in areas like atomic energy and satellite communication and provides the trained manpower for our economic development.

10.4. The expansion of educational facilities has also helped to some extent in the correction of regional and other imbalances and in achieving progress towards equality of educational opportunity and social justice. The annual non-Plan expenditure on education from the Central and State budgets has increased more than fifty times over the past 35 years, from Rs. 114 crores in 1950-51 to more than Rs. 6,000 crores in 1984-85.

10.5. Although the Indian education scene since independence has been characterised by massive quantitative expansion at all levels, it is still to undergo the kind of transformation envisaged in the National Policy. It is faced with a staggering backlog; the level of illiteracy is as high as 63 per cent; to achieve universal elementary education, as enjoined by the Constitution. There will be need to enrol fifty million more children; vocationalisation of secondary education has yet to make headway; there is very significant pressure on the higher educational system and a decline in the standards of quality. There is an urgent need for a new design for education. The Approach to the Seventh Plan has emphasised that one of the primary tasks is the harnessing of the country's abundant human resources and improving their capability for development with equity. It is recognised that programmes for alleviation of poverty, reduction of social and economic inequalities and improving productivity can and should be integrated with educational development. Further, the strategies for educational programmes and training and their organisational designs should particularly focus on women, youth and economically weaker groups so that they can make increasing contribution to the socio-economic development of the country.

Sixth Plan Review

10.6. The Sixth Plan provided, *inter alia*, for mass education through programmes of elementary education (formal and non-formal streams) and adult education. The Plan also envisaged increased bias towards the practical secondary education, vocationalisation of higher secondary education and restructuring of undergraduate courses with a vocational bias. Forging beneficial linkages between education, employment and development was another objective in the field of higher education.

10.7. An enrolment target of 18 million additional children was set for the Sixth Plan period under the formal system of elementary education. According to the available reports, the additional enrolment is likely to be nearly 22 million. Although the target has thus been exceeded on an all-India basis, there have shortfalls in a few States, especially in regard to the enrolment of girls. Also, the enrolment ratio in 1984-85 was 92 per cent for primary and 53 per cent for middle stages of education. For girls it was only 69 per cent and 38 per cent respectively. Some of the notable measures taken for the promotion of elementary education were: 'earn while you learn' scheme, mid-day meals for children, innovative curriculum renewal schemes, and special emphasis on appointment of women teachers. Funds available under the National Rural Employment Programme (NREP) and Rural Landless Employment Guarantee Programme (RLEGP) were also utilised for construction of school buildings.

10.8. Under the programme of non-formal education, although no specific targets were laid down, 8 million children were expected to be enrolled during the Sixth Plan. This was an experimental programme under which diverse models were to be worked out to suit the area-specific or beneficiary-group-specific requirements. It is estimated that over 3 million children would have been enrolled under this programme. Besides the non-formal education centres organised by the State Governments, innovative and experimental projects were taken up by a number of voluntary and academic institutions. Syllabus and instructional materials for use of learners enrolled in non-formal centres were developed following the integrated approach covering areas of health, hygiene, home science, agriculture, physics, chemistry, biology, history, geography and civics.

10.9. The position at the end of the Sixth Plan is that 80 per cent of the out-of-school children are in the nine States of Assam, Andhra Pradesh, Bihar, Jammu and Kashmir, Madhya Pradesh, Orissa, Rajasthan, Uttar Pradesh and West Bengal, but there is need in all States and Union Territories to improve the quality, relevance and effectiveness of the elementary education system, to improve enrolment and retention rates and to promote girls' education.

10. The Sixth Plan indicated the goal of reaching 100 per cent literacy in the age-group 15-35 years by 1990. While no definite physical target was laid down for the Sixth Plan, the adult education programme was to be developed on a large scale for the age-group 15-35 years to combat the problem of illiteracy among the productive segment of the population in general and, in particular, among the rural poor. The Central Government funded 386 rural functional

literacy projects in the States besides giving assistance to 380 voluntary agencies and 49 universities for adult education programmes. In addition there were programmes of the State Governments. It is estimated that 20 million adult illiterates would have been covered by these programmes during the Sixth Plan. Fifteen States Resources Centres provided the resource support to adult education centres in terms of curriculum formulation, preparation of teaching and learning material, development of methods and media, training of functionaries, monitoring and evaluation, and research and innovation. Development of learning materials for women and weaker sections was given special attention.

10.11. Enrolment in secondary and higher secondary levels has increased from about 10 million in 1979-80 to about 17 million in 1984-85. The 10+2 pattern of education has been adopted by 20 States and 9 Union Territories although it is yet to be fully implemented in some of these States. The National Council of Educational Research and Training, the State Councils of Educational Research and Training and the State Institutes of Education continued their efforts towards improvement in science and environmental education, value-orientation including national integration and curriculum reforms. Propagation of community singing in schools was launched as a national movement.

10.12. In the context of INSAT utilisation, State Institutes of Educational Technology (SIET) were set up in six States, namely, Andhra Pradesh, Bihar, Orissa, Gujarat, Maharashtra and Uttar Pradesh, to produce educational television programmes. A Central Institute of Educational Technology (CIET) was set up for the production of programmes, training of personnel from the States as well as for providing guidance in the development of the programmes.

10.13. Vocationalisation of education at the higher secondary stage was one of the importand reforms included in the Sixth Plan. This programme has made limited progress with an enrolment of about 55,000 students in vocational education, confined to nine States and three Union Territories where it has been introduced. Measures have been initiated to establish the necessary links combining vocationalisation, skill training, in-plant apprenticeship and placement in gainful employment as composite parts of an integrated effort to raise the level of utility of the programme, and its wider acceptance and success. The organisational requirements for the planning, implementation, supervision and evaluation of the integrated programme, along with the mechanism for effective coordination among the concerned agencies, are being assessed and defined.

10.14. Enrolment in higher education is estimated to have increased from 2.5 million in 1979-80 to 3.5 million in 1984-85. Efforts were made for the consolidation of existing institutions and to equip universities and colleges with essential facilities within the limited resources available. Other important programmes taken up during the Sixth Plan included restructuring of under-graduate courses, improvement in standards of teaching of sciences and the humanities, strengthening of postgraduate education and promotion of research within the university system. A one-hour daily telecast on higher education was also initiated for the benefit of colleges. On the recommendation of the Science Advisory Committee to the Cabinet, a new scheme was introduced in 1983-84 for strengthening the infrastructure facilities for research and post-graduate education in science and technology within the university system.

10.15. During the Sixth Plan period, the major emphasis in technical education was on diversification and optimum utilisation of existing courses and institutional resources. Efforts were made to provide facilities in areas such as computer sciences, instrumentation, product development, maintenance engineering, bio-sciences and material sciences. Forty-six selected polytechnics were assisted and supported to develop them into a network of "community Polytechnics" which would help transfer and apply available technology with the object of modernising rural structures. New manpower training programmes were undertaken for emerging areas in technology such as micro-processor application, remote sensing, laser technology, atmospheric sciences and energy sciences. Programmes of management, education, particularly in the Institutes of Management, were reviewed by an Expert Committee and on its recommendation, the establishment of a new Institute at Lucknow was taken in hand.

10.16. The Resolution on National Sports Policy was laid before Parliament in 1984 to serve as a policy frame for the Central and State Governments and all organisations connected with sports. The policy gives a new thrust to sports activities towards achieving excellence in as many areas of sports and games as possible and at the same time making "sports for all" a reality. The Eastern Regional Centre, Calcutta, of Netaji National Institute of Sports, Patiala (NIS) started functioning from 1983 providing additional training courses for coaches. The national coaching scheme now has an authorised cadre strength of 800 coaches. Twenty five Regional sports coaching centres have been developed in State capitals and district headquarters. Besides its regular training programme. NIS implemented on behalf of the Central Government, programmes of National Sports Festival for Women, All India Rural Sports Tournament and Sports Talent Search Scholarship.

10.17. The Sports Authority of India was established in 1984 and it undertook several sports activities in addition to maintaining and managing infrastructure and other facilities created for ASIAD 1982. Sports Councils with the assistance of Central and State Governments have jointly undertaken programmes for improving and developing facilities for the promotion of sports and games. Specifically, assistance was given for development of playfields, construction of stadia and swimming pools, construction of sports complexes, establishment and maintenance of rural sports centres, running annual coaching schemes and for purchase of sports equipment. The ceilings of financial assistance for these purposes were also enhanced. National Sports Federations were also assisted for organising coaching camps for preparing the Indian teams and competitors to participate in approved international competitions. Under the scheme of National Sports Organisation, financial assistance was provided for developing physical facilities for sports and games in colleges and universities, especially for developing playfields, and construction or gymnasia.

10.18. Youth programmes for student and non-student youth were continued and expanded during the Sixth Plan. A National Service Scheme originally launched in 1969-70 as a pilot scheme with 40,000 students, covered over six lakh students in the year 1984-85. The scheme enabled students to participate during their first degree studies in various programmes of social service and national development and provided them an opportunity to understand the conditions and problems of social environment. The activities undertaken by the students included environmental conservation, plantation of trees, cleaning of village ponds, construction of wells, health and family welfare programmes, family welfare education for rural women and sanitation drives in urban slums. They also undertook some production-oriented programmes. Nehru Yuvak Kendras set up to cater primarily to the needs of rural student and non-student youth, organised several social service camps, slum clearance schemes and environmental awareness schemes as well programmes for training of youth leadership. In the year 1984-85, 120 youth leadership camps and 180 work camps were organised, involving 65,000 participants.

10.19. Programmes for preservation of monuments and sites of national importance were taken up on a priority basis. An expert group on archaeology carried out a professional study to prepare an overall plan of action. The number of archaeological circles which look after the preservation of monuments and sites of national importance was raised from 12 to 16. The number of excavation branches was also raised from three to five. Assistance was also provided to Indian National Trust for Art and Cultural Heritage (INTACH) for promoting the conservation ad propagation of works of Indian art and culture. A large number of conservation programmes were taken up for repair and preservation of monuments and sites of national importance. The facilities at the National Museum, New Delhi, were further improved through taking up the first phase of its construction programme. The National Museum organised several aided tours and short-term in-service course. The Indian Museum, Calcutta, the Salar Jang Museum, Hyderabad, the National Gallery of Modern Art, New Delhi, the Nehru Memorial Museum and Library, the National Museum of Man and the National Archives were the other institutions whose programmes received support during the Sixth Plan. The National Council of Science Museums was also supported to undertake the task of popularising science and technology, among students in particular, through a wide range of programmes. The National Research Laboratory for Conservation of Cultural Property in Lucknow undertook a number of research programmes for technical studies with a view to improving conservation methods.

10.20. The Anthropological Survey of India was supported through funding of its several research projects on physical and cultural anthropology and allied disciplines. The Survey also undertook exploratory studies in the Himalayas, Narmada Valley and Costal Andhra Pradesh.

10.21. Library programmes were another area of importance during the Sixth Plan. The construction programme at National Library, Calcutta, was taken up. The Raja Ram Mohan Roy Library Foundation which renders assistance to States and Union Territories for development of public libraries was further strengthened. Promotion and dissemination of culture was another major programme of the Department of Culture. The Sangeet Natak Akademi, the Sahitya Akademi and the Lalit Kala Akademi, besides the National School of Drama, undertook several programmes in this area. The Centre for Culture Resources and Training, New Delhi, organised a number of in-service training programmes for the benefit of teachers drawn from primary and high or higher secondary schools in different parts of the country. Financial assistance was also provided to dance, drama and theatre ensembles and to selected cultural organisations.

Strategy and Thrust Areas in the Seventh Plan

10.22. The Seventh Plan provides for re-orientation of the education system so as to prepare the country to meet the challenges of the next century. The main thrust areas in the Seventh Plan would be:(i) achievement of universal elementary education; (ii) eradication of illiteracy in the age-group 15-35 years; (iii) vocationalisation and skill-training programmes at different levels of education; (iv) upgradation of standards and modernisation at all stages of education with effective links with the world of work and with special emphasis on science and environment and on value orientation; (v) provision of facilities for education of high quality and excellence in every district of the country; and (vi) removal of obsolescence and modernisation of technical education.

10.23. The major strategies for achieving these objectives would include effective decentralised planning and organisational reforms, promotion of non-formal and open learning systems, adoption of low cost alternative and optimum use of resources, forging of beneficial linkages with industry and development agencies, and mobilisation of commodity resources and social involvement.

Elementary Education

10.24. Overriding priority will be given to realising universalisation of elementary education for children in the age group 6-14 years by 1990; this will continue to be part of the Minimum Needs Programme. The emphasis will shift from mere enrolment to retention of pupils in schools and to the attainment by them of basic elements of learning. The objective is sought to be achieved through a combination of formal and non-formal methods, focusing sharply on the needs of girls and of children belonging to the economically and socially weaker sections.

10.25. The enrolment at the elementary stage is estimated to have reached nearly 112 million by the end of the Sixth Plan period. For achieving the goal of universalisation by the end of the Seventh Plan, over 50 million children will have to be additionally enrolled. A projection of enrolment in full-time elementary schools is given in Table 24.1 Increasing enrolment in full-time schools beyond this level of 137 million in classes I to VIII might not be feasible due to socio-economic reasons and other factors. Even to achieve this level effectively, sustained efforts will have to be made to reduce the number of drop-outs.

TABLE 24.1: Expansion of Elementary Stage Education: Projection-during Seventh Plan

(Enrolment figures in million)

Sl. no.	Classes/Age Group	Likely enrolment (1984-85)	Projected enrolment (1989-90)	Additional enrolment (1985-90)
1	2	3	4	5
I.	I-V (6-11)			
	Boys	51.20 (117.48)	55.00 (110.00)	3.80
	Girls	34.17 (69.20)	40.96 (88.15)	6.79
	TOTAL	*85.37* *(91.84)*	*95.96* *(99.89)*	*10.59*
II.	VI-VIII (11-14)			
	Boys	17.46 (66.90)	25.12 (92.56)	7.66
	Girls	9.27 (38.19)	16.55 (65.44)	7.28
	TOTAL	*26.73* *(53.07)*	*41.67* *(79.46)*	*14.94*
III.	I-VIII (6-14)			
	Boys	68.66 (90.96)	80.12 (104.24)	11.46
	Girls	43.44 (64.02)	57.51 (80.28)	14.07
	GRAND TOTAL	*112.10* *(78.21)*	*137.63* *(92.60)*	*25.53*

Note: Figures in parentheses indicate enrolment ratio relative to population in the corresponding age-group.

10.26. Non-formal education would be the other important programme for the achievement of universalisation of elementary education as this can be useful to those who are not able or willing to attend full-time schools. The number of children to be covered by the non-formal programme is reckoned to be of the order of 25 million. Non-formal education in the Seventh Plan will, therefore, have to be expanded at a fast pace and made acceptable with a variety of forms to suit the varying needs of the target groups. Non-formal system should be made flexible and appropriately linked to the formal system. Adequate textual material with area-specific background and supplementary reading material would be developed and made available to students. Adequate teacher-training arrangements will be made for teachers participating in the non-formal system. For optimum use of resources, the schools, the non-formal education centres and adults education centres should develop linkages and be educationally integrated with development programmes.

10.27. The enrolment projections in paras 10.24 and 10.25 above are indicative figures, worked out at the macro-level and disaggregated to the State level. Specific operational targets will require to be worked out by the State Governments concerned block-wise and village-wise through decentralised planning. Once such targets are worked out for the catchment area of each school or a cluster of schools, it would be expected that the authorities responsible for the achievement of the target would adopt the most appropriate strategies of implementation and monitoring of progress.

10.28. The role of the teacher is most crucial in achieving universal elementary education, especially in the motivation of children as well as their parents. They can play a leading role in improving the quality of primary education, bringing in environment and health education and value orientation. In-service training of teachers thus becomes a programme of high priority. The training of teachers will include, apart from pedagogy, the use of mass media, science and technology, planning and curriculum design for local environment-based courses, mobilisation and use of community resources and other relevant subjects. There will also be special emphasis on teaching methods and other measures particularly required for first generation learners and for reducing the number of dropouts. Teacher training institutions will be developed and strengthened accordingly.

10.29. Facilities will have to be created for the training of additional teachers required during the Seventh Plan period. There is as yet no infrastructure in the country for training of teachers in non-formal and early childhood education. Training of such teachers would have to be organised by suitably strengthening the existing teacher training centres.

10.30. Considering the numbers involved (over 2.5 million teachers), institutionalised in-service education of teachers will be difficult to organise not only due to the huge costs involved but also due to lack of facilities for training. It is, therefore, necessary to think of a variety of training arrangements. Among others, these would include:

(a) In-service education by utilising the mass media, as was done during SITE;
(b) adoption of schools of lower levels of education by institutions of higher levels for upgrading of teacher competencies;
(c) dispatch of teacher guidance notes by training schools;
(d) publication of bulletins informing teachers of new developments; and
(e) use correspondence course materials supported by occasional contact.

10.31. Drop-outs and non-attendance of children at the primary stage of education are due to poor school facilities, unrelated curriculum, poor methods of teaching and poverty. The reorientation of teacher training referred to above will help to a large extent in tackling these factors. In addition, suitable supportive programmes for the provision of incentives, the improvement of facilities, increasing community awareness, curricular reforms, adjusting of school timings, utilisation of local community resources and earn-while-you-learn scheme, etc., will be introduced or expanded selectively according to local requirements.

10.32. Enrolment of girls has been lagging behind despite special measures taken in the past. Towards the end of the Sixth Plan some steps were taken to promote enrolment of girls and for providing non-formal education to them wherever necessary. In the Seventh Plan, the focus of effort will be on promotion of girls' education through appointment of women teachers, attachment of pre-school centres, provision of free uniforms and other incentives.

10.33. Special emphasis will be given to the enhancement of quality and efficiency of elementary education. The Seventh Plan will seek to provide specific funds for those programmes which will enhance the efficiency of the system. There is need to have a fresh look at the design and construction of school buildings as well as at the text-books in use. Various projects like population education, environment and wild life education and curriculum renewal have helped in the preparation of suitable teaching-learning material and this material will be utilised.

10.34. Due to the difficult resource position and the magnitude of the task involved in the implementation of the programme of universalisation of elementary education, optimal use should be made of the available infrastructure and funds. The Plan and non-Plan budget provision for elementary education and the existing teacher resources should be reviewed and redeployed on the basis of actual requirements and attendance in classes. Part-time teachers or helper-teachers on fixed salary, selected from among locally available educated men and women will be utilised to augment teaching resources and also improve relevance and cost-effectiveness of elementary education. Community support and financial contributions will be mobilised especially for clearing the backlog of physical facilities and school buildings. The construction of school buildings will be taken up also under the National Rural Employment Programme (NREP) and similar programmes.

10.35. Early childhood education is important both from the point of view of the personality development of the child and for inculcating in the children a healthy attitude to school-going to help increase their retention rate in schools. This programme will be dovetailed with nutrition, health care and social welfare as a package within the broad framework of the programme of Integrated Child Development Service (ICDS). Voluntary efforts to undertake innovative experiments in respect of early childhood education will be supported.

10.36. The National Policy Resolution on Education recommends the placement of disabled children in regular schools. The scheme of integrated education of disabled children was started by the Ministry of Social Welfare as a Centrally-sponsored scheme where handicapped children were sought to be integrated in the normal school system with a view to promoting their psychological acceptance. The scheme is now being implemented by the Ministry of Education. One of the difficulties facing this scheme is the lack of trained teachers in special education. As such, during the Seventh Plan, greater emphasis will be laid on teacher training.

Adult Education

10.37. Eradication of adult illiteracy and the development of a programme of continuing adult education is a major thrust area in the Seventh Plan. The task of covering all the illiterates in the age-group 15.35 years by 1990 is a formidable one. As motivation of the learner is crucial for success and as the number to be covered is about 90 million, the strategy to achieve the goal can only be through a mass movement involving social institutions, voluntary organisations, students, teachers, employers and the community. The programme will also have to be linked effectively with various development programmes especially the Integrated Rural Development Programme (IRDP). Active participation of village panchayats, mahila mandals, community centres, etc., is essential. Employers will be required to impart necessary functional education to all their illiterate employees. The programmes of Nehru Yuvak Kendras (NYK) and the National Service Scheme (NSS) will also focus on eradication of illiteracy. Programmes for motivating the learners by holding community meetings and through publicity through posters, films, broadcasting, etc., will be implemented on an adequate scale and with sufficient intensity to create a conducive climate. A network of libraries and the development of literature for neo-literates will also be initiated as a follow-up programme to avoid lapse into illiteracy. Community participation in all literacy programmes will be an essential feature from village level upwards to give proper direction and orientation and lend effective support to the national programme.

10.38. Another aspect of education of adults relates to training in functional skills relevant to their respective economic activities. Programmes for this purpose will be strengthened and adequate resource support provided for organising technical and vocational skill-based courses for the benefit of adult learners through Shramik Vidyapeeths and other similar institutions. As a part of the post-literacy and follow-up services, short-duration condensed training courses will be organised for upgrading the skills of the neo-literates and for increasing their awareness of various social events. The existing programmes on rural functional literacy and State adult education programmes and various training programmes for adult learners will be consolidated and dovetailed in the new mass movement programmes of adult education. Citizenship education including adult education, will be a necessary part of the entire education system, and will be specially promoted.

Secondary Education

10.39. The demand for secondary education has been growing. The expansion and effectiveness of elementary education will provide a further impetus to this growth. The projected demand for additional facilities will, to some extent, be met by better utilisation of resources in the existing schools. Provision has been made for this purpose and for promoting distance learning techniques and open school systems. Unplanned growth of high/higher secondary schools will be checked. Norms for the establishments of secondary school will be evolved and strictly observed in order to avoid proliferation of economically non-viable and educationally inefficient institutions. In expanding the facilities, special attention will be given to the needs of backward area, of under-privileged sections of the population and of girls. Girls education will be free up to the higher secondary.

10.40. The teaching of science and mathematics at high/higher secondary stage of education will be strengthened and made universal. Efforts will be made to update and modernise science curricula, improve laboratories and libraries in schools and ensure the quality of science teachers through large-scale in-service training programmes. Environment education will from an important aspect of science education.

10.41. The socially useful productive work (work experience) programme component seeks to highlight the link between work and education and to develop positive work ethics and work habits. The programme would allow for better utilisation and integration of community expertise in the teaching-learning process and the use of facilities available with local industry and development institutions. Besides, the support system for development, training, management and supervision available for vocationalisation programmes, will also be utilised for the programme of socially useful productive work at the secondary stage. Some courses/activities of pre-vocational character will also be introduced for move effective implementation of this programme.

10.42. In view of the importance of linking education with productivity, a major impetus will be given in the Seventh Plan to vocationalisation of the higher secondary stage. Facilities for vocational education will be suitably diversified to cover a large number of fields in agriculture, industry, trade and commerce and services. It will be ensured that there is no duplication of courses between technical and vocational institutions and the schools. The skills imparted, will be of adequate standard for securing gainful employment or self-employment. At the same time, opportunities for pursuing higher general and professional education would be provided.

10.43. Vocational/career courses in educational institutions will be introduced in a flexible manner linked to emerging work opportunities. The current intake will be considerably increased by introducing vocational courses in may more institutions.

10.44. Based on the evaluation of the on-going scheme of vocationalisation, States are taking steps to re-organise and improve the programme. An Expert Committee has been set up to suggest ways and means of implementing an expanded programme of vocationalisation fully coordinated with the education system and manpower needs of economic development. The report of this Committee will provide guidelines for further development.

10.45. The present wide reach of the media will be used for improving education, especially at the secondary stage. Facilities for production of the requisite audio-visual material including educational software for broadcasting and telecasting will be augmented substantially in the Seventh Plan. During the Sixth Plan, a small beginning was made in providing computer literacy to students in selected secondary schools, based on this experience steps will be taken to extend the programme to cover different aspects of computer appreciation and application.

10.46. One of the essential conditions for continuous improvement in the quality of secondary education is an effective system of in-service training of teachers. The existing facilities will be assessed, additional requirements identified and steps taken to meet them. The opportunity provided by the new communication technology will be explored for this purpose. Here again, special attention will be paid to the development of requisite software. Training of personnel required for effective use of modern communication technology and computers in education will be given very high priority. The NCERT which has already initiated programmes in this regard will help the States build a network for this purpose.

10.47. Education has a crucial contribution to make towards promoting national integration, understanding and a sense of togetherness and harmony. There is, therefore, great need for an integrated and value-oriented education with a national perspective. This programme should be so designed that its various threads can be women into curricular and co-curricular activities. Suitable revision of text-books, strengthening of school libraries and training of teachers would be important from this point of view.

University Education

10.48. The main emphasis in higher education will be on consolidation, improvement in standards and reforms in the system to make higher education more relevant to national needs and to forge forward and backward linkages of higher education with employment and economic development. Expansion of general higher education facilities will be carefully planned so as to take care of the need to provide large access to weaker sections and first generation learners from backward areas. In doing so, emphasis will be laid on providing access to existing institutions through appropriate reservation, scholarships, provision of hostel facilities. A network of facilities will be provided through open universities, correspondence courses and part-time education to meet social demand and the needs of continuing education.

10.49. The need and urgency for restructuring of undergraduate courses so as to bring in the necessary concern for relevance and use, application orientation, flexibility and diversification is well recoganised. The guidelines for restructuring of courses of study indicated by the University Grants Commission (UGC) provide for addition of groups of courses that may be relevant and useful according to local or regional needs. Extension activities will be developed as components within each subject/discipline. Beneficial linkages will be developed between colleges and development institutions and programmes. Application oriented courses will be given due emphasis.

10.50. The Indira Gandhi National Open University, which is being established as a pace setting institution, will besides offering courses in higher education based on the principles of the open learning system, be also responsible for training of personnel, production of programmes and development of material for utilisation through the electronic media. The National Open University will function as a nodal resource centre for coordination of programmes and development of models for distance education, documentation and dissemination of information and organisation of appropriate support programmes. Besides this, six centres of educational technology being developed by UGC would serve as regional centres for the production of software for educational technology and training of personnel engaged in the programme of distance education and correspondence courses for higher education.

10.51. In the area of post-graduate education and research, emphasis will be placed on promoting quality programmes, inter-disciplinary studies and on new emerging frontiers. Research within the university system will get due emphasis and be coordinated with national research efforts under the Science and Technology programme. The programme of strengthening infrastructure facilities for research in science and technology and of post-graduate education within the university system, which was started on the recommendation of the Science Advisory Committee to the Cabinet, will be further developed.

10.52. Training of teachers in higher education is another area which needs special attention in the Seventh Plan. The faculty improvement programmes will be designed to impart knowledge of new methods and techniques of teaching, learning and evaluation, to develop a national value system, and to prepare the teachers for the task of restructuring under-graduate courses.

10.53. Many of the reforms initiated earlier, such as autonomous colleges and examination reform, seem to have faced obstacles and delays in the process of implementation. The Seventh Plan will give high priority to the speedy implementation of various reforms already initiated and to the modernisation of university administration.

10.54. Besides concerted efforts to increase the enrolment of Scheduled Castes/Scheduled Tribes students the most significant programmes for these students will consist of remedial teaching, preparatory training and special coaching. These programmes will be implemented on a large scale by institutions with sizeable student population drawn from the Scheduled Castes and Scheduled Tribes and other weaker sections. These institutions will be strengthened to impart a better quality of education. The scope of these programmes will also be enlarged to include training for employment, coaching for competitive examinations for recruitment to various services and adult and continuing education programmes.

Technical Education

55. In the context of the rapid modernisation of the economy envisaged in the near future and given the Seventh Plan objective of improvement in productivity, technical education has to play a leading role. The main emphasis in the field of technical education during the Seventh Plan period will be on the following:

(i) Consolidation of infrastructure and facilities already created;
(ii) Optimum utilisation of the existing facilities with attention to cost effectiveness;
(iii) Identification of critical areas with a view to strengthening the facilities in the fields where weaknesses exist in the system at present;
(iv) Creation of infrastructure in new areas of emerging technology vital for the development of the country and provision of necessary facilities for education, training and research in those fields;
(v) Improvement of quality and standards of technical education;
(vi) Removal of obsolescence;
(vii) Modernisation of engineering laboratories and workshop in the technical education institutions;
(viii) Effective management of the overall system of technical education for an optimum return on investments made;
(ix) Innovative measures to improve existing facilities to provide low-cost alternatives to achieve various goals and objectives laid down in the Plan; and
(x) Institution linkages between technical education on the one hand, and rural development and other development sectors, on the other.

10.56. To achieve these objectives there would be a balanced development of institutions of technical education at all levels. The Indian Institutes of Technology, which have been set up as pace-setting institutions, would be further developed as advanced centres of excellence. The institutes have already initiated research work in a number of new areas. An expert committee has been set up to look into the requirements of these Institutes in the context of the challenges ahead. The regional and other engineering colleges would also be developed further, particularly with a view to their modernisation and to making their courses relevant to the emerging requirements. The upgradation of standards and modernisation of polytechnics will also be accorded a high priority. A major task in the Seventh Plan will be the removal of obsolescene in equipment and revision of courses in all technical education institutions, many of which were drawn up more than two decades ago. The All India Council for Technical Education has recommended that it is necessary also to restructure polytechnic education with a view to:

(a) improving the standard and contents of technical courses;
(b) providing a lateral entry to the vocational stream from 10 + 2 stage;
(c) restoring the balance in the employment pattern of engineering graduates and diploma holders; and
(d) providing multi-point entry to the various courses.

Besides the improvement on these lines, polytechnic education for women will be given greater attention to meet their special requirements. Further, as a result of reorganisation of school education in the 10 + 2 system and with vocationalisation becoming the major thrust in it, the polytechnics will play a significant role in the promotion and development of vocational education, particularly in engineering and allied trades. Besides modernising polytechnics and removing obsolescence in courses and equipment, special attention will be paid to emerging technologies and computerisation. Development of interaction between the technical institutions and industry will be taken up. Removal of regional imbalances would be another major objective in the development of technical education at all levels. The faculty in the technical institutions have to keep themselves, abreast of the latest knowledge and advances taking place elsewhere in the world and also have to be in constant touch with industry. A number of schemes have already been instituted under the quality improvement programme including M. Tech. and Ph.D. courses, short-term and mid-term courses and industrial training for engineering college and polytechnic teachers. However, these arrangements need considerable strengthening. Special attention will be paid to the problems of staff training and the retraining and to continuing education for staff, including those of the polytechnics, to facilitate academic and professional advancement.

10.57. A reliable manpower information system is a prerequisite to planning in the field of technical education. A national manpower information system is being developed for storage, updating, retrieval and analysis of manpower information to assist in technical education planning. It has at present 17 nodal centres and is coordinated by the Technical Education Division of the Department of Education with the assistance of the lead centre located at the Institute of Applied Manpower Research. The manpower information system will be considerably strengthened and integrated with the planning of technical education.

10.58. Besides general improvements, polytechnics will be assisted to undertake extension services for the benefit of the community. The programme of community polytechnics, already initiated in the earlier Plans, will be expanded in the Seventh Plan to cover as many polytechnics as possible.

10.59. Curriculum changes need to be introduced periodically in the light of emerging trends in technology. This will require more effective collaborative linkages with industry and research and development establishments and agencies. The allocations provided from budgetary funds for technical education have to be supplemented by contributions from user industries and organisations, which will be facilitated when closer collaborative arrangements are established.

S and T Component

10.60. Considerable emphasis will be laid on the improvement of the quality of teaching science and technology at all levels of education. At school level NCERT at the centre and SCERTs/SIEs in States will provide training to teachers on all aspects of science and technology including design, development and production of science kits and strengthen science laboratories of secondary schools. A National Science Centre will be established for displaying experimental models and projects.

10.61. The quality of higher science and technology education has to match the best in the world. In this connection, university departments and colleges will be selected for providing special assistance to bring about improvements in science education.

10.62. Modernisation of laboratories in Indian Institutes of Technology, Regional Engineering Colleges and other institutions of technical education will be accorded priority for providing research in technology. An International Centre for Science and Technology

Education will be established. This will operate through a net work of existing institutions and serve as a resource centre for cooperative research, and will also disseminate ideas, methods an materials to bring about basic improvement and modernisation in Science and Technology education. The total estimated outlay for S & T component in the education sector will be of the order of Rs. 180 crores, including Rs. 35 crores for the programmes recommended by the Science Advisory Committee to the Cabinet.

Examination Reforms

10.63. The present examination-oriented system has distorted the very character of education and has converted it into a mere system of certification to regulate the flow of manpower to the labour market. The dominance of the examination system over the educational process has led not only to the wrong type of learning, but has also led to many attendant malpractices. Examination reforms to remedy the present malaise would be given the utmost priority. At the same time, the employing sector should be helped to devise its own selection procedures, lay down academic qualifications, prepare assessment tests and evaluation systems in keeping with job content and the ability and skill for performance of the tasks attached to a job.

Other Programmes

10.64. The Seventh Plan provides for the continuation and limited expansion of on-going programmes relating to scholarships, development of languages, book promotion, educational planning and administration as well to effective monitoring, particularly of elementary (including non-formal) and adult education.

10.65. The existing schemes of scholarships will be reviewed and, if necessary, re-oriented to help talented students to develop their full potential. The Central Government schemes of national scholarships including that for talented children from rural areas will continue in the Seventh Plan. Financial assistance by itself is not adequate for the development of talented children, especially from the poorer sections of society and from backward areas. Their access to, and placement in, good academic institutions is equally necessary. Placements in residential schools will be particularly helpful and a scheme for this purpose is already in operation.

10.66. To provide good quality modern education with Indian values to talented children, particularly from the rural areas, it is proposed to set up 432 model secondary schools, one in each district, during the Seventh Five Year Plan. These schools will offer a common core curriculum, ensuring comparability in standards and promoting National Integration and National Values. They will bring together students from different parts of the country, providing opportunities to talented children to fully develop their potential. Admission to these schools will be through a test conducted at tahsil/block level, in which the best performers from every primary school in the district will be eligible to appear. The test would be designed by the NCERT, and it will be associated in conducting and evaluating the test. Residential facilities will be provided in these schools. An autonomous organisation, registered under the Registration of Societies Act, will be set up for establishing and running these schools.

Development of Languages

10.67. The development of languages is of basic importance for all educational development programmes. The activities and programmes undertaken in the field of languages comprise : (i) promotion of Hindi (as envisaged under Article 351 of the Constitution); (ii) promotion of modern Indian languages (as provided in National Policy of Education); (iii) promotion of English and other foreign languages; and (iv) promotion of Sanskrit and other classical languages such as Arabic and Persian. Other languages for which the Centre has special responsibility, like Urdu and Sindhi, have also received attention. These activities will be further developed in the Seventh Plan, with special attention being paid for raising the standards of language competency, spoken as well as written.

10.68. The capabilities of existing institutions will be strengthened, particularly, with a view to enabling them to undertake a much larger programme of in-service training, publication of textual and other materials. Production of software for transmission through radio and television and to work at the grass-roots level. A selective approach will be adopted in respect of publications, so as to ensure that materials of good quality become available and are widely disseminated. Instead of entrusting publication of dictionaries, terminologies, text-books, etc., exclusively to governmental agencies, it is proposed to involve creative scholars, university departments and literary organisations with publication activities. Voluntary organisations working for the development and promotion of various languages will be supported, particularly, for undertaking innovative and experimental projects the experience from which will assist in more effective teaching and learning of languages, whether by formal or informal methods.

10.69 In Sanskrit, emphasis will be given to activities which will ensure preservation of Shastric and Vedic traditions in oral and written forms, preservation, editing and cataloguing of rare manuscripts, publications of rare and out-of-print books, and training of teachers. It is proposed to assist selected institutions for audio and video taping of recitations of various *sakhas* which for want of continuing training of scholars in the oral tradition, are becoming extinct. Support will be provided for inter-disciplinary research, particularly with a view of identifying the scientific and technical advancement that had taken place in the past and has been recorded in various Sanskrit texts.

10.70. The programmes being undertaken for the development of modern Indian languages, including Urdu and Sindhi, and also classical languages like Arabic and Persian will be continued and additional support provided to increase their coverage.

Art and Culture

10.71. In Art and Culture the main thrust in the Seventh Five Year Plan would be on the development of culture in all aspects, with emphasis on dissemination, and on the promotion and development of regional cultures and building up of a sense of the oneness and underlying unity and cohesiveness of India. This would require the involvement of the masses in cultural activities. In order to achieve these objectives, the programmes of the Seventh Plan would include:

(i) Zonal Cultural Centres being set up in different regions of the country. The essential thrust of the creative development efforts of these zonal centres would be to bring about awareness and participation at the grass-root level, cutting across-territorial/linguistic boundaries.

(ii) The existing activities of various cultural organisations for dissemination of culture would be stepped up on a wide scale with adequate financial inputs.

(iii) Introduction of a cultural component into the educational system at different levels. The Departments of Education and Cultural Affairs would work together in close coordination for inter-linking education and culture through appropriate programmes.

(iv) Cultural inputs would be integrated in youth activities, rural development activities, domestic tourism, etc.

(v) For the dissemination of culture to the masses, the mass media would be utilised.

(vi) Besides the national cultural organisations, the State agencies would also strengthen their programmes. The Central and State Agencies would work with greater coordination towards this objective.

10.72. It is proposed to set up seven zonal cultural centres which while developing the unique cultural identities of various areas in the States would also stress and explore their cultural kinship in relation to the totality of India's composite culture, highlighting the essential unity in diversity of the Indian cultural heritage. The Centres would provide facilities for creative development of arts; with special emphasis on folk arts as also the revival of vanishing arts.

10.73. The traditional fairs and festivals which provide the continuing link with the rich traditions of the past would be supported through the State agencies and Zonal Cultural Centres. Appropriate programmes would be taken up to provide exposure to youth to the cultural diversity of the country to raise their awareness of the rich heritage that exists in the country.

10.74. Preservation, documentation and conservation of our rich and varied cultural heritage would continue to receive priority in the Seventh Plan. This would mean greater attention to the development of archaeology museums, archives, manuscript libraries, Buddhist Tibetan studies, and to folk-lore and oral traditions. It is recognised that strands of cultural heritage run through a wide range of development sectors and programmes. These need to be identified and demonstrated as diverse aspects of our rich traditions. Art forms and cultural institutions provide a powerful medium to foster national integration as well as national development. Necessary co-ordination links will be established and co-operative programmes will be undertaken for this purpose.

10.75. Greater emphasis will be laid on strengthening of arts through institutions, such as the Akademies. Assistance would continue to be provided to voluntary organisation engaged in the promotion of art and culture. Library systems would be strengthened throughout the country with special attention to improving the facilities in the National level institutions.

10.76. Some of the rich art forms existing are in the realm of tribal and folk art. The development of folk and tribal arts, especially those which are facing extinction such as the folk art of the Himalayan regions, threatened ecologically as also culturally, would be supported through assistance to voluntary organisations engaged in these fields and areas.

10.77. In the field of anthropology, new projects have been identified to study the people of India and promote dissemination of culture. The Rashtriya Manav Sangrahalaya which is expected to be completed in the Seventh Plan, would recreate the history of human evolution, the evolution of culture and the range of living cultures in India.

10.78. The Indira Gandhi National Centre for Art will be set up at New Delhi as a resource centre and data base for the arts. It will also develop a major informatics library of cultural materials. The National Theatre will also be established on the same premises to support and project activities particularly in the field of visual arts, including folk and tribal arts.

Youth and Sports

10.79. According to the 1981 Census, 220 million or about 30 per cent of our population is in the age-group of 15-34 years, with 63 per cent living in the rural areas. The majority of them do not have the benefit of formal education. The problems of youth, therefore have to be identified, with existing programmes being strengthened and new programmes devised to involve their participation and development. The two existing programmes of National Service Scheme (NSS) and Nehru Yuvak Kendras (NYKs) have proved useful in promoting the involvement of youth, both student and non-student, and urban and rural, and in creating awareness among them of nationally accepted objectives and motivating them to work towards their fulfilment. Both these programmes will be further developed and expanded in the Seventh Plan. The strength of the NSS will be raised from six hundred and ten thousand at the end of the Sixth Plan to one million at the end of the Seventh Plan. Activities of Nehru Yuvak Kendras will be expanded to cover all the districts in the country and will also be diversified. The organisational structure of the Yuvak Kendras will also be revamped to impart greater flexibility in the development of programmes for youth, their speedier execution and closer monitoring. The aim will be to make the Kendras effective by ensuring coordinating links between youth and the various agencies of Government and public sector in the national development effort. Programmes of scouting and guiding, mountaineering and adventure, Commonwealth youth programmes and International Youth Exchange Delegations, and National Service Volunteer Schemes will be continued.

10.80. A major step will be taken during the Seventh Plan to translate into action the newly adopted Resolution on National Sports Policy, by giving high priority to the development of infrastructure and facilities for sports and games at grass-root levels and developing the potential of our human resources both in the rural and urban areas. Efforts will be made to raise national standards in games and sports. Programmes for spotting and nurturing potential sports talent through coaching, training and nutrition required for helping the talented to realise their highest level would be continued. Present schemes like Rural Sports Tournaments, Women's Sports Festivals, National Talent Search Scholarships, grants to National Federations and State Sports Councils, etc., will be expanded. The activities of the Netaji Subhash National Institute of Sports, Patiala, will be intensified and its coverage enlarged. The Sports Authority of India will be assisted to pursue its main objective of promotion and broad-basing of sports in the country and creation of health consciousness among citizens through appropriate and meaningful schemes.

Outlays

10.81. The Seventh Plan outlay for education is of the order of Rs. 6,383 crores of which the States sector outlay is Rs. 3,994 crores.

10.82. The provision for education is mainly in the States' sector. The Centre will play a coordinating role and provide leadership and guidance for new and innovative programmes. Out of the total non-

Plan budget estimates of education in 1983-84, amounting to Rs. 5,229 crores, nearly 91 per cent was in the States' Sector. Nearly 87 per cent of the total national expenditure on education is incurred on non-Plan side. In view of the constraints on resources for education, the structure and pattern of utilisation of Plan and non-Plan funds needs to be reviewed, to ensure the optimal use of funds in relation to the goals of the Seventh Plan. It is proposed to adopt low cost designs and devices for effecting economy and for reducing unit costs. Besides, non-budgetary resources have to be tapped and substantial resources mobilised from the community especially for replenishing and augmenting physical facilities in educational institutions.

10.83. It is also necessary to emphasise the non-monetary inputs in educational development, i.e., better planning, advanced technologies and practices, careful block level and institutional planning, and school mapping; better systems of supervision and administration; monitoring and evaluation; a good information system; dedicated efforts by teachers, students and educational administrators; intensive utilisation of existing resources and facilities; and above all, commitment and active involvement of the local community. Educational research and training, and planning and administration of education needs to be streamlined. The State level capabilities particularly require to be built up under the leadership of the National Council of Educational Research and Training and National Institute of Educational Planning and Administration.

SECTION III

SELECTED EDUCATIONAL STATISTICS
AND
CLASSIFIED INDEX TO TABLES

25

EDUCATIONAL STATISTICS

Although up to date and comprehensive statistics are indispensable to the educational administrators, planners and research workers, there seems to be no uniform system of maintaining educational statistics in India with the result that at times it becomes rather difficult to reconcile data collected even by National Agencies. Nevertheless new methods are constantly developed and it can be said that in spite of their limitations statistics provide the framework for looking at situations in a logical way. Numerical data derived from surveys and other sources constitutes the raw material on which interpretations, analysis and decisions are made and it is essential to know how to squeeze usable information from such data.

Tables in this volume have been compiled/adapted/reproduced primarily from the following sources:

1. *Annual Report(s), 1988, 1989* and *1990*, Ministry of Human Resource Development, Department of Education, New Delhi.
2. *Annual Report(s)*, University Grants Commission, New Delhi.
3. *Census of India, 1991*, Registrar General and Census Commissioner of India, New Delhi, 1991.
4. *Five Year Plan(s)*, Planning Commission, Government of India, New Delhi.
5. *Education For All by 2000 A.D : Indian Perspective*, National Institute of Educational Planning and Administration, New Delhi, 1991.
6. *A Handbook of Educational and Allied Statistics*, Ministry of Human Resource Development, Department of Education, Government of India, 1987.
7. *India, 1990 : A Reference Manual*, Publication Division, Ministry of Information and Broadcasting, Government of India, New Delhi, 1990.

8. *Selected Educational Statistics, 1988-89, 1989-90* Ministry of Human Resource Development, Department of Education, Government of India, New Delhi, 1990, 1991.

TABLE 25.1: Literacy and Demographic Data at a Glance, 1991

INDIA, 1991	
Population	
Total	843,930,861
Males	437,597,929
Females	406,332,932
Decennial Population Growth 1981-91	
1. Absolute	160,606,764
2. Percentage	+ 23.50
Density of Population	267 per sq. km.
Sex Ratio	929 Females per 1,000 Males
Literacy Rate	
Total	51.11 per cent
Males	63.86 per cent
Females	39.42 per cent

Notes: 1. Population of India includes projected population of Jammu & Kashmir where the 1991 Census is yet to be held.
2. Density has been worked out on comparable data.
3. Literacy rates relate to population aged seven years and above.
4. Literacy rates exclude Jammu & Kashmir.

TABLE 25.2: Literacy and Demographic Data, 1981 and 1991

	1981	1991
1. Total Population	683,929,097	843,930,861
2. Sex Ratio (Females per 1,000 males)	934	929
3. Density of Population	216	267
4. Literacy Rate %	43.56	51.11
(i) Males %	56.37	63.86
(ii) Females %	29.75	39.42

TABLE 25.3: Literacy, Population and Density: States and Union Territories, 1991

Sl. No. Rank	State/Union Territory	Population	Percentage to Total Population	Decadal Population Growth 1981-1991	Density	Literacy %		
						Total	Male	Female
1	2	3	4	5	6	7	8	9
1.	Uttar Pradesh	138,760,417	16.44	25.16	471	41.71	55.35	26.02
2.	Bihar	86,338,853	10.23	23.49	497	38.54	52.63	23.10
3.	Maharashtra	78,706,719	9.33	25.36	256	63.05	74.84	50.51
4.	West Bengal	67,982,732	8.06	24.55	766	57.72	67.24	47.15
5.	Andhra Pradesh	66,304,854	7.86	23.82	241	45.11	56.24	33.71
6.	Madhya Pradesh	66,135,862	7.84	26.75	149	43.45	57.43	28.39
7.	Tamil Nadu	55,638,318	6.59	14.94	428	63.72	74.88	52.29
8.	Karnataka	44,817,398	5.31	20.69	234	55.98	67.25	44.34
9.	Rajasthan	43,880,640	5.20	28.07	128	38.81	55.07	20.84
10.	Gujarat	41,174,060	4.88	20.80	210	60.91	72.54	48.50
11.	Orissa	31,512,070	3.73	19.50	202	48.55	62.37	34.40
12.	Kerala	29,011,237	3.44	13.98	747	90.59	94.45	86.93
13.	Assam	22,294,562	2.64	23.58	284	53.42	62.34	43.70
14.	Punjab	20,190,795	2.39	20.26	401	57.14	63.68	49.72
15.	Haryana	16,317,715	1.93	26.28	369	55.33	67.85	40.94
16.	Delhi	9,370,475	1.11	50.64	6,319	76.09	82.63	68.01
17.	Jammu & Kashmir	7,718,700	0.91	28.92	76	N.A.	N.A.	N.A.
18.	Himachal Pradesh	5,111,079	0.61	19.39	92	63.54	74.57	52.46
19.	Tripura	2,744,827	0.32	33.69	262	60.39	70.08	50.01
20.	Manipur	1,826,714	0.22	28.56	82	60.96	72.98	48.64
21.	Meghalaya	1,760,626	0.21	31.80	78	48.26	51..57	44.78
22.	Nagaland	1,215,573	0.14	56.86	73	61.30	66.09	55.72
23.	Goa	1,168,622	0.14	15.96	316	76.96	85.48	68.20
24.	Arunachal Pradesh	858,392	0.10	35.86	10	41.22	51.10	29.37
25.	Pondicherry	789,416	0.09	30.60	1,605	74.91	83.91	65.79
26.	Mizoram	686,217	0.08	38.98	33	81.23	84.06	78.09
27.	Chandigarh	640,725	0.08	41.88	5,620	78.73	82.67	73.61
28.	Sikkim	403,612	0.05	27.57	57	56.53	64.34	47.23
29.	Andaman & Nicobar Islands	277,989	0.03	47.29	34	73.74	79.68	66.22
30.	Dadra & Nagar Haveli	138,542	0.01	33.63	282	39.45	52.07	26.10
31.	Daman & Diu	101,439	0.01	28.43	906	73.58	85.67	61.38
32.	Lakshadweep	51,681	0.01	28.40	1,615	79.23	87.06	70.88
	INDIA	843,930,861	—	23.50	267	52.11	63.86	39.42

TABLE 25.4: Plans Outlay and Expenditure on Education: Share of the Centre and States First Plan to Seventh Plan.

Sl. No.		Outlay for Education (Rs in crores)	% of Outlay for Education to Total Plan	Expenditure on Education (Rs in crores)	% of Expenditure on Education to Total Plan
1.	*First Plan*				
	Centre	44	4.9	32	6.36
	State	126	8.7	131	8.32
	Total	170	7.2	153	7.86
2.	*Second Plan*				
	Centre	70	2.7	70	2.75
	State	207	9.2	203	9.49
	Total	277	5.8	273	5.83
3.	*Third Plan*				
	Centre	148	4.1	152	3.61
	State	412	10.6	437	10.01
	Total	560	7.5	589	6.87
4.	*Fourth Plan*				
	Centre	271	3.1	241	2.35
	State	551	7.8	454	7.43
	Total	822	5.2	786	9.94
5.	*Fifth Plan*				
	Centre	405	2.1	—	—
	State	880	4.5	—	—
	Total	1285	3.3	912	—
6.	*Sixth Plan*				
	Centre	735	1.6	601	
	State	1789	3.6	2288	
	Total	2524	2.6	2889	
7.	*Seventh Plan*				
	Centre	1739	—		
	State	3994	—		
	Total	5733	—		

Source: A Handbook of Educational Statistics and Allied Statistics, Ministry of Human Resource Development, Government of India, New Delhi, 1987.

TABLE 25.5: Plan Outlay of the Seventh Five Year Plan on Education

Sl. No.	Sector	Rs. in Crores
1.	Elementary Education	1963 (34)
2.	Adult Education	360 (6)
3.	Secondary Education	
4.	University Education	2595 (45)
5.	Other Educational Programmes	
6.	Cultural programmes	132 (2)
7.	Total General Education	5051 (88)
8.	Technical Education	682 (12)
9.	Total Education	5733 (100)

Note: Figures in Parentheses indicate percentage to total distribution among different sectors of Education.
See also Table 1.1 and 1.2

Source: *A Handbook of Educational and Allied Statistics*, Ministry of Human Resource Development, Government of India, New Delhi, 1987.

TABLE 25.6: Number of Primary Schools, Enrolment, Percentage of Enrolment, Percentage of Trained Teachers and Number of Teachers, 1950-51 to 1989-90

Year	No. of Primary School	Enrolment in Classes I to IV (lakh)	Percentage of Enrolment to total Population in the Age Group 6-11	Percentage of Trainee Teachers	No. of Teachers
1950-51	2,09,671	191.5	42.6	58.8	5,37,918
1960-61	3,30,399	349.5	62.4	64.1	7,41,515
1968-69	4,00,621	543.7	78.1	76.9	10,05,282
1978-79	4,72,519	689.6	81.6	87.1	12,96,639
1979-80	4,82,476	715.58	82.7	86.8	13,28,700
1982-83	5,11,106	795.07	86.8	86.9	14,23,639
1984-85	5,21,048	856.6	93.6	85.8	14,85,305
1986-87	5,37,399	899.6	95.96	87.26	15,22,108
1987-88	5,43,677	929.4	97.9	88.41	16,16,685
1988-89	5,48,059	957.3	99.6	89.44	16,03,058
1989-90	5,50,700	973.1	99.9	89.44	16,01,717

TABLE 25.7: Number of Middle Schools, Enrolment, Percentage of Enrolment, Percentage of Trained Teachers and Number of Teachers, 1950-51 to 1989-90

Year	No. of Middle Senior Basic School	Enrolment in Classes VI to VIII (lakh)	Percentage of Enrolment to total Population in the Age Group 11-14	Percentage of Trainee Teachers	No. of Teachers
1950-51	13,590	31.2	12.7	53.3	85,496
1960-61	49,663	67.0	22.5	66.5	3,45,228
1968-69	84,246	125.4	33.5	81.0	5,95,733
1978-79	1,12,801	181.8	38.0	87.4	8,25,126
1979-80	1,15,117	192.79	39.6	88.7	8,35,608
1982-83	1,25,446	236.31	45.5	89.7	8,82,506
1984-85	1,31,249	262.2	48.1	89.5	9,27,623
1986-87	1,37,196	287.8	53.14	89.64	9,79,073
1987-88	1,41,014	299.1	55.14	90.10	10,14,162
1988-89	1,44,145	309.4	56.9	91.25	10,32,534
1989-90	1,43,747	3.21	59.1	91.74	10,47,588

TABLE 25.8: Number High/Higher Secondary Schools, Enrolment, Percentage of Enrolment and Number of Teachers, 1950-51 to 1989-90

Year	No. of Schools High/Higher Secondary	Enrolment of Pupils in Classes IX-XI/ XII (lakhs)	Percentage of Enrolment to Total Population in the Age Group 14-17	No. of Teachers
1950-51	7,288	12.2	5.3	1,26,504
1960-61	17,257	28.9	1.06	2,96,305
1968-69	33,487	61.5	18.3	5,81,618
1978-79	46,874	84.1	18.8	8,18,507
1979-80	48,905	98.14	21.9	8,69,,842
1982-83	52,716	115.88	18.6	9,93,093
1984-85	62,186	154.8	23.5	10,86,589
1986-87	64,240	155.0	N.A.	11,99,367
1987-88	71,305[1]	178.5[1]	N.A.	12,,42,827
1988-89	73,365[1]	185.2[1]	N.A.	12,35,530
1989-90	76,119[1]	199.5[1]	N.A.	12,64,249

N.A. stands for not available

1 includes data of Intermediate/pre-degree/junior colleges/10+2 Higher Secondary and High/Higher Secondary.

TABLE 25.9: Number of Teachers Training Schools and Colleges, 1950-51 to 1989-90

Year	No. of Teachers Training Schools	No. of Teachers Training Colleges or Colleges of Education
1950-51	782	53
1960-61	1138	478
1968-69	231	1377
1978-79	118	1286
1979-80	138	1283
1982-83	111	1310
1984-85	223	367
1986-87	973	462
1987-88	990	485
1988-89	992	485
1989-90	1315	485

TABLE 25.10: Number of Universities and Colleges, Number of Students and Teachers, 1950-51 to 1988-89

Year	Univer-sities	Colle-ges	UC	Enrolment in (000's)			No. of Teachers		
				Total*	AC	% in AC	Total	UD/UC	AC
1	2	3	4	5	6	7	8	9	10
1950-51	28	695	—	174	—	—	21264	—	—
1955-56	32	1025	—	295	—	—	33208	—	—
1960-61	44	1542	—	557	—	—	55460	—	—
1961-62	46	1783	107	664	—	—	63053	9313	53740
1962-63	54	1938	133	752	—	—	66370	11044	55326
1963-64	55	2111	128	842	690	82.0	68634	11522	57112
1964-65	62	2360	147	950	781	82.2	77120	13637	63483
1965-66	64	2572	163	1067	881	82.6	84676	14291	70385
1966-67	70	2749	166	1191	990	83.1	93251	14900	78351
1967-68	700	2899	170	1370	1135	82.8	103180	17456	85724
1968-69	76	3112	181	1566	1306	83.4	110943	19058	91885
1969-70	79	3297	185	1793	1522	84.9	119052	19757	99295
1970-71	84	3604	206	1954	1655	84.7	128876	21619	107257
1971-72	86	3896	208	2065	1773	85.9	139204	22842	116362
1972-73	90	4158	229	2168	1855	85.6	145524	24704	120820
1973-74	95	4308	230	2234	1905	85.3	156562	26659	129903
1974-75	102	4388	240	2367	2013	85.0	161782	27830	133952

Contd.

TABLE 25.10 *Contd.*

1	2	3	4	5	6	7	8	9	01
1975-76	102	4508	305	2426	2059	86.0	167623	31624	135999
1976-77	105	4569	302	2432	2069	85.1	169615	32142	137473
1977-78	105	4375	351	2565	2160	84.2	178344	37142	141202
1978-79	108	4460	352	2618	2178	83.3	181659	38835	142824
1979-80	108	4558	352	2649	2210	83.5	188502	39838	148664
1980-81	112	4722	411	2753	2299	83.5	193341	39964	153377
1981-82	118	4886	495	2952	2455	83.3	199904	42186	157718
1982-83	120	5039	501	3133	2610	83.3	209017	44596	164421
1983-84	124	5246	—	3308	2749	83.1	216500	46859	169641
1984-85	125	5590	—	3404	2846	83.6	220101	47382	172719
1985-86	132	5816	—	3571	2975	83.3	226909	49008	177901
1986-87	136	6512	—	3682	3067	83.3	234388	51150	183238
1987-88	142	6647	—	3814	3177	83.3	241973	53165	188808
1988-89	144	6912	—	3948	3293	83.4	249068	54973	194095

Source: UGC Reports

* Excluding Pre-university/Intermediate/Pre-professional level 1977-78 onwards. Number of colleges excludes junior colleges and colleges having only diploma/certificate courses.

Note: UC = University Colleges
UD = University Department
AC = Affiliated Colleges.

TABLE 25.11: Levelwise Enrolment in Higher Education 1950-51 to 1988-89

Year	Undergraduate		Postgraduate		Research		Total Enrolment	
	No.	%	No.	%	No.	%	No.	%
1950-51	145389	83.7	19992	11.5	1434	0.83	173696	100.00
1951-52	166935	84.1	21903	11.3	1774	0.89	198543	100.00
1952-53	182775	84.9	23751	11.3	1715	0.80	215350	100.00
1953-54	201258	84.7	26191	11.0	2071	0.87	237668	100.00
1954-55	219917	84.5	27801	10.7	2464	0.95	260121	100.00
1955-56	248690	84.4	30866	10.5	2692	0.91	294815	100.00
1956-57	276999	84.7	33516	10.3	2992	0.92	326926	100.00
1957-58	314783	84.7	38298	10.3	3087	0.83	371446	100.00
1958-59	359829	84.1	45543	10.6	3745	0.87	427868	100.00
1959-60	407415	84.6	52244	10.8	4867	1.01	481534	100.00
1960-61	471658	84.7	58908	10.6	5083	0.91	556559	100.00
1961-62	571485	86.1	67610	10.2	5249	0.79	663661	100.00
1962-63	651805	86.7	71297	9.5	5297	0.70	752095	100.00
1963-64	739607	87.8	76685	9.1	5895	0.70	842110	100.00
1964-65	835804	88.0	84201	8.9	7104	0.75	950277	100.00
1965-66	944015	88.5	91830	8.6	8633	0.81	1066884	100.00
1966-67	1053750	88.5	101798	8.5	9668	0.81	1190713	100.00
1967-68	1211083	88.4	117250	8.6	11479	0.84	1370261	100.00
1968-69	1388335	88.6	135469	8.6	12145	0.77	1566103	100.00
1969-70	1603898	89.5	146804	8.2	12474	0.69	1792700	100.00
1970-71	1746090	89.4	161182	8.2	13311	0.68	1953640	100.00
1971-72	1835077	88.9	180343	8.7	14995	0.73	2065041	100.00
1972-73	1920364	88.6	195307	9.0	16443	0.70	2168107	100.00
1973-74	1964432	88.0	214691	9.6	16417	0.70	2234385	100.00
1974-75	2075039	87.7	234114	9.9	17977	0.80	2366451	100.00
1975-76	2146919	88.5	219826	9.1	18381	0.70	2426109	100.00
1976-77	2141542	88.1	218128	9.0	21910	0.90	2431563	100.00
1977-78	2255306	87.9	233644	9.1	26659	1.10	2564972	100.00
1978-79	2294785	87.7	249528	9.5	30078	1.10	2618228	100.00
1979-80	2307924	87.1	265251	10.0	29570	1.10	2648579	100.00
1980-81	2401485	87.2	273337	9.9	32171	1.20	2752437	100.00
1981-82	2588759	87.7	285892	9.7	34558	1.20	2952066	100.00
1982-83	2757893	88.0	296103	9.4	36731	1.20	3133093	100.00
1983-84*	2912487	88.0	313110	9.5	36249	1.10	3307649	100.00
1984-85*	2999621	88.0	322541	9.5	38160	1.10	3404096	100.00
1985-86*	3142389	88.0	339235	9.5	39280	1.10	3570897	100.00
1986-87*	3240046	88.0	349778	9.5	40500	1.10	3681870	100.00
1987-88*	3356687	88.0	362370	9.5	41958	1.10	3814417	100.00
1988-89*	3474171	88.0	375053	9.5	43427	1.10	3947922	100.00

* Estimated

TABLE 25.12: Statewise Percentage of Literates to Estimated Population Aged Seven Years and Above, 1981-1991

Sl. No.	State	1981			1991		
		Persons	Males	Females	Persons	Males	Females
	India	43.56	56.37	29.75	52.11	63.86	39.42
1.	Andhra Pradesh	35.66	46.83	24.16	45.11	56.24	33.71
2.	Arunachal Pradesh	25.54	35.11	14.01	41.22	51.10	29.37
3.	Assam	N.A.	N.A.	N.A.	53.42	62.34	43.70
4.	Bihar	32.03	46.58	16.51	38.54	52.63	23.10
5.	Goa	65.71	76.01	55.17	76.96	85.48	68.20
6.	Gujarat	52.21	65.14	38.46	60.91	72.54	48.50
7.	Haryana	43.85	58.49	26.89	55.33	67.85	40.94
8.	Himachal Pradesh	51.17	64.27	37.72	63.54	74.57	52.46
9.	Jammu & Kashmir	32.68	44.18	19.55	N.A.	N.A.	N.A.
10.	Karnataka	46.20	58.72	33.16	55.98	67.25	44.34
11.	Kerala	81.56	87.74	75.65	90.59	94.45	86.93
12.	Madhya Pradesh	34.22	48.41	18.99	43.45	57.43	28.39
13.	Maharashtra	55.83	69.66	41.01	63.05	74.84	50.51
14.	Manipur	49.61	64.12	34.61	60.96	72.98	48.64
15.	Meghalaya	42.02	46.62	37.15	48.26	51.57	44.78
16.	Mizoram	74.26	79.37	68.60	81.23	84.06	78.09
17.	Nagaland	50.20	58.52	40.28	61.30	66.09	55.72
18.	Orissa	40.96	56.45	25.14	48.55	62.37	34.40
19.	Punjab	48.12	55.52	39.64	57.14	63.68	49.72
20.	Rajasthan	30.09	44.76	13.99	38.81	55.07	20.84
21.	Sikkim	41.57	52.98	27.35	56.53	64.34	47.23
22.	Tamil Nadu	54.38	68.05	40.43	63.72	74.88	52.29
23.	Tripura	50.10	61.49	38.01	60.39	70.08	50.01
24.	Uttar Pradesh	33.33	47.43	17.18	41.71	55.35	26.02
25.	West Bengal	48.64	59.93	36.07	57.72	67.24	47.15
26.	A & N Islands	63.16	70.28	53.15	73.74	79.68	66.22
27.	Chandigarh	74.81	78.89	69.31	78.73	82.67	73.61
28.	Dadra & Nagar Haveli	32.70	44.69	20.38	39.45	52.07	26.10
29.	Daman & Diu	59.91	74.45	46.51	73.58	85.67	61.38
30.	Delhi	71.93	79.28	62.57	76.09	82.63	68.01
31.	Lakshadweep	68.42	81.24	55.32	79.23	87.06	70.88
32.	Pondicherry	65.14	77.09	53.03	74.91	83.91	65.79

NA stands for not available.

Literacy rates for 1981 excludes Assam where the 1981 census could not be held and the literacy rates for 1991 exclude Jammu and Kashmir where the 1991 census is yet to be conducted. The literacy rates for India for 1981 and 1991 excluding Assam and Jammu and Kashmir works out as under:

	Persons	Males	Females
1981	43.66	56.49	29.84
1991	52.07	63.90	39.31

TABLE 25.13: Educational Institutions Statewise, 1989-90

(As on 30th Sept., 1989)

Sl. No.	State/U.Ts.	Primary	Middle	Sec/ Hr. Sec.	Colleges for General Education	Colleges for Prof.@ Education	Universities*
1.	Andhra Pradesh	47216	5827	6366	403	86	17
2.	Arunachal Pradesh	1101	241	108	4	0	1
3.	Assam	28875	5703	3137	179	15	3
4.	Bihar+	52181	12530	4006	552	31	11
5.	Goa	996	118	361	14	4	1
6.	Gujarat	13103	16794	5021	227	57	10
7.	Haryana	4922	1321	2266	119	22	4
8.	Himachal Pradesh	7522	1101	1037	39	4	3
9.	Jammu & Kashmir+	8712	2320	1097	27	9	3
10.	Karnataka	23538	16318	5062	403 +	132 +	9
11.	Kerala	6812	2892	2547	132	31	6
12.	Madhya Pradesh+	65867	13453	3449	448	37	12
13.	Maharashtra	38796	18145	10071	571	189	18
14.	Manipur	2771	443	393	33 +	4 +	1
15.	Meghalaya	4162	685	298	23	1	1
16.	Mizoram	1084	522	185	13	1	0
17.	Nagaland+	1286	343	124	16	1	0
18.	Orissa	39593	9396	4695	232	30	5
19.	Punjab+	12357	1413	2740	171	26	4
20.	Rajasthan	30022	8600	3642	138 +	41 +	9
21.	Sikkim	512	127	68	1	0	0
22.	Tamil Nadu	29491	5651	4949	209	71	15
23.	Tripura	2043	437	428	13	2	1
24.	Uttar Pradesh	74275	14549	5946	414	24	25
25.	West Bengal+	50827	4179	6804	302	62	11
26.	A & N Islands	186	42	63	1	1	0
27.	Chandigarh+	43	31	70	12	2	2
28.	Dadra & Nagar Haveli	120	41	11	0	0	0
29.	Daman & Diu	43	20	19	1	0	0
30.	Delhi	1851	397	1043	52 +	6 +	11
31.	Lakshadweep+	19	4	11	0	0	0
32.	Pondicherry	344	104	102	6	2	1
	INDIA	550700	143747	76119	4755	891	184

* Includes Deemed Universities and Institutions of National Importance.

@ Includes only Colleges of Engineering Technology, Medical and Teacher Training.

\+ Figures relate to the year 1988-89.

Source: Selected Educational Statistics, 1989-90.

TABLE 25.14: Statewise: Enrolment Per Lakh Population, 1989-90

Sl. No.	State/U.T.	Total		Scheduled Castes		Scheduled Tribes	
		Primary	Middle	Primary	Middle	Primary	Middle
1.	Andhra Pradesh	11591	3219	15213	2548	12866	1630
2.	Assam	14178	5085	21287	7440	20626	4674
3.	Bihar	9797	2284	8279	1511	9936	1913
4.	Gujarat	13647	4126	16828	5984	14052	2972
5.	Haryana	10467	4280	12285	3291	0	0
6.	Himachal Pradesh	13734	6662	13558	5171	11978	4359
7.	Jammu & Kashmir	10246	4046	10017	4028	0	0
8.	Karnataka	12327	3945	12967	3469	9990	2644
9.	Kerala.	10833	6148	12500	6748	13321	5030
10.	Madhya Pradesh	12284	4003	12624	3051	10192	1824
11.	Maharashtra	13331	5120	27149	9644	13379	3075
12.	Manipur	14698	4086	14273	6091	19314	3119
13.	Meghalaya	14289	4079	36971	12814	14905	4283
14.	Nagaland	14012	4373	0	0	16089	4259
15.	Orissa	11606	3153	15001	3221	10943	1889
16.	Punjab	10691	4138	13151	3365	0	0
17.	Rajasthan	10395	3014	9330	2366	9140	1991
18.	Sikkim	16414	3349	16824	2580	15103	3297
19.	Tamil Nadu	13790	5448	14966	5415	10002	2844
20.	Tripura	15085	4509	17676	4589	15267	3301
21.	Uttar Pradesh	10095	3103	8333	1381	11785	2331
22.	West Bengal	14308	4232	10240	1751	12380	1588
23.	A&N Islands	13726	6337	0	0	11082	4894
24.	Arunachal Pradesh	13296	3077	8225	2700	14067	2939
25.	Chandigarh	6225	3215	11243	4306	0	0
26.	Dadra & Nagar Haveli	12493	3354	11900	6933	13181	2901
27.	Delhi	10311	5599	13059	4853	0	0
28.	Goa, Daman & Diu	11134	6683	12976	4603	12962	8508
29.	Lakshadweep	18260	6696	0	0	19288	6863
30.	Mizoram	16584	5223	0	0	17568	5525
31.	Pondicherry	13984	7210	17061	7620	0	0
	INDIA	11795	3901	11854	3018	12179	2450

TABLE 25.15: Statewise: Enrolment by Stages, 1989-90

(*As on 30.9.1989*)

Sl. No.	State/U.Ts.	Primary			Middle			Sec./Hr.Sec.			Hr. Education *		
		Boys	Girls	Total	Boys	Girls	Total	Boys	Girls	Total	Boys	Girls	Total
1	2	3	4	5	6	7	8	9	10	11	12	13	14
1.	Andhra Pradesh	4205423	3115165	7320588	1304111	728839	2032950	878456	419125	1297581	188168	77439	265607
2.	Arunachal Pradesh	62454	44846	107300	15226	9603	24829	10073	4952	15025	1251	244	1495
3.	Assam	2302022	1165381	3467403	792046	451561	1243607	370180	236747	606927	72052	33415	105467
4.	Bihar	5581656	2719530	8301186	1435922	499111	1935033	990827	223558	1214385	401154	94041	495195
5.	Goa	72444	65815	138259	44004	37406	81410	30530	25087	55617	5692	5534	11226
6.	Gujarat	3153000	2357000	5510000	1022000	644000	1666000	682000	402000	1034000	141050	92020	233070
7.	Haryana	954490	734917	1689407	439601	251214	690815	283906	126104	410010	44943	29204	74147
8.	Himachal Pradesh	371102	319123	690225	188667	146131	334798	171205	105178	276383	7269	3357	10626
9.	Jammu & Kashmir +	450374	288386	738760	190878	100860	291738	122903	58410	181313	16395	10958	27353
10.	Karnataka	2969753	2524279	5494032	1038292	719914	1758206	733785	370794	1104579	178459 +	76858 +	255317 +
11.	Kerala	1649072	1564532	3213604	936091	887824	1823915	558666	573109	1131775	76351	86046	162397
12.	Madhya Pradesh +	4788209	2956283	7744492	1759302	764218	2523520	757511	248236	1005837	162421	69721	232142
13.	Maharashtra	5338000	4554000	9892000	2269664	1529632	3799296	1892450	958380	2850830	383683	234334	618017
14.	Manipur	138800	120200	259000	39600	32400	72000	39618	26878	66496	12178 +	9197 +	21375 +
15.	Meghalaya	124023	117853	241876	36754	32292	69046	31016	26801	57817	4271	2763	7034
16.	Mizoram	60506	53660	114166	18290	17663	35953	9530	8462	17992	1494	761	2255
17.	Nagaland +	78800	75000	153800	26200	21800	48000	12392	9821	22213	1415	694	2109
18.	Orissa	2150000	1439000	3589000	548000	427000	975000	477601	215605	693206	50322	17330	67652
19.	Punjab +	1131340	960955	2092295	462549	347246	809795	320232	218004	538236	75600	37290	112890

Contd.

TABLE 25.15 *Contd.*

1	2	3	4	5	6	7	8	9	10	11	12	13	14
20.	Rajasthan	3151738	1367515	4519253	1024132	286025	1310157	635931	149690	785621	132621 +	38689 +	171310 +
21.	Sikkim	38656	32859	71515	7824	6767	14591	4658	2929	7587	486	178	664
22.	Tamil Nadu	4140009	3537807	7677816	1756874	1276142	3033016	946514	610822	1557336	152270	87324	239594
23.	Tripura	211572	170061	381633	65954	48128	114082	39841	24975	64816	7276	3810	11086
24.	Uttar Pradesh	8687102	4809214	13496316	3029011	1120012	4149023	2215833	668891	2884724	349757	112063	461820
25.	West Bengal +	5313432	3960689	9274121	1578095	1164672	2742767	1058516	540100	1598616	196157	134837	330994
26.	A. & N. Islands	20538	18320	38858	9838	8102	17940	6902	5560	12462	681	655	1336
27.	Chandigarh +	24361	20615	44976	12752	10577	23229	15501	11964	27465	7061	6160	13221
28.	D & N Haveli	9650	6629	16279	2812	1558	4370	1484	942	2426	0	0	0
29.	Daman & Diu	5373	4764	10137	4099	3565	7664	3284	2252	5546	168	102	270
30.	Delhi	489395	429318	918713	278015	220878	498893	206099	160105	366204	66045 +	50825 +	116870 +
31.	Lakshadweep +	4464	3954	8418	1765	1322	3087	1090	596	1686	0	0	0
32.	Pondicherry	53776	48910	102686	29563	23383	52946	14532	10977	25509	2669	2091	4760
	INDIA	57731534	39586580	97318114	20367831	11819845	32187676	13523066	6447144	19970210	2739359	1317940	4057299

* Excludes enrolment in Ph.D/M.Phil and all Professional courses except Engineering (B.E./B.Tech/B.Arc.), Medicine (MBBS) and Teacher Training (B.Ed/B.T.).

\+ Figures relate to the year 1988-89.

Source: Selected Educational Statistics, 1989-90.

TABLE 25.16: Statewise: Number of Teachers, 1989-90

Sl. No.	State/U.Ts.	Primary Schools			Middle Schools			Sec./Hr. Secondary Schools		
		Male	Female	Total	Male	Female	Total	Male	Female	Total
1	2	3	4	5	6	7	8	9	10	11
1.	Andhra Pradesh	74495	28749	103244	28128	13321	41449	54924	24251	79175
2.	Arunachal Pradesh	1936	406	2342	1329	336	1665	1746	407	2153
3.	Assam	56600	14300	70900	31120	6180	37300	31456	9908	41364
4.	Bihar+	95160	20345	115505	77327	17742	95069	40213	6220	46433
5.	Goa	1067	1703	2770	422	521	943	3117	3692	6809
6.	Gujarat	22208	13607	35815	75007	59728	134735	40458	11739	52197
7.	Haryana	9012	6449	15461	7167	4648	11815	28047	19168	47215
8.	Himachal Pradesh	10980	6020	17000	5700	1300	7000	9100	3800	12900
9.	Jammu & Kashmir+	8159	5565	13724	11822	5807	17629	12987	6015	19002
10.	Karnataka	30110	11149	41259	57195	37332	94627	37135	12146	48281
11.	Kerala	18619	31315	49934	19584	30533	50117	36014	56732	92746
12.	Madhya Pradesh+	129167	35980	165147	60045	17844	77889	37130	10918	48048
13.	Maharashtra	71800	44996	116796	91993	53564	145557	130801	57708	188509
14.	Manipur	7030	2030	9060	3120	950	4070	4704	1906	6610
15.	Meghalaya	4242	2485	6727	1887	1108	2995	1490	1442	2932
16.	Mizoram	2133	1710	3843	2489	579	3068	1119	246	1365

Contd.

TABLE 25.16 *Contd.*

1	2	3	4	5	6	7	8	9	10	11
17.	Nagaland +	4691	1807	6498	2601	678	3279	1744	786	2530
18.	Orissa	77755	25785	103540	30996	6368	37364	30189	8476	38665
19.	Punjab +	21965	25528	47493	5518	4321	9839	26727	21162	47889
20.	Rajasthan	54808	18697	73505	52901	17404	70305	47807	13472	61279
21.	Sikkim	1542	611	2153	1103	498	1601	1201	810	2011
22.	Tamil Nadu	72381	46541	118922	33826	31842	65668	67218	46110	113328
23.	Tripura	4973	3314	8287	3143	915	4058	5802	3866	9668
24.	Uttar Pradesh	213698	47761	261459	76382	18831	95213	104619	21714	126333
25.	West Bengal +	144112	40636	184748	18092	7139	25231	78326	41691	120017
26.	A. & N. Islands	432	252	684	349	346	695	1101	966	2067
27.	Chandigarh +	30	389	419	66	449	515	586	2053	2639
28.	D & N Haveli	114	50	164	163	206	369	102	43	145
29.	Daman & Diu	137	140	277	132	53	185	131	46	177
30.	Delhi	8378	13548	21926	2165	3245	5410	15754	22094	37848
31.	Lakshadweep +	157	66	223	151	66	217	132	31	163
32.	Pondicherry	1061	831	1892	1035	676	1711	1657	1094	2751
	INDIA	1148952	452765	1601717	702958	344630	1047588	853537	410712	1263249

\+ Figures relate to the year 1988-89.

Source: *Selected Educational Statistics*, 1989-90.

TABLE 25.17: Statewise Dropout Rates, 1986-87

Sl. No.	State/U.T.	Class I—V			Class I—VIII		
		Boys	Girls	Total	Boys	Girls	Total
1.	Andhra Pradesh	57.70	62.17	59.60	78.03	85.14	81.08
2.	Assam	62.00	66.95	64.16	70.31	73.20	71.56
3.	Bihar	64.11	68.23	65.42	77.25	84.68	79.53
4.	Gujarat	41.30	48.65	44.49	58.65	67.90	62.53
5.	Haryana	26.95	32.77	29.26	29.79	48.30	36.38
6.	Himachal Pradesh	30.90	32.36	31.56	15.23	31.04	22.04
7.	Jammu & Kashmir	39.74	38.20	39.16	46.91	57.37	50.89
8.	Karnataka	49.48	62.93	55.98	67.27	77.60	72.06
9.	Kerala	−0.44	1.30	0.41	19.09	18.32	18.71
10.	Madhya Pradesh	38.38	49.19	42.40	51.77	69.79	58.07
11.	Maharashtra	37.42	47.64	41.42	37.41	72.15	64.15
12.	Manipur	72.00	73.82	72.86	76.63	80.51	78.44
13.	Meghalaya	64.29	69.83	66.99	86.35	86.87	86.60
14.	Nagaland	29.12	18.39	24.31	78.26	79.21	78.68
15.	Orissa	49.80	53.49	51.34	61.38	74.05	66.66
16.	Punjab	38.74	40.12	39.38	60.26	67.73	63.73
17.	Rajasthan	49.06	56.58	51.08	58.96	69.83	61.63
18.	Sikkim	62.38	62.90	62.61	66.11	65.37	65.80
19.	Tamil Nadu	19.86	25.06	22.28	44.89	55.23	49.67
20.	Tripura	62.46	62.46	62.46	71.10	71.30	71.19
21.	Uttar Pradesh	54.52	46.48	45.82	50.49	64.20	54.94
22.	West Bengal	61.20	64.72	62.72	78.20	79.57	78.75
23.	A & N Islands	23.99	27.54	25.65	31.61	41.27	36.15
24.	Arunachal Pradesh	65.54	62.55	64.46	78.06	75.53	77.25
25.	Chandigarh	8.22	1.71	5.32	13.41	16.27	14.63
26.	Dadra & Nagar Haveli	37.85	50.17	42.81	71.56	75.00	73.03
27.	Delhi	8.24	20.64	14.26	15.15	30.06	22.30
28.	Goa, Daman & Diu	9.44	13.00	11.13	23.67	32.81	28.01
29.	Lakshadweep	19.01	21.45	20.16	41.00	46.94	43.76
30.	Mizoram	40.16	40.95	40.54	77.03	77.08	77.06
31.	Pondicherry	N.A.	N.A.	N.A.	N.A.	N.A.	N.A.
	INDIA	46.86	51.17	48.60	61.44	70.16	64.90

Drop-out rate is calculated as follows:

Drop-out rate from Class I to V for the year 1986-87 =

$$\frac{\text{(No. of students enrolled in Class I in 1982-83)} - \text{(No. of Students enrolled in Class V in 1986-87)}}{\text{No. of students enrolled in Class I in 1982-83}} \times 100$$

Drop-out rate from Class I to VIII for the year 1986-87 =

$$\frac{\text{(No. of students enrolled in Class I in 1979-80)} - \text{(No. of students enrolled in Class VIII in 1986-87)}}{\text{No. of student enrolled in Class I in 1979-80}} \times 100$$

This ratio does not take into account:

(i) Repeaters; and

(ii) Children who enter the system after Class I.

TABLE 25.18: Statewise Enrolment by Stages: Scheduled Castes, 1989-90

(*As on 30.9.1989*)

Sl. No.	State/U.Ts.	Primary			Middle			Sec./Hr.Sec.			Hr. Education *		
		Boys	Girls	Total	Boys	Girls	Total	Boys	Girls	Total	Boys	Girls	Total
1	2	3	4	5	6	7	8	9	10	11	12	13	14
1.	Andhra Pradesh	819177	609325	1428502	152909	86332	239241	183927	83776	267703	23239	7440	30679
2.	Arunachal Pradesh	215	114	329	71	37	108	56	28	84	N.A.	N.A.	N.A.
3.	Assam	170067	154777	324844	64904	48623	113527	30758	17965	48723	5394	2396	7790
4.	Bihar+	745163	272495	1017658	149526	36235	185761	56183	8496	6479	N.A.	N.A.	N.A.
5.	Goa	1749	1608	3357	613	440	1053	317	156	473	56	40	96
6.	Gujarat	278000	208000	486000	109315	63498	172813	71796	31392	103188	12100	4435	16535
7.	Haryana	211603	166541	378144	69753	31549	101302	33879	7924	41803	3689	625	4314
8.	Himachal Pradesh	92265	75450	167715	39397	24570	63967	23428	9855	33283	681	137	818
9.	Jammu & Kashmir+	36200	23800	60000	15700	8430	24130	6420	2340	8760	N.A.	N.A.	N.A.
10.	Karnataka	479636	391112	870748	142035	90902	232937	95917	39615	135532	19105 +	4869 +	23974
11.	Kerala	191180	180205	371385	102984	97498	200482	55858	60424	116282	5003	5180	10183
12.	Madhya Pradesh+	765231	357176	1122407	210962	60302	271264	88794	18275	107069	14777	2649	17426
13.	Maharashtra	791123	646412	1437535	318817	191816	510633	229055	95682	324737	43112	8896	52008
14.	Manipur	1490	1650	3140	760	580	1340	795	563	1358	296 +	190 +	486 +
15.	Meghalaya	1311	1277	2588	524	373	897	854	425	1279	139	91	230

Contd.

TABLE 25.18 *Contd.*

1	2	3	4	5	6	7	8	9	10	11	12	13	14
16.	**Mizoram**	@	@	@	@	@	@	@	@	@	@	@	@
17.	**Nagaland+**	@	@	@	@	@	@	@	@	@	@	@	@
18.	**Orissa**	415000	265000	680000	105000	41000	146000	55145	16840	71985	3755	773	4528
19.	**Punjab+**	389980	301621	691601	108752	68223	176975	55836	29463	85299	7195	2613	9808
20.	**Rajasthan**	524720	170993	695713	155320	20001	175321	84929	6190	91119	N.A.	N.A.	N.A.
21.	**Sikkim**	2239	1967	4206	348	297	645	171	107	278	13	9	22
22.	Tamil Nadu	844591	684156	1528747	329691	223459	553150	154453	85302	239755	23010	9612	32622
23.	Tripura	37404	30117	67521	10671	6860	17531	5330	2697	8027	814	318	1132
24.	Uttar Pradesh	1712827	644126	2356953	315496	75210	390706	311780	45902	357682	52354	3966	56320
25.	West Bengal+	875964	583280	1459244	165098	84470	249568	1202254	50844	171098	17364	7753	25117
26.	A. & N. Islands	@	@	@	@	@	@	@	@	@	@	@	@
27.	Chandigarh+	6337	5131	11468	2507	1885	4392	1279	865	2144	47	164	634
28.	D & N Haveli	191	166	357	123	85	208	98	60	158	N.A.	N.A.	N.A.
29.	Daman & Diu	219	187	406	126	156	282	180	101	281	4	3	7
30.	Delhi	119125	90735	209860	47355	30628	77983	31750	13684	45434	5350 +	2507 +	7857 +
31.	Lakshadweep	@	@	@	@	@	@	@	@	@	@	@	@
32.	Pondicherry	9722	10239	19961	4646	4269	8915	1340	945	2285	258	96	354
	INDIA	9522729	5877660	15400389	2623403	1297728	3921131	1799527	643706	2443233	238178	64762	302940

* Excludes enrolment in Ph.D/M.Phil and all Professional courses except Engineering (B.E./B.Tech/B.Arc.), Medicine (MBBS) and Teacher Training (B.Ed/B.T.).

\+ Figures relate to the year 1988-89.

@ No castes were scheduled by the President of India for Nagaland, A & N Islands and Lakshadweep.

Source: *Selected Educational Statistics*, 1989-90.

TABLE 25.19: Statewise Enrolment by Stages: Scheduled Tribes, 1989-90

(*As on 30.9.1989*)

Sl. No.	State/U.Ts.	Primary			Middle			Sec./Hr.Sec.			Hr. Education *		
		Boys	Girls	Total	Boys	Girls	Total	Boys	Girls	Total	Boys	Girls	Total
1	2	3	4	5	6	7	8	9	10	11	12	13	14
1.	Andhra Pradesh	297962	1844009	481971	42170	18895	61065	39529	14162	53691	3272	833	4105
2.	Arunachal Pradesh	46169	33031	79200	10375	6174	16549	7193	2843	10036	893	117	1010
3.	Assam	306376	248051	554427	72674	52966	125640	34657	20723	55380	6193	2183	8376
4.	Bihar +	467248	232413	699661	97898	36808	134706	40708	14081	54789	N.A.	N.A.	N.A.
5.	Goa	87	63	150	23	4	27	5	1	6	1	1	2
6.	Gujarat	470000	337000	807000	111865	58801	170666	59713	29548	89261	9695	4950	14645
7.	Haryana	@	@	@	@	@	@	@	@	@	@	@	@
8.	Himachal Pradesh	15642	12146	27788	6793	3319	10112	4244	1689	5933	255	56	311
9.	Jammu & Kashmir +	@	@	@	@	@	@	@	@	@	@	@	@
10.	Karnataka	119864	99008	218872	34533	23393	57926	19466	9983	29449	4318 +	832 +	5150 +
11.	Kerala	21122	19506	40628	7997	7345	15342	3644	3363	7077	320	262	582
12.	Madhya Pradesh +	1032983	443210	1476193	205121	59116	264237	95108	43008	138116	9904	1866	11770
13.	Maharashtra	528640	384058	912698	138480	71308	209788	71086	26486	97572	8398	2004	10402
14.	Manipur	50100	42800	92900	8200	6800	15000	6971	5269	12240	2060 +	1141 +	3201 +
15.	Meghalaya	104390	98910	203300	30121	28295	58416	25164	21900	47864	2574	1858	4432
16.	Mizoram	59638	53497	113135	18067	17513	35580	9473	8421	17894	1451	740	2191

Contd.

TABLE 25.19 *Contd.*

1	2	3	4	5	6	7	8	9	10	11	12	13	14
17.	Nagaland+	77039	71301	148340	21227	18039	39266	7683	6373	14056	1149	567	1716
18.	Orissa	516000	243000	759000	93000	38000	131000	33628	13010	46638	2903	617	3520
19.	Punjab+	@	@	@	@	@	@	@	@	@	@	@	@
20.	Rajasthan	373292	111834	485126	95273	10410	105683	53498	3088	56586	N.A.	N.A.	N.A.
21.	Sikkim	8140	7114	15254	1705	1625	3330	969	655	1624	78	22	100
22.	Tamil Nadu	34216	25598	59814	10215	6794	17009	4491	3006	7497	441	142	583
23.	Tripura	65503	44416	109919	15215	8550	23765	6224	2493	8717	363	107	470
24.	Uttar Pradesh	21092	12024	33116	5004	1545	6549	5819	1474	7293	1211	497	1708
25.	West Bengal+	316631	134878	451509	43094	14830	57924	20092	10560	30652	775	284	1059
26.	A. & N. Islands	2013	1755	3768	894	770	1664	443	360	803	6	3	9
27.	Chandigarh+	@	@	@	@	@	@	@	@	@	@	@	@
28.	D & N Haveli	8205	5371	13576	2044	944	2988	849	401	1250	N.A.	N.A.	N.A.
29.	Daman & Diu	792	743	1535	569	510	1079	305	144	449	51	8	59
30.	Delhi	295	272	567	245	146	391	222	155	377	390 +	251 +	641 +
31.	Lakshadweep+	4398	3896	8294	1706	1245	2951	1004	511	1515	N.A.	N.A.	N.A.
32.	Pondicherry	@	@	@	@	@	@	@	@	@	@	@	@
	INDIA	4947837	2849904	7797741	1074508	494145	1568653	552188	243707	795895	56701	19341	76042

- * Excludes enrolment in Ph.D/M.Phil and all Professional courses except Engineering (B.E./B.Tech/B.Arc.), Medicine (MBBS) and Teacher Training (B.Ed/B.T.).
- \+ Figures relate to the year 1988-89.
- @ No tribes were scheduled by the President of India in Haryana, Jammu and Kashmir, Punjab, Chandigarh, Delhi and Pondicherry.

Source: *Selected Educational Statistics*, 1989-90.

TABLE 25.20: Statewise Dropout Rates: SC and ST, 1986-87

Sl. No.	State/U.T.	Class I to V SC	Class I to V ST	Class I to VIII SC	Class I to VIII ST
1.	Andhra Pradesh	66.37	72.38	85.19	89.09
2.	Assam	61.54	73.77	71.13	77.25
3.	Bihar	69.42	73.41	83.35	86.70
4.	Gujarat	44.93	62.03	62.68	80.40
5.	Haryana	39.06	—	48.85	—
6.	Himachal Pradesh	36.27	40.63	34.37	35.79
7.	Jammu & Kashmir	28.72	—	52.97	—
8.	Karnataka	52.99	39.37	69.27	58.71
9.	Kerala	14.83	21.54	10.34	52.33
10.	Madhya Pradesh	32.40	58.08	51.68	74.10
11.	Maharashtra	49.31	60.15	68.37	75.43
12.	Manipur	83.63	77.71	86.47	85.10
13.	Meghalaya	47.68	69.12	N.A.	78.71
14.	Nagaland	—	56.30	—	83.46
15.	Orissa	55.49	75.54	75.97	87.71
16.	Punjab	50.96	—	78.02	—
17.	Rajasthan	62.96	75.40	73.28	76.61
18.	Sikkim	66.02	59.39	78.55	66.96
19.	Tamil Nadu	29.09	6.88	58.03	24.97
20.	Tripura	66.48	78.59	79.96	84.57
21.	Uttar Pradesh	46.59	54.75	59.06	65.62
22.	West Bengal	58.04	64.68	81.02	85.24
23.	A & N Islands	—	23.27	—	31.60
24.	Arunachal Pradesh	5.26	67.87	88.64	81.32
25.	Chandigarh	N.A.	—	13.13	—
26.	Dadra & Nagar Haveli	N.A.	51.48	36.36	81.03
27.	Delhi	39.13	—	60.96	—
28.	Goa, Daman and Diu	47.66	44.96	66.93	72.05
29.	Lakshadweep	—	20.69	—	44.05
30.	Mizoram	N.A.	43.26	N.A.	76.46
31.	Pondicherry	3.72	—	34.58	—
	INDIA	50.79	66.12	69.15	80.19

Census was not conducted in Assam.

Source: (i) *Fifth All Educational Survey.*
(ii) Annual Statistics of the Department of Education.

Remarks: No castes were scheduled by the President of India for Nagaland, A & N Islands and Lakshadweep and no tribes were scheduled in Haryana, Jammu & Kashmir, Punjab, Chandigarh, Delhi and Pondicherry.

TABLE 25.21: Sectorwise and Statewise Plan Expenditure for Education during the Seventh Plan Period, 1985-90

(*Rs. in lakhs*)

Sl. No.	State/U.Ts.	Elementary Education	Adult Education	General Education	Technical Education	Arts & Culture	Sports	Total
1	2	3	4	5	6	7	8	9
1.	**Andhra Pradesh**	16063.96	1152.45	28911.50	2172.87	759.55	812.95	32656.87
2.	**Arunachal Pradesh**	3878.36	222.69	6189.78	34.95	425.92	218.70	6869.35
3.	**Assam**	14538.88	823.12	23498.69	2075.12	1607.12	553.00	27733.93
4.	**Bihar**	22940.00	3865.00	34056.90	1261.15	532.40	817.81	36668.26
5.	**Goa**	736.80	68.69	3673.74	727.25	536.53	1410.49	6348.01
6.	**Gujarat**	7712.10	769.80	11646.78	1883.24	419.68	1487.95	15437.65
7.	**Haryana**	6806.77	76.57	13972.88	1909.07	229.43	761.01	16872.39
8.	**Himachal Pradesh**	3558.52	94.05	8061.36	1190.74	543.69	587.52	10383.31
9.	**Jammu & Kashmir**	5571.48	185.87	12368.11	490.98	355.14	829.88	14044.11
10.	**Karnataka**	5686.81	934.02	12696.19	583.62	1333.74	548.22	15161.77
11.	**Kerala**	746.37	30.00	3763.36	2387.84	596.12	682.27	7429.59
12.	**Madhya Pradesh**	21320.30	1041.52	43452.85	3940.34	1287.23	416.94	49097.36
13.	**Maharashtra**	7790.55	1321.39	28555.25	6114.83	545.76	1078.36	36294.20
14.	**Manipur**	1580.00	203.69	3710.61	184.94	348.13	619.60	4863.28
15.	**Meghalaya**	2247.97	105.00	3407.55	129.19	212.06	508.30	4257.10

Contd.

TABLE 25.21 *Contd.*

1	2	3	4	5	6	7	8	9
16.	Mizoram	1048.20	46.26	2157.05	273.00	161.60	242.92	2834.57
17.	Nagaland	1076.25	46.72	2381.18	208.62	414.00	545.43	3549.23
18.	Orissa	11883.41	447.58	24597.19	1938.38	932.97	1752.16	29220.70
19.	Punjab	1873.73	53.67	6170.40	1743.27	524.67	1445.24	9883.58
20.	Rajasthan	15965.38	502.31	29483.94	1552.20	790.53	311.72	32138.39
21.	Sikkim	2064.84	28.28	3768.65	—	294.39	123.51	4186.55
22.	Tamil Nadu	17837.27	1247.34	29746.19	2456.53	830.40	502.76	33535.88
23.	Tripura	5620.84	123.42	9811.78	42.22	66.29	378.60	10298.89
24.	Uttar Pradesh	27209.98	1899.46	45759.94	9321.23	2309.85	5227.59	62618.61
25.	West Bengal	6885.68	740.86	19665.12	2095.02	930.14	1618.98	24309.26
26.	A. & N. Islands	1264.37	15.56	1805.00	174.84	29.03	75.02	2083.89
27.	Chandigarh	565.49	24.42	1712.34	419.01	126.09	588.09	2845.53
28.	D & N Haveli	317.13	8.38	491.93	171.50	18.59	7.70	689.72
29.	Daman & Diu	164.72	5.32	253.55	178.84	2.51	22.48	457.38
30.	Delhi	12669.23	82.60	18719.46	3343.79	1479.61	516.15	24059.01
31.	Lakshadweep	141.20	4.85	428.27	—	47.86	74.16	550.29
32.	Pondicherry	808.02	15.07	2183.93	1379.88	151.75	523.21	4238.77
	INDIA	228533.61	16185.96	437101.47	50384.46	18842.78	25288.72	531617.43

TABLE 25.22: Percentage of Sectorwise and Statewise Plan Expenditure to Total Plan Expenditure on Education in Seventh Plan Period, 1985-90

Sl. No.	State/U.Ts.	Elementary Education	Adult Education	General Education	Technical Education	Arts & Culture	Sports	Total
1.	Andhra Pradesh	49	4	89	7	2	2	100
2.	Arunachal Pradesh	56	3	90	1	6	3	100
3.	Assam	52	3	85	7	6	2	100
4.	Bihar	63	11	93	3	1	2	100
5.	Goa	12	1	58	11	8	22	100
6.	Gujarat	50	5	75	12	3	10	100
7.	Haryana	40	0	83	11	1	5	100
8.	Himachal Pradesh	34	1	78	11	5	6	100
9.	Jammu & Kashmir	40	1	88	3	3	6	100
10.	Karnataka	38	6	84	4	9	4	100
11.	Kerala	10	0	51	32	8	9	100
12.	Madhya Pradesh	43	2	89	8	3	1	100
13.	Maharashtra	21	4	79	17	2	3	100
14.	Manipur	32	4	76	4	7	13	100
15.	Meghalaya	53	2	80	3	5	12	100
16.	Mizoram	37	2	76	10	6	9	100
17.	Nagaland	30	1	67	6	12	15	100
18.	Orissa	41	2	84	7	3	6	100
19.	Punjab	19	1	62	18	5	15	100
20.	Rajasthan	50	2	92	5	2	1	100
21.	Sikkim	49	1	90	0	7	3	100
22.	Tamil Nadu	53	4	89	7	2	1	100
23.	Tripura	55	1	95	0	1	4	100
24.	Uttar Pradesh	43	3	73	15	4	8	100
25.	West Bengal	28	3	81	9	4	7	100
26.	A. & N. Islands	61	1	87	8	1	4	100
27.	Chandigarh	20	1	60	15	4	21	100
28.	D & N Haveli	46	1	71	25	3	1	100
29.	Daman & Diu	36	1	55	39	1	5	100
30.	Delhi	53	0	78	14	6	2	100
31.	Lakshadweep	26	1	78	0	9	13	100
32.	Pondicherry	19	0	52	33	4	12	100
	INDIA	43	3	82	9	4	5	100

TABLE 25.23: **Sectorwise** and Statewise Approved Plan Outlay, 1990-91

(*Rs. in lakhs*)

Sl. No.	State/U.Ts.	Elementary Education	Adult Education	General Education	Technical Education	Arts & Culture	Sports	Total
1	2	3	4	5	6	7	8	9
1.	**Andhra Pradesh**	2556.00	376.00	4730.00	300.00	148.00	122.00	5300.00
2.	**Arunachal Pradesh**	1176.00	77.00	2200.00	N.A.	135.00	80.00	2415.00
3.	**Assam**	3211.00	423.00	6009.00	617.00	522.00	147.00	7295.00
4.	**Bihar**	7850.00	1250.00	11060.00	1685.00	150.00	220.00	13115.00
5.	**Goa**	210.00	20.00	1162.00	181.00	188.00	425.00	1956.00
6.	**Gujarat**	933.00	350.00	1850.00	1708.00	148.00	100.00	3806.00
7.	**Haryana**	1500.00	N.A.	3100.00	675.0	70.00	100.00	3945.00
8.	**Himachal Pradesh**	N.A.	N.A.	3250.00	425.00	105.00	105.00	3885.00
9.	**Jammu & Kashmir**	2350.00	114.00	4787.00	156.00	100.00	275.00	5318.00
10.	**Karnataka**	1511.00	259.00	5055.00	750.00	285.00	175.00	6265.00
11.	**Kerala**	162.00	N.A.	824.00	1205.00	175.00	165.00	2369.00
12.	**Madhya Pradesh**	8094.00	500.00	14413.00	1704.00	270.00	150.00	16537.00
13.	**Maharashtra**	1598.00	110.00	3500.00	1700.00	260.00	600.00	6060.00
14.	**Manipur**	430.00	50.00	1045.00	80.00	100.00	225.00	1450.00
15.	**Meghalaya**	764.00	67.00	1485.00	20.00	71.00	272.00	1848.00
16.	**Mizoram**	290.00	28.00	797.00	60.00	70.00	90.00	1017.00

Contd.

TABLE 25.23 *Contd.*

1	2	3	4	5	6	7	8	9
17.	Nagaland	N.A.	N.A.	837.00	110.00	110.00	240.00	1297.00
18.	Orissa	3171.00	291.00	8427.00	1285.00	310.00	470.00	10492.00
19.	Punjab	—	—	416.00	1000.00	339.00	106.00	1861.00
20.	Rajasthan	N.A.	N.A.	7007.00	970.00	371.00	129.00	8477.00
21.	Sikkim	N.A.	N.A.	850.00	75.00	80.00	45.00	1050.00
22.	Tamil Nadu	1914.00	345.00	3203.00	229.00	192.00	97.00	3721.00
23.	Tripura	800.00	44.00	1738.00	25.00	30.00	180.00	1973.00
24.	Uttar Pradesh	N.A.	N.A.	13900.00	3343.00	325.00	1115.00	18683.00
25.	West Bengal	1849.00	N.A.	6815.00	642.00	377.00	637.00	8471.00
26.	A. & N. Islands	335.00	6.00	809.63	200.00	5.00	30.00	1044.63
27.	Chandigarh	133.00	0.64	530.00	191.00	26.00	150.00	897.00
28.	D & N Haveli	50.00	2.00	84.54	95.00	7.00	2.00	188.54
29.	Daman & Diu	32.00	2.00	80.87	84.30	6.00	2.10	173.27
30.	Delhi	N.A.	N.A.	5354.00	1300.00	307.00	300.00	7261.00
31.	Lakshadweep	23.00	2.50	92.45	30.00	30.35	14.12	166.92
32.	Pondicherry	N.A.	N.A.	846.00	289.00	60.00	255.00	1450.00
	INDIA	409[illegible]2.00	4308.14	116257.49	21134.30	5372.35	7023.22	149787.36

TABLE 25.24: Percentage of Sectorwise and Statewise Approved Plan Outlay, 1990-91

Sl. No.	State/U.Ts.	Elementary Education	Adult Education	General Education	Technical Education	Arts & Culture	Sports	Total
1.	Andhra Pradesh	48.23	6.92	89.25	5.66	2.79	2.30	100
2.	Arunachal Pradesh	48.70	3.19	91.10	N.A.	5.59	3.31	100
3.	Assam	44.02	5.80	82.37	8.46	7.16	2.02	100
4.	Bihar	59.86	9.53	84.33	12.85	1.14	1.68	100
5.	Goa	10.74	1.02	59.41	9.25	9.61	21.73	100
6.	Gujarat	24.51	9.20	48.61	44.88	3.89	2.63	100
7.	Haryana	38.02	N.A.	78.58	17.11	1.77	2.53	100
8.	Himachal Pradesh	N.A.	N.A.	83.66	10.94	2.70	2.70	100
9.	Jammu & Kashmir	44.19	2.14	90.02	2.93	1.88	5.17	100
10.	Karnataka	24.12	4.13	80.69	11.97	4.55	2.79	100
11.	Kerala	6.84	N.A.	34.78	50.87	7.39	6.96	100
12.	Madhya Pradesh	48.94	3.02	87.16	10.30	1.63	0.91	100
13.	Maharashtra	26.37	1.82	57.76	28.05	4.29	9.90	100
14.	Manipur	29.66	3.45	72.07	5.52	6.90	15.52	100
15.	Meghalaya	41.34	3.63	80.36	1.08	3.84	14.72	100
16.	Mizoram	28.52	2.75	78.37	5.90	6.88	8.85	100
17.	Nagaland	N.A.	N.A.	64.53	8.48	8.48	18.50	100
18.	Orissa	30.22	2.77	80.32	12.25	2.95	4.48	100
19.	Punjab	N.A.	N.A.	22.35	53.73	18.22	5.70	100
20.	Rajasthan	N.A.	N.A.	82.66	11.44	4.38	1.52	100
21.	Sikkim	N.A.	N.A.	80.95	7.14	7.62	4.29	100
22.	Tamil Nadu	51.44	9.27	86.08	6.15	5.16	2.61	100
23.	Tripura	40.55	2.23	88.09	1.27	1.52	9.12	100
24.	Uttar Pradesh	N.A.	N.A.	74.40	17.89	1.74	5.97	100
25.	West Bengal	21.83	N.A.	80.45	7.58	4.45	7.52	100
26.	A. & N. Islands	32.07	0.57	77.50	19.15	0.48	2.87	100
27.	Chandigarh	14.83	0.07	59.09	21.29	2.90	17.72	100
28.	D & N Haveli	26.52	1.06	44.84	50.39	3.71	1.06	100
29.	Daman & Diu	18.47	1.15	46.67	48.65	3.46	1.21	100
30.	Delhi	N.A.	N.A.	73.74	17.90	4.23	4.13	100
31.	Lakshadweep	13.78	1.50	55.39	17.97	18.18	8.46	100
32.	Pondicherry	N.A.	N.A.	58.34	19.93	4.14	17.59	100
	INDIA	27.33	2.88	77.62	14.11	3.59	4.69	100

TABLE 25.25: Budget of Education Department ranked in Order of Percentage of Budget of Education Department to Total State Budget, 1989-90

(*Rs. in lakhs*)

Sl. No.	State/U.T.	Budget of Education Department			Percentage of Education Budget to Total State Budget
		Plan	Non-Plan	Total	
1.	Delhi	46.52	183.05	229.57	27.40
2.	West Bengal	95.22	928.93	1024.15	26.04
3.	Kerala	38.42	534.45	572.87	25.29
4.	Daman & Diu	0.81	2.63	3.44	23.61
5.	Rajasthan	105.11	483.77	588.88	22.66
6.	Tripura	19.41	74.45	93.86	22.12
7.	Punjab	55.96	389.34	445.30	21.81
8.	Chandigarh	3.94	27.81	31.75	21.81
9.	Bihar	59.43	758.70	818.13	21.77
10.	Karnataka	63.84	706.82	770.66	21.70
11.	Manipur	9.90	46.17	56.07	21.41
12.	Orissa	114.02	314.48	428.50	21.39
13.	Tamil Nadu	73.55	803.29	876.84	21.21
14.	Gujarat	27.91	704.84	732.75	20.94
15.	Andhra Pradesh	165.60	796.80	962.40	20.66
16.	Assam	91.62	270.56	362.18	20.36
17.	Himachal Pradesh	26.82	122.22	149.04	19.68
18.	Meghalaya	10.53	43.09	53.62	19.35
19.	Pondicherry	8.26	19.44	27.70	19.22
20.	Goa	10.21	37.44	47.65	18.77
21.	Sikkim	8.88	12.04	20.92	18.28
22.	Maharashtra	94.92	1191.72	1286.64	18.17
23.	Madhya Pradesh	92.94	532.70	625.64	17.01
24.	Haryana	49.38	214.45	263.83	16.25
25.	Arunachal Pradesh	12.66	22.69	35.35	15.34
26.	Uttar Pradesh	166.30	1136.10	1302.40	15.07
27.	Jammu & Kashmir	23.95	114.15	138.10	14.43
28.	Mizoram	6.91	25.20	32.11	13.75
29.	Nagaland	6.24	34.94	41.18	13.39
30.	Lakshadweep	0.98	2.88	3.86	13.31
31.	A & N Islands	2.38	11.64	14.02	11.37
32.	Dadra & Nagar Haveli	0.73	1.84	2.57	10.14
	TOTAL	1493.36	10548.62	12041.98	19.94

TABLE 25.26: Statewise Percentage of Budgeted Expenditure of Education Department to State Net Domestic Product, 1987-88

Sl. No.	State/U.T.	% of Budget of Education Deptt. to State N.D.P.
1.	Andhra Pradesh	4.8*
2.	Arunachal Pradesh	8.3*
3.	Assam	5.1
4.	Bihar	3.3
5.	Goa	0.2
6.	Gujarat	3.9*
7.	Haryana	2.8*
8.	Himachal Pradesh	6.4*
9.	Jammu & Kashmir	6.1*
10.	Karnataka	4.3
11.	Kerala	7.2*
12.	Madhya Pradesh	3.3
13.	Maharashtra	2.9
14.	Manipur	9.2
15.	Meghalaya	7.1*
16.	Mizoram	10.4*
17.	Nagaland	8.5*
18.	Orissa	3.8
19.	Punjab	2.5
20.	Rajasthan	4.6
21.	Sikkim	8.3*
22.	Tamil Nadu	3.6
23.	Tripura	10.8*
24.	Uttar Pradesh	3.2*
25.	West Bengal	3.6
26.	A & N Islands	N.A.
27.	Chandigarh	N.A.
28.	Dadra & Nagar Haveli	N.A.
29.	Daman & Diu	N.A.
30.	Delhi	3.6
31.	Lakshadweep	N.A.
32.	Pondicherry	7.6

* Figures relate to 1986-87.

Source: 1. *Estimates of State Domestic Product, 1970-71 – 1987-88.*
2. *Analysis of Budgetted Expenditure on Education, 1987-88.*

TABLE 25.27: Statewise Annual Cost Per Student in Elementary Education, 1989-90

Sl. No.	State/U.T.	Enrolment I to VIII (000)	Expend. on Ele. Edn. (B.E.) (Rs. in '000)	Cost Per Student (Rs.)
1.	Andhra Pradesh	9354	4362797	466.41
2.	Arunachal Pradesh	132	217547	1648.08
3.	Assam	4711	2115832	449.13
4.	Bihar	10236	5253543	513.24
5.	Goa	220	133850	608.41
6.	Gujarat	7176	3690478	514.28
7.	Haryana	2380	1061937	446.19
8.	Himachal Pradesh	1025	845375	824.76
9.	Jammu & Kashmir	1030	617385	599.40
10.	Karnataka	7252	3924023	541.10
11.	Kerala	5038	2915196	578.64
12.	Madhya Pradesh	10268	3949530	384.64
13.	Maharashtra	13691	5747786	419.82
14.	Manipur	331	253703	766.47
15.	Meghalaya	311	285781	918.91
16.	Mizoram	150	182538	216.92
17.	Nagaland	202	257075	272.65
18.	Orissa	4564	2313094	506.81
19.	Punjab	2902	1287228	443.57
20.	Rajasthan	5829	2932294	503.05
21.	Sikkim	86	73630	856.16
22.	Tamil Nadu	10711	3630383	338.94
23.	Tripura	496	373233	752.49
24.	Uttar Pradesh	17645	6902356	391.18
25.	West Bengal	12017	3176425	264.33
26.	A & N Islands	57	82988	1455.93
27.	Chandigarh	68	65666	965.68
28.	Dadra & Nagar Haveli	21	17446	830.76
29.	Daman & Diu	18	15900	883.33
30.	Delhi	1418	500784	353.16
31.	Lakshadweep	12	17740	1478.33
32.	Pondicherry	156	116142	744.50
	TOTAL	129507	57319685	442.60

TABLE 25.28: Educational Expenditure in India by Sources (Percentage)

Year	Government Funds	Local Body Funds	University Funds	Fees	Endowment and Other Sources	Total
1950-51	57.1	10.9	—	20.4	11.6	100.0
1960-61	68.0	6.5	—	17.1	8.4	100.0
1970-71	76.2	3.6	1.4	12.9	5.9	100.0
1979-80	80.8	5.0	1.3	8.7	4.2	100.0
1984-85*	86.2	2.5	1.2	7.3	2.8	100.0
1985-86*	86.6	2.5	1.2	7.0	2.7	100.0
1986-87*	86.8	2.7	1.1	6.9	2.5	100.0

* Author's Estimate.

Source: 1. Computed on the basis of data collected from *A Handbook of Educational and Allied Statistics*, Ministry of Human Resource Development, Government of India, New Delhi, 1987.

2. *Higher Education in India* (Edited by Moonis Raza), Association of Indian Universities, New Delhi, 1991.

TABLE 25.29: **Recurring** Cost Per Student by Faculty of Study, 1986-87

(In Rs.)

Faculty	Universities								
	Delhi	Aligarh	Banaras	Madras	Annamalai	Kurukshetra	Ravi Shanker	JNU	Coefficient of Variation (%)
1. Arts	3335	8040	4737	13247	8751	2599	2500	4282	64
	(3112)	(9108)	(7592)	(43316)	(15551)	(6245)	(10819)	(8429)	(98)
2. Science	5878	6804	9274	17447	3677	6525	4703	12004	55
	(5499)	(7709)	(14863)	(50404)	(6747)	(15675)	(20347)	(23620)	(81)
3. Law	1957	3463	1622	2659	–	4021	2000	–	36
	(1827)	(3935)	(2590)	(10923)	–	(9663)	(8706)	–	(63)
4. Commerce and	3070	2993	1413	4660	3011	2196	–	–	37
Management	(282)	(3395)	(2273)	(19132)	(5539)	(5264)	–	–	(99)
5. Education	7247	–	3531	–	2833	3101	–	–	49
	(6731)	–	(5683)	–	(5198)	(7452)	–	–	(16)
6. Engineering and	–	9932	16149	–	4048	–	–	–	60
Technology	–	(11253)	(25871)	–	(7427)	–	–	–	(66)
Average	3883	10859	11005	10364	3592	3415	3149	5283	56
	(3629)	(12305)	(17635)	(42577)	(6589)	(8204)	(13627)	(10396)	(85)

Note: Figures in parentheses () indicate the unit costs of general administration attributed to the respective faculties.

– Faculty does not exist.

Source: Higher Education in India, edited by Moonis Raza, Association of Indian Universities, New Delhi, 1991.

26

CLASSIFIED INDEX TO TABLES

Educational Expansion

APPENDIX

INTERNATIONAL CONGRESS ON PLANNING AND MANAGEMENT OF EDUCATIONAL DEVELOPMENT, 1990*

Introduction

From 26th to 30th March, 1990, the International Congress on 'Planning and Management of Educational Development' was held in Mexico City. It was organized by UNESCO, in collaboration with the Government of Mexico. There were 402 participants, including 323 national specialists from 113 countries attending in their individual capacity, three observers from three Member States and 76 inter-Governmental organizations and nine organizations of the United Nations system.

The purpose of the Congress, which followed on from the International Conference on Educational Planning held by UNESCO in Paris in 1968, was to start up a wide debate and foster a broad exchange of experience and information in order to formulate suggestions and recommendations at a professional level on:

(a) the way to revitalize the planning and administration of education so as to improve the management of education systems; and
(b) the new forms that might be assumed by international co-operation in the context of the democratization of basic education and the worldwide elimination of illiteracy at the beginning of the twenty first century.

The Congress also examined the possible implications for educational planning and management of the decisions adopted during the

* *Final Report*, UNESCO, Paris, 1990.

World Conference on Education for All (Jomtien, 5–9 March, 1990), this being the first follow-up meeting at an international level of educational planning and administration professionals.

The Conference discussed the following topics in detail:

(a) The role of educational planning and administration in the context of the renewal and universalization of basic education and the eradication of all forms of illiteracy throughout the world.
(b) Educational planning and the development of human resources.
(c) Modernization and development planning and type of educational management needed in a time of crisis.

RECOMMENDATIONS

The participants in the International Congress on Planning and Management of Educational Development.

1. *Being aware* that:

   (a) the dynamics of change that are generated by the reform and restructuring of State institutions present a new challenge for educational planning and management,
   (b) the human dimension of development includes, besides job-oriented training, basic education, improvement of the quality of life, conservation of natural resources and the environment in general and the needs arising from longer life expectancy,
   (c) the need for a concept of development that is compatible with modernization and economic growth together with a fairer distribution of resources, demands that education should play a fundamental role,
   (d) the economic, environmental and cultural crisis in many countries — and, particularly for some developing countries, the problems arising from their external debt — has a social and political impact that affects the development of education,
   (e) there exist unsatisfied educational needs in every country which are revealed in different ways and at different levels.

2. *Recognizing* that these situations constitute an unprecedented challenge regarding both changes in the very concept of education and the approaches to and processes of educational planning and management.
3. *Noting* that despite the considerable progress made over the last three decades, often with the support of UNESCO, the role of educational panning and management must be redefined in order for it to be adapted to the many factors that determine the progress of education and its contribution to overall development.
4. *Taking into account* the results of the World Conference on Education for All, recently held in Jomtien (March 1990), and particularly the World Declaration on Education for All and the Framework for Action to Meet Basic Learning Needs adopted by that Conference.
5. *Endorsing* the objectives of International Literacy Year (1990), the Plan of Action for the Eradication of Illiteracy by the Year 2000, adopted by the UNESCO General Conference at its twenty-fifth session (November 1989), the World Decade for Cultural Development (1987-1997) and the Fourth United Nations Development Decade (1990-1999).
6. *Recognizing* the decisive role that must be played by educational planning and management in helping to mould the societies of the future.

I. General Considerations

Draw attention to the need to bear in mind the following general considerations when formulating national policies and strategies for education:

1. The right to education as a factor in personal development and in preparing the individual for participation in the political, social and productive processes must be ensured.
2. The conditions must be created for education to become available for all, especially by:

   (a) democratizing access to and improving the quality of the education offered;
   (b) obtaining significant results by ensuring that students

complete their studies at each level of education;

(c) promoting special supporting measures to ensure access to and effective participation in the learning process by women in rural areas, refugees, the disabled and other disadvantaged groups;

3. Steps must be taken to meet the growing demand for better social services by making education into a continuing lifelong process and by taking into account the profound changes in the economic, information, communication, science and technology sectors.

II. Basic Requirements Regarding the Planning Process

Suggest that the following basic requirements be emphasized in national planning processes:

1. Forward-looking scenarios need to be constructed in order to explore the future and initiate processes of social change through education, while encouraging the use of the various ways and means available in formal and non-formal education.
2. The planning and management process should be democratized, with greater participation by all the relevant social actors, in order to improve strategic planning and management capabilities, mainly with regard to consultation, supervision and guidance and to the formulation of more precise standards of quality and performance.
3. Planning activities at the intermediate, local and institutional levels need to be strengthened or introduced in the process of reforming State institutions, by incorporating programmes that are better adapted to the diversity of regional and local situations, thereby promoting decentralization and social participations.
4. Training and further training programmes for planners and managers need to be re-examined, updated, strengthened and institutionalized in the light of the new demands on educational planning and management.
5. Better working conditions must be provided for teachers and, given the diversity of the actors directly affected by the processes of planning and management, an attempt must be

made to develop in teachers a mental attitude which is receptive to the working methods and procedures specific to educational planning and management.

6. Information systems should be strengthened through the construction of new indicators, more systemic use of data and more extensive development of qualitative analysis.
7. New avenues of research must be developed and ongoing studies on the improvement of the learning process, better knowledge of learning outcomes, the preparation and introduction of incentive measures in both formal and non-formal education and the evaluation of innovative paradigms for planning involving new actors and systems must be consolidated.

III. Recommendations to UNESCO

Recommend that UNESCO:

1. *Intensify and diversify* its regional and international co-operative efforts in the field of educational planning and management, especially in the strategic areas identified by the International Congress on the Planning and Management of Educational Development, namely:

   (a) educational planning and management in the context of the renewal and universalization of basic education and the eradication of all forms of illiteracy throughout the world;
   (b) educational planning with reference to the human dimension of development;
   (c) educational planning and management in a time of crisis.

2. *Encourage* the setting up of flexible co-operative networks in order to establish links among educational researchers, planners, decision-makers and information and experience and providing access to the latest information on the subject of educational planning, policy-making, administration, monitoring and evaluation; and, with due regard for regional networks, *organize* a worldwide network of specialists and institutions involved in training, research, information and innova-

tions in educational planning, management and evaluation.

3. *Undertake and encourage* activities that strengthen analytical and managerial capabilities in the field of education, from policy analysis and planning through administration and financial management to the preparation and introduction of specific programmes and projects, for example in relation to the planning of educational facilities or planning in small states.
4. *Devote special attention* to co-operation for the wider application of new information technologies.
5. *Assist* Member States in achieving the goals set forth in the World Declaration on Education for All and the Framework for Action to Meet Basic Learning Needs by contributing to the planning and monitoring of programme involving all forms of education.
6. *Strengthen* its training and research activities in the fields of educational planning, management, evaluation and research, taking into account future needs, through its substantive division at Headquarters, Regional Offices, IIEP and other units, acting in close liaison with specific projects, programmes and bodies pursuing the same objectives at the national, sub-regional and regional levels.
7. *Undertake*, in co-operation with member States and international governmental and non-governmental organizations, studies on the key themes examined by the Congress, in order to enrich the international store of information and experience, mainly in respect of new concepts and renewed practices in educational planning.
8. *Seek* innovative formulae in order to overcome the main financial constraints affecting education, by stimulating and mobilizing financial and other forms of external aid to developing countries and by encouraging an increase in national contributions based on an assessment of the various domestic possibilities.

CICIL LIST

CONCEPTS IN COMMUNICATION, INFORMATICS & LIBRARIANSHIP

(CICIL)

General Editor: S.P. AGRAWAL

CICIL-1 Development of Library Services in India: Social Science Information
S.P. Agrawal Rs. 150

CICIL-2 Development of Documentation in India: Social Science Information
S.P. Agrawal Rs. 250

CICIL-3 UNESCO and Social Sciences: Retrospect and Prospect
S.P. Agrawal and **J.C. Aggarwal** Rs. 250

CICIL-4 INDIANA : A Bibliography of Bibliographical Sources
M.K. Jain Rs. 200

CICIL-5 Dimensions of Library and Information Science: Kaula Festschrift
V. Venkatappaiah (Eds.) Rs. 600

CICIL-6 Book Numbers: Some Indian Methods
M.P. Satija and **S.P. Agrawal** Rs. 100

CICIL-7 National Policy for University Libraries in India: Problems and Perspectives
N.B. Inamdar and **L.S. Ramaiah** (Ed.) Rs. 250

CICIL-8 Media Utilisation for the Development of Women and Children
B.S. Thakur and **Binod C. Agrawal** Rs. 150

CICIL-9 Terrorism: An Annotated Bibliography
Susheela Bhan (Ed.) Rs. 275

CICIL-10 Transnational Library Relations: The Indo-American Experience
M.B. Konnur Rs. 175

CICIL-11 Geography of Marketing and Commercial Activities in India (Documentation on Research Information)
R.S. Dixit Rs. 130

CICIL-12 Information India 1988: Global View
S.P. Agrawal and **J.C. Aggarwal** Rs. 200

CICIL-13 Women's Education in India: Historical Review, Present Status and Perspective Plan
S.P. Agrawal and **J.C. Aggarwal** Rs. 360

CICIL-14 Cultural Communication in India: Role and Impact of Phonograms
J.M. Ojha Rs. 220

CICIL-15 Second Historical Survey of Educational Development in India: Select Documents 1985-1989
S.P. Agrawal and **J.C. Aggarwal** Rs. 490

CICIL-16 Documentation Encyclopaedia of UNESCO and Education
J.C. Aggarwal and **S.P. Agrawal** Rs. 800 (set of 2 parts)

CICIL-17 Attitude Towards Information: A Study of Post-Graduate Teachers and Researchers in Social Sciences
N.G. Satish (in press)

CICIL-18 Librarianship and Bureaucratic Organisation: A Study in the Sociology of Library Profession in India
P.K. Jayaswal Rs. 175

CICIL-19 Literature Search
K.A. Isaac Rs. 150

CICIL-20 Child Education in India: Index to Scholarly Writings in Indian Educational Journals and Newspapers since independence
S.P. Agrawal and **Naresh Kanta** Rs. 100

CICIL-21 Lok Sabha and Vidhan Sabha Elections in India 1989 & 1990: Process and Results with Comparative Study of Manifestos
S.P. Agrawal and **J.C. Aggarwal** Rs. 250

CICIL-22 Islamic Studies in India: A Survey of Human, Institutional and Documentary Sources
Mohamed Taher Rs. 180

CICIL-23 Panchayati Raj: An Annotated Bibliography
N.B. Inamdar, N.G. Satish and **Anil Takalkar** 290

CICIL-24 Information India 1989-90: Global View
S.P. Agrawal and **J.C. Aggarwal** Rs. 500

CICIL-25 First Handbook of Psychological and Social Instruments
Udai Pareek and **T. Venkateswara Rao** Rs. 500

CICIL-26 Educational and Social Uplift of Backward Classes: At What Cost and How? Mandal Commission and After
S.P. Agrawal and **J.C. Aggarwal** Rs. 275

CICIL-27 Mass Media and New Horizons: Impact of TV & Video an Urban Milieu
H.R. Trivedi Rs. 180

CICIL-28 Indian Writings on Education : An Indicator to Indian Educational Journals Grouped by Subject Deseriptors 1979 to 1986 (in two parts)
S.P. Agarwal Rs. 900 (per set)

CICIL-29 Nation in Crisis
S.P. Agrawal and **J.C. Aggarwal** Rs. 200

CICIL-30 Information India 1990-91: Global View
S.P. Agrawal and **J.C. Aggarwal** Rs. 500

CICIL-31 Development of University Libraries in India After Independence
O.P. Gupta Rs. 270

CICIL-32 Handbook on Child : With Historical Background
Pramila Pandit Barooah Rs. 320

CICIL-33 Weaker Section in Indian Society : Undiscovered Past, Uncertain Present and Unpredictable Future Index to Writings in Indian Scholarly Journals and 10 National Newspapers Classified under 1500 Descriptors 1886-1990
S.P. Agrawal and **Rajeev Kumar Sharma** Rs. 600

CICIL-34 Communication Informatics and Librarianship in India : An Introductory Guide to Publications Based on a Survey of Libraries in Capital of City India
S.P. Agrawal and **Pushpa Rani Sharma** Rs. 720

CICIL-35 Problems of Collection Development in Special Libraries
M.S. Sridhar Rs. 225

CICIL-36 National Information Resources for Social Sciences in India : Mobilisation, Dispersal and International Enhancement
S.P. Agrawal Rs. 225

CICIL-37 Modern History of Punjab : A Look Back into Ancient Peaceful Punjab Focusing Confrontation and Failures Leading to Present Punjab Problem, and a Peep Ahead : Relevant Select Documents
J.C. Aggarwal and **S.P. Agrawal** Rs. 400

CICIL-38 India Information Sources : Economics and Business
Kyllikki Ruokonen and **Manohar Lal** Rs. 270

CICIL-39 Educational Planning in India : With a Slant to Educational Financing and Administration, Vol. 1, Reports of Committees and Commissions, Five Year Plans, Statistical Tables
J.C. Aggarwal and **S.P. Agrawal** Rs. 550

CICIL-40 Integrated Library System : Two Case Studies : Latin America and India
Maria Luiza Rigo Pasquarelli, Rosaly Favero Krzyanowski, Ines Maria M. Imperatriz and S.P. Agrawal
Rs. 160